the BRIMSTONE DECEIT

An In-Depth Examination of Supernatural Scents, Otherworldly Odors, and Monstrous Miasmas

JOSHUA CUTCHIN

ANOMALIST BOOKS
*San Antonio * Charlottesville*

An Original Publication of ANOMALIST BOOKS
The Brimstone Deceit
Copyright © 2016 by Joshua Cutchin
ISBN: 9781938398643

Cover image: Aliaksandr Vlasik/123RF

All rights reserved, including the right to reproduce this book or portions thereof in any form whatsoever.

For information, go to anomalistbooks.com, or write to: Anomalist Books, 5150 Broadway #108, San Antonio, TX 78209

Contents

Part I: Introduction
Chapter 1 – Why Smells?..1
Chapter 2 - An Olfactory Primer..9
Chapter 3 – Sulfur..23

Part II: Spirit Smells
Chapter 4 - A History..41
Chapter 5 - Pleasant Fragrances...45
Chapter 6 - Smoke...59
Chapter 7 - Decay And Sulfur 67
Chapter 8 - Miscellany...81
Chapter 9 - Loose Ends And Theories...87

Part III: UFO Smells
Chapter 10 - A History..97
Chapter 11 - Miscellany...105
Chapter 12 - Sulfur..117
Chapter 13 - Ozone...133
Chapter 14 - Chemicals 145
Chapter 15 - Burning Odors..159
Chapter 16 - Misidentification and Speculation 169

Part IV: Sasquatch Smells
Chapter 17 - A History..183
Chapter 18 - Animal Odors and Scent Glands..........................197
Chapter 19 - Garbage, Decay, B.O., and Burning 219
Chapter 20 - Sulfur, Strangeness, and Screen Memories............231

Part V: Other Anomalous Smells
Chapter 21 – Various Entity and Monster Odors 245

Part VI: Speculation
Chapter 22 – Observations..277
Chapter 23 – Altered States 285

Epilogue: An Alchemical Answer..305

Acknowledgements 319
Endnotes 321
Bibliography 379
Index...423

Fortosmia - n., *the experience of smelling something that is not supposed to exist.*

Part I: Introduction

Chapter 1
Introduction: Why Smells?

There is something rotten out there, and it isn't from Denmark.
— John Keel

In the beginning was the great creator, who called himself Taikomol. After two failed attempts to fill the universe with life—one world sank, the second burned—he at last made the Earth, sweeping down from the north until the great ocean in the east could be seen no more. Pleased with his work, Taikomol anchored the land with a great deer, elk, and coyote, whose stirrings cause the land to tremble to this day.

Like all creators, Taikomol had loneliness in his heart, and sought companionship. Taking up sticks, the great creator breathed life into them as human beings, and bade them feast. Following the celebration, Taikomol bestowed upon mankind the *hulk'ilal wok*, the dance of the dead, by which boys could become men and draw closer to the spirit world.

In his haste to learn the *hulk'ilal wok*, one of these first men made a fatal error, fell ill, and perished. Taikomol saw no reason why death should be permanent, and thus decreed: "I shall dig a hole and bury you, but in the morning you will come back."[1]

Indeed, just as prophesied, the man returned to the door of the dance house the following day, but the overwhelming stench his body emanated made everyone sick. Taikomol abandoned his plans for resurrection on the spot, instead entreating his people to enjoy their finite days by continuing the *hulk'ilal wok* tradition.

"The dead smell bad," Taikomol's people say.

Such is the power of smell, and the reason why the Huchnom—a subset of California's indigenous Yuki people—say the dead must remain buried.[2]

Modern mysterious miasmas

Eons later, thousands of miles south, and seemingly unrelated to the Huchnom legend, Ivete Clemência Felipe and her relatives encountered their own unearthly stench near São Vicente, Brazil. One evening in 1978, the 23-year-old witness was alone in the home of her sister-in-law when she suddenly noticed a "little blue light in the sky quite far away." As it approached the house with frightening rapidity, the anomaly grew in size and began to strobe a startling array of colors.

"I could hear a buzzing sound," Felipe recalled. "It was going around and around. All the doors and windows were shut, but it lit up the inside of the house. I was so scared that I ran and hid under a bed."

Her cousin and sister-in-law, both of whom observed the object upon their return home, corroborated the event. A follow-up interview by members of the Belo Horizonte UFO group CICOANI and investigator Bob Pratt revealed that both women detected "a smell of gas, like sulphur" during the incident.[3]

***

Five years earlier, the town of Murphysboro in southwest Illinois found itself under siege by a "7-foot-tall mud-covered and light-haired man" dubbed the Big Muddy Monster.[4] The beast was renowned for its overpowering odor, which many townsfolk attributed to the river of its namesake. They speculated the beast was using the waterway as a transportation corridor.

One of the more famous encounters during the Big Muddy

Monster flap took place on June 26, 1973. Witness Cheryl Rath (nee Ray) was stargazing on her back porch when she and her boyfriend, Randy Creath, heard rustling in the nearby bushes. Upon investigating the noise, the couple was amazed to see a manlike creature Rath described as "real tall, hairy. I think it was white, but [the hair] was dirty, matted. It had a real bad odor. It was really rank. I never smelled anything like it."

After a few moments, the Big Muddy Monster simply turned and walked away. When asked later about the overpowering stink, Creath agreed with the common opinion that it was due to a layer of "river slime" covering the beast.[5] Other witnesses over the years would describe the smell as rotten or sewage-like.

* * *

The Battle of Bentonville took place March 19-21, 1865, in North Carolina, marking the final clash between Union Major General William Tecumsah Sherman and Confederate General Joseph E. Johnston. Johnston's subsequent defeat, coupled with the April surrender of Confederate General Robert E. Lee, effectively marked the end of the War Between the States.

As the largest Civil War battle in the Old North State, the site of the Battle of Bentonville has been preserved as a state park. Today, it welcomes thousands of history aficionados coming to pay their respects or relive the past—quite vividly, on occasion.

According to author Christopher K. Coleman, a man whose farm bordered the historical park was busily cutting wood in March 1990 when he found himself surrounded by the sounds and smells of battle, as though he had been transported 125 years back in time. Startled, he dropped his chainsaw and fell beside it on the ground, terrified by the sensation of bullets and artillery audibly passing over him. Swirling smoke appeared and "the acrid smell of gunpowder" filled the air, adding to the terror.

The entire occurrence stopped just as abruptly as it had begun, as if a switch had been flipped. The witness fled, his chainsaw remaining where it had fallen for weeks before enough courage was summoned to retrieve it.[6]

About the book

If "seeing is believing," then smelling is trusting; for, as the adages go, "the nose knows" when something "fails to pass the smell test." "A rose by any other name would smell as sweet," wrote the Bard, and it is for this reason that scent is often regarded as something of an intuitive sense, able to parse the true nature of things even when deception occludes truth. Thus, it should come as little surprise that Forteana—anomalous phenomena whose existence was first investigated in earnest by pioneering researcher Charles Fort—has its reality reinforced when accompanied by odors, as the gullible eye is more easily fooled than the skeptical nose.

The three contemporary examples above are a mere handful of the cases detailing scents in conjunction with the supernatural. On some level, it isn't particularly surprising that encounters with the unknown are accompanied by specific odors—lots of experiences have closely-associated smells, from visits to the hospital to walking into a humidor—and it wouldn't be at all rude to question why we should even bother looking into this niche subject in greater detail.

But, as C.S. Lewis once wrote of the faerie folk, "if I may risk the oxymoron, their unimportance is their importance."[7] Smells seem quite inconsequential upon cursory examination, a mere byproduct, an afterthought to bigger, much grander, events. Upon examining the literature, however, certain patterns take shape, some more immediately apparent than others; and, if consistent odor trends between various paranormal encounters can be established, it certainly implies a deeper meaning to their appearance in eyewitness (nosewitness?) testimony.

Those collecting data on esoterica have long noted the consistency of supernatural odors. Over the course of his career as a paranormal writer, the late John Keel paid a great deal of attention to the consistency of smells in his investigations, dedicating space in several of his books to his observations.

"With the exception of the European stories and some of those reports from Canada, it seems that the majority of these creatures are accompanied by a pungent, very unpleasant odor," he wrote of hairy hominids in *The Complete Guide to Mysterious Beings*. "This stink seems to exceed normal animal smells and could, eventually, offer some kind of clue to the body chemistry of the creatures."[8]

This quote represents neither the extent nor the depth of Keel's analysis, and his thoughts will prove invaluable to our discussion throughout the book. Similar observations were made by Capt. Robert White, Pentagon spokesman for the United States Air Force's UFO study, Project Blue Book, who admitted in a 1955 press conference that the most common "ufonaut" reported to the USAF were the "little, green, luminous, smelly types."[9] In *The Encyclopedia of Ghosts and Spirits*, researcher Rosemary Ellen Guiley wrote that "distinctive, unusual, and out-of-place odors are one of the most common phenomena associated with hauntings," often appearing foul in poltergeist and demonic cases.[10]

If John Keel, a Pentagon spokesman, and Rosemary Ellen Guiley feel paranormal smells are worth noting, then perhaps we should pay attention—they are neither uninformed nor alone in noticing the prominence of odors in strange and unusual cases. Perhaps this line of research is worth pursuing.

If we are truly dedicated to deciphering the nature of all things unexplained, it behooves us to scrutinize every possible aspect of these encounters. No stone is too small to leave unturned, yet many ghost hunters, UFOlogists, and Sasquatch seekers frustratingly gloss over the importance of minute details when preparing their reports, neglecting these (possibly crucial) bits of evidence in favor of the Sisyphean goal of "proving" such phenomena.

This study surveys not only the three most common subjects of paranormal speculation—the aforementioned spirits, UFOs, and Sasquatch—but also digs deeper into less prominent areas, such as lake monsters, faeries, Men-in-Black, Black Eyed Kids, and much more. It may displease some readers to see such a wide array of entities represented in one book. After all, what does a Sasquatch reeking of rotten eggs have to do with the smell of a ghostly cigar, or the odor of ozone accompanying a flying saucer?

Perhaps UFOs are extraterrestrials in nuts-and-bolts craft, ghosts are the spirits of the deceased, and Sasquatch is a flesh-and-blood giant ape. Perhaps they aren't. Lines blur and cross with uncomfortable irregularity: visitations from Venusians are occasionally nigh indistinguishable from visions of the Blessed Virgin Mary (BVM); Sasquatch can appear alongside a UFO; faeries consort with the spirits of the deceased.

It would be easy to interpret this catchall approach as a tacit declaration that all paranormal *phenomena* are merely multiple faces of a singular *phenomenon*. Although this is a possibility, the reader is invited to consider whether these different phenomena merely utilize similar methods (e.g. though faeries, angels, and aliens are presaged by a bright light, this doesn't necessarily mean the entities are one-and-the-same—perhaps it only means that their modes of manifestation are the same, or that our limited senses perceive them similarly). The patterns in paranormal smells may only indicate commonalities, not the substructure of some underlying pan-supernatural theory. Ergo, it may be more useful to think of our approach as less of a pie chart and more of a Venn diagram.

Limitations and disclaimers

This book is the first of its kind, solely dedicated to the smells of spirits, UFOs, Sasquatch, and other strange creatures of the outer fringe. It is critical to remember that, by virtue of the subject matter, it is impossible for such a collection to be comprehensive. Paranormal reports are replete with descriptions of smells, and for every one represented in this book, 20 more were omitted. Researching the subject at hand could take decades and still remain incomplete—not only are there a myriad of cases, but there is also a wealth of explanations and interpretations to analyze and consider.

In retrospect, it is likely the reason why this particular project has never been tackled in the past.

While such a large data set can be daunting, it can also prove beneficial, the sheer volume of cases strengthening patterns and revealing strong consistencies. Every effort was made to avoid skewing or misrepresenting the odor trends that emerged during the collection process. Cases where witnesses described odors in great detail, particularly when those descriptions raised additional questions, were naturally given greater attention.

Another disclaimer, also serving as a plea for patience: in order to fully grasp the subject at hand, a working knowledge of several peripheral subjects must be established. Before focusing on contemporary accounts and their implications, the following pages will first address the basics of olfaction, scent philosophy, smell memory, odors and the occult, etc. These areas have been discussed in great depth by a variety of authors and scholars in other publications; unfortunately, there is too much information on these fields to exhaustively include here. Supplemental literature is recommended whenever possible.

Many witnesses to unexplained phenomena claim to have received strange substances from their captors, from drinks to pills and ointments. These offerings quite often have a smell associated with them, and while of great interest to anyone interested in the unexplained, we do not have enough room to discuss the topic here. Anyone interested in learning more about the odors (and tastes) of food, drink, and medicinal offerings is encouraged to read this book's companion piece, *A Trojan Feast: The Food and Drink Offerings of Aliens, Faeries, and Sasquatch*.

It should also be noted that the goal of this book is not to prove the objective reality of any of the phenomena discussed herein. More than enough ink has been spilt attempting to validate the existence of the unexplained, and there are countless others books that make sound arguments that at least *some* of this activity is real.

Finally—and perhaps most vitally in Fortean studies—we

must remember that a majority of these cases are strictly anecdotal. Stories are only as reliable as their witnesses, and not every tale contained herein is pristine. No assertions are made equating anecdotes with quasi-scientific evidence; at final reckoning, it may well be revealed that all unexplained phenomena have a psychosocial solution. Those reading with an open mind should realize that the absolute, factual validity of each case isn't the driving force behind this study—our focus lies rather on their overarching trends.

Regardless of each claim's validity, it is sincerely hoped that the following chapters will not only reveal consistent themes, but also provoke insightful discussion and shed some light on one of the most criminally overlooked aspects of the unexplained.

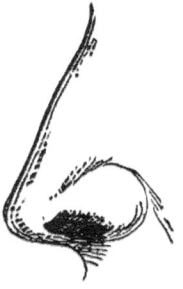

Chapter 2
Introduction: An Olfactory Primer

Hence, if the facts be at all as here stated, it is clear that—if one should explain the nature of the sensory organs in this way, i.e. by correlating each of them with one of the four elements,—we must conceive that the part of the eye immediately concerned in vision consists of water, that the part immediately concerned in the perception of sound consists of air, and that the sense of smell consists of fire.
— Aristotle, *Sense and Sensibilia*

The nose is nature's chemical receptor. It categorizes the unseen, allowing us to "identify friend, foe, or quarry, and further differentiate between edible and nonedible foods," in the words of environmental engineering professor Paul N. Cheremisinoff. The affect may be unconscious, like subtle arousals when smelling the opposite sex, or it may be overt, as when the scent of smoke alerts us to fire. It isn't until we are faced with the terrifying notion of dangerous, odorless substances like carbon monoxide that we fully appreciate olfaction's alerting power.[11]

Alarming smells may well be our first indicator of the unexplained. In November 1999, a semi truck driver near Holtville, California, pulled off the road to relieve himself around 10:00 p.m. He immediately noted a "strong dead decaying skunk smell" and left his headlights on to avoid stepping in anything unpleasant. The witness had just reached the vehicle's passenger side when the stench intensified to "a gagging type of a smell." At that instant, something with long hair and a large frame rushed down the mountainside, grunting as it passed through his headlights and across the road.

The panicked driver vacated the area immediately.[12]

Philosophy: A brief overview

It is strongly recommended that anyone interested in the fascinating development of olfactory philosophy read historical anthropologist Annick Le Guérer's *Scent: The Essential and Mysterious Powers of Smell*, a masterpiece winding the evolution of odor in culture through history, mythology, and the occult.

In 1929, neurologist Sigmund Freud published *Civilization and Its Discontents*, a seminal work highlighting the inherent tension between the individual's desire for independence and civilization's need to impose order. In his classic fashion, Freud posited that one of the main sources of this friction was mankind's primitive sexual drives, further speculating that the diminished role of smell in modern man was thanks to evolution: as human ancestors assumed an upright position, noses lifted farther from the fragrant ground, allowing smell to take a backseat to vision. Sexually stimulating odors were surpassed in favor of visual arousal—olfaction was, to Freud's mind, a base, animalistic sense.[13]

Millennia before *Civilization and Its Discontents*, Plato laid the groundwork for Freud's theory, declaring the eye and ear superior organs to the nose; to the Greek philosopher, vision and hearing, which allowed mankind to appreciate geometry and music, were "noble" senses.[14] Plato cited the source of smell's shortcomings as inferiorities in the nose's "veins," too narrow to accommodate the "particles" of water and earth, too wide for those of air and fire.[15]

The sentiment was obviously passed from master to student, for Aristotle elaborated on the notion in his short treatise *Sense and Sensibilia*, pointing out the inferiority of olfaction in mankind as compared to beasts. Aristotle placed smell between the tactile senses of touch/taste and the medium-delivered senses of sight/

hearing—it was the most liminal of all senses, generated neither within nor without.

While both Plato and Aristotle wrote extensively on the subject (as did their contemporary Theophrastus and Roman successor Lucretius), smell received scant philosophical attention until Christendom. Though the Old Testament unabashedly relishes smell—the Song of Solomon is replete with positive olfactory imagery—the New Testament seems less tolerant. In the latter half of the Bible "we continually sense a veiled criticism of the profane use of scent," wrote Le Guérer, citing Judas' objections when Mary fragrantly anointed the feet of Christ.[16]

Early church officials, who condemned all earthly delights, adopted this aversion. Even though it sought to upset the status quo of thought, the Age of Enlightenment continued to degrade olfaction, which it held could lead the intellect astray. It wasn't until the eighteenth and nineteenth centuries, with the renewed interest in medicine, that smell came to the forefront of scholarly attention.[17]

Misguided doctors and researchers determined that diseases were caused by foul smells, or *miasmas*. Even in the 1700s, the idea was by no means new—ancient India had its own version of the theory in the east,[18] while second century philosopher Galen of Pergamon had pioneered the concept in the west (as early as the 1300s scholars attributed the Black Plague to a "deadly corruption of the air").[19] Nor was the notion restricted to the old world: the native people of upstate New York held that, circa 700 B.C., a horned serpent rose from the depths of Lake Ontario, spreading disease and killing by the score[20] with its foul breath.[21]

In short, smells were ascribed supernatural powers. Hateful beliefs from medieval Christianity re-emerged in popular culture, where "menstrual blood, the devil and Jews, for example, were all believed to have a distinctive smell, thus sneakily invading the Christian male through his nostrils."[22] During the alleged four-year possession of Ursuline nuns known as the Loudun Possessions of 1630, the scent of "a bouquet of musk roses" was blamed for allowing Satan access to the sisters (the events were likely exaggerated by the church).²³ By the 1800s, European miasmatic beliefs were so widespread that fires were lit to cleanse the air during times of pestilence, jars of bodily odors were collected for examination,²⁴ and—naturally—pleasant smells were ascribed positive, curative effects, a notion that survives in modern aromatherapy practice.²⁵

Eventually, miasma theory gave way to modern concepts of germs and viruses, and the study of smell evolved into a scientific examination of olfaction. In the modern era, the Mad Gasser of Mattoon and the Flatwoods Monster—both cases discussed at length in this book—would illustrate that the key conceits of miasma theory were not entirely without basis. Smells can, in some sense, harm the smeller.

Basic science

On April 26, 1969, Calgary, Canada, resident David Arychuk was taking his dog on an evening walk when he saw a circular object land in the distance, topped by three throbbing red lights.²⁶ Halfway between Arychuk and the craft were two tall humanoids; a smell of "sweet bitterness" clung to the air, producing a nauseating effect. The witness yelled to the creatures, who wordlessly returned to their craft. Arychuk wished to follow, but his dog was too frightened. When he returned the next day, the craft was gone, but the queasy odor lingered.²⁷

To outline the complex olfactory process in full would fill up the remainder of this book. What follows is a rough, greatly simplified version of a complex physiological process.

When we smell, scent molecules bind to specific sensory cells high in our nose; this interaction has been described as a sort of key-lock configuration, with each cell corresponding to specific molecules. If a "key" (molecule) and "lock" (cell) are compatible, the ensuing stimulation is eventually relayed to the olfactory bulb, a neural structure in the brain.²⁸ Once here, this stimulation fires electrical impulses at the amygdala, a neuron cluster that serves as the hub for memory, emotions, and decision-making. This complex brain-body interaction links directly with the limbic system, a series of nerves and networks governing visceral and behavioral reactions. Olfaction is the first sense to become dominant in infants[29]—the entire nervous system is affected by odors, from our pulse and breathing to more complex digestive, sexual, and emotional responses.[30]

Smell's deep, reflexive triggers regularly cause paranormal witnesses to experience physical reactions. Reports of nausea and dizziness are among the most common effects attributed to smells and the unknown.

- Two luminous fireballs landed in the cow pasture of a pregnant housewife in Bowling Green, Missouri, one summer evening in July 1972. The event was accompanied by a nauseating stench of decomposition and strange, unearthly grunts and screams.[31]

- Russian city leader V.A. Ivanov returned abruptly after disappearing for eleven months in 1987. Ivanov claimed that he had been returning home when, on a whim, he stopped by a favorite childhood haunt, a gully near River Irtysh. Dipping his hand to the water for a drink, he noticed an unpleasant dizzying odor. Ivanov immediately feared asphyxiation and tried to claw his way out of the gully but was paralyzed. After blacking out, he awoke in a surreal, tropical location, complete with pink sky and unrecognizable wildlife. Ivanov claimed that when he tried to move again, he suddenly found himself back in Russia. The entire experience, to his estimation, had taken no more than a few hours. Ivanov was purportedly of sound mental health, and some reports claimed the soil samples taken from his boots were not native to the area.[32]

- Chilean citizen Cariaga Gonzales noticed a large, monkey-like animal by the side of the road the evening of June 24, 2000. When he stepped out of the vehicle to investigate, Gonzales was nauseated by a strong smell. "It's something similar to a decomposing animal," he said later. Gonzales came within 25 feet before a blood-curdling howl forced him to flee.[33]

Was it the sound that made Gonazles flee, or the smell? Studies have shown time-and-again that human beings are highly susceptible to scent manipulation. For example, the aroma of cleaning products can make people more honest and fair in business dealings. Foul smells have an even greater impact. In October 2010, New York governor hopeful Carl Paladino trounced his rival in the Republican primary by issuing flyers infused with the smell of rotting garbage that read "end the stink of corruption in Albany."[34]

"Unconsciously influenced by a smell, we may be prompted to do or avoid doing or feeling something without fully understanding why," wrote Dutch psychologist Piet Vroon.[35] Odors can even influence the character of dreams—in one study, dreamers exposed to rose scent (phenyl ethyl alcohol) had more pleasant dreams than those exposed to the scent of rotten eggs (hydrogen sulfide).[36]

Despite its importance and ability to viscerally impact us, olfaction remains largely under-researched and poorly understood, especially when compared to Plato's "noble senses." Science still lacks a consensus opinion on exactly how the key-lock system of odor coding and perception functions; some posit that molecular shape determines which cells react, while others have begun to invoke more controversial theories including quantum effects.

There are two key concepts in olfactory science that will prove critical to our discussion moving forward: thresholds and hedonics.

Thresholds measure the concentration of an odor. When half a population can detect a scented versus a scent-free sample, the *detection threshold* has been reached. When that population can *identify* the odor, the *recognition threshold* has been reached. Some smells are quite detectable, even recognizable, in minute concentrations, while others require a more substantial presence.[37] Note that longer exposures lead to desensitization, a condition known as olfactory fatigue or adaptation, until the odor is no longer noticeable.[38]

Hedonics describe the pleasant or unpleasant nature of a smell. Though some might assume that universal hedonic values are present in every human from birth (e.g. garbage smells bad, bacon smells good), the truth of the matter is that specific odors are only perceived as pleasant/unpleasant because they possess corresponding learned associations. To the garbage man, trash smells of money, but to a vegan, bacon smells of death (in an exception to this rule, research indicates that unknown odors are generally less likely to be deemed pleasant).[39] This factor is one of the main reasons for the inability of the United States military to create a universal stink bomb; with few exceptions, a representative sample of the world's ethnic groups cannot agree upon a consistently revolting odor.[40]

This same associative logic extends to encounters with the unknown: generally speaking, benevolent entities—BVM, angels, female ghosts, Adamski-style space brothers—smell pleasant, while malevolent beings like devils, demons, and Grey aliens smell unpleasant. These hedonic associations extend to near-death experiences (NDEs) as well. Pope Gregory wrote in the sixth century of a soldier who had died and returned, but not before seeing the intersection of Heaven and Hell:

> He said that there was a bridge, under which ran a black, gloomy river which breathed forth an intolerably foul-smelling vapor. But across the bridge there were delightful meadows carpeted with green grass and sweet-smelling flowers. The meadows seemed to be meeting places for people clothed in white. Such a pleasant odor filled the air that the

sweet smell by itself was enough to satisfy the hunger of the inhabitants who were strolling there.[41]

Mystics have long spoken of odors of sanctity, and today the hedonic associations of Heaven and Hell remain engrained in culture. One NDE collected by psychologist Margot Grey told of a survivor who, after attempting suicide, was suddenly "in a place that I can only describe like Dante's *Inferno*. I saw a lot of other people who seemed grey and dreary and there was a musty smell of decay."[42]

Scientists steeped in the materialist paradigm have long sought to write off NDEs as last minute misfirings within the brain. The appearance of uncommon odors would not be out of place in such explanations, as there are a variety of olfactory disorders, mostly of neurological origin. *Anosmia* is the inability to smell; *dysosmia*, a distortion of smell; *cacosmia*, the unpleasant interpretation of pleasant smells. Not inconsequential to our discussion is *phantosmia*, the hallucination of odors in the absence of noticeable smells. These phantom scents are often unpleasant (cacosmic) and are frequently caused by brain damage or seizures in the temporal lobe. As such they are common in schizophrenics and those suffering from brain tumors.[43]

It is imperative to understand that phantosmia does *not* refer to spirit smells. Unfortunately, some paranormal researchers have begun erroneously using the term to describe any odor without a source, particularly in haunted locations. The difference is simple: phantosmia generates odors smelled only by an individual, while several witnesses can notice spirit smells. By definition, phantosmia is a neurologically generated medical condition that is entirely internal. It is individual-based and not location-based, though it may provide an explanation for odors in single-witness sightings and accounts of clairscent (psychic smells).

While hallucinogens such as LSD (lysergic acid diethylamide) and DMT (N,N-Dimethyltryptamine) do not usually generate odor hallucinations, it is possible for the power of suggestion to create imagined scents. In one such example, painter and Holocaust survivor Avigdor Arikha, upon reopening his old concentration camp sketchbook, was hit with the overpowering stench of corpses. Those around him denied the stench.

"Did he actually experience the odor of the concentration camp," wrote odor psychologist Trygg Engen, "or, rather, the memory of a terrible situation associated with an odor?"[44]

Memory and language

Benjamin Davidson was traveling from Portsmouth, Ohio, to Cincinnati on a spring evening in the mid-1960s when he was forced to a halt. In the middle of the road sat an elliptical metallic craft, flashing a dazzling array of multicolored lights. Despite this startling scenario, Davidson remained calm as several tall, praying mantis-like beings escorted him from his vehicle to the waiting structure.

Once inside the well-lit interior, Davidson allegedly met 20 of the creatures, which placed him on a table and began examining him. They performed a variety of procedures, including scraping skin from his hands, clipping his fingernails, and extracting blood. Most chillingly, Davidson noticed the body of a dead girl on an adjacent table. "I know she was dead," he later said. "I didn't know who she was or where she came from, but it was quite obvious that she was dead."

Davidson reappeared several hours later at a traffic light near Portsmouth before returning home to a very upset and suspicious wife. He claimed no recollection of the event until, while smoking at his kitchen table in the early 1990s, his cigarette singed the hair of his arm. The odor of burnt hair brought back memories of the unwelcome medical examination he had repressed for nearly three decades.[45]

Few senses have a more profound effect upon memory than smell. Any adult who has experienced a fragrance from childhood is well aware of the tight coupling between scent and memory, and it is not at all uncommon to have memories flood back, unbidden, by catching a nostalgic whiff. Memories of odors are persistent and permanent, especially when the associated event is particularly significant to our lives. British veterinarian James Herriot, who served in the Royal Air Force, used a popular soap in the shower the first night of his service; the day's events, which included medical examinations, ornery corporals, and saying goodbye to his wife, made him unable to use the soap again the rest of his life.[46]

"It is actually better to think of this ability in terms of not forgetting rather than remembering," writes Engen. "While visual and auditory memory usually decrease with time, often exponentially in light of new experiences, odor memory remains intact." In many cases this recall is a primitive, protective act, designed to safeguard us against repeating unpleasant encounters of the past.[47] Not only does scent memory fail to diminish, but it is also impervious to *retroactive interference*, the tendency for newer memories to overwrite and mix with older recollections.[48] Notably, Alzheimer's patients show a severe impairment in odor memory.[49]

So why is our sense of smell—in actuality, robust and powerful, inviolable in memory—so often overlooked and taken for granted? The confounding element masking the power of human olfaction lies not in our physiology or psychology but rather, unsurprisingly, in our language. Olfactory researchers playfully call this the "tip-of-the-nose" phenomenon, a riff on the phrase "tip-of-the-tongue"; like a word on the tip of our tongue, we can recognize odors and yet have their names elude us. On average, we experience this once out of every 10 scents we perceive. This occurrence is compounded by the difficulty of identifying odors in the absence of context clues. Our language actively affects the way we perceive smells: unknown odors are more likely to be perceived as negative,[50] while any smell that can be named will actually be perceived more sharply.[51]

The difficulties of language are endemic in the descriptions provided by paranormal witnesses, as odors are described in equal parts "strange, foul, or unpleasant." In his unparalleled two-volume work *UFO Abductions: The Measure of a Mystery*, Thomas Bullard lists smells that are "sharp-smelling, sickly, burning," or, even more frustratingly, "strange" or "odd."

A good example of such nebulous descriptions comes from "Jane," one of the abductees studied by the late Karla Turner. On December 2, 1992, she noticed an "unrecognizable odor" in the air of her home: "'acrid, strong, heavy, sharp, pungent, and tangy,' unrelated to food or smoke odors, and unlike anything she'd ever smelled." That evening she witnessed a UFO, and was taken early the following morning.[52]

Odor and the occult

The role of scents in occult rituals can be traced back to prehistoric sacrificial rites. Ancient faiths worldwide embraced the concept of burnt offerings, wherein a sacrifice—exclusively an animal in Abrahamic religions, occasionally a human in pagan ceremonies—was burned as an offering to supernatural forces. Being invisible, these deities found solid food unfit for consumption and thus relied upon fire to release the essence of the food, changing the tangible into the ethereal. (These concepts, studied in depth in *A Trojan Feast*, are echoed in the Celtic faerie faith, wherein earth elementals consume not the physical food, but rather its essence, or *foyson*.) When the ritual was complete, the burnt husk would remain, but the essence itself had risen to the Heavens in the form of smoke. Naturally, the odor of the smoke and the offering itself were conflated.[53]

Even older religious rites used incense to similar effect. The ancient Egyptians used perfumed smoke to not only please the gods, but also for pragmatic purposes like removing odors, a practice mirrored in Babylon and later Greece and Rome, where incense was used while praying to divining oracles.[54] In some sense, the burning of incense is a variation on the burnt offering writ small; it is the immolation of plants instead of flesh, essential oils combusting in the place of blood and fat.[55]

The Christian church adopted the use of incense in medieval times, though not without criticism—smell, as it has been noted, was viewed suspiciously. Again, the decision was partly spiritual and partly practical, as the smoke no doubt helped to alleviate the smell of dozens of unwashed congregants crammed in for Mass.[56]

The ability for scent to transcend the physical plane naturally appealed to those dabbling in magic. Occult communities seized upon this attribute along with the entrenched hedonic qualities of odor: the rituals for fell deeds required foul scents, while conjuration for a positive outcome demanded pleasant perfumes.[57]

The purpose of incense in magic was two-fold, not only carrying prayers to the Heavens but also focusing the mind of the magician and providing an atmosphere conducive to their goals.[58] We can see similar thematic parallels in modern psychedelic use, which emphasizes how set and setting—the user's state-of-mind and surrounding environment—are as important to the experience as the substance itself.

"Present-day writing on astral magic also emphasizes perfumes," writes Le Guérer. "According to one theory, odors created by the volatilization of particles of matter emit vibrations that have a profound effect on the behavior of all living creatures and on one's astral twin." These "vibrations"—conceptually familiar to anyone with any experience in the New Age community—supposedly reinforce the natural abilities imbued to us under our zodiacal sign.[59]

Such techniques extend to the summoning of demons and familiars in witchcraft, a subject we will return to in short order. Conversely, smells have long been used to repel supernatural entities. Popular culture tells how vampires are repelled by garlic (a curious bit of folklore when compared to garlic's newfound popularity as a "superfood" to repel harmful health problems), and it is not uncommon to find modern wiccans, demonologists, and ghost hunters participating in "smudging" ceremonies, using burned sage to cleanse an area of evil spirits. Lesser known is the purported ability of saffron oil and henna to repel the Arabic *djinn*,[60] that the odor of pomade frightens Japan's *kuchi-sake-onna*,[61] or the fact that *duendes*, South America's faerie folk, cannot abide the odor of "culantro," the regional term for the herb *Eryngium foetidum*.[62]

Odors have a legion of applications in conjuration, and it is not our goal to chronicle every possible use. Rather, it is the aim of this chapter to provide a solid understanding of the way olfaction works, and to underscore its importance to our reality. It occupies an integral place in our psychology and perception of the world around us, worthy of the attention of anyone interested in the unexplained; for, when taken in aggregate, all existing research points to olfaction as a sense ripe for exploitation by occult forces.

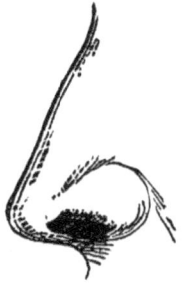

Chapter 3
Introduction: Sulfur

And the beast was taken, and with him the false prophet that wrought miracles before him, with which he deceived them that had received the mark of the beast, and them that worshipped his image. These both were cast alive into a lake of fire burning with brimstone.
— Revelation 19:20

The people of Tedworth thought they had heard the last of the drummer.

He arrived in the Wiltshire village in 1661, his incessant drumbeating quickly irritating the populace, in particular local landowner John Mompesson. Mompesson won a judgment against the unlicensed drummer, exposing him as a conman, and the drummer fled town, his instrument turned over to Mompesson by the local bailiff.

From that day forward, disembodied drumming plagued the Mompesson estate. The beating would stretch for days on end, accompanied by frightful animal noises and disembodied voices. Objects moved of their own volition, occasionally launching at family members, and the Mompesson children were assaulted in their sleep, sometimes bodily levitated. Apparitions were spotted in the home, including a dark form with red, glowing eyes. The activity lasted for two years and was experienced by many witnesses until the drummer once more found himself in custody, where he bragged about harassing the Mompessons. Convicted of witchcraft, he was condemned to leave the area but returned to Tedworth from time-to-time, always accompanied by strange activity in the Mompesson home.[63]

The Drummer of Tedworth (modern-day Tidworth) is often cited as one of the first *poltergeist*, or "noisy ghost," accounts. Like most poltergeist cases, the events of 1661 involved the dramatic manifestation of physical phenomena, including the moving of inanimate objects, strange sounds, and unpleasant odors: on the morning of November 6, 1662, according to witness Joseph Glanvill, the spirit "left a sulphurous smell behind it, which was very offensive."[64]

Spoiler alert: an inordinate amount of the accounts in this book involve the smell of sulfur.

There is no need to be coy about this fact. Even if one is unfamiliar with the commonly held folklore that Hell smells of brimstone, the following chapters quickly demonstrate that a plurality of witnesses report sulfurous odors. Acknowledging this tendency now rather than at discussion's end will allow us to highlight these consistencies from the start, bringing a deeper appreciation to the encounters throughout.

Do not be mistaken—in spite of this overall trend, there are plenty of other odors reported by witnesses. While smells of sulfur may be common to spirit, UFO, and Sasquatch cases, each of these discrete phenomena possess other unique odor categories, themselves rife with further questions. In other accounts, subtler trends emerge; subsets of sulfurous smells reveal themselves; some cases obviously, explicitly describe sulfur, while others do not reveal their connection to the element until investigated in depth. In short, it matters little that we already know *what* many paranormal witnesses report smelling, for the question is not *what*, but *why?*

The observation that *sulfur*—the official spelling of the element since 1990 according to the International Union of Pure and Applied Chemistry—is commonly smelled in paranormal encounters was keenly noted by John Keel. In 1976's *The Eighth Tower*, he wrote:

> Ancient dragons, monsters, and demons supposedly reeked with the smell of brimstone (sulfur). Burning sulfur smells like rotten eggs. Modern witnesses often complain that the monsters—and some UFOs—smelled like rotten eggs. Sometimes the smell is even more rancid and is compared with the wretched stench of marsh gas.[65]

Keel had much more to say on the subject, which we will return to throughout this book. Setting aside some pedantic (but important) conflations about his "rotten egg" connection, we should take note of Keel's keen invocation of mythology. It is true that all things supernatural have long been reported to smell of brimstone (burn stone), an archaic term for sulfur. As such, we must acknowledge that reports of sulfurous odors have undoubtedly become their own self-reinforcing popular culture paranormal meme. Liars and hoaxers have no doubt embraced this stereotype and are quick to add it as the sort of detail "expected" when encountering something demonic.

An additional wrinkle comes in the power of suggestion, which can change the way witnesses perceive smells. One olfactory study, for example, determined that when a cherry beverage is colored orange, subjects are much more likely to actually *smell* an orange odor coming from the drink.[66] For a fun experiment, blindfold a friend, put a piece of Parmesan cheese under their nose, and tell them someone vomited. They will recoil. Tell them you're making Italian tonight, and they will smile.

What role do these expectations play when we witness the supernatural?

This is not a book written from a purely Christian perspective, though naturally much of the following is mired in Christian belief. This is not to suggest that spirit, UFOs, and Sasquatch are demonic—though it would be foolish to write off that possibility entirely—nor to unjustly emphasize one faith over another. Christianity has had an enormous impact upon Western thought, and any discussion of mythology and sulfur in the Americas, Europe, or Australia would be impossible without addressing Christianity and its interpretation of demonic activity.

Sulfur and Hell

Sulfur has a longstanding cultural association with the devil, demons, and Hell. Folklorists have yet to reach a clear consensus for exactly how this connection arose.

Curiously enough, of all the numerous mentions of brimstone in the Bible, most are tied not to demonic forces, but rather those of Heaven: sulfur comes from above, not below. The first mention is Genesis 19:24: "Then the Lord rained upon Sodom and upon Gomorrah brimstone and fire from the Lord out of Heaven." Later, in Isaiah 30:33: "… the pile thereof is fire and much wood; the breath of the Lord, like a stream of brimstone, doth kindle it."

These examples are representative of most Biblical depictions of sulfur. Notably, the element is not presented in an evil context, but rather given the role of sanctification or purification (more on that later). The apocryphal Book of Enoch describes a vision of Hell:

> And I saw that valley in which there was a great convulsion and a convulsion of the waters. And when all this took place, from that fiery molten metal and from the convulsion thereof in that place, there was produced a smell of sulphur, and it was connected with those waters… Through that valley also rivers of fire were flowing, to which those angels shall be condemned, who seduced the inhabitants of the earth.[67]

The Book of Revelation also depicts hellish waters, where God casts Satan into a "lake of fire and brimstone." In *The Eighth Tower*,

Keel mentions the propensity for the unexplained to smell of sulfur, an observation immediately followed by a discussion of how "monsters" tend to appear near water; it is tempting to wonder if he was making this connection.

In any case, note that both the lake of Revelation and the river of Enoch are not things to be relished by the damned, but rather a form of torturous, cleansing fire: sulfur is the wrath of the divine. Thus, rather than thinking of sulfur as simply "the stench of Satan," it makes more sense to frame it as "the stench of God's attempt to purify evil."

It is not surprising that brimstone is a tool of God in Abrahamic thought. In ancient Greek, "brimstone" (*theion*) and "divine" (*theios*) share a common root, an etymology shared in modern English with the word "thiol," which describes certain sulfur compounds. In antiquity, sulfur often came from the Heavens, as evidenced in classic literature.

In the *Odyssey*, Homer writes, "Zeus thundered and hurled his bolt upon the ship and she quivered from stem to stern, smitten by the bolt of Zeus, and was filled with sulphurous smoke." The *Iliad* similarly tells of a moment when Zeus "thundered horribly and dashed it to the ground… a ghastly blaze of flaming sulphur shot up and the horses, terrified, both cringed away against the chariot." Today, we attribute the smell after a lightning strike to ozone rather than sulfur. This confusion still continues into the modern era and makes our discussion all the more difficult. The topic deserves a great deal more discussion than given here, and it is covered in greater depth later.

This ozone-sulfur conflation helped shift the origin of lightning from divine to demonic. In the 1700s, demonologist Nicholas Rémy determined that the jagged slashes left at strike sites were the claw marks of the devil, the lightning itself a physical manifestation of mingled demons. This, to his mind, was reinforced by the "sulphurous smell" left in lightning's wake.[68]

So if brimstone comes from Heaven, why is Hell found underground? Hell exists below simply because its exact opposite,

Heaven, exists above. It is easy to imagine a volcano, leading below ground to a channel of magma, interpreted as a lake or river of fire and brimstone. Volcanoes seem like portals to Hell even to the modern imagination; they exude deadly gases and can also, in some sense, rain "fire and brimstone" from the sky during an eruption. They are also traditionally the home of monsters, dragons, and giants; in the Comoros islands off the coast of Africa, for example, Mount Karthala is home to the giant "Red Headband," who stalks the volcano's summit, snatching the unwary.[69] In the modern era, witnesses claim to see UFOs dart in and out of active volcanic sites.

These parallels are further reinforced by the presence of sulfur deposits and the odor of hydrogen sulfide, a sulfur compound important to later discussion, around volcanic sites.[70] Caves, caverns, and hot springs can all feature this distinctive "rotten egg" odor, and the underworld—home not only to Hell, but also faerie mounds, secret alien bases, and Sasquatch lairs in modern mythology—would naturally smell the same. When miasma theory was at its height, it was believed that "the bowls of the earth contained a quite dangerous 'stench laboratory,' capable of making mankind sick."[71]

Hell, however, was not always depicted as literally subterranean. Outside Jerusalem lies Gehenna, known as the Valley of the Son of Hinnom, a Biblical garbage dump where fires burned constantly and the bodies of criminals were dumped. The rank smell and low-lying topography, along with its reputation as the final resting place of the wicked, led to its frequent translation as "Hell."[72] The connotation is paralleled in the Islamic Qu'ran, which names *Jahannam* as Hell's equivalent.[73]

Another, less popular earthbound contender for Hell is the Serbonian Bog, or the modern day Lake Bardawil in Egypt. In 440 BC Herodotus visited the site and declared its shores to be where Zeus exiled Typhon, the terrifying beast of Greek mythology;[74] the parallels between such a clash and God tossing Satan into a lake of fire are obvious, and were not at all lost upon nineteenth century writer Kersey Graves. In *The Biography of Satan*, he wrote:

> This lake was chosen as the place of consignment for the great Arch-Demon or Arch-Enemy of the human race... Hence it became universally execrated. Bearing these facts in mind, let us observe that when the Nile overflowed its banks, as it did semi-annually, and spread over the country for many miles around, it reached this lake Sirbonis and submerged it with its putrid waters. And, as it receded into its channel by the subsidence of the current, it deposited in the lake a great amount of debris, putrefying vegetation, and nauseating substances of various kinds. And it is a matter of fact or fable, that upon its stagnant waters, there accumulated a scum bearing a strong analogy in taste, color and smell, to that of brimstone or sulphur. In fact, some authors speak of it as being veritably and truly brimstone in solution—*i.e.* sulphur.

Graves further speculates that this decaying scum on the surface of the lake, when illuminated by the sun, could give the appearance of being on fire, "while the steam, gas, vapor, or miasma created and eliminated by the action of the sun upon the deposits of mud and slime around the margin of the lake, ascending upward, formed the imaginary smoke."[75]

Sulfur and Satan

In his 1820 treatise on honoring the Sabbath, John Willison told of one particular Northampton church congregation who could not be moved to church on Sunday. Defying pleas from Pastor Hugh Clarke, the flock failed to rectify their evil ways until "upon a Sabbath day at night, when they were retired to their several homes, there was heard a great noise and rattling of chains up and down the town, which was accompanied with such a smell and stink of fire and brimstone, that many of their guilty consciences suggested to them, that the devil was come to fetch them away: and now, and not till now, they began to think in good earnestness of a reformation."[76]

Regardless of its historical origins, the concept of Hell remains powerful, as does the lore surrounding its ruler, Satan. Originally created as an angel, wise and righteous, he fell from the sight of the Lord for the sin of pride, seeking God's glory for himself. The ensuing schism ignited a rebellion in Heaven, where the archangel Michael cast Satan and his followers (traditionally a third of the angels) to the Earth.

In the fifth century, the Council of Toledo codified many of our modern concepts surrounding Satan: embodying all things foul and wicked, he was portrayed with horns, cloven hooves, donkey ears, blazing eyes, a large phallus, and an overpowering stench of sulfur.[77]

"In a motif common to the later Middle Ages, Satan squats down to defecate writhing sinners through his anus while simultaneously ingesting them through his mouth above," writes Brenda S. Gardenour Walter, associate history professor at the St. Louis College of Pharmacy. "In this upside-down schema, Satan's anus likewise becomes a mouth to be kissed by his worshippers, while his mouth is an anus that defecates lies, curses, and the foul stench of flatulence, sulfur, and dead fish."[78] When combined with his prominent phallus, this anal imagery represented Satan's association with the lowest and basest of bodily functions: defecation and ejaculation.

This odor of brimstone extended not only to Satan but also to his cadre of fallen angels, the demons, as well as anyone who followed him. In 1611, Father Louis Gaufridi confessed to witnessing demonic baptisms at which "water, sulphur and salt are employed: the sulphur renders the recipient the Devil's slave while salt confirms his baptism in the Devil's service."[79] Indeed those in Satan's thrall, especially witches, often smelled foul, partially due to their grave robbing habits but largely because of the stink of evil (the word for "witch" in the Pyrenees is derived from *putrere*, meaning one who smells foul).[80] One sixteenth century account described Satan's workers as reeking of "sulphur and cannon powder and stinking flesh all intermingled."[81] Even when disguised as an animal, their rank odor would give them away. A British pamphlet of 1661 described a baker's ghost that could appear not only as a human, but as a goat or black cat, in each case leaving "the hellish whiff of brimstone after it."[82]

Sulfur also appears in magic, alchemy (a topic for later discussion), and the conjuration of demons. Johann Georg Faust—the inspiration for Goethe's eponymous drama—detailed a recipe including garlic, sulfur, pitch, and special herbs that would summon an evil spirit if placed upon hot coals.[83] Special requests could even be made for demons to appear "in human guise noiselessly and without foul scents," as in the Grand Grimoire, a famous book of magic spells.[84] Anyone summoning Ashtaroth, the Great Duke of Hell, was warned to hold a magical ring beneath his or her nose to combat his stench.[85]

Oddly, sulfur was believed to *repel* demons as well, leading to its use in exorcisms. Girolamo Menghi advised in the 1500s that the possessed should inhale burning sulfur, while exorcist Piero Antonio Stampa advised holding the demoniac above flames fueled by pitch and sulfur.[86] In the Loudun Possessions, a confession was coaxed out of one of the sisters after a bit of burning sulfur fell upon her lip.[87]

Similarly, demons could be imprisoned with the aid of sulfur. Using the "Curse of Chains," a magician could punish unruly demons by writing their name and seal on a scrap parchment, then securing it within a black wooden box alongside sulfur and other malodorous substances.[88] Sulfur also found use among black slaves of the American south, who would fashion "witch balls" to ward off supernatural creatures. These were purportedly composed of "animal excrement found in the woods, human semen, spit, sulphur, foxfire, and camphor," all bound in women's hair."[89]

This duality—to both lure and repel spiritual intelligences—reflects the manner in which sulfur is at once divine and demonic in Christian tradition. It seems that, from a folkloric perspective, sulfur is possessed of an ever-changing character, shifting like a chemical trickster, echoing the liminal, contradictory phenomena reported by so many modern paranormal witnesses.

Science of sulfur

In 1677, Swedish miner Fat-Mats Israelsson was presumed dead when a tunnel in his mine collapsed. Forty-two years later, explorers in the old tunnel discovered a body, perfectly preserved, and brought it to the surface, only to have its identity confirmed by Israelsson's former fiancée, Margareta Olsdotter. The miracle of the preserved miner was put on display; when naturalist Carolus Linnaeus saw the exhibition, he declared that Israelsson's body had been preserved in vitriol, a type of sulfate, and would decompose once this initial coating evaporated.[90]

Predictably for someone of his reputation, Linnaeus was proven correct. The entire affair of Fat-Mats calls to mind archaic tales of people who visited Fairyland only to emerge decades later, having not aged a day. In these narratives, the unfortunate sojourners crumble into dust shortly after their return.

There is a bit of mythology in science and a bit of science in mythology. Any understanding of one is incomplete without the other. An overwhelming amount of literature exists regarding sulfur, and we could spend chapters discussing the element. Again, patience is required while we lay the groundwork of the discussion to come.

Sulfur (symbol S, atomic number 16), has been known to mankind since antiquity.[91] In its pure state, it presents as a bright yellow solid element, quite soft with a low specific gravity. It is so susceptible to heat that simply holding it in one's hand can cause it to expand and fracture, and it is destroyed if left in direct sunlight.[92] This susceptibility to heat is responsible for its "brimstone" name, and when set on fire the element releases a blue flame. When melted, sulfur thickens and turns reddish black; at more extreme temperatures, it becomes a dark orange-yellow gas. It is present in a wide variety of minerals, such as galena, pyrite, and cinnabar, as well as sulfur compounds like hydrogen sulfide, sulfur dioxide, and sulfuric acid.[93] We will examine several of these compounds in depth over the course of our discussion.

Sulfur is essential to life on this planet. It is a key component in many polypeptides, proteins, and enzymes. All organisms on Earth are built of the same six elements: carbon, hydrogen, nitrogen, oxygen, phosphorus, and sulfur.[94] The element's association with foul odors arises from its presence wherever biological material is broken down. In decomposition, sulfate-reducing bacteria convert sulfate into hydrogen sulfide;[95] similar processes in the gut, along with the substances indole and skatole, contribute to the ill-smelling bouquet of feces and flatus (interestingly enough, the largest component of flatus—methane—is actually odorless,[96] with the malodorous components only making up 1% of the total composition).[97]

Scientists estimate that sulfur is the 15th most common element in the universe. Naturally occurring deposits can be found worldwide, particularly in Sicily, Central Europe, Canada, the Arabian Peninsula, Texas, Louisiana, and beneath the Gulf of Mexico.

Sulfur moves to and from living systems via the sulfur cycle: decaying biological material, volcanic eruptions, hot springs, and the ocean all release sulfur compounds into the air, which react in the atmosphere and fall to the earth in the form of rain.[98] A little acid deposition is good, but mankind has increased the incidence of acid rain worldwide by burning fossil fuels, which releases excess sulfur dioxide into the air.[99]

It is ironic that, although associated with Satan, sulfur actually has a number of beneficial qualities and applications. The *Odyssey* describes its preclassical Grecian use as a fumigant. Pliny the Elder later cited its medicinal applications—indeed, sulfur's mild antimicrobial attributes make it a popular additive in modern pharmaceuticals (sulfonamides) and acne medications. This medicinal quality is one possible reason the breath of God was equated with brimstone in the Bible, and sinners were cast in the lake of fire as a cleansing attempt. (Not all sulfur derivatives are positive, however: keeping the theme of duality as in sulfur's demonic/divine origin, some compounds—particularly hydrogen sulfide and sulfuric acid—are actually quite dangerous.)

Other contemporary applications for sulfur involve the production of sulfuric acid, gunpowder, fertilizers, batteries, soaps, matches, desiccants and bleaching agents, plastics, pesticides, and paints. Vulcanized rubber, preferred for its extra strength and durability, is produced with sulfur.[100]

If sulfur is so useful and prevalent, why does it stink? Actually, it doesn't. One hundred percent pure sulfur only smells when burned. What we describe as the "smell of sulfur" is actually one of a handful of sulfur compounds—the smell of burning sulfur, for example, is actually sulfur dioxide (SO_2), wherein sulfur has combined with oxygen via combustion. This naturally raises the question of *exactly what compound* people smell when they report sulfur in paranormal encounters. As each of these compounds appears in our discussion, we will investigate them in greater depth.

Although sulfur itself doesn't smell, most of us agree its compounds stink. No one enjoys the odor of decay, rotten eggs, or flatus (or, at least, the flatus of others). Out of the 26 most common major offensive odorants derived from chemical and petroleum plants, 12 contain sulfur.[101]

Yet we may also recall that hedonic associations are acquired, not innate. Perhaps the learned association between sulfur compounds and revulsion is in fact not universal, but tied to universally-shared human experiences: as Vroon noted, "man is looking for a suitable biotrope, which explains the human preferences for certain plants and foods, as well as our dislike of rotting; likewise, in order to avoid infection it is sensible to avoid contact with feces."[102]

Even if we are not hardwired to despise sulfur compounds, we are hardwired to detect them. The ability of human beings to perceive sulfur compounds in our environment is practically unmatched by any other scent, with a detection threshold as low as 0.5 parts per *billion* for hydrogen sulfide.[103] Put in perspective, one drop of ink in a large semi-trailer tank is twice that concentration.[104] Other sulfur compounds, including thiocresol, ethyl mercaptan, and methanethiol, have similar sensitivities.[105]

Recent research suggests that it is an abundance of copper in our bodies that allows us to detect sulfur compounds at such low levels. In 2012 scientists at Duke University Medical Center and the University of Albany were examining a chemical attractant in mouse urine when they discovered that the detectability of sulfur is linked to the amount of copper in mammalian bodies. Subsequent experiments demonstrated that, when copper is unavailable to scent receptors, mice have a much greater difficulty in detecting sulfur compounds.[106]

Modern mythmaking

An oft-circulated urban legend tells the story of a young lady who wished to dance at the local discotheque, to her mother's protestations. "If you go, I hope you meet with the devil," she yells as her stubborn daughter walks out the door.

The young lady arrives at the club to find all her friends atwitter. It seems a preternaturally handsome young man in dapper dress entered just prior to her arrival. After some time, this man asks the young lady to dance. Enchanted, she accepts the invitation. It isn't until she looks at his feet, however, that she spies his cloven feet floating above the parquet floor. She tries to extricate herself, to no avail; his touch burns her shoulders as well as the hands of the friend who tries to rescue her. The handsome man disappears, leaving behind disembodied laughter and a sulfurous stench.[107]

The medieval belief that the devil smells of sulfur has perpetuated through the years. As the ages waned on, legendary monsters were eventually ascribed similar sulfurous traits. Dragons (synonymous with Satan in the Bible) were ascribed a stench of sulfur and other foul smells. The concept is no doubt partially responsible for the belief in their fiery, lethal halitosis. Lindorms, for example—the dragons of Scandinavia—would exude an overpowering stench when slain.[108]

Many of our modern monsters still reflect these expectations. On Saturday, January 20, 1996, in Varginha, Brazil, Liliane da Silva (16 years old), her sister Valquíria (14), and friend Kátia Xavier (22) saw a strange being covered in "oily brown skin with big eyes and three 'horns' on its head" crouching in a vacant lot. "We thought it was the Devil," they said upon later reflection. The three girls fled and returned with their mother 20 minutes later. The "devil" was gone, "but we could see the grass mashed down and we could smell sulfur or ammonia," Kátia said. UFO investigator Ubirajara Franco Rodrigues linked the sighting to an event earlier in the month, when NORAD detected an anomalous object on radar and predicted a Brazilian impact point.[109]

In addition to smell, many have noted the similarities between UFOs, their purported pilots, and demonic entities. In a 2000 *MUFON Journal* editorial, Ann Druffel and Jean Sider outlined the manner in which tall, blond "Nordic" space brothers evoke angels, while short, malignant "Grey" abductors call to mind demons of the past. Sider pursued some particularly compelling connections between the purported names of alien entities and demonic monikers—for example, George van Tassel's contact "Solganda," she argued, appears to be a portmanteau of "Sol" (sun, an alchemical symbol for sulfur) and "Gandarewa," a demon found in the Zoroastrian Avesta.[110] Ashtar, another extraterrestrial entity supposedly invoked during channeling sessions, shares an etymological root with Ashtaroth, the aforementioned Great Duke of Hell. Even some factions within the United States government entertained the UFO-demon idea, as chronicled by author Nick Redfern in his book *Final Events*.

Demonic Sasquatch are not uncommon either, despite how ridiculous that phrase looks on paper. A seven-foot-tall, hairy beast with glowing "reddish pink eyes" was seen in September 1975 by farmer Kenneth Tosh on his Noxie, Oklahoma, ranch. It first appeared a mere 20 feet from the farmhouse, and all of Tosh's rifle shots seemingly passed right through the hominid. It left three-toed tracks, screamed like a crying baby, and emitted a noxious (Noxie?) odor of "rotten eggs or sulphur."[111]

What do all these similarities mean? No promises are made that we will arrive at any real conclusions to such a question, but we will certainly leave better informed. With a solid understanding of olfaction and the history of sulfur behind us, we can at last turn our attention to unraveling the secrets behind the smells of spirits, UFOs, Sasquatch, and other things that go bump in the night.

Part II: Spirit Smells

Chapter 4
Spirit Smells: A History

Under the ground, the well-perfumed stink just as bad.

— Martial

On a winter night in the early 1980s, author Paul Gater "awoke to an atmosphere in [his] bedroom supercharged with cold and a strong smell of sulphur." Peering into the darkness, Gater could clearly see a shape hiding among the shadows: stooped and clad in black rags, hideous, even though a hood obscured its face. The author later reminisced that he was more surprised than afraid and responded by simply flicking on the bedside lamp. The stench and apparition vanished, though the cold lingered for some time afterward.[112]

Was it a ghost? A demon? Or a simple bout with sleep paralysis?

All cultures hold beliefs about the spirit world, a realm of existence populated by the souls of the dead, elemental earth spirits, angelic beings, and demonic forces. Unlike religious dogma, which internalizes spirituality, most concepts of the spirit world posit an objective sphere of existence for these entities, concomitant with the world of the living. For those who believe, this reality constantly influences our own, replaying echoes of humanity's past and facilitating interactions with benevolent beings from Heaven or malevolent forces from Hell. In some traditions, like the Celtic faerie faith or the *yokai*—Japan's elaborate taxon of spirit beings—

the inhabitants of this world are quite diverse. By contrast, the strictest interpretations of Christianity only allow for the Trinity, angels, and demons to influence the living.

Of all paranormal phenomena, spirits exhibit the widest variety of odors in contemporary accounts. This is in no small part because they are the *only* phenomena to present pleasant (or at least non-offensive) odors on a regular basis during encounters. Roughly speaking, apparitions of saints are associated with floral smells, demonic and poltergeist activity involve foul and sulfurous smells, and ghosts run the gamut, depending upon which scents echo the pastimes of their former lives. This is particularly true in the case of smoking gentlemen and fragrant ladies; Rosemary Ellen Guiley writes that, in her research, she has found tobacco and lilac to be two of the most common aromas.[113] Other typical examples include perfumes, the odor of cooking food, and candied odors like cinnamon and chewing gum.

Many world cultures harbor beliefs about how the spirit world smells. Australian Aborigines hold that ghosts smell "stale" and cannot abide the scent of pregnant women.[114] The *yokai* are frequently attributed distinctive odors, often of a foul, decaying nature.[115]

Ghosts do not smell at all in African folklore, with the peculiar exception of their fingernails. In one legend, a spirit wished to strengthen its thumbnail for the express purpose of sawing bones, a task it attempted by heating it in the village campfire. The resultant stench alerted everyone in the village, and the plan was foiled.[116]

"A common belief in modern ghost lore is that if a smell is connected with a ghost, it often defines whether the spirit is good or evil," writes Brian Haughton in *Famous Ghost Stories: Legends and Lore*. "A pleasant smell, often of flowers, is associated with a friendly ghost, while a stale, rank odor is associated with an unpleasant or threatening phantom."[117] Such hedonic associations are unsurprising.

What *is* curious is the fact that, prior to the mid-1800s, smells were rarely connected with ghosts in the West. Instead, pre-Victorian spirit smells were associated almost exclusively with saintly apparitions and demonic visitation. Haughton speculates that the rise of spiritualism, "when just about every form of communication from the dead imaginable was recorded," led to an increased awareness of odors with an invisible, "supernatural" source.[118]

It is true that spirit cases are the only paranormal reports where an entity need not be visually sighted to be associated with a smell. This is particularly problematic, as smells not only arise from a variety of mundane, unnoticed sources, but can also linger for years. Anyone who has worked with horses knows that long-abandoned stables retain their equine smell years after disuse, particularly if they remain shut; certainly that odor is not (always) attributable to ghost horses. The suggestible bed-and-breakfast lodger, primed by hours of paranormal reality television, may catch the whiff of a cigar and believe their non-smoking room is possessed by the spirit of Herbert Hoover, who stayed there one night in 1931… when in reality, the last lodger simply decided to break the rules and tossed a butt into the potted plant. To be fair, this is not always the case; visitors to America's Gettysburg National Military Park, which has been exposed to a century-and-a-half of weather since the climactic Civil War battle ended, have every right to think that the scent of gunpowder is anomalous, in spite of annual reenactments.

Still, skepticism is advisable when discussing spirit smells, particularly when odors are unaccompanied by other phenomena. By their very nature, "ghost stories" are apocryphal. At the end of this discussion, once the common motifs have been collected and examined, we will look into theories about scents from the spirit world, and possible mundane explanations.

Before proceeding further, an important note on nomenclature: for simplicity's sake, the word "spirit" is used as a catchall term to encompass all non-corporeal entities. This not only includes ghosts, but also poltergeists, demons, angels, *yokai*, and Blessed Virgin Mary (BVM) apparitions (the faerie folk are tabled for later discussion).

Do not be misled by this umbrella term, however, and assume that these entities are all of the same nature, or come from the same source. It is entirely likely—probable, even—that each of these spirits are fundamentally different. It is equally possible that ghosts are not the spirits of the dead, demons don't come from Hell, and angels don't come from Heaven. For all we know, ghosts could be time-travelers, demons and angels may come from the collective unconscious, and BVM apparitions might be more akin to UFO activity than spiritual revelation. We may mistake a demon for a ghost, or a ghost for an angel.

As with all things unexplained, the true nature of the spirit world remains elusive. All we have are our best guesses.

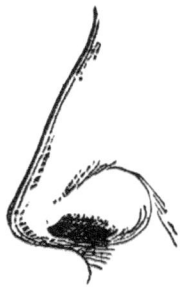

Chapter 5
Spirit Smells: Pleasant Spirit Fragrances

During the Easter season of 1666, I smelled a very sweet fragrance for around seven minutes; I had never smelled anything like it in my life, and it gave me such deep satisfaction that I was enraptured.
—Judge François Grimaud on Our Lady of Laus

The Lady and child were beautiful beyond compare, and even though the strange old man had told Benôite to look for her in Vallon des Fours, the young shepherdess could not believe she was looking at the Mother of God. Benôite greeted the beautiful Lady and offered her some bread. She accepted graciously and wordlessly.

This small act of communion began a half-century of visits with the Blessed Virgin Mary, beginning with four months of contact in 1664 during which Benôite Rencurel was instructed to pray for sinners and work toward their salvation. To accomplish this, the apparition charged Benôite with the foundation of a mission in Laus, France. "If you wish to see me again," she said, "Go to Laus. You will find there a chapel from which a beautiful perfume comes."[119]

After much searching, Benôite located a ramshackle chapel exuding an exquisite odor of perfume and flowers. Mary appeared to the girl once again, and it was here that she was instructed to build her church. The tiny congregation that followed soon swelled, and in 1666 an expansion of the chapel began.

The wonderful fragrance persisted, having a pervasive, joyous affect on anyone who smelled it. During the construction process, one historian wrote, "The earliest historians of Laus are unanimous in reporting the sweet, Heavenly fragrance of the place; they mention it as a public occurrence to which a great number of people attested. These fragrances were sometimes so intense that their odor spread from the chapel all across the valley."[120] An investigation into Benôite's claims led by Judge François Grimaud confirmed their veracity, citing the aroma's overpowering beauty.[121] The odor was so beautiful that Honore Pela, a sculptor from Gap, was inspired to donate a marble statue of Madonna and Child.

Of the 10 Marian Apparitions recognized by the Holy Roman Catholic Church, Our Lady of Laus is considered one of the more obscure, largely due to its exclusively French reportage. The Vatican only recently recognized its authenticity in May 2008.[122] Though fragrances appear in most official and unofficial BVM apparitions, none feature odor as prominently as the vision at Laus, and to this day, flowers are not allowed at the church, for fear visitors might conflate their fragrance with Mary's blessed scent.[123]

The bulk of pleasant odors in spirit encounters are reserved for saints or female ghosts, with the rare exception of male cologne. Such pleasant odors can be roughly subdivided into floral smells and perfume smells, though there is naturally some overlap (flowers, especially rose and lilac, are popular fragrances).[124] Flower pageantry is particularly strong in BVM apparitions, where literal petals sometimes accompany visions. In the 1531 appearance of Our Lady of Guadalupe, Mary appeared and instructed Juan Diego to collect flowers from a once-barren hill; he threaded them into his *tilma* (cloak), and upon returning to the archbishop, they fell away to reveal the shape of the Virgin in the fabric.[125] These floral connotations owe a debt to St. Bernard, who described Mary as "the rose of charity, the lily of chastity, violet of humility," and the "golden gilly-flower of Heaven."[126]

The hedonic associations are obvious. In spite of the unfair patriarchal tendencies of Western society, women have long been ascribed the traits of virtue, warmth, love, and gentility; similarly, saints of either sex lived existences of divinity, kindness, and good deeds.

"We are hardly surprised that a pleasant smell should be associated with holiness," writes Le Guérer. "After all, the saint has a special contact with the beyond, and even during his or her lifetime the true saints resides, as it were, in the anterooms of Paradise. Paradise itself was a region traditionally described as filled with exquisite odors, a notion derived directly from pagan antiquity."[127]

Having given the devil his due, it is only fitting we discuss the scent of the divine.

The fragrance of Heaven

Like Hell, Heaven's olfactory origins lie in antiquity. Plutarch wrote that the river Lethe emitted "a delicate and suave exhalation of strangely voluptuous odors, causing an intoxication like that achieved by becoming drunk on wine"—drinking of these waters led one to forget their former life, serving the same purpose as the draught of oblivion, *nepenthe*.[128] Early Christian theologians echoed similar ideas, describing Heaven as "a broad prairie from which rises at all times an extraordinary perfume" (Gregory of Tours), filled with "an inimitable ambrosial odor that emanated from the loveliest of lovely springtime flowers" (Saint Maximus).[129]

The hedonic association of pleasant smells and Heaven is by no means exclusive to the West. In Hindu tradition, the afterlife is filled with perfumes and flowers, including "a blue flower which, Brahmins say / Blooms nowhere but in Paradise," while the Qu'ran tells us that the very ground of the Islamic afterlife is "composed of pure wheaten flour mixed with musk and saffron."[130] Fragrant oils were also used worldwide when preparing corpses for the afterlife, from the ancient Egyptians to the Aztecs.[131]

These fragrances naturally extended to the Heavenly host. In Hinduism, the deity Krishna is thought to give off the aroma of flowers.[132] Classical literature is rife with the association of deities and their holy fragrances, to the extent that Homer and his contemporaries rarely invoked a Greek goddess without mentioning her holy fragrances. "Celestial Venus hovered o'er his head / And roseate unguents Heavenly fragrance shed," it is said of Cupid's mother in the *Iliad*.[133]

In Christianity, God, the Holy Ghost, and angels were all thought to smell exquisite. Though the breath of the Lord was compared to brimstone, He himself was said to smell fragrant—there is confusion, however, whether these divine odors are to be taken literally or as a metaphor for God's pervasive, ethereal love. For example, in 2 Corinthians 2:14 the Apostle Paul speaks of the Lord's power to spread "the fragrance of His knowledge in every place. For we are to God the fragrance of Christ among those who are being saved and among those who are perishing."

In the *Ars Notoria* portion of the *Lesser Key of Solomon*, the Lord is called upon to "illustrate and confirm [the spell caster's] understanding with the sweet odor of thy Spirit." In the *Ars Almadel* section of that selfsame grimoire, it is written that a departing angel "will fill the whole place with a sweet and pleasant smell, which will be smelled for a long time."[134]

Three times in the Bible, Mary of Bethany—sister to Lazarus—falls at Christ's feet, each time noting an odor. In Luke 10, Mary sits at His feet and listens to His word, smelling an odor of food; in John 11 she falls to His feet to share her woe, smelling death; and in John 12, she smells perfume as she worships at Christ's feet. Not coincidentally, each scent appears in spirit smell literature.

The Holy Spirit was often responsible for spreading this "fragrance." Psychiatrist Carl Jung discussed the "sweet odour" of the Holy Ghost at length, prompted in part by visions during his 1944 hospitalization. In his autobiography he recalled the transformation of his hospital room into a garden of pomegranates: "For me the presence of sanctity had a magical atmosphere... I understood then why one speaks of the odor of sanctity, of the 'sweet smell' of the Holy Ghost. This was it. There was a *pneuma* of inexpressible sanctity in the room, whose manifestation was the *mysterium coniunctionis*."[135]

The fragrance of saints

Residing as they do in "the anterooms of Paradise" while alive, saints were often believed to exude pleasant smells. What exactly they were and how many different odors were involved seems to vary between individuals—Lidwina, Dutch mystic and Catholic saint, was said to give off the scent of "cinnamon, cut flowers, ginger, clove, lily, rose, and violet,"[136] while Pio of Pietrelcina ("Padre Pio") was accompanied by "a mixture of violets and roses."[137]

This "smell of sanctity" occasionally extended beyond saints. In Scandinavian mythology, the blood of all Christians is said to smell distinctive to supernatural entities.[138] In the East, yogis are often said to smell like fragrant flowers, while magical healers in pre-Christian Russia were said to maintain impeccably tidy living spaces, emitting the pleasing smell of medicinal herbs.[139] Many researchers attribute this hedonic association (holy persons smell good, demons smell bad) with the reason why modern ghosts are ascribed positive or negative attributes based upon their odor.[140]

What could have caused this fragrance from living saints? While Christianity holds that the cause is self-evident, there may be a scientific explanation. Some have suggested these fragrant saints, eschewing pleasures of the flesh, may have developed ketosis from their restrictive diet. This metabolic state is created by fasting or a diet low in carbohydrates, and imparts to breath and urine a sweet smell likened to alcohol or nail polish remover.[141] These odors, however, do not satisfactorily fit the array of olfactory profiles attributed to saintly perfumes.

Another possible answer lies in the work of scientists Michael Persinger and Stanley Koren, who pioneered "neurotheology" in the 1980s with the "God helmet," a device placed upon the head that stimulates the right temporal lobe via weak magnetic fields. In his experiments, Persinger was able to induce visions, sensed "presences," and other sensory stimuli in subjects evocative of a host of anomalistic phenomena, from religious revelations to alien abductions.

To Persinger, this frontal lobe stimulation in mystics could have caused their sweat to emit pleasant odors. "Areas of the temporal lobe probably affect the metabolism in such a way that your sweat has a certain smell," he told author Barbara Bradley Hagerty in 2006. "Many of the classic mystics are often described as having a smell about them that is very fragrant, like roses, and all of this is tied to temporal lobe function."[142]

Aside from his tenuous link between the temporal lobe and metabolism, Persinger's hypothesis does not posit a *cause* of the stimulating magnetism in the first place. It also fails to explain one of the more peculiar aspects of saintly smells: their ability to linger, even change, after death.

Upon her death in 1582, the odors of lily and orris emitted by Saint Teresa of Ávila ripened to incorporate violet and jasmine.[143] Saints who defy decomposition by miraculous preservation are referred to as "the Incorruptibles," and the phenomenon is not at all uncommon; Joan Carroll Cruz's eponymous 1977 study detailed over one hundred such cases. Some corpses seem to exude living smells like sweat and blood, while others continue to give off more pleasant aromas.

In 1130, St. Isidore the Laborer was buried in a simple farmer's grave in Madrid, only to be exhumed for transfer to a more dignified resting place four decades later. "It was found to be perfect as if it had but just died although it had been lying in the earth for forty years," a contemporary historian reported of the body. "Not only was no sign of decay perceptible but a sweet ravishing odour proceeded from it, an odour which all extolled." In May 1969, the body was displayed in Madrid's cathedral, where it allegedly appeared "darkened, rigid, but perfect."[144] The similarities to Fat-Mats Israelsson, while tangential, are apparent.

The scent of the BVM

According to Christian tradition, Mary's similarly incorrupt body was assumed directly into Heaven at the end of her earthly life. It is of little doubt, therefore, that blissful aromas often accompany her appearances in the modern era. Though the church only endorses 10 Marian Apparitions, researcher Gilbert Cornu estimates around 230 took place between 1928 and 1975 alone (to say nothing of unreported cases).[145]

One of the most celebrated Marian apparitions took place in Fátima, Portugal, where three young children— Lúcia, Jacinta, and Francisco—claimed to have encountered an angel while shepherding in 1916. The angel commanded them to live pious lives. On May 13 the following year, a bright, shining lady who identified herself as "The Lady of the Rosary" appeared to them and asked them to engage in penance, Acts of Reparation, and personal sacrifices for sinners. As a result, the children became unsettlingly devout, engaging in self-flagellation and fasting.

After one particular encounter, the children snapped a branch that had brushed up against Mary's cloak and presented it to Jacinta's aunt as evidence of the encounter. The branch was reportedly infused with a smell that was "not spicy, not the smell of roses… but a very fine perfume."[146] Friends and neighbors bore witness as the reportedly "wonderfully sweet" fragrance filled the entire house.[147]

Our Lady of Fátima remains compelling for two main reasons: the Three Secrets and the Miracle of the Sun, both of which supported the children's claims. The Three Secrets featured a vision of Hell; foretold of the end of World War I and the beginning of World War II; and predicted a twentieth century Christian persecution and the botched 1981 assassination attempt of Pope John Paul II (much controversy surrounds the last secret's interpretation). The Miracle of the Sun, on the other hand, occurred during the last of the BVM apparitions before an enormous crowd—estimates range 30,000-100,000—where the Sun appeared as a spinning disc, dancing to and fro in the sky and releasing multicolored beams of light.[148]

Modern UFOlogists, including Jacques Vallee, view the Miracle of the Sun through different eyes than the Holy See. They certainly have a right to do so. In his seminal work *Daimonic Reality*, author Patrick Harpur clearly highlights the ambiguity of the BVM: like nymphs of pagan lore, the BVM has an affinity for appearing near water; the lights and flashes of her visions evoke UFO encounters; and, most tellingly, Mary rarely explicitly identifies herself in such encounters, preferring vague pseudonyms, as at Fátima.[149]

In Cairo, more than 100 witnesses experienced spontaneous healing when a woman appeared in 1968 atop St. Mary's Coptic Church, accompanied by red, perfume-scented clouds. She never said a word, but the crowd nonetheless identified her as Mary.[150] Even when her identity is obvious, the BVM sometimes appears in a ridiculous guise, such as the three-foot version that visited Mary Fowler of Conyers, Georgia, in the 1990s—yet crowds flocked to hear Mary's messages from Fowler and often experienced visions and the smell of roses.[151]

Let's play a game: BVM or UFO?

A girl from Roccagloriosa, Italy, was working the fields in 1929 when she allegedly beheld a white ball of light in the sky that descended slowly to the ground. Dimming, the sphere opened in a sort of portal, out of which stepped a lady in a "sumptuous black garment." The witness noticed several smaller entities within the light as the woman floated toward her, then abruptly turned for the tree line. Frightened, the girl ran and returned with her father, but the light was gone. The landing site, however, was permeated with the scent of roses.[152]

Given the female entity, historically Catholic setting, and smell of roses, it reads like the BVM; given the slowly descending light and short entities, a UFO. To what side do we award this case? Perhaps there are no sides; or perhaps the deciding vote should be cast in favor of the pleasant smell, as our noses rarely seem to lie to us.

Fragrance of female ghosts

As noted, not every pleasant-smelling apparition is a saint—some are thought to be merely the souls of the departed, those who had an affinity for pleasant fragrances in life. In the warden's private bathroom at the Ohio State Reformatory, witnesses claim to detect the faint smell of perfume;[153] visitors to the Baker Hotel of Mineral Wells, Texas, say that Virginia Brown's lavender perfume hangs in the air;[154] and the Bush House of Index, Washington, still manifests perfume on the second floor, even when no guests are present.[155] The examples are literally endless. Such accounts resonate with more veracity when the odors can be matched to a specific individual who frequented a haunted location during life, e.g. Chicago's Red Lion pub, where the persistent smell of lavender on the second floor matches the perfume favored by a former tenant who passed away in the building.[156]

- The Gold Hill Hotel of Virginia City, Nevada, is known for two ghosts: former owner "William" (who manifests cigar smoke) and "Rosie," a prostitute who died in the building and whose presence is known by her (you guessed it) cheap rose perfume. Psychic investigator and author Richard Senate was bathing when he detected the odor himself. "It wasn't like a real smell—it was overpowering," he wrote. "I checked the soaps, the windows, everything, and then the aroma vanished instantly in an unnatural way."[157] This sudden cessation is a hallmark of spirit smells and is one of the few ways to differentiate them from random aromas.[158] Senate believes he was visited by Rosie, and took efforts to ensure no one was in the hall or balcony with an atomizer (highly unlikely, given the incident took place at 2:00 a.m.).[159]

- Log Cabin Village, an attraction in Fort Worth, is home to several historic log cabin homes. Foster Cabin, built in

1853, is one of the oldest homes in Texas and is regarded as the most haunted of the six buildings. Staff members claim that the spirit of Miss Jane Holt lingers about the cabin, making her presence known by the scent of lilac perfume. The fragrance is particularly noticeable on the upper level, where she treated her son after he returned home wounded from the American Civil War, and is often accompanied by the sound of footsteps, the creak of a rocking chair, and cold spots.[160]

- One of the few negative entities associated with floral smells is the *kuntilanak* of Indonesia. Always depicted as female, this spirit smells of flowers or strong perfume and lurks in roadside trees or old buildings, waiting for her victims to drive by. When they are close, she covers their eyes and causes an automobile accident, from which she takes human blood to strengthen herself.[161]

- Paranormal aficionado Lon Strickler claims to have encountered the ghost of a woman in a bonnet on the property of an old Maryland plantation in 1984. Strickler claims that the entity appeared in the weeds before rushing toward him, passing through his body. Following the encounter, he reeked of honeysuckle, even though it was too early in the season for him to have encountered any outdoors. "When I got home… my ex-wife wouldn't even let me come in the bedroom for about a week because it smelled that bad," he later recalled. "It just made her nauseous."[162]

- One ghost in an antique mall (formerly the Mineral Springs Hotel) in Alton, Illinois, is explicitly defined by her smell. The "Jasmine Woman," as she has come to be known, was staying at the hotel with her husband when she was caught in an affair. She fled her room and fell to her death down the stairway, where the scent of jasmine lingers to this day.¹⁶³ The experience of former building owner and skeptic Bob Love, who claimed to have smelled the "strong, almost putrid jasmine scent" before learning of the legend, seems to rule out the power of suggestion.¹⁶⁴

Jasmine, a commonly detected perfume in hauntings, is also smelled in conjunction with the Grey Lady of Bath, England's Theatre Royal.¹⁶⁵ It is interesting to note that the distinctive odors of many flowers (including jasmine and honeysuckle) are due in part to the presence of skatole and indole.¹⁶⁶ Human digestion also generates these compounds, converting them from tryptophan, an essential amino acid. In small amounts, indole and skatole are pleasant; in higher concentrations, they impart a fecal odor.¹⁶⁷

These foul-smelling undertones allow flowers to take on a more unpleasant odor profile. In Hebrew tales, *dybbuk* boxes—wine cabinets purportedly haunted by a malevolent spirit—plague their owners with ill luck and foul smells. One American antique collector who had acquired such a box claimed that "all of the owners have said they catch scents of jasmine—sweet, sickly smells, and very bad smells like cat urine."¹⁶⁸

Feline spirits are responsible for aromas as well. According to researcher and author Randy Russell, Castillo de San Marcos in St. Augustine, Florida, is home to a spectral cat that carries with it the scent of rose perfume. Legend holds the cat was once the pet of Colonel Luis Gaspar and his wife, Marianna. Gaspar was so focused on the fortress's 1740 renovations that he failed to notice his wife's affair with a dashing young captain. Marianna employed a strong rose perfume, fashioned by the camp doctor, to mask the sexual smells of her affair. Eventually, their indiscretions were revealed and the couple was imprisoned; the doctor, taking pity on them, fashioned a poison. Covering the foul taste with Marianna's rose scent, the doctor strapped the vial to the cat's collar and sent it to the dungeon. The walled-in lovers were rediscovered centuries later, but visitors claim the phantom feline can still be seen—and smelled—on its macabre errand.¹⁶⁹

In *The Ghost Files*, researcher Jeff Belanger relates the tale of a young girl named Elaine who, while searching for her lost dog in Chicago, Illinois, found herself alone in a cemetery. She was surprised to discover the dog, shaking like a leaf, tethered to the high branch of a tree. The leash was too high and tight to have been secured by the wind. "I began to smell a very strong scent of men's cologne," she wrote. "It was very, very distinct, and smelled good." There was no one around at the time, nor any empty cologne bottles—though it certainly possible a good albeit lazy Samaritan had fastened the leash.[170]

This anecdote aside, it is interesting that fragrances of masculine cologne appear infrequently in hauntings. Like perfume, cologne has been worn around the world for several centuries, and yet rarely are pleasant spirit smells as attributed to men. Cologne cases are much harder to come by than their feminine counterparts.

One rare, if apocryphal, story involves a pleasant odor of the non-floral variety, though a feminine interpretation remains. "Dr. Beachcombing," a historian who moonlights as a well-regarded Fortean researcher, came across the tale of a European couple who, after deciding to spend the night at a friend's home in southern Italy, arrived to find their room already taken. Double booked, the host instead took them to the renovated guesthouse, informing the husband that the ghost of a nun haunted the building. Returning to bed, the husband fell into a deep sleep, despite his wife's complaints about a sickeningly overwhelming scent of talcum powder. The next morning, she remarked how the smell had suddenly disappeared, to which the husband absent-mindedly offered their host's warning as an explanation. The wife fled immediately, convinced the nun's ghost was responsible.[171]

The tale isn't especially exciting or well vetted, but it is still notable as an outlier, not *quite* falling within the perfume/floral categories. The actual scent components of talcum powder are hard to pin down—the Johnson & Johnson's formula is proprietary, it seems—but its fragrance is traditionally a mixture of white musk and orange blossom, the latter of which, like jasmine and honeysuckle, contains skatole and indole.[172]

Chapter 6
Spirit Smells: Smoke

I smoke in moderation. Only one cigar at a time.
— Mark Twain

If the fragrance of perfume or flowers suggests the presence of female spirits, their male counterparts are implied by the odor of smoke. As with pleasant spirit smells, there are countless examples of smoke in association with hauntings; the frequency of this occurance cannot be overstated. This makes logical sense if one ascribes to the theory that ghosts are the souls of the deceased—tobacco products were ubiquitous in yesteryear, and what other pastimes were as aromatic as enjoying a pipe or cigar?

Visitors to the former Red Rooster Inn of Key West, Florida (now the Chelsea House) occasionally report a distinctively smooth cigar smoke odor wafting into their rooms. "It was during the late 1800s that the cigar business began booming in Key West and the Delgados were one of the largest manufacturers," said Jim Durbin, former co-owner of the building. "The Red Rooster was built around 1870 and it served as the Delgado family home for a number of years. It is the ghost of Mr. Delgado that is supposed to be the cause of the hauntings, and the sweet, rich cigar scent is said to have been his favorite brand."[173]

It is not at all uncommon for tobacco lovers to leave behind an odor of smoke.

- The crew quarters of Michigan's Whitefish Point Light House station are said to house a spirit affectionately called "Stinky," so named for his strong smoke smell. The odor is so powerful that some guests look for a living smoker to reprimand, only to discover no culprit exists.[174]

- Tombstone, Arizona, is home to the O.K. Corral, location of the most famous shootout of the old west, as well as the Bird Cage Theatre, where many of the shootout's participants passed their time. Today, employees of the establishment remark that the coin-operated music box smells of cigars when opened. The laughter of carousing cowboys, accompanied by music and the odors of smoke and whiskey, is common as well.[175]

- A fan of late American actor James Dean related one particularly charming anecdote to Indiana researcher Bob Freeman. The fan, "Marc," told of a visit to Dean's gravesite: "… as we started to leave, I thought I smelled a cigarette burning… just a whiff. I turned around, and the smoke I had left for Jimmy was gone and I could see a pinpoint of fire just off by the old Sycamore tree. I called out and it disappeared."[176]

- The staff of New York's Burrville Cider Mill not only smell cigar smoke in the building, but also discover old cigars on freshly swept floors. In one instance, a floor had been completely cleared and repainted, only to have a cigar appear in the very center, covered in cobwebs. Caretakers credit this activity to the spirit of John Burr, a pirate captain of the early 19th century for whom the original settlement was named. The smell of cigar smoke in the mill can often become overwhelming—one worker reported the smell was so strong that it stung her nostrils, and seemed to cling to her clothes. As with many spirit smells, the odor dissipated before she came home for the evening.[177]

Smoking was once a common habit, and it appears as if modern efforts to curb it receive protests from the grave. Many taverns in Old New Castle, Delaware, fill with the fragrance of pipe tobacco, in spite of a statewide ban on smoking in public buildings.[178] The RMS *Queen Mary*— permanently docked at Long Beach, California, and refurbished as a hotel and tourist attraction—also has a no-smoking policy, yet visitors hear strange noises and report the odor of cigar smoke.[179] As one of the American South's largest antebellum homes, Cedar Grove in Vicksburg, Mississippi, has a strict no smoking policy to aid in the building's preservation; still, the gentleman's parlor smells of smoke from time to time, just as it did when former owner John Klein lit his nightly pipe.[180] One wonders how the recently departed gentlemanly spirits of today, with our recent societal stigma on smoking, will make themselves known in a hundred years' time.

Physical smoke can manifest in conjunction with these odors. At McPike Mansion in Illinois, visitors frequently smell tobacco and witness the spontaneous formation of cigarette smoke.[181] Similar activity is reported in Parkersburg, West Virginia, where former mayor William N. Chancellor refuses to vacate the Blennerhassett Hotel. According to witnesses, Chancellor—who built the hotel in 1889—not only appears as a full-bodied apparition, but also manifests the smell of cigars and coils smoke around his portrait in the lobby.[182]

The nature of smoke odors is not solely restricted to tobacco. In Cambridge, England, a medieval thoroughfare that passes alongside the city's oldest pub is known for "a persistent pungent odor like a perfume being burned"—subsequent research revealed that the pub had been a 19th century opium den where an intoxicated sailor burned to death after dropping his pipe in a dreamy haze.[183]

Doug Shoback compiled a fieldwork collection of supernatural stories in 1999 that included the collegiate tale of "Stoney Ghosty," a spirit whose fondness for marijuana haunts the University of Northern Colorado at Greeley. According to the legend, a young stoner who died in his dormitory room returns regularly to smoke, causing disembodied voices and leaving a strong pot smell in his wake. At the time Shoback collected this story, four young ladies lived in the dorm room and claimed no drug use of their own; nonetheless, one wonders if the story wasn't simply a cover for strange male voices and a little "recreational use" of their own.[184]

Burning buildings

In addition to their affinity for loud rapping, levitating objects, and throwing stones, poltergeists are also fond of generating smoke, particularly from spontaneous fires. In a well-documented 1695 Scottish case, smoke almost suffocated the family of Andrew Mackie after an unseen force set handfuls of peat ablaze.[185] Flameless smoke was seen during the 10-year reign of the Borley Rectory poltergeist in England, an ominous precursor to the building's mysterious arson on February 27, 1939.[186]

During the famed Amherst, Nova Scotia, case of the late 1870s, the Teed family was often alerted to fires in the home by the smell of smoke. According to Walter Hubbell, who documented the event, poltergeist activity manifested in the home shortly after an attempted sexual assault of Olive Teed's sister, 18-year-old Esther Cox. The girl began suffering from seizures, strange noises knocked about at night, and household objects moved on their own, sometimes taking flight. Among his descriptions, Hubbell detailed the poltergeist's predilection for arson.

> ... I say, candidly, that until I had had that experience I never fully realized what an awful calamity it was to have an invisible monster, somewhere within the atmosphere, going from place to place about the house, gathering up old newspapers into a bundle and hiding it in the basket of soiled linen

or in a closet, then go and steal matches out of the match-box in the kitchen, or somebody's pocket, as he did out of mine; and after kindling a fire in the bundle, tell Esther that he had started a fire, but would not tell where; or perhaps not tell her at all, in which case the first intimation we would have was the smell of smoke pouring through the house, and then the most intense excitement, everybody running with buckets of water.[187]

Though some hauntings may also include poltergeist activity, most paranormal researchers differentiate the two, positing that poltergeists are not spirit infestations but rather psychic energy generated from a living person—perhaps a physical expression of repressed emotions, sexual tension, or trauma. The Amherst case certainly adheres to this scenario.

Contrary to the old adage, it would seem that where there is smoke there is *not* always fire. The Market Square in Oakville, Ontario, has served as the community hub since the early 19th century, hosting both the town hall and jailhouse; both buildings were burned to the ground twice. Investigator Jennifer Tyrrell reports that "close to Halloween, the acrid smell of something burning is very distinctive" around the market.[188] Of course, given the outdoor setting and the great distances it can travel, smoke from an actual bonfire cannot be ruled out, particularly in autumn.

More compelling is the testimony from author Steve Stockton, who once worked at Bally's Casino. The Las Vegas establishment was erected on the former site of the MGM Grand Hotel and Casino, which caught fire in 1980, tragically killing 87 people. Stockton claims the fallout from that day still lingers in the form of an odd burning smell.

"It's this really odd smell, and it doesn't smell like any other kind of burnt smell," Stockton said. "I used to keep a fan going, and when it showed up it would come against the fan… from the opposite direction."[189]

Witnesses also report smelling long-extinguished building fires on or near the anniversary of their destruction. Journalist Peter Haining related how he and his wife, Philippa, would detect the scent of wood smoke on their Suffolk estate each summer around June 6. After catching a glimpse of a mysterious figure with long hair at their home around the same time, Philippa encouraged her husband to research the building's history. The locals—whose ancestors had worked on the property since its construction in the 1500s—informed them that French prisoners had been brought in to work the land in the early 19th century, lodging in the out buildings. During their stay there, an unfortunate fire at the home claimed the life of one of the laborers, an event local lore placed in early June.[190]

Smoky spirits and speculation

Guy Routh, an anesthetist from Andoversford, England, was driving near Naunton when he noticed a woman with dark, shoulder-length hair standing by the side of the road in a sleeveless cream-colored dress. Routh came to a stop as the woman smiled and waved, causing him to wonder if she needed assistance. After glancing away for a moment, he was perplexed to find she had vanished. The car was adjacent to an empty field, making it impossible for her to have fled. As if things couldn't get any stranger, the aroma of wood smoke immediately filled his car. Routh stepped out to see if he could determine the source of the odor; outside, everything smelled normal.[191]

There is no apparent reason the entity—we assume a ghost, though it could have been anything—should smell like wood smoke. Moreover, the absence of an odor outside the car suggests a targeted locality, i.e. it was projected *into* the vehicle. This line of thought raises more questions than answers. Do we always smell what we think we smell? How often do we conflate the smell of the *entity* with the smell of the *environment*? Where does reality end and expectation begin?

Another question worth asking is why tobacco smoke is exclusively associated with male spirits when smoking was quite common between both sexes in the nineteenth century (the Vanity Fair brand even offered petite-sized, monogrammed cigarettes targeted specifically to women in 1863).[192] Is it possible our hedonic expectations of femininity lead us to stereotyped assumptions?

Symbolically, smoke is at once physical and nonphysical. The ancients understood this—like the burnt offerings of old, smoke seems to possess the ability to transcend the barrier between this world and the next. It is the corporeal rendered non-corporeal, just as human beings are believed to transcend the earth into the spirit world. Though some appear quite solid, many witnesses describe spirits, as well as ectoplasm—the alleged vaporous substance by which spirits manifest—as smokelike, wispy, ethereal. We say they "disappear like a puff of smoke."

Smoke smells from spirits also highlight a theme crucial to our discussion of paranormal odors: the scent of burning. There is something significant about combustion odors in paranormal phenomena (recall how ghosts in African lore do not smell unless their fingernails are burned). Keel hinted at this connection in his work, noting how the smell of smoke featured in more than your typical hauntings—for example, Linda Scarberry, one of the original "Mothman" witnesses, reported the anomalous odor of cigar smoke in her basement apartment.[193]

Sulfur, odorless in pure form unless burnt, also fits this combustion trend. It may be noted that the scent of gunpowder smoke, very common in spirit cases, is absent from the above discussion. Due to its distinctive odor and composition, gunpowder is addressed in the following chapter.

Chapter 7
Spirit Smells: Decay And Sulfur

*All the diseases in one moat were gathered
Such was it here, and such a stench came from it
As from putrescent limbs is wont to issue.*
— Dante's *Inferno*, Canto XXIX

In the heart of Ireland lies Leap Castle, a jagged and imposing fortress of stone nestled amongst the lush greenery of the emerald isle. Built in the 13th century by the O'Bannon clan, the grounds passed by marriage to the Darby family in 1659. Some 250 years later, Mildred Darby, fascinated with the burgeoning spiritualist movement, decided to hold a series of séances at the castle.

It was a bad idea.

Darby had awakened something with her gatherings, a predictable result given the property's oubliette housed the bones of 150 people. Writing under the pseudonym "Andrew Merry," she submitted her encounters to the December 1908 edition of *Occult Review*. According to Darby, she felt something lay its hands upon her shoulders one evening in the gallery and turned to see a "gray elemental" approximately "the size of a sheep." Thin and gaunt, its face had neither eyes nor nose, and gave an animalistic impression on account of its thick fur coat and paws.

"Its lustreless eyes, which seemed half-decomposed in black cavities, and looked incredibly foul, stared into mine, and the horrible smell which had before offended my nostrils, only a hundred times intensified, came up into my face, filling me with a deadly nausea," Darby wrote. "I noticed the lower half of the creature was indefinite and seemed semi-transparent—at least, I could see the framework of the door that led into the gallery *through* its body." The apparition began to fade as Darby unloaded her revolver into it. She stumbled to the floor unconscious.[194]

The smell of decay

Darby compared the stench to a decomposing corpse.[195] Though not as pervasive as smells of smoke, perfume, or flowers, the odor of decomposition is still relatively frequent in hauntings. Investigators are quick to deem such cases demonic (curiously, no one has ever blamed the benign ghost of their Uncle Dudley or Aunt Gertrude for foul odors, no matter how renowned they were for flatulence while living—one imagines this scenario would have occurred by now).

In addition to demonic activity, researchers also cite poltergeist phenomena as a common source of foul smells. In the 1938 case of the Thornton Heath poltergeist, the Forbes family was besieged by an assortment of disruptive activity: shattering ceramics, levitating eggs, moving furniture, etc. The activity seemed to center around the family's 35-year-old mother, who was "constantly assailed by the smell of decomposition, suffered from periodic bouts of blindness, and spontaneous burns appeared on her neck." It was later determined that Mrs. Forbes had been sexually assaulted in her youth, a possible source of traumatized psychic energy.[196]

There are also accounts of séances manifesting similar odors. The famous Brazilian medium Carmine Carlos Mirabelli was once enlisted in a search for the missing remains of a mentally disturbed woman. After pinpointing the unmarked grave in São Paulo's Araçá cemetery, "a terrible smell of decomposed corpse filled the room, as bones began to materialize one after the other and fall on people's heads."[197]

In Japanese legends *nuribotoke*, a type of fish-tailed zombie with oily skin, emits a foul, pungent odor. Another *yokai*, a short, lumpy, anthropoid mound of decaying flesh known as *nuppeppō*, is known for its revolting rotten meat stench; it lurks around rundown temples and cemeteries with the goal of disgusting anyone unlucky enough to pass by. Legends tell of castle guards fainting from the smell when dispatched to drive these spirits out. Curiously, if one could get past the odor, the flesh of *nuppeppō* is said to have magical curative properties.[198]

The First Nations Ojibwe people feared possession by the *wendigo*, a hungry spirit known for turning men into bloodthirsty cannibals. The entity appeared as an emaciated skeleton, and, according to scholar Basil Johnson, "gave off a strange and eerie odor of decay and decomposition, of death and corruption."[199]

Once again, we find instinctive hedonic associations at play. Much has been said on the link between unpleasant odors and evil; the Christian church doubled down on such connections, its early saints employing smell to discern the true nature of others. According to early church writer Sulpicius Severus, Satan attacked Saint Martin of Tours numerous times, appearing in his prison cell in the guise of Christ—a ruse revealed when the entity "vanished like smoke, and filled the cell with such a disgusting smell, that he left unmistakable evidences of his real character."[200] To Saint John Chrysostom, sinners emitted "black and stinking smoke," each bearing "a dead soul eaten up by worms and filled with rottenness."[201] Saint Antony could smell demons within the possessed, famously sniffing out a demoniac while aboard a ship loaded with stinking fish.[202]

The experiences of "Barbara," a young lady from New Zealand, were of great interest to researcher John Stuart.[203] One evening in the 1950s, the victim—who was in all likelihood Stuart's colleague, Doreen Wilkinson—returned to her apartment and immediately noticed an overpowering stench while lying naked in bed.[204] The next thing she knew some unseen force with sandpapery skin sexually assaulted her, leaving signs of the encounter on her body in the form of small scratches. Stuart claimed to have later confronted the entity, which bears a striking resemblance to the Leap Castle elemental: "Its body resembled vaguely that of a human... Its flesh, stinkingly putrid, seemed to hang in folds. It was a grayish color... the slack mouth was dribbling, and the lips began to move, but there was no sound."[205]

Martin, Antony, and Chrysostom would have labeled the attacker an *incubus*, a male demon known to rape Christian women. One wonders how they would have classified Barbara's UFO sightings, or the odd, anonymous phone calls she received.

The odor and fleshy guise of Barbara's entity bears a passing resemblance to the experiences of a young girl from London who encountered a spirit in 1908 that smelled "like a charnel house." The account was described in Volume 7 of *The Annals of Psychical Science*:

> The girl, who is about fourteen years of age, had fallen asleep, when she was suddenly aroused by the consciousness of the presence of someone standing by her bedside in the dark. Startled, she was about to cry out, when a flabby, large clammy hand was pressed firmly over her mouth.
>
> She was a strong-minded girl. With an effort she sat bolt upright in bed, trying to tear the hand from her mouth. To her horror she found the hand of the invisible intruder strongly forcing her back on to her pillow, and at the same time she was conscious of an intolerable odour. Hastily pulling the bedclothes over her head, she went fervently over her prayers—I may say it is a Catholic family—and, to her great relief and delight, the grasp of the hideous Invisible relaxed, and she went to sleep.
>
> In the morning she thought it might have been a nightmare, and said nothing about it. The next

time, however, when she had to sleep in that room the same horrible haunting occurred. Again there was the presence in the room, again the horrible odour as of decaying flesh; again the gruesome, flabby, clammy hand pressed on her mouth. She screamed, jumped out of bed, and went down to her mother, declaring that nothing would induce her to sleep in that room.[206]

According to the author, the odor—also likened to that of a "pest house"—would cling to the interior in spite of efforts to air out the home.

One unsettling spirit encounter took place at a hospital in Houston, Texas. In a 1997 *Strange Magazine* article by Mark Chorvinsky, a nurse rushing to exchange duties with a coworker noticed something odd in one of the rooms. Backing up for a closer look, she saw an elderly female patient lying in bed, a tall figure in a hooded robe by her side.

"His face was a skull with tiny red fires for eyes," she said. "His hands, skeletal, were patiently folded over each other inside the dark sleeves." The character—obviously evocative of the folkloric Grim Reaper—brought with it a terrible smell of death, "like something rotting in the sun."[207]

Any discussion of death smells would be incomplete without mentioning the famous "Death Car" urban legend. Many versions exist, but the broad strokes remain the same: a late-model automobile in fantastic shape is sold cheaply at a dealership because the original owner's corpse had been discovered rotting inside, and any attempt to remove the smell is met with failure. A variation on the tale features a cheap mattress instead of a car.[208]

"Many legends suggest that the smell of death, like an ineradicable bloodstain, never disappears completely," wrote folklorist Elizabeth Tucker. "This insistence on an everlasting smell reminds [ghost story] listeners of death's inevitability… no matter how hygienically dead bodies are separated from living ones, death is the inescapable endpoint of human life."[209]

A handful of malodorous cases, however, are *not* overtly suggestive of evil activity.

- John Cameron found himself working alone one evening in the 1930s while renovating Castle Stuart in Inverness, Scotland. From his perch atop a ladder, he noticed that a portion of the ceiling sounded hollow when struck. Determining it was part of the long-sealed (and allegedly haunted) East Tower, Cameron began chiseling away in earnest. He soon broke through to empty space, hearing a voice yell "No!"—but continued on, ascribing it to his imagination. The next blow was answered with a violent shove to the floor, accompanied by the smell of rot.[210]

- One of the most haunted sites in Australia is reportedly Port Arthur, an old penal facility on the island of Tasmania. Though all of the camp's buildings are home to paranormal activity, the Parsonage is most notorious. It reportedly features the entire spectrum of spirit activity: temperature drops, unexplained raps, eerie moans, strange lights, and, of course, the smell of decaying flesh.[211]

- North Wales' Gwydir Castle (actually a mansion) boasts a "Ghost Room" frequented by a lady in gray who smells of rotting flesh. Legend holds that she was murdered and walled into the building, doomed to haunt the house for eternity. During renovations in the 20th century, a hollow space was discovered within a chimneybreast adjacent to the Ghost Room, adding credibility to the tale.[212]

- The historical Nelson House of Yorktown, Virginia, served as the headquarters for British General Cornwallis during the American Revolution. Later during the Civil War it was retrofitted to serve as a hospital. In addition to strange breezes, full-bodied apparitions, and disembodied voices, visitors report a putrid decaying corpse odor.[213]

- "Mr. Boots," the specter in the South Bridge Underground Vaults in Edinburgh, Scotland, allegedly enjoys sneaking up behind visitors on guided tours. "We call him that because he wears knee-length boots," said Des Brogan, tour founder and author. "He's unkempt and unshaven, and he has very bad breath. We know this because people can smell it… as soon as he's spotted, he disappears."[214]

The stink of rot is also attributed in folklore to undead entities such as zombies and vampires. These revenants rise from their graves to stalk the living, and naturally smell of decay. It is peculiar that ghosts—whose appearance, actions, and aromas most often reflect their living existence, not their current state of decomposition—should stink in this manner as well.

In some cases, such as the Gwydir Castle example, it would appear as though the smell of rot serves a specific purpose, i.e. to reveal the corpse of someone who met with foul play. This suggests that there is, at least occasionally, intent behind spirit smells.

What exactly is the odor of decay? A variety of factors add to the rancid bouquet. As soon as four minutes after death, carbon dioxide buildup begins breaking down cells, setting microorganisms to work and producing a variety of gases in the process. Skatole and indole, aforementioned components in feces, contribute to the overall stench, as do cadaverine and putrescine. These two compounds have a low detection threshold and are also present in urine and halitosis (recall Mr. Boots). As the process progresses, bacteria continue to release compounds like methanethiol, dimethyl disulfide, dimethyl trisulfide, and hydrogen sulfide.[215]

All of these, naturally, contain sulfur.

Sulfur

In 1896's *Myths & Legends of our Own Land*, Charles M. Skinner tells of one Mr. Francis Woolcott, by all accounts a nineteenth century warlock who demanded tribute from the people of Copake, New York. Anyone foolish enough to refuse would find themselves cursed, such as the farmer whose pigs were made to dance and speak. To collect his fines, Woolcott summoned 13 hellish "night-riders," who served him until his dying day when the devil returned to collect his soul. Skinner writes of Woolcott's death: "There was a burst of purple flame at the window, a frightful peal, a smell of sulphur, and Woolcott was dead."[216]

How many "foul" cases actually refer to sulfurous smells? It stands to reason that many witnesses conflate sulfur and the odor of decay. When a demonic presence is suspected, claims of sulfur are commonplace; as already noted, this association has existed for millennia. Such odors manifested during New York's famed (and controversial) Amityville Haunting, a case that included cloven hoof prints in the snow and sightings of a demonic pig child.[217] Sulfur's smell can even function as a warning of impending damnation—in the 16th century case of Mistress Kingesfielde, the London housewife proclaimed herself doomed one morning in church after "a smoke or mist came before her eyes with an extreme air of brimstone in her nose."[218]

Those who conjure demons can expect an accompanying odor of sulfur. This applies not only to occult magicians, but the unwitting as well: after children were found playing with a Ouija board, investigators were called to a home in Memphis, Tennessee, where they noted strange noises in the attic, overwhelming feelings of negativity, and "a horrible smell like sulfur."[219]

Once summoned, the stench may provide a clue as to the vicinity of such entities. In *The Demon of Brownsville Road: A Pittsburgh Family's Battle with Evil in Their Home*, a family combating demonic activity held mass in their second story living room, complete with candles and holy water. By focusing their efforts on the area where the stench of "sulfuric burning rubber" was strongest, they were able to force the foul odor—and presumably its source—downstairs.[220]

Not surprisingly, the possessed emit a sulfurous stench too, as with Margaret Rule, a case documented by none other than Cotton Mather. In September 1693 Rule's neighbor was suspected of putting a spell on her, an allegation supported by witness testimony that Rule had levitated from her bed to the ceiling, and that smells of sulfur would fill and vacate her home without warning.[221] In the modern era, German missionary and theologian Kurt E. Koch chronicled the story of an Englishwoman who returned from South Africa cursed by a Bantu shaman. The possession was accompanied by poltergeist phenomena in her home, as well as "an unpleasant smell, as of a rotting corpse… they could smell sulphur." An Anglican priest advised the girl to destroy all souvenirs of her trip, and to be born again, a course of action that seemed to do the trick.[222]

Even when not explicitly demonic, odors of sulfur are still often associated with negative energy.

- Cathy Chadwick-Ciccone of Mount Holly, New Jersey, reports the marching of boots and a strong sulfur smell in her gift shop. She attributes the phenomena to the ghost of a Hessian soldier who served in the American Revolution and was killed after raping a young girl.[223]

- In Freeport, Illinois, the former home of Charles Guiteau—the man who assassinated United States President James A. Garfield—was plagued by a variety of phenomena following his execution, including "an oppressive, dark presence and the smell of sulfur."[224]

- The West Virginia State Penitentiary, vacant since 1995, is regarded as one of the state's most haunted locations, filled with the spirits of angry inmates. One area is renowned for its particularly rancid odor. "The putrid stench of sulfur can fill the room making visitors gag and vomit," wrote Trent Brandon in *The Ghost Hunter's Bible*.[225]

- While assessing an old Victorian house in Ealing, the father of English ghost investigator Andrew Malcolm Green noticed an odd sulfur odor in a small mezzanine room. Though they replaced the room's floor and plaster, the smell persisted, accompanied by footsteps, shutting doors, and moving objects. The home was later revealed to be the site of 20 suicides and one murder.[226]

A peculiar entity known as "the Eggman," short and thin, dressed in a tattered suit and fedora, is said to prowl the streets of Manitou Springs, Colorado. In one hand he clutches a black cane, in the other a basket or sack of rotten eggs. Because of his malodorous load, he naturally smells of sulfur and is notorious for accosting lonely travelers at night. His victims are often infused with this potent stench; in fact, author Stephanie Waters interviewed a hapless recluse who claimed to have been twice spurned by lovers because of the spirit's lingering odor. A 1912 *Pikes Peak Journal* article seems to provide a clue to the haunting's genesis: on May 31, a man carrying a sack of eggs walked into a local saloon and shot himself in the temple.[227]

Unlike floral and smoke odors, sulfurous spirit smells can generate visceral physical reactions in individuals. Returning to Gettysburg—the site of so many spirit tales—one witness named Kendra encountered a particularly foul-smelling spirit in the town's old orphanage. The building is home to one of the few hauntings not associated with the battle; rather, a particularly malicious caretaker named Rosa Carmichael bound and tortured her wards at the site in the 1870s.

Late one evening Kendra, who worked as a tour guide at the orphanage, realized she had left her lantern in the cellar. Returning downstairs, she was soon assailed by an awful stench. "It was so rancid that I gagged, then raced past to get to the stairs," she said. She retrieved her manager, who failed to detect the odor. "After literally gagging, I asked them why they couldn't smell the rotten eggs and rancid smell of rot… I said, 'It's right here! You can't tell me you don't smell this. It's awful!'"

Her manager asked Kendra to describe the smell in detail, then revealed that the year prior a psychic visiting the orphanage had sensed a young boy in a checkered shirt and woolen pants at that exact spot; he had also gagged when approaching him, claiming the boy smelled revolting. "Chills went up my spine, because in all my life I had never smelled a spirit before," Kendra recalled.[228]

Since sulfur is odorless, it is anyone's guess as to exactly what sulfur compounds witnesses were detecting in these cases (hydrogen sulfide, which we discuss in depth later, is a good candidate, at least in the Manitou Springs and Gettysburg examples). However, we can occasionally pinpoint the exact sulfur compound in spirit sightings—specifically, sulfur dioxide.

Sulfur dioxide

The 1993 film *Gettysburg* is historic in that it marked the first time the United States National Park Service allowed a production company to film on the actual battlefield, with real Civil War reenactors filling out the armies as extras. According to one story, a bedraggled looking gentleman in a Union uniform who smelled strongly of sulfur met several of these reenactors on set. The figure gave them a handful of musket balls and asked, "Rough one today, eh, boys?" He then disappeared into the bushes. The perplexed extras later took the musket balls to be appraised in Gettysburg, where they were deemed authentic, more than 130 years old.[229]

Sulfur is one of three key components in gunpowder (black powder), the other two being charcoal and potassium nitrate. The potassium nitrate, more commonly known as saltpeter, oxidizes the mixture, while charcoal and sulfur—prized for its low ignition temperature—serve as fuel for the reaction.[230] Theoretically, this ignition process only produces carbon dioxide, nitrogen, and particles of potassium sulfate and potassium carbonate. In reality, impurities (common in gunpowder of centuries past) and variations in the exact mixture generate nitrogen oxides and sulfur dioxide,[231] as well as minute quantities of hydrogen sulfide.[232]

Sulfur dioxide (SO_2) is one of the main smells associated with gunpowder, fireworks, and just-lit matches.[233] In the story of the 1974 Bridgeport, Connecticut, poltergeist, sulfur was noted with great regularity and was, at least on occasion, likened to burning matches.[234] The Manner family of Pennsylvania, whose matriarch was clairvoyant, noted similar smells when they moved into a home in Stoystown: burning matches, occasionally conjoined with the scent of perfume and tobacco smoke.[235]

SO_2, which is easily generated by burning sulfur, was one of the very first chemicals ever used, held in high regard as a bleaching agent and disinfectant as early as 4,000 years ago. Today, it is released as a byproduct in coal and fossil fuel combustion, making it the chief cause of acid rain.[236] Despite its production and use in the human cardiovascular system, large amounts of SO_2 are highly toxic and react with the moisture of mucus membranes to form dangerous sulfurous acid (H_2SO_3).[237]

Like many sulfur compounds, SO_2 occurs naturally at volcanic sites. This underground source can cause some confusion, as detailed by Robert Allen Baker and Joe Nickell in their book *Missing Pieces: How to Investigate Ghosts, UFOs, Psychics, and Other Mysteries*.

> Another unusual case involved a family in the coal mining area of western Kentucky who were religious fundamentalists. Periodically they would smell sulfur dioxide (SO_2) which they interpreted as the smell of brimstone, which the Bible says indicates the presence of the Devil... When we first investigated, no smell was encountered nor could we discover where the smell came from or how it

could have entered the house. We requested that someone call us the next time the smell was encountered. When we returned a few weeks later, we found the house filled with SO_2 but could not discover its source until we went outside and inspected the foundation of the house. When the area sustained a dry spell, the earth pulled away from the house foundation and large fissures were opened in the soil, allowing the natural gas in the area to well up from the coal deposits below and enter the house through the ventilators. Following a normal amount of rain, the soil filled up and closed the fissures, thus shutting off the gases.[238]

In spirit encounters, SO_2 is mostly noted at military sites, particularly in the United States. Harpers Ferry, West Virginia, where abolitionist John Brown clashed with army forces in 1859, is plagued to this day by smoke, sulfurous smells, and the sounds of gunfire and bayonets.[239] At the Antietam National Battlefield, site of the bloodiest single-day battle in American history, visitors report "the acrid sulfurous scent of gunpowder" along Bloody Lane—the spot where 5,600 men died.[240] An accidental explosion on July 4, 1809, at New Hampshire's Fort Constitution killed nine people, causing smells of gunpowder and fire today.[241] In 1955, a U.S. Navy officer took a photo aboard the USS *Constellation* showing the blurry form of a man in nineteenth century seaman's garb, supposedly the spirit of a young "powder monkey" who died aboard while running his errands; the officer noted "a faint scent in the air—a certain something not unlike gunpowder" during the sighting.[242]

The pungent smell of gunpowder lies at the intersection of two common spirit smells, i.e. smoke and sulfur. The connection is deeper than one might think: many tobacco casings and flavorings involve added sulfur.[243] Tobacco smoke contains a lethal cocktail of chemical compounds, among them SO_2, which has the ability to paralyze cilia lining the respiratory tract.[244] SO_2 has also been recently applied to the tobacco curing process, used to artificially ripen green harvests.[245] The underlying, unifying quality of sulfur grows ever more apparent.

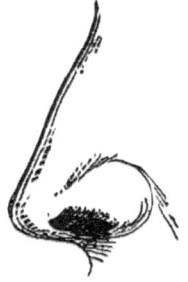

Chapter 8
Spirit Smells: Miscellany

ELEANOR: Oh! I can't go in there... my mother...
DR. MARKWAY: Yes?
ELEANOR: ... that smell...
DR. MARKWAY: It's just stale air, Eleanor.
ELEANOR: No, no, that other smell... awful....
— *The Haunting* (1963)

With the discussion of how prevalent perfume, smoke, decay, and sulfur are, one might assume all spirit cases involve just these core smells. While they *most often* fall into those categories, spirit smells *can* be just about anything—visitors to the Parisian catacombs, for example, report the aroma of sandalwood, a smell unexpected in the resting place of six million people.[246]

Food, candy, and makeup

Witnesses occasionally report the smell of cooking food at haunted locations. Each Friday the Bradley family of Lampasas, Texas, would note the scent of frying liver and onions in their haunted home.[247] Food smells are said to waft from the abandoned kitchen at Waverly Hills Sanatorium (Louisville, Kentucky), while San Diego's Whaley House occasionally fills with the aroma of freshly baked bread and apple pie.[248] One homeowner in Memphis, Tennessee, claims that it is quite common for disappointed houseguests to expect breakfast, thanks to the scent of cooking bacon in the morning that breezes through her historic 1917 home.[249] Could cooking be seen as a variation on combustion? It doesn't seem too much of a stretch, as intense heat is applied in each case.

At first blush, it seems odd that odors of cooking would appear in hauntings, which are normally associated with traumatic events like battles, murders, betrayal, etc. However, if we accept the notion that strong emotions play a role in establishing hauntings, the tendency makes a bit more sense. Eating together is a communal act, strengthening relationships and serving as one of life's focal points. All of us have fond memories of meals made incredible not by the chef's culinary prowess, but rather by the enjoyable company involved. Food evokes powerful emotions. Taking this logic a step further, it is worth pointing out that taste, like smell, shares a strong relationship with involuntary memory.

Along these lines, though not exactly foods per se, are accounts involving candy. Psychics have noted the smell of bubblegum at the Emmitt House in Waverly, Ohio, an 1861 hotel built upon the banks of the Erie Canal.[250] On one trip to Gettysburg, investigator Troy Taylor was baffled when he noticed the scent of peppermint along Baltimore Street; he later discovered that, to mask the stench arising from dying soldiers, citizens liberally employed peppermint and vanilla following the battle.[251]

Taylor was also involved in another unique spirit smell case. While investigating Illinois' Springfield Theatre Center, he noticed the tangy pong of a facial cream used by stage actors to remove makeup. Unbeknownst to Taylor, the odor in this particular dressing room was closely associated with the ghost of actor Joe Neville, who had committed suicide in the 1950s. Taylor initially thought nothing of the smell (it could have come from any number of productions), but in reality the theatre had forbidden use of that specific cream for years on account of the haunting.[252]

Body odor

Though body odor is not common in hauntings, one special case is worth mention. In September 2015, Dana Matthews, blogger for the popular *Week In Weird* website, embarked on a ghost hunting trip to Michigan's Mackinac Island in Lake Huron. While there, she and fellow investigators visited Mission Point Resort, a locale renowned for its peculiar activity.

Matthews experienced a variety of unsettling incidents: feelings of being touched, cold spots, electromagnetic field fluctuations, etc. She was particularly affected, however, by "a very strong scent, the kind of musk given off by a man who hadn't bathed in many, many weeks." The odor became overwhelming, but she held her tongue, fearful of offending someone else in the group.

Eventually, her investigation partner mentioned the odor, and both agreed that the stench of "body odor and general uncleanliness" did not seem to have precedent elsewhere in the hotel. The team member then revealed an additional twist: she was anosmic, having lost her sense of smell years earlier.

"How did a woman with no sense of smell, well, smell the phantom odor?" Matthews wrote. "And stranger still, how was it that she and I were the only two people to experience it? What does that say about a ghosts ability to effect us? Can they draw upon our memories, influence parts of our brain, even causing us to 'smell' something that isn't physically there?"[253]

Pets

If ghosts are tied to the earth by strong emotions, it seems logical to assume that the love shared with our furry friends can generate hauntings as well. Owners have reported smelling their old dog's shampoo, or even the odor of phantom litter boxes.[254] These animal scents are not always positive: during the late 1800s at Ballechin House in Perthshire, Scotland, one woman was violently brushed aside by an invisible dog, her only warning the overpowering odor she experienced moments before.[255]

Both cats and dogs have long been thought to perceive the supernatural more readily than humans. Few have suggested a reason for this ability. Having established that paranormal phenomena often manifest odors, perhaps the greatly refined olfactory senses of pets play a role in this heightened detection. A cat's sense of smell is 14 times greater than that of a human,[256] while dog noses are even more powerful—though it varies from breed to breed, their olfactory nerves are 10,000 to 100,000 times as acute.

"Let's suppose they're just 10,000 times better," said former director of the Sensory Research Institute at Florida State University James Walker. "If you make the analogy to vision, what you and I can see at a third of a mile, a dog could see more than 3,000 miles away."[257]

Perhaps *all* spirits emit an odor, but in amounts so miniscule that humans cannot smell them until a greater concentration is reached. Pets, on the other hand, would have no trouble detecting these otherworldly fragrances at their lowest levels.

Blood

The smell of blood—and sometimes *actual* blood—is common in poltergeist and possession cases. During the Amityville Haunting, the Lutz family "reported overwhelming smells of dried blood" in their cellar, which served as ground zero for much of the house's activity.[258] If manifesting in a physical sense, the fluid typically oozes from a house's walls: in March 1985, blood spurted from the walls of an Ivory Coast home and appeared on clothing, doors, and kitchen utensils, though no one in the home appeared injured. The substance gave off a foul smell.[259]

Blood odors are not exclusive to poltergeist activity. Catholic tradition is replete with statues, saints, and Incorruptibles that weep blood and exude the odor. The Alzheimer's ward of Iowa's decommissioned Jasper County Care Facility is infused with "the very strong metallic scent of blood," which comes and goes as it pleases.[260] Evil entities can make their presence known by the smell of blood as well—Japan's *kubikajiri* carries with it the aroma of fresh blood while scouring cemeteries for its missing head. If it spies a hapless passerby, it will take their head instead.[261]

Recent research suggests that the characteristic odor associated with blood is actually an illusion. A 2006 study led by University of Leipzig chemist Dietmar Glindemann found that the odor of iron is nonexistent; rather, it is the scent of human skin oil *reacting* with iron.

"The odors humans perceive as 'metallic' when they touch iron are really volatilized compounds of skin," said Virginia Polytechnic Institute and State University professor Andrea Dietrich, who contributed to the study. "These odorous aldehydes and ketones split off of a kind of rancid skin fat (lipid peroxides) due to their decomposition by 'bivalent' iron ions. This reactive form of iron (also called green rust) is a result of partial dissolution (corrosion) of the iron metal with acidic sweat from the skin. Since skin fat sticks to metal surfaces, a coin or a door handle containing iron or copper will smell via the decomposed lipid peroxides from all the human users that have previously touched them."[262]

This reaction also takes place when iron-rich blood makes contact with skin, arguably the most common context in which blood is smelled.[263] In this sense, the smell of blood is more related to decomposition or body odor than standing alone as its own discrete category.

Ozone

We've all smelled it, even though we don't all realize what it is—that clean, pungent, almost peppery smell after a thunderstorm.

The odor is that of ozone (from the Greek *ozein*, literally "to smell"), and it is one of the more unconventional outliers of spirit cases. As already noted, there is a great deal of historical confusion between ozone and sulfur; its presence is much more prevalent in

UFO lore than spirit cases. As such, this relationship, as well as a detailed description of ozone, is covered later.

For the time being, a brief description of exactly what ozone is and how it is created will have to suffice. Oxygen (O) in our atmosphere normally exists as molecules that contain two oxygen atoms (O_2). When a great amount of energy is imparted to these diatomic molecules (e.g. lightning), the atoms are fragmented. Known as radicals, these fragments readily bond to surrounding diatomic molecules, forming O_3, or ozone. Expressed as a chemical equation, the reaction is $3O_2 \rightarrow 2O_3$. This method of production resonates with the theme of combustion—imparting large amounts of energy generates both burning smells and the odor of ozone.

Ozone is notable in spirit cases because it appears almost exclusively in ceremonies. During the height of the spiritualist movement, mediums were said to posses the ability to manifest ectoplasm from their orifices. This peculiar, milky-white substance, either material or vaporous, could allegedly take the form of spirits' bodies. Witnesses claimed it gave off the smell of ozone. In one famous 1920 Parisian séance, Polish medium Franek Kluski manifested ectoplasm that took the shape of faces, feet, and hands, all accompanied by the "strong odor of ozone."[264]

Aside from séances, ozone also appears after exorcisms. While foul smells like sulfur, decomposition, and feces normally accompany demonic possession, they are sometimes replaced by the scent of ozone following the rite of exorcism.[265] This is particularly interesting because ozone has disinfectant properties, often used to eliminate microorganisms and remove foul odors in air and water sources (more on this later). Both exorcism and ozone cleanse—just as the rite of exorcism removes the demon from the demoniac, ozone removes the stench from the air.

Could a powerful manifestation of energy during paranormal activity account for this odor?

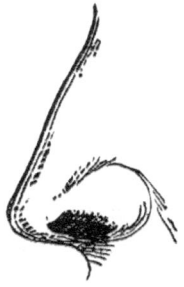

Chapter 9
Spirit Smells: Loose Ends And Theories

As a psychologist, I wondered what might be the cause of this peculiar olfactory hallucination. But I was unable to discover any convincing connection between it and my present state of consciousness.
— Carl Jung

In the summer of 1920, Carl Jung and a friend vacationed at a rented cottage in Buckinghamshire, England. On the second night of their stay, Jung's nostrils were assailed by a putrid odor whose stench kept him from falling asleep; the next morning, he informed his host, who experienced nothing of the sort. The following night, the odor returned.

"It was hard to identify the smell, despite my best efforts to establish its nature," he wrote. "The only thing that came into my head was that there was something sickly about it." Jung finally recalled the smell of an elderly patient with an open carcinoma. "This was quite unmistakably the same sickly smell I had so often noticed in her room."

Jung's stay included a nonexistent dripping tap, nightly rapping, and the impression of a phantom dog. Servants confirmed his suspicions: the property was haunted. The events came to a head when, opening his eyes from sleep, Jung beheld "the head of an old woman," missing half its face, staring at him.[266]

Sleep paralysis and astral projection

Most rational individuals—including Jung himself—would find mundane ways to explain the events. The noises were exaggerated in his mind, he concluded, and the smell was simply left over from a previous cancerous tenant (cancer can indeed have a distinctive smell—one New York physician of the 1930s famously diagnosed a man by smell alone, without even setting foot upstairs).[267] To Jung's credit, this odor was the most difficult aspect to dismiss.

Less difficult, however, was the vision. Jung ascribed the old woman's presence to hypnagogia, or sleep paralysis, an altered state of consciousness between sleep and full wakefulness. In simple terms, a hypnagogic state occurs when the mind has awoken but the body is still asleep. This state is often accompanied by sightings of ominous figures, sensed presences, and an inability to move. Modern science has embraced sleep paralysis as an explanation for a host of paranormal encounters, including spirit sightings and alien abduction.

However, scientists have difficulty explaining some of the finer points of the sleep paralysis experience. If the mind fabricates these bedroom intruders, why do victims without their corrective lenses see entities as blurry? Why are some sufferers left with physical marks afterward? And how do we account for realistic smells during sleep paralysis?

Revolting odors are commonly reported in encounters with the Old Hag, the hideous female entity responsible for sleep paralysis in medieval thought.[268] One experiencer described the entity as "very old, with deep crevices in her face… she also had a hard-to-describe but strong musty odor… The smell was horrible and I wanted to throw up."[269]

Ronald K. Siegel, psychiatrist with the University of California, Los Angeles School of Medicine, observed his Old Hag experience with a clinical eye—though he was nonetheless terrified by the "whiff of a dusty odor," a peculiar smell "like something that had been in an attic too long." He recalled a figure with foul, tobacco-smelling breath mounting him on the bed, crushing the life out of him until he was able to fully awaken.[270]

While most sleep paralysis odors are musty, there are still outliers. Skirting dangerously close to UFOlogy, a case collected by researcher Peter Davenport featured a young New Hampshire witness who claimed to have awoken twice one evening in the summer of 1987, once to the presence of her dead grandmother and a second time to a blue beam of light that vanished and left behind a smell of burning paper or wood (again, note the theme of combustion).[271] Investigator William F. Hamilton recalled an instance when "three little white-skinned beings [appeared] at the foot of my bed while I was in a hypnagogic state. When they departed suddenly, a pungent odor of ozone permeated the air of the bedroom."[272]

Curiously, odor has also been used to ward off sleep paralysis in traditions around the world. Women in Newfoundland once slept with bottles of urine under their beds, while Czechs placed feces-streaked towels over their bodies.[273] Given research that foul smells can induce nightmares, this preventative measure seems counterproductive.

Those who claim the ability to astrally project—that is, to produce out-of-body experiences on command—report smelling their surroundings in the astral realm. Usually the odors noticed in this state correspond to their environment. Robert Bruce allegedly experienced the smell of rain and grass, all from indoors, during one astral travel session. Less mundane are Bruce's claims to have smelled the "intoxicating perfume" of flowers in "The Summerland," his nomenclature for the afterlife.[274] While possibly a tall tale, the description fits nicely with many historical accounts of the scent of Heaven.

One apocryphal story tells of a young man in China who was taking a nap, only to awake in an out-of-body state. Enjoying his newfound freedom, he began flying about the room but soon heard strange, otherworldly singing. According to the story, the young man turned and saw two women and a small boy flying next to him. He described them as having long hair and, in the popular Chinese idiom, a smell "stinky enough to kill me." The beings tried to pull the boy out of the room, but he resisted, instead calling out to his dog. The canine bit the boy's physical body, which jolted him back to the realm of the living.[275]

Such tales strain credulity and are wholly unverifiable. Still, it is interesting to entertain the notion that smell, intangible in its own right, may be just as functional in the ethereal realm as it is on earth.

Theories: Odor absorption and phantosmia

It is obvious that spirit smells can be just about anything. Some reflect the nature of the entity, as with the smell of roses in BVM interactions, others reflect the actions attributed to the deceased, such as smoking or cooking, and a handful of accounts seem tied to past events, rather than spirits themselves.

Investigator Andrew Malcolm Green posited that a variety of smells could be absorbed into materials like wood and remain trapped for extended periods of time, only to reappear when specific environmental criteria, in particular temperature and humidity, were met. Such a notion seems logical enough—we have all experienced the smoky smell of a fireplace long after its disuse, or the way the smell of a loved one clings to their clothes. Even something as simple as friction can release long dormant odors.

Green had direct experience with this phenomenon. Rosemary Ellen Guiley writes in her *Encyclopedia of Ghosts and Spirits*:

> A mutual friend [of Green and his fiancée, Norah] asked him to look into a mysterious smell of perfume in her old farm cottage. The perfume pervaded the sitting room inexplicably at times, usually in the evenings. Norah was not worried or frightened, but was curious to find an explanation.

Together they established that the smell was that of an old Victorian perfume based on the mignonette flower. It had been used heavily for years by a previous tenant, an old woman thought to have died in the cottage. The perfume aroma apparently seeped into the exposed oak beams. When a fire was lit in the inglenook fireplace in the evenings, the heat warmed the beams and released the smell.

Smells needn't be absorbed into buildings to have a mundane explanation, either. Broken sewer pipes, backed up drains, smells from other buildings, and simple misidentification are all possible causes—recall Robert Allen Baker's experience with SO_2. In the absence of an actual apparition, it is safe to assume that there is usually a mundane explanation for disembodied odors. This being said, the odor absorption idea fails to explain actual manifestations of smoke, such as at Blennerhassett Hotel, nor does it account for the punctuality of smells on event anniversaries.

Another possible explanation for spirit smells is phantosmia, the aforementioned medical condition where a sufferer detects nonexistent smells. As already discussed, true phantosmia only affects one individual at a time and should be dismissed as an explanation involving multiple witnesses.

The line between phantosmia and clairscent blurs quite often. Like clairvoyance, clairscent is the use of a sense—in this case, smell—to obtain psychic information. Those possessing this ability are the only ones to detect such odors, and may retrieve information about past events, or be warned of future ones.

Laura Dickson of Kent, England, claims to smell fish just before negative events occur in her life, an ability she first noticed as a child prior to a relative's stroke. "In a way, the spirits' whiffy warning had helped prepare me," she said. "The pong always appeared right before something bad happened."[276]

Expectations

Upon cursory examination, unexplained smells seem to reveal the nature, if not the very identity, of spiritual presences. Pleasant scents are feminine, smoke scents masculine, unpleasant scents demonic; it seems nice and tidy. But, as noted, these associations run contrary to historical record when scrutinized. We should expect more feminine smoke scents, more masculine perfumes, and ghosts—usually reflections of the living—shouldn't smell of decay.

These incongruities between reality and expectation are highlighted in the case of George Washington Vanderbilt II, original owner of the Biltmore House, America's largest privately owned residence. Today, the palatial mountain estate is a popular destination for tourists visiting Asheville, North Carolina, and the internet is filled with claims of spooky happenings on the property. Some even claim to have seen and smelled Vanderbilt's ghost smoking his pipe.

The problem with these accounts is that, as a self-described "red-hot prohibitionist," Vanderbilt neither drank nor smoked, and certainly had no pipe[277] (the home has a gentlemen's smoking lounge, but that was common to the era). Nor does Biltmore boast a particularly rich haunting tradition from the pre-internet era. Most would assume these witnesses are fabricating tall tales.

However, it seems more likely that those whose testimony conflicts with historical fact are not lying. We always trust our noses, the most difficult-to-fool of our senses. In *Gothic Realities: The Impact of Horror Fiction on Modern Culture*, L. Andrew Cooper writes, "The relative obscurity of the nose's capacity for deceit combined with its data's unconventional appearance allows it to communicate a strong suggestion of objective existence."[278]

Setting aside deception and misidentification, let us consider a third option: reports of Biltmore's haunting are a reaction to the fact that—as an imposing, 135,280-square-foot chateau from the nineteenth century—it is *supposed* to be haunted. Similarly, the ghost of its owner is *supposed* to be smoking, as so many men of the era did, just as feminine spirits are *supposed* to exude perfume, and demons are *supposed* to emit brimstone. Expectations trump reality.

The 1908 spirit sightings that plagued Alma, Colorado, highlight the role of the witness in describing the unknown:

> Alma had a sensation this week in the shape of a ghost, which appeared at night. People coming from the saloons about midnight saw a strange sight, or imagined they did. One night the phantom was seen near the Thomas saloon, another time it was at the bridge, on Main Street. The courageous Almaites gave chase, but when they arrived at the spot the apparition had mysteriously disappeared. Some describe it as a beautiful woman, clad in the finest white lingerie. The spot where the beauty disappeared was fragrant with the perfume of roses and violets. Others again say it looked to them like a huge elephant, with streams of fire issuing from its trunk, and when they arrived at the spot where it had vanished, the smell of sulphur and brimstone permeated the air.[279]

So which was it: the specter of a fragrant woman, or a sulfurous pachyderm? The descriptions are about as disparate as they could possibly be. If the Alma witnesses were honest, perhaps the discrepancy can be explained by suggesting the apparition possessed no objective form or smell at all—whatever the spirit was, it may have simply mirrored witness expectations, causing the fearful to behold a demonic elephant and the curious to perceive a lady in white. If beauty is in the eye of the beholder, perhaps fragrance is in the nose.

An alternative suggestion is that appearances (and, by extension, odors) are deliberately chosen by these "spirit" intelligences, tailored to individual witnesses for the purpose of deliberate manipulation. Specific scents could be selected for specific effects, or to reinforce different identities, like olfactory masks. To what end remains uncertain—what *is* apparent is that the hedonic odor associations prime the way we react to, interact with, and ultimately perceive these spirits, be they souls of the dead or something else entirely.

This is by no means the final word on this complex issue. Broader, cross-phenomenal trends are outlined in our final chapters. For now, this discussion has hopefully highlighted the stronger themes surrounding spirit smells, and will continue to provide deeper insight as our studies progress.

We now turn our attention to the skies.

Part III: UFO Smells

Chapter 10
UFO Smells: A History

Aliens use all manner of deodorants, perfumes, or lotions to disguise their natural scent, which is offensive to humans.
— *Weekly World News*,
"10 Ways to Tell if Your Co-Worker is an Extraterrestrial!"
(1/28/2003)

After Vatican museum Egyptologist Alberto Tulli passed away in the mid-twentieth century, Italian nobleman Boris de Rachewiltz discovered a mysterious papyrus in the old man's belongings. An amateur Egyptologist himself, de Rachewiltz set to translating the document, only to discover it belonged to the *Annals of Thutmose III*, dated between 1594 and 1450 B.C. He was astounded by what the ancient text revealed.

> In the year 22, in the third month of winter, in the sixth hour of the day, the scribes of the House of Life noticed a circle of fire that was coming from the sky [...] From the mouth it emitted a foul breath. It had no head. Its body was one rod long and one rod wide. It had no voice. And from that the hearts of the scribes became confused and they threw themselves down on their bellies... Now after some days had passed, these things became

more and more numerous in the skies. Their splendor exceeded that of the sun and extended to the limits of the four angles of the sky [...] High and wide in the sky was the position from which these fire circles came and went... Then these fire circles ascended higher into the sky and they headed toward the south. Fish and birds then fell from the sky.[280]

Though some may erroneously think that UFO sightings began with Kenneth Arnold's famous 1947 "flying saucer" sighting, mankind has seen (and smelled) strange things among the clouds since we first gazed skyward. The "Tulli Papyrus," as it has become known, may be the earliest written account of an unidentified flying object, and is certainly the earliest account of one emitting foul odors. The document should still be viewed with a skeptical eye—neither its chain of custody nor pedigree are pristine.[281]

UFOs exist. It is a fact—people see unidentified flying objects in the sky on a near-daily basis. The true question is whether or not these unexplained aerial phenomena are evidence of extraterrestrial visitation, a subject very much open to debate.

It is unfortunate that the popular lexicon no longer distinguishes between "UFOs" and "alien spacecraft." The truth of the matter is that these strange things haunting our skies could very well be misidentification of aircraft or satellites, unrecognized natural phenomena, or clandestine military aircraft. Even in sightings where these causes are ruled out, there is no need to make the leap of logic that UFOs are non-terrestrial, save for a handful of cases where their "pilots" proclaim otherwise... and even when they do, why should we believe them? Why trust these intelligences, which have obfuscated their origin for millennia, to be so forthcoming?

The evidence connecting lights in the sky with the perceived "alien abduction" phenomenon is on similarly shaky ground. Not every abductee recalls being pulled into a flying saucer. What people are experiencing could well be extraterrestrial... or it could be ultraterrestrial, interdimensional, or spiritual, to list just a few alternate scenarios.

As with spirits, we should assume nothing about UFOs or their "occupants." Many researchers, including Jacques Vallee, have demonstrated that modern UFO lore shares much with worldwide faerie traditions. The abduction experience also has commonalities with the near-death experience: bright lights, levitation, passing through walls, even the occasional appearance of deceased loved ones. We may be dealing with physical, structured, nuts-and-bolts spacecraft, or perhaps something far stranger.

We still must somehow deal with this terminology. The most parsimonious method is to adopt the existing nomenclature and refer to UFOs as "craft" and their occupants as "aliens." Note that this is not an endorsement of the Extraterrestrial Hypothesis (ETH), nor is this lengthy disclaimer a condemnation of it either. To reiterate, all unexplained phenomena may not come from one source—but all unexplained phenomena *have undeniable similarities.*

Smells in UFO Sightings

Regardless of the veracity of accounts like the Tulli Papyrus, there are countless historical descriptions of strange, smelly things in the sky. In past centuries, such anomalies were not signs of extraterrestrials visiting Earth in spacecraft, but rather divine portents. Many such historical encounters are detailed in Jacques Vallee and Chris Aubeck's excellent book *Wonders in the Sky*: a 137 A.D. sighting of a glowing celestial object that "left a smell like burning wood" in Forli, Italy; a 1444 Italian sighting of a glowing orb "leaving a smell of remarkable sweetness" in its wake; an 1845 sighting of three luminous objects emerging from the sea near Turkey, accompanied by "an overpowering heat and a stench of sulfur"; two "rolling wheels" of fire that exploded over the Arabian sea, leaving a sulfurous odor.[282]

With so many cases exhibiting an olfactory component, it is

baffling why some researchers like Joan Woodward would claim UFO witnesses "rarely report an odor."[283] While it is true that many UFO sightings take place at a distance, precluding an olfactory component, a cursory survey of the past half-century of *Mutual UFO Network Journals* alone yields hundreds of close range sightings accompanied by odors.

On the contrary, some consider smells to be a hallmark of UFO close encounters. Researchers Norman J. Briazack and Simon Mennick noted as early as 1978 that many UFO occupants emanate "an obnoxious sulfurous odor," and stated, "In any event, more study is needed in the entire field in order to unravel these interlocking problems and mysteries."[284]

The old guard of anomalous research certainly gave the subject of UFO smells a great deal of thought. In *The Eighth Tower*, John Keel stated that many unexplained entities and UFOs smell like "rotten eggs," theorizing that the smell was attributable to large amounts of energy released when these beings manifest in our reality.[285] Ivan Sanderson tackled the subject in *Uninvited Visitors*, roughly breaking accounts down into metallic, aromatic, and sulfurous odors, further subdividing the last category into cabbage, whale oil, and rotting odors. The metallic smells, he felt, indicated the presence of hot hydrocarbon oil from nuts-and-bolts spacecraft.[286] James McCampbell, on the other hand, saw more tendencies toward ozone odors, SO_2, and chemical components such as benzene.[287] Thomas E. Bullard, author of 1987's seminal *UFO Abductions: The Measure of a Mystery*, noted that a quarter of abductee cases describe breathing difficulties or odd smells aboard craft, including "ozone or something described in similar terms—sulphurous, pine-like, or rain like. Exceptions include a burnt-sugar smell, a smell like chicken, or something burnt, or simply a bad odor."[288]

Over the years, witnesses have accused these noxious fumes of causing a variety of unpleasant symptoms, including nausea, dizziness, upset stomach, vomiting, low blood lymphocyte counts, and irritation of the skin, ear, eyes, nose, and throat. On the whole, the foul odors associated with UFOs tend gain notice immediately following a sighting, rather than during the event itself. We must ask ourselves what exactly witnesses smell: the craft, its exhaust, or a reaction in the environment? In cases where entities are seen, do they smell the craft's occupants, their gadgetry, or the gases they are breathing?

Existing research

Of the three primary areas of inquiry in this book—spirits, UFOs, and Sasquatch—UFO odors have the richest existing research (while a lot of *thought* has been put into spirit smells, a lot of *science* has been put into UFO smells). As such, this section of the book is a great deal longer than our discussion of spirit smells; there is simply more for us to hang our proverbial hat on.

Most literature has been preoccupied with determining what these odors are, rather than what they might mean. Thomas M. Olsen was the first to scientifically tackle the subject with "UFO Odours and Origins," an article that first appeared in a 1980 issue of *Flying Saucer Review* (and later in the *MUFON Journal*). Olsen's work is to be commended for giving the subject the attention it deserves, if not for being particularly open-minded; he came to a conclusion similar to Sanderson's, that UFO odors suggest physical, structured craft utilizing hydrocarbon fuel. Olsen's approach was flawed from the outset for three main reasons: first, he used a tiny data set (16 cases, although this may be a limitation of the era); second, he adopted a constrictive materialist paradigm, assuming such smells *must* come from machine emissions; and third—perhaps most egregiously—he dismissed witness testimony of "burning sulphur" as misidentified ozone.[289]

While we have certainly noted the precedent for ozone/sulfur misidentification (and will further do so in the following chapters), Olsen's assumption fails to take into account how keen human noses are at detecting sulfur compounds in our environment. It also conflates misidentification with abundance; just because city slickers might misidentify mules as horses, it doesn't mean they aren't actually seeing horses, nor that horses aren't, in fact, more common. Assuming eyewitness misidentification from the start renders all Fortean inquiry moot. Why not assume people smelled what they smelled? Researchers certainly assume they saw what they saw. If we decide that modern witnesses are mistaking ozone for sulfur, we might as well second-guess the visual component of sightings too, and proclaim that every UFO witness has mistaken Venus for a flying saucer.

Research into the subject remained sporadic for the next two decades. One notable exception is a 1998 *MUFON Journal* article by R.J. Durant cataloguing the sounds and smells of *Majestic*, a fictionalized retelling by Whitley Strieber of the purported UFO crash at Roswell, New Mexico. Durant counted more than twenty different references to smell in the book, including burning rubber, sulfur, decay, gardenias, and perfume. It is a bit baffling why so much effort was put into studying a fictionalized account, other than the fact that Strieber claims to have had extraterrestrial contact himself. Still, Durant's article at least represents a useful compendium of popular culture assumptions on how UFOs smell, even if the article presents little in the way of analysis.[290]

Finally in 2000, the subject of UFO smells found a true champion with researcher Antonio F. Rullán's essay "Odors from UFOs: Deducing Odorant Chemistry and Causation from Available Data." In what is the finest scholarship on the subject, Rullán presented a comprehensive literature review and sound scientific analysis of UFO smells—it is not recommended reading, it is *required*. The only downside to the essay is Rullán's relatively small research pool of 26, a sample that is also entirely American.[291]

Rullán's research strongly disagreed with Olsen's findings, though not explicitly. In the course of his study, he identified burning, metallic, and various chemical odors, as well as their perceived effects upon witnesses. Overall he determined that "sulfur appears to be a predominant component of the odor chemistry in UFO cases," and attributed these smells to a variety of sulfur compounds:

hydrogen sulfide, sulfur dioxide, carbonyl sulfide (COS, the smell of burnt rubber), carbon disulfide (CS_2, a burnt/iodine/medicinal/ rotten egg smell), and methyl mercaptan (CH_3SH, found in putrid cabbage).[292]

The essay also provides a useful system for classifying odor sources, one that can be conceptually applied to virtually all unexplained phenomena.

- **EE: Environmental source, environmental cause** – In this model, the smell exists in the environment and is unrelated to the sighting.
- **EO: Environmental source, object cause** – The UFO acts upon components in the environment, producing the odor.
- **OE: Object source, environmental cause** – The environment acts upon components from the UFO, producing the odor.
- **OO: Object source, object cause** – The UFO releases the odorant itself with the environment playing no role whatsoever.[293]

Of the four choices, Hypothesis EE seems the least likely, as it posits that anomalies only manifest at sites with existing sulfur odors. Still, some would correctly point out the propensity for unexplained phenomena to occur in swamps, which often smell of decay, or the West Virginia Mothman's affinity for appearing at "the TNT area," where sulfurous explosives were manufactured in World War II, or the famous Socorro, New Mexico sighting of 1964, which was also in close proximity to a dynamite shack.[294]

"There's a lot of incidents—a lot of low-level close encounter-type UFO events—that occur in the vicinity of energy sources," said Pennsylvania investigator Stan Gordon. "High tension power lines, power-generating stations, gas wells, gas lines, communication towers, railroad tracks, water reservoirs—and I've believed for quite a while that a lot of the phenomena we're dealing with seems to have some kind of type of energy connection to it."[295]

We will return many times to Rullán's model and work throughout this section of the book, particularly in our concluding chapter.

It is interesting to note that Rullán threw out cases where smells were remembered under hypnotic regression, a common method for retrieving memories of alleged UFO abductees. Though our discussion does not adopt a similar position, there is certainly wisdom in this approach. Scientists have long debated whether or not humans can create "smell pictures" with their memory or imagination, and at least 40% of the population openly admits the inability to do so.[296] Even those who claim the ability to recall specific odors are likely exhibiting "the confusion of odors with other sensations," according to Trygg Engen—put succinctly, we never forget smells when exposed, but lack the ability to create a "picture" of them in the "mind's nose."[297] Hypnotic regression (already viewed skeptically by many) would naturally be rife with such complications.

Chapter 11
UFO Smells: Miscellany

Our first clue is, therefore, the awful smell. It can be so bad it makes dogs and people ill. I've received a powerful whiff of this myself in my travels.

— John Keel, *The Eighth Tower*

In *The UFO Silencers*, Timothy Green Beckley interviewed Sarah Hines, a young Canadian girl who claimed to have been taken aboard an arrowhead-shaped craft on August 4, 1979. The neighborhood had seen the objects for several days prior, and when they appeared again, she found herself wandering to a nearby field. Under hypnotic regression she recalled entering the craft and meeting seven short, football-shaped, "shadowy creatures" that appeared crystalline. Among the dreamlike things Hines noted during her experience were a housecat, buzzing sounds, a view of the Earth from space, and "the odor of chicken" (no clarification on whether that meant alive, dead, raw, or cooked).[298]

Though it may seem out-of-order to begin our coverage of UFO smells by addressing the outliers, later chapters discussing the most common odors build upon one another. To interrupt that flow with the inclusion of this chapter, which focuses on more ambiguous and less common scents, would be ill advised. Thus—having briefly established several of the larger trends in the previous chapter—we shall first discuss the exceptions to the rules.

Tip-of-the-nose

A majority of the odors in UFO sightings are unplaceable. Such nebulous descriptions naturally frustrate researchers. Sometimes the hedonic quality—good or bad—is all that witnesses are able to articulate. In other instances, they recall a slightly more specific albeit still generic scent, like the "musky" UFO interior noted by a 1942 Texan abductee,[299] or the "waxy" smell left at a 2002 Ukrainian landing site.[300]

"Unpleasant," "putrid," and "foul" are the most common descriptors. Like foul spirit smells, it is possible (likely?) that some of these odors are sulfurous, though there is no way to be certain. These vague adjectives are used not only to describe the stench from anomalous craft, but also the odor of trace evidence, like the foul-smelling green substance discovered in the snow after Bill Gowan's 1973 North Carolina sighting.[301] The odors of UFO occupants can be equally ambiguous. For example, "Jane Murphy," a recurring British experiencer, claimed a "foul-smelling" entity sexually assaulted her while aboard a UFO in 1975.[302]

Unidentifiable odors appear in some of the earliest modern reports, such as the controversial sighting of Florida resident "Sonny" DesVergers. DesVergers was driving three boy scouts home on August 19, 1952, when a strange light in the palmettos caught his eye. Curious, he stopped the car to investigate and began to make his way through the thick underbrush. He soon noticed a peculiar aroma, and after a few moments reached a large, oval object hovering 30 feet above a clearing. The object was emitting a red mist that washed over DesVergers, who passed out. When he regained consciousness, he fled the scene, running into the scouts further down the road.[303]

DesVergers, who was familiar with acids in his workplace, could not place the odor, only describing it as an "acute, sharp smell."[304] He believed these "sickening, nauseating" qualities were the reason he lost consciousness. After the USAF examined the case as part of its infamous Project Blue Book, rumors circulated that the affair was a hoax; though impossible to be sure, it is suspicious that DesVergers's recollection of the odor changed as he grew older (this revised description is discussed later).

Graham Conway, late founder of UFO British Columbia, investigated a case prominently featuring another affecting, unidentified smell. "Salina Quail," an experiencer since childhood, discovered in 1980 that she was pregnant, though paradoxically her husband was sterile. Six weeks after this revelation, Salina rose in the night to use the bathroom and detected a strange, unidentifiable scent. Frightened, she shuttered the window and returned to bed, only to find herself paralyzed. A dark shape appeared by the bedside, telling Salina it was there to check on the baby. After a brief medical inspection, the entity disappeared.[305]

Had the smell somehow induced her paralysis?

Musty Odors: Cheese, cinnamon, and the problem with Whitley Strieber

The Old Hag often smells musty, a stale, moldy odor with overtones of dampness. The stench is one of the more common outliers in UFO cases—Travis Walton, perhaps the most famous of all alien abductees, described the UFO interior during his encounter as "hot and humid," full of air that "smelled slightly stale and muggy."[306] The rooms where these odors manifest are predictably drab: "Dave," one of the abductees studied by John Mack, recalled being taken to "a round, gray room in which there is an 'earthylike' smell,"[307] identical in description to a 1973 abduction from Henry County, Georgia.[308] Australian abductee Irene Sander claimed that in 1996 her captors took her inside a ship that was "dull silver in colour with a horrible musty smell."[309]

Karla Turner's husband, who was also an abductee, recalled visiting an underground cavern during one of his experiences, an unsurprising locale given rampant speculation of subterranean extraterrestrial bases over the years. He described the location as "musty" and "dank," and visited a similar space that gave the impression of "an old gym, an old locker room."[310]

The comparison is apt, alluded to in other accounts. Brian Scott, who claimed to have been taken by large, reptilian aliens near Phoenix in 1971, was examined inside a mist-filled craft that smelled of "rotten socks, as if someone hadn't taken their shoes off for twenty years."[311] One would be hard-pressed to find a more fitting description of an old locker room odor. Similarly, witnesses in a 1981 case from Stone Mountain, Georgia, recalled being snatched from their car into a cold, dim room with a musty quality. Inside were tables stretching as far as the eye could see, each holding a moaning human being, all smelling like "dirty clothes."[312] Compare this image—hundreds of agonized people, accompanied by a musty odor—to the aforementioned near-death vision of Hell recorded by Margot Gray.

Such odors emanate from the alleged entities as well, sometimes in conjunction with sleep paralysis. In July 1990, a visitor to Las Vegas claimed to have spotted two discs in the sky, only to have half a dozen Grey aliens appear by his bedside that evening, manifesting a musty odor.[313] Similarly, a witness from North Berwick, Scotland, awoke in the night to find a diminutive shape leaning over her, exuding the smell of burnt cardboard or paper[314] (again, themes of combustion).

This cardboard smell—undeniably a "musty" odor—has become something of a minor motif in abduction accounts. Author Eve Lorgen claims that 59% of abductees notice a "sulphur smell, moldy cardboard or wet leather odor in presence of aliens"[315] (having spent so much time parsing out the minute differences between odors, asking witnesses about such a broad set of smells is cringeworthy).

Author Whitley Strieber doubtlessly popularized this cardboard description with his bestselling book *Communion*. Strieber claims that he was taken from his upstate New York cabin the day after Christmas 1985, as part of an ongoing contact scenario. In one early instance, he asked his alien abductors to reinforce their reality by letting him smell them.

The one to my right replied, "Oh, OK, I can do that," in a similar voice, speaking very rapidly, and held his hand against my face, cradling my head with his other hand. The odor was distinct, and gave me exactly what I needed, an anchor in reality. It remained the most convincing aspect of the whole memory, because that odor was completely indistinguishable from a real one. It did not seem in any way a dream experience or a hallucination. I remembered it was an actual smell.

There was a slight scent of cardboard to it, as if the sleeve of the coverall that was partly pressed against my face were made of some substance like paper. The hand itself had a faint but distinctly organic sourness in its odor. It was not a human smell, but it was unmistakably the smell of something alive. There was a subtle overtone that seemed a little like cinnamon.[316]

Before proceeding further—since the following section becomes a bit problematic—a note on Strieber, who has become a contentious figure in UFOlogy. As a bestselling author, he had everything to lose and nothing to gain by coming out with his experiences... anyone involved in the subject will tell you that expressing an interest in UFOs is not exactly a sound career decision (present author included). Moreover, as a master of fictional storytelling, he could have undoubtedly crafted a better, more logical narrative than the one he has perpetuated for the past 30 years. Whether or not he experienced everything he claims to have is up for debate, but he himself seems to believe it.

The cinnamon odor appears more frequently than expected in alien abductions. Author Jenny Randles asserted in the early 1990s that British abductees report cinnamon with regularity.[317] In 1988,

Randles herself investigated the case of a woman who claimed to have levitated from her bed and into a waiting spaceship that smelled of cinnamon.[318] The odor also appears in American reports—John C. Thompson wrote in 1998 of a man abducted from the American South who presented purple stains on his hands and a clinging "cinnamon like odor" as "proof" of his encounter.[319] Witnesses also report odors mildly evocative of cinnamon: a "dry sweet burning smell," the odor of burnt sugar or burnt chocolate, incense, or frankincense (not to belabor the point, but note again the theme of combustion).

Perhaps the most prominent case involving an odor of cinnamon is the infamous November 11, 1987 case from Gulf Breeze, Florida. Ed Walters claimed to have photographed a flying saucer after investigating a strange glow among the pine trees outside his home office. While trying to get closer, Walters claimed that a bright blue beam paralyzed him and lifted him bodily from the ground. The event was accompanied by a voice that robotically proclaimed, "We will not harm you," and an odor of ammonia mixed with cinnamon, which clung to his clothes. The event kicked off a series of visitations and impressive photographs.[320]

The fantastic story caught the attention of Strieber, who came to Walters's defense in the June 1988 edition of the *MUFON UFO Journal*. Strieber cited the odor, with its cinnamon overtones, as evidence of the story's veracity. Unfortunately for Strieber, time has not been kind to Ed Walters and the Gulf Breeze photos.[321] Accusations of double-exposures (wherein one photograph can be superimposed over another) took root and, even more damning, the new owner of Walters's home discovered a flying saucer model in the attic several years later.[322] While the whole Gulf Breeze flap is not a certain fake—there were many witnesses to odd events—it at least casts Walters' photographs into doubt.

It is painful to admit that there are other inconsistencies with Strieber's olfactory memories, contradictions made even more unpalatable after siding with an all-but proven hoaxer. After cherishing the reality-reinforcing, conscious memory of smelling cinnamon and cardboard, Strieber revised the odor of his encounter. Under hypnotic regression, Strieber said, "… it smells funny. Smells somethin' like cheese in here. Smells kind of nasty, to tell you the truth."[323]

"What cheese?" wrote sensory psychologist Avery Gilbert in 2009. "This olfactory detail—that the UFO's reception room smelled like cheese—is an entirely new feature brought up under hypnosis. Strieber has just revised his 'totally real' smell memory." Gilbert also notes how, later in *Communion*, Strieber revises the odor a third time, incorporating the odor of sulfur.[324]

Every scientist who has ever studied olfaction and memory agrees that smells are not forgotten. They are impervious to the reevaluation and degradation that other memories experience over time. Long-term odor memory can be established after just *one single exposure*,[325] and can spontaneously trigger memories.

Strieber even acknowledges the strength of olfactory memory during *Communion*, describing how the odor of his abductors made him recall an experience from his childhood when he encountered a small entity in his house and detected "a distinct odor as if of smoldering cardboard."[326] The unique odor triggered this memory, yet Strieber presents us with an ever-evolving description of the odor he experienced in 1985.

In Strieber's defense, there are a handful of explanations for the discrepancies. Perhaps he was simply wrestling with the tip-of-the-nose phenomenon, and getting closer each time to his actual memory. Alternately, much has been made of "screen memories" in abduction lore, where false memories are implanted to keep witnesses from having full recall—perhaps one of these mistaken olfactory profiles is a result of such meddling. Finally, there may be a subtle distinction between *what* Strieber smelled in each example, e.g. the entity vs. the room.

Strieber's exact description continues to change. In his follow-up book *Transformation*, he described the odor as "pungent, organic,"[327] while in a 2012 interview he simply described the odor of Grey aliens as "hot."[328] Taste—closely related to smell—has also been revised in Strieber's writing. In *Communion*, he recalled consuming something like a "rotten pomegranate" during his abduction, while in *Transformation*, the fruit has become a fig.[329]

In the end, Strieber's testimony underscores the need to treat hypnotic regression—if not witness testimony as a whole—with skepticism.

Nuts, sweets, and fruit

Even when recognized, UFO smells are sometimes an olfactory *non sequitur*. Consider the dome-shaped object that touched down near Cape Cod, Massachusetts, in August 1975, whose occupants left behind a white gauzy material and an almond smell.[330] It is difficult to discern why extraterrestrials would smell like nuts—perhaps, if it was a bitter smell (like the Arychuk case), the witnesses were detecting cyanide, a compound almonds are known to create.

Just as confounding are sweet, sickly odors.

- On August 13, 1975, a USAF sergeant was sky-watching in New Mexico when a gray disk landed next to his car. He regained consciousness inside what he presumed was the craft, paralyzed and enveloped by a "sickeningly sweet" odor. After making his way home, he reported a puncture at the base of his spine, red skin rashes, hair loss, headaches, and personality changes.[331]

- Alan Godfrey, a police officer in Yorkshire, England, was on patrol just before dawn on November 28, 1980, when he saw a flying saucer. During his abduction he recalled a similar sickly smell.[332]

- In 1990, young Alisher Sabirov claimed to have been taken from a road in Urgench, Uzbekistan, by a beautiful lady in a triangle-shaped craft. The odor of the interior was described as "light and aromatic, somewhat sweet-smelling."[333]

A highly suggestive case, if not explicitly an alien abduction, comes from the UFOs Northwest investigative group. In June 2010, an Oregon security guard saw a strange figure on the campus of George Fox University. As he approached it, the figure disappeared, leaving the guard to guess where the last three hours had gone, why his identification was misplaced, and why his jacket smelled of ozone and sickly sweet, rotten fruit[334] (missing time, of course, is common in both alien abductions and faerie lore).

Skeptics would likely chuckle at society's "fruits and nuts" smelling fruits and nuts. Nonetheless, these accounts resonate with spirit smell research, which not only features food odors, but repulsively strong sweet scents.

Pleasant smells

Though negative alien abductions have gained much attention in recent decades, extraterrestrial contact of the 1950s and early '60s was marked by positive experiences. Those taken weren't abductees but instead contactees, their encounters marked by fanciful travel to other planets, wise and beautiful humanlike beings, and messages of universal peace and love. Naturally, odors reported by contactees were pleasant, often floral in nature.

Pleasant fragrances are less common in UFO cases than in spirit reports, even taking the testimony of these early contacts into account. This being said, the interpretation of BVM apparitions as UFO activity—a stance held by some—would drastically increase the number of sightings. The association is not as outlandish as it first seems. In 1982, Migdalia Cintron and Aida Rivera witnessed a BVM in Puerto Rico who smelled of roses; bystander Felito Felix saw the entity transform into a large-headed, three-foot-tall little man with "oriental eyes" and "pointed ears" before it disappeared.[335]

The BVM comparisons are particularly strong in the contactee literature. Take Lyra, one of the entities encountered by Orfeo Angelucci in 1953: dazzlingly beautiful, clad in "a kind of Grecian gown of glowing silvery-white substance," with lush golden hair and expressive blue eyes, Angelucci compared her to a goddess. When she departed, Lyra left behind "an exquisite fragrance… as if bowers of invisible flowers were everywhere."[336] Similarly, the home planets of these entities evoke historical depictions and scents of Heaven. One of the more obscure contactees, Calvin C. Girvin, allegedly traveled in 1954 to a distant planet complete with exotic flowers, babbling brooks, and an overpowering floral fragrance that filled him with joy.[337] George Adamski, the most famous and controversial contactee, capitalized on these associations to lend credence to his fictional claims of meeting a coalition of wise Saturnians in 1962; their conference room was filled with "12 small fountains… Each was a different color and odor which blended as one, producing a pleasant atmosphere throughout the building."[338]

These phenomena blend in perplexing ways. It is not uncommon for poltergeist activity to manifest following a UFO sighting. On July 2, 1968, Canadians Fred and Wayne Coulthard saw "an object with rotating red lights" perturbing their livestock, only to find the house under siege by poltergeist activity less than two hours later. Among the disturbances were shattered glass, objects tossed, and a "strong odor of roses" in the kitchen.[339]

Though rare, floral fragrances still occur in the modern UFO era from time-to-time. United States congressman Dennis Kucinich saw a UFO outside his Graham, Washington home, according to friend and actress Shirley MacLaine. In private correspondence, Kucinich told MacLaine that he had been lured onto the balcony by "the smell of roses," then observed a "gigantic triangular craft" in the sky for ten minutes before it shot away at frightening speed.[340] In 2003, witnesses reported five dark silhouettes that walked out of a blinding bright light at a roadside near Murchison, Australia, then disappeared, leaving the witnesses in a new location with an hour of missing time and the scent of roses in the car.[341]

The scent of violets and hyacinth have also been reported. One particularly fascinating and difficult-to-categorize case was relayed in the September 1980 issue of *Flying Saucer Review*. Walter Rizzi was traveling through Italy's Dolomite Mountains in July 1968 when he pulled off the road to catch some sleep. He was roused by "a strong odour as though something was burning," so pungent that he thought his car was on fire (burning smells are thoroughly covered later). Rizzi observed a bright light in the distance, a sight that triggered earlier memories during his service in the Italian Army.

In 1942, Rizzi had befriended a young girl on the Greek island of Rhodes who had the habit of taking food to an old holy man. Through much cajoling, he secured a meeting with the wizened hermit, and the two began a master-pupil relationship. The old man claimed to be over a century old and had the ability to astrally travel the universe. He told Rizzi that, using a special ancient prayer, "he would be able to give me a sign of his presence, and this would be simply by means of a powerful odour. Finally, after so many years, I did manage... to reach such concentration that, wherever I might be, I would receive a strong smell of roses and lily-of-the-valley."

The holy man also predicted that Rizzi would meet "beings from the Cosmos," a prophecy fulfilled in his 1968 encounter with several glass-hooded spacemen in the Dolomites. Like so many other encounters, the aliens relayed spiritual and apocalyptic messages before departing, leaving Rizzi to cope with a month of fatigue and hair loss.[342]

Rarely are pleasant, non-floral fragrances noted. Two notable examples are the October 4, 1973, sighting by Gary J. Chopic, who noticed a flying-wing style craft hovering near Simi Valley, California, which released a fog with "a sweet odor, not flowery... but perhaps close to certain incense scents;"[343] and a 1979 Brazillian case where the witness was brought aboard a craft that smelled like—in a strange parallel to the story of the Italian nun ghost—baby powder.[344]

Chapter 12
UFO Smells: Sulfur

There stood a Hill not far whose griesly top
Belch'd fire and rowling smoak; the rest entire
Shon with a glossie scurff, undoubted sign
That in his womb was hid metallic Ore,
The work of Sulphur.

— Milton, *Paradise Lost*

"A mysterious odor—a potent mix of sulfur and rotten eggs—has been hitting noses at the intersection of Quincy Shore Drive and East Squantum Street," reads the subtitle of a 2013 article from *The Patriot Ledger* of Quincy, Massachusetts. "The city has hired chemists from UMass Boston to test water samples for the presence of any bacteria that could contain clues about the smell's origin."[345]

Mysterious odors are nothing new to city dwellers. Researcher and author Greg Newkirk, however, astutely pointed out that, on May 9, 2013—the same publication date as *The Patriot Ledger* article—WBZ-TV Boston ran a story about a mysterious aircraft in the skies over Quincy.[346] The object would mysteriously ascend with a hum each evening like clockwork before descending around 5:00 a.m. It was never confirmed as belonging to any government agency.

"We're as frustrated as our constituents," said Quincy Mayor Tom Koch. "We'd like to be able to give our citizens some answers, but we don't have any answers."[347]

Sulfurous smells are the most commonly reported odors in UFO sightings. Their presence is pervasive, appearing at the beginning, middle and end of encounters, emanating from structured craft, alleged occupants, and trace evidence alike.

"The smell of rotten eggs—hydrogen sulfide… frequently surrounds the fabled flying saucers and their space-suited pilots," Keel wrote in *The Mothman Prophecies*.[348] Anyone doubting the prevalence of sulfur should refer to the work of Jacques Vallee who, in *Dimensions*, alluded to "the smell of sulphur" as a UFO hallmark, [349] and detailed a compelling Brazilian case in his follow-up book, *Confrontations*.

In 1982, a prospector named Manuel was sleeping after a successful deer hunt when two luminous objects in the sky fired a red beam of light towards him. The objects, according to one witness, were *chupas*, Latin American UFOs shaped like refrigerators. Manuel discharged his rifle to no affect before fleeing the scene, one of the *chupas* in hot pursuit. It followed him for seven hours through the jungle and into caves before finally breaking off pursuit.

In spite of burns, fatigue, and irritated eyes, the object's odor made the greatest impact on Manuel. "It was penetrating, like burning sulphur, and it made his nose run," Vallee wrote. "It did not impair his breathing, but forced him to clear his throat at frequent intervals. He believes that it was the smell rather than the light that made him fall, and that it was the piece of cloth over his nose that saved him." [350]

This rapid-fire timeline of selected sightings illustrates the prevalence of sulfurous odors.

- **Skåne County, Sweden: October 1936.** Five bright orbs in the sky follow a pair of boys through the countryside. The witnesses note a sulfurous odor, confirmed by their mother upon returning home.[351]

- **Dai-el-Aouagri, Morocco: July 20, 1952.** A saucer lands and gives off a smell akin to "burning sulfur."[352]

- **Connersville, Indiana: Autumn 1966.** Two paperboys report a curved object with glowing lights, noting "the odor of sulphur in the air, and a high-pitched whirring."[353]

- **Jonestown, Pennsylvania: April 1967.** John H. Demler's car stops and is buzzed by a black UFO that smells of "sulphar [sic] and oil."[354]

- **Cussac, France: August 29, 1967.** Two schoolchildren observe "four little devils" floating into a luminous orb, which ascends with a soft whistling noise and a "sulphurous" odor.[355]

- **Ross, Ohio: November 10, 1975.** Two gas station attendants note a bright light in the sky that suddenly blinks out, leaving a strong sulfur odor.[356]

- **Ragusa, Italy: December 15, 1978.** A truck driver notices an illuminated object in conjunction with two humanoids in coveralls. Following the encounter, his radio begins working again, and "a strong smell of sulfur" fills the air.[357]

- **Saquarema, Argentina: October 15, 1979.** Luli Oswald and a student are taken aboard a craft and given sexual examinations, all the while their breathing made difficult by "a sulphurous odor."[358]

- **Dauphin County, Pennsylvania: December 4, 1988.** A police officer notices "a strong odor similar to sulphur," after seeing a mysterious aerial object.[359]

- **Dallas, Oregon: October 16, 1990.** A glowing disk is seen above a pasture, gliding out of sight with a high-pitched noise and "a strong sulphur odor."[360]

- **Silbury Hill, England: July 1994.** Multiple witnesses camping atop the historic mound notice the smell of sulfur and burning rubber, accompanied by the approach of floating, translucent objects. Small, luminous beings are seen within the pyramidal shapes, each topped by "orange fireballs."[361]

- **Near Indianapolis, Indiana: August 23, 2005.** Dottie Phillips is traveling with her husband when she notices several lights rise from a "fire" in the distance and follow their car, accompanied by an odor "similar to creosol, burnt tar, and sulfuric acid." The next evening they pass directly under the craft, complete with smell, and Dottie's brand new shoes begin to crumble and peel.[362]

- **Toledo, Spain: August 21, 2014.** While meditating, a witness spots a large sphere in the sky that vanishes and leaves "a very strong sulfuric odor." A large creature with glowing eyes is observed shortly thereafter.[363]

To further underscore the pervasiveness of sulfur in UFO accounts, sometimes witnesses aren't even aware they are describing sulfurous smells. Australian Andrea Richards and her two children experienced car trouble during a September 16, 1974, encounter with a brilliant light in the sky. Richards noted facial numbness and a smell akin to household gas, albeit stronger.[364] Two months later, a Pennsylvanian witness described a glowing object that landed in a pond, accompanied by the smell of a gas stove.[365]

Household natural gas is odorless—its distinctive smell comes from methanethiol (CH_3SH) added to the mixture with the express purpose of providing an olfactory warning of leaks. The main malodorant in methanethiol is, naturally, sulfur, to which the human nose is so very, very sensitive. Similar thiols (also called *mercaptans*) are the reason skunk spray—an odor noticed in a 1979 UFO sighting from Massachusetts[366]— smells unpleasant.[367]

Sulfurous odors linger well after sightings in a variety of ways. A Miami, Florida, police officer picked up Filiberto Cardenas in 1979 after several witnesses watched him disappear into a luminous UFO two hours earlier.[368] Cardenas told a fanciful story of underwater travel with humanlike beings who examined him, leaving over 100 pinpricks on his skin and a stench of sulfur clinging to him.[369]

A sulfurous presence can be a lifelong stigma for abductees long after the smell disappears. Jesse Long claimed to have lived with an alien implant for 32 years before having it surgically removed in 1989. Seven years later he had the sample analyzed—its composition was phosphorous, calcium, and, most surprisingly, nearly a full quarter sulfur. "No glass or transparent ceramic was available in the 1950s… with sulfur at any measurable level, let alone 24.42%," the report read.[370]

In addition to remnants left in and on witnesses, sulfurous smells are detected at alleged UFO landing sites for days afterward from a variety of sources, including burn marks, gelatinous goo, and powders. A rash of sightings in Israel in Spring 1993 were noted for leaving behind a white powder whose sulfurous odor made witnesses nauseous,[371] similar to a yellow substance detected in Querétaro, Mexico, after a landing in 1975.[372] Such samples have been collected and analyzed, as Vallee did with a sample from a sighting at the University of Bogotá; results revealed the presence of sulfur, if not much else.[373]

Some have even reported crop circles infused with the odor. Allegedly, the area of the famed 1966 Tully "saucer nests" of Queensland was infused with the smell of sulfur; the reeds at the site were flattened in a 30-foot circle, swirled clockwise.[374] Any inclusion of crop circles in this chapter, of course, is based on the assumption they are somehow linked to UFOs—a tenuous conclusion (it seems just as possible that most are hoaxes, or that psychic phenomena plays the primary role in their creation).

One of the most famous residual cases comes from 1967. At 11:20 p.m. on October 4, a large, unidentified, glowing object crashed into the water near the tiny Nova Scotia fishing village of Shag Harbour. Multiple witnesses described the light sitting in the harbor, surrounded by frothy yellow foam, before submerging.

When boats reached the area, the object had disappeared, but the slick remained, stretching some 80 feet wide by a half-mile long.[375] The brave few who touched the foam noted it left an oily residue on their hands, and everyone agreed the smell of sulfur lingered.[376]

Author Carl W. Feindt reprinted some speculative correspondence with UFOlogist Don Ledger in his 2010 book *UFOs and Water*:

> Some claimed there was the odor of sulfur and additionally there was some evidence of bubbling below and "roiling" of the water. It's not claimed that the bubbling caused the foam. If the Shag Harbour object was hot, it might have caused the water to release or gel agents in the water such as plankton. If there is an electrical field around the object, then perhaps that could cause plankton-rich water [Nova Scotia's waters are plankton rich] to react with the production of some foaming agent.[377]

A reaction with the water may have created the foam, but needn't be cited as a source of the odor—UFOs just as often smell sulfurous in air. Shag Harbour clearly illustrates the difficulty in determining whether trace effects—including odor—are the direct result of the object or the object's interaction with the environment.

This all implies that sulfur is somehow involved in the propulsion of extraterrestrial spacecraft. However, even that straightforward assumption is undermined when perusing reports of alleged

UFO occupants, who often smell sulfurous themselves. Could their "craft" be so odoriferous as to infuse these beings with this stench? Maybe. But even terrestrial truck drivers—who drive upwards of 70 hours weekly—don't always smell like diesel fumes.

It seems as though the smell of sulfur is fundamentally associated with these entities. During a UFO flap in 1978, Douglas Gould spotted several helmeted Grey aliens—short, pasty, with large heads and almond eyes—with his brother and cousins near South Middleton, Massachusetts; all detected a pervasive sulfur odor in the area.[378]

Earlier that same year, three New Jersey children were playing in the snow when they saw two square objects in the sky, one of which emitted a red beam of light (shades of Vallee's Brazilian case). Both objects departed, and the boys' attention was drawn to a group of sulfurous, bald, caped figures walking parallel to them.[379]

More contemporary descriptions are consistent with this theme. In 1994, Alice Leavy, an abductee interviewed by hypnotist Yvonne Smith, described her diminutive captors as "kind of cute, but they stunk, they smelled like sulphur… they smelled really bad." By contrast, she also reported taller insectoid abductors who were odorless, suggesting that sulfurous odors are specific to Grey aliens.[380]

Sulfur-exuding aliens certainly open the door to misidentification as demons, or vice versa. Hedonically speaking, it is obvious why beautiful entities in Contactee lore smell wonderful and malicious, abducting Greys smell bad. UFOs themselves, however, should be hedonically neutral, perched as they are at a distance in the nighttime sky, neither threatening nor benign. Yet witnesses still report unpleasant smells and feelings of intense fear. Could odors from UFOs be the root cause of witnesses' terror? If we believe olfaction alerts us to the true nature of that which is smelled, perhaps our noses are warning us.

Just as with spirit stories, multiple sulfur compounds are at play. Evidence exists for two primary culprits: SO_2 and, more commonly, H_2S—hydrogen sulfide.

Sulfur dioxide: SO_2

In *The Eighth Tower*, John Keel described an encounter similar to the one Vallee recorded in Brazil. Night watchman Harry Sturdevant was making his rounds in Trenton, New Jersey, in 1956 when he saw a cigar-shaped craft that released a smell like "sulfur or brimstone, but it was different." The stench made him nauseous, deadened his taste and smell, and made it difficult to swallow. "My stomach felt worse than the time I was overcome with mustard gas in France in World War I," he said.[381]

Like Vallee's Brazilian witness, Manuel, Sturdevant saw no gas, only inferring its presence from an odor—perhaps it was SO_2. As previously noted, the gas causes irritation to respiratory passages and eyes, resulting in a sore throat, coughing, a runny nose, and eye irritation.[382] During his time in Brazil, Vallee interviewed another witness who described a yellow, acrid-smelling cloud of smoke—both qualities associated with burning sulfur—in a sighting where an orb kidnapped his father.[383]

SO_2 appears throughout UFO literature. Raymond Fowler investigated a 1967 case where a couple from Haverhill, Massachusetts, saw a metallic saucer hovering above a pond, piloted by two lobster-like creatures—their departure included a "lit match" smell.[384] This exact same odor left a Scottish witness weak and dizzy in 1980 after seeing a bright light and three figures covered in dark, one-piece metallic suits.[385]

Skeptics would convincingly argue that any predominantly Christian country would attribute sulfur to paranormal activity, on account of its close association with Hell. Sulfurous smells from UFOs, however, are not a strictly Western phenomenon—Sunin Bhowmick of Islampur, India, explicitly identified SO_2 in her harrowing UFO encounter. In July 1979, villagers observed a ball of fire hovering over her school for two minutes, ripping metal roofing off nearby buildings.

"I fell over one of these metal sheets—and was amazed to find that it was hot," Bhowmick said. "The air was filled with a burning smell, like gunpowder. The odor was so strong that I nearly became sick." The object's "magnetism" also ripped the copper bracelet off one woman, in spite of copper's weak magnetism (another sulfur-copper connection?).[386]

Given its presence as an industrial pollutant, Rullán speculated that UFOs might induce chemical reactions that transform atmospheric SO_2 into malodorous compounds (Rullán's Hypothesis EO). A majority of the reactions he posited are endothermic, requiring large heat input[387]—perhaps another reference to our combustion theme (e.g. smells of smoke, gunpowder, etc.).

Recall how James McCampbell felt SO_2 was the most common UFO smell, likely because it implies some sort of machine exhaust. Although found in volcanic activity and a handful of other natural sources, 99% of atmospheric SO_2 is from human activity, in particular vehicle emissions.[388] SO_2 fits nicely with nuts-and-bolts, structured-craft UFOs, wherein mechanical cause produces atmospheric effect.

In reality, the most commonly identified odor is hydrogen sulfide (H_2S), a compound with *deep* organic ties. We have referenced H_2S numerous times; it is overdue for examination.

Hydrogen sulfide: H_2S

Researcher Stan Gordon's world changed one autumn evening in 1973. A major UFO flap was rocking Pennsylvania, with hundreds of sightings reported throughout the state. In late October, Gordon was called out to a farm where, 90 minutes earlier, 15 people had witnessed a giant red sphere dip into a nearby pasture.

Three witnesses had grabbed their guns and were approaching the 100-foot object when they spotted two apelike figures, each eight-feet tall, walking the fence line. Frightened by their glowing green eyes, the witnesses fired upon the creatures, which seemed unaffected by the rounds. The sphere abruptly disappeared—as if a switch had been flipped—and the beasts ambled toward the woods.

The story doesn't end there. Livestock avoided the still-luminescent landing site, and everyone was set on edge by the bizarre events. During his early morning investigations, Gordon visited the farmhouse of the primary witness, who was visibly agitated. Within moments, the witness began growling and screaming like an animal, viciously attacked one of Gordon's fellow investigators, ran toward the field, and collapsed.

Back in the farmhouse, Gordon's team began wheezing, the air suddenly filling with the odor of rotten eggs. Composing themselves, the investigators stepped outside to recover the witness. Though free from his trance, he still seemed powerfully affected, and began rambling about the apocalypse. Gordon and company wisely contacted a psychiatrist for professional help.[389]

This surreal tale ties together UFOs, Sasquatch, and demonic possession in an untidy little bow; Gordon called it "the case that caused him to reconsider Bigfoot." Such accounts illustrate the deep interconnectivity of paranormal phenomena, an interconnectivity accentuated by the presence of H_2S. Its ubiquitous presence across tales of spirits, UFOs, and Sasquatch suggests some type of commonality to all "supernatural" events.

Most of us associate the generic "sulfur smell" with rotten eggs, a distinctive odor created by anaerobic bacterial digestion of proteins within their shells—fibrous protein structures known as keratin found in feathers, horns, fingernails, and hair are high in sulfur, which serves the same strengthening role as in vulcanized rubber (in each of these examples, sulfur is what imparts their foul odor when burnt).[390] H_2S is present anywhere decomposition takes place in the absence of oxygen: swamps, sewers, hot springs, and the human digestive tract.[391] As such, it is the primary malodorous component of flatus,[392] and is also among the many toxic gases in volcanic emissions.[393]

It stands to reason that most eyewitnesses who report smells of "sulfur" in sightings are identifying H_2S, even when not making direct comparisons to rotten eggs. After examining numerous witness descriptions, Rullán determined in his 2000 study that, although no chemical compound matched *all* common physiological effects reported in UFO cases, H_2S and CS_2 (carbon disulfide) matched the most parameters.[394]

John Keel was keenly aware of H_2S's ubiquitous presence in the paranormal, having encountered the smell himself throughout his investigations. He compared it to the stink bombs of his youth, and briefly speculated in *The Eighth Tower* that the smell could be the result of sulfur oversaturation in our atmosphere, converted to H_2S by energy released during paranormal manifestation. In his typically insightful manner, Keel left the door open as to exactly what this suggested about the *nature* of such entities: this energy release could come from extraterrestrial technology, or from the immense amount of energy needed to jump between dimensions. In either scenario, this "force or energy unnatural to the earth's atmosphere," he contended, would generate "a sudden new mixture to be formed in areas where the sulfuric content is high. The result is a potent cloud of hydrogen sulfide or, where there is more fluoride gas than sulfuric gas, hydrofluoride [hydrogen fluoride]."[395]

Following the 1961 Hill case—widely though erroneously regarded as the first modern alien abduction—Betty Hill noted a pink powder on her dress; though it was odorless at the time, researchers said "a 'putrid' odor was noted in the water used for the soluble extracts of the stained samples," akin to "the odor resulting from a bacterial attack on water bottoms from fuel service tanks."[396] Diesel workers describe this odor as similar to rotten eggs (i.e. H_2S).[397] Analysis of the powder revealed sulfur, sodium, chlorides, and silicon.[398]

Descriptions of H_2S are not confined to sightings of structured craft. Those encountering alien entities frequently report the distinctive stench.

- Credo Mutwa, a colorful abductee portrayed in John Mack's *Passport to the Cosmos*, described the entities he encountered as having "a strange smell, a throat-tightening, chemical smell, which smelled like rotten eggs." Mutwa also characterized the odor as "like hot copper"[399]—recall recent research linking copper to sulfur detection in mammals.

- "Jim," another of Mack's subjects, was sitting in his living room prior to an encounter when "he felt as if his body were surrounded by static electricity, and then he sensed a foul, sulfurous smell like rotten eggs."[400]

- Laci, a friend of abductee Alice Leavy, described her companion's "cute" Greys as "disgusting" and smelling "really bad like rotten eggs."[401]

- According to a 1977 article by Rufus Drake, a security guard at Williams Air Force Base in Arizona saw a light descend on a construction site. Upon investigation, he found a large disk and an eight-foot-tall, stumpy-legged being with teardrop eyes. As it began moving toward him, he felt a humming in his skull accompanied by the odor of rotten eggs. A passing car scared the being back into its craft.[402]

- In 1985, a Spanish man named Xavier underwent hypnotic regression after discovering missing time and peculiar, demonic photos on his camera. He relayed an incredible story in which he was taken to an underground cave stinking of rotten eggs, where he was covered in a thick liquid by malicious entities. The story also involved a medical examination, clones, and stolen sandwiches (obviously psychiatric issues are possible, though his photos remain interesting).[403]

- Nazar Kopov of Ukraine claimed to have experienced rumbling and whistling sounds in his ears before being pulled into the sky in 1995. His slow descent to earth culminated in a meeting with several tall, reptilian entities smelling of rotten eggs. They informed him Earth was dying, and he had been selected as one of many to "establish a harmonious world order."[404]

The presence of H_2S suggests a biological component to these entities. Outside the digestive tract, small amounts of the gas are produced endogenously in human beings, where they serve a critical role in cell growth.[405] Like serotonin or the indole alkaloid DMT, H_2S functions as a neuromodulator within the human brain, assisting in the creation of long-term memory by increasing the response of NMDA receptors.[406] There is also evidence for its role as a smooth muscle relaxant and vasodilator, protecting against cardiovascular disease[407] (garlic's reputation as a panacea for disease and repelling vampires is likely due to its polysulfide content, whose conversion into H_2S produces cardioprotective qualities).[408]

Even with all this internal production, humans do not smell like H_2S (insert flatus joke here). By comparison, extraterrestrial visitors seem to exude the stuff. In *The Mothman Prophecies*, Keel discusses the curious interactions of Long Island talk-show host Jaye P. Paro with one "Princess Moon Owl," an otherworldly being who arrived "by flying saucer." Left-of-field zaniness gravitated toward Keel and his contacts, and the princess was no different. Tall and dark-skinned, with large eyes and clad in a cloak of feathers, Princess Moon Owl delivered a wheezy monologue to Paro in her studio about life on the planet Ceres, which was recorded on tape.

Over the course of the conversation, however, the princess' host began to grow uncomfortable. "She stank like rotten eggs," Paro said. The odor had begun inoffensively enough, but grew stronger until it was overwhelming. Keel was dubious as to the recording's veracity, but admitted that Princess Moon Owl, whatever she was, seemed to know an awful lot of private information regarding local UFO buffs.[409]

Keel asserted that "no mere animal could produce such a huge volume of gas by itself, no matter how long it had gone without a bath,"[410] an argument unsupported by science; huge volumes need not be produced. On the contrary, humans possess *extreme* sensitivity to sulfur compounds. H_2S is particularly detectable, with an odor threshold of 0.47 ppb.[411] Unlike most foul-smelling compounds, H_2S is revolting even in small doses.[412] This hedonic quality changes as the concentration increases, becoming more offensive at 3-5 ppm, then "sickeningly sweet" at 30 ppm and undetectable in higher doses due to olfactory adaptation.[413] It is possible that both "rotten egg" odors and "sweet" odors could be the same gas, albeit in different amounts (curiously, some describe higher H_2S concentrations as evocative of sandalwood—recall the odor detected in the Parisian catacombs).[414]

Our sensitivity to H_2S is due to the fact that it is more than just stinky—it's dangerous. In addition to eye and throat irritation, coughing, nausea, shortness of breath, and fluid in the lungs, low-level exposure over extended periods of time can lead to fatigue, appetite loss, headaches, irritability, memory loss, and dizziness.[415] These symptoms are, of course, emblematic of those experienced by alien abductees. Chronic, low-level exposure was also linked to miscarriages and reproductive issues in Russian and Finnish wood pulp factory workers, another feature that resonates with tales of missing fetuses in abduction lore.[416]

Massive buildups of H_2S are to blame for multiple mass extinctions in prehistory, including the Permian-Triassic extinction event of 252 million years ago.[417] The gas is instantaneously fatal in high concentrations, as evidenced by a 2008 wave of Japanese suicides where household ingredients were mixed to produce the gas.[418] Its ability to deaden the sense of smell makes it particularly dangerous in industrial applications. Acute H_2S poisoning can be remedied by an injection of sodium nitrite; though the connection is tenuous, one cannot help but wonder if the folkloric qualities of salt, said to dispel a host of paranormal entities from faeries to spirits, have some realistic grounding in this fact.[419]

Such knowledge re-frames miasma theory, nevermind legends

like the serpent of Lake Ontario, whose lethal breath could kill. Consider also the classic tale relayed by Jerome Clark in the November 1967 edition of *Flying Saucer Review*:

> On a day in late summer 1939, a military transport left the Marine Naval Air Station in San Diego, California, for a routine flight to Honolulu. About three hours afterwards, several urgent distress signals sounded from the plane, and then silence. Later, the craft came limping back to execute an emergency landing. When Air Station personnel entered the plane, they found every man on the crew, including the co-pilot, who had lived long enough to pilot the craft back to its base, dead of unknown causes.
>
> Each of the bodies had large, gaping wounds, and the outside of the ship was similarly marked. Air Station men who touched parts of the craft came down with a mysterious skin infection.
>
> One of the most puzzling aspects of the whole affair was that the .45 automatics carried by the pilot and co-pilot as service pieces had been emptied and the shells lay on the floor. A smell of "rotten eggs" pervaded the atmosphere inside the plane.[420]

The implication is that some unknown entity slaughtered the crew. It may not have been the entity, but rather its stench, that carried the blame.

Given its presence in subterranean sources—volcanoes, hot springs, etc.— H_2S has hellish connotations. Such belief is not restricted to old-world Christianity. Ancient Mayans believed that water-filled sinkholes called *cenotes* led to the spirit world. A layer of H_2S, created by organic decomposition, flows at the bottom of these pools, appearing as an underwater river that immediately conjures comparisons to the River Styx, the malodorous boundary of the Grecian underworld.[421] In the modern era, apocryphal tales on the internet describe subterranean caverns inhabited by reptilian entities, presumably from other planets, all of which exude hellish odors of sulfur.

Be it Gehenna, Lake Sirbonis, or cenotes, all inspirations for the underworld evoke decomposition. In UFO reports, the stench of decay is normally reserved for peripheral phenomena (e.g. entities, post-sighting strangeness, etc.) rather than the craft themselves. Naturally we must wonder whether rotten odors, like the smell of "dead bodies" noted by the Knowles family during their 1988 Australian UFO encounter,[422] are actually H_2S. Strange activity in Kent, England, in late 1963 included anomalous lights in the sky and a shadowy figure accompanied by the stench of something dead.[423] Two months after sighting multiple UFOs in July 1970, one New Jersey housewife noticed "a smell in the bedroom, rotten: like death" that made her nauseous and affected her sleeping patterns.[424]

Given all the possible descriptions, determining just how many UFO cases involve the odor of sulfur is tricky. This complex task is made even more difficult by centuries of confusion with another common scent: ozone.

Chapter 13
UFO Smells: Ozone

Aliens could exhibit colors that are not in our spectrum. Aliens could look like coke bottles, or could be composed of magnetic forces and undetectable to the human eye. They could be just a strange smell in the air. They could be completely digital and look like beautiful strange fractal chaotic swirls. Who knows?

— Cameron McKechnie

It all started with an itch on her leg—harmless enough. Virginia Horton had gone to fetch eggs from the barn when she felt the need to scratch. It was then she realized she was in the yard, not the barn, and that the itch was from a small, painless, bloody cut beneath her undamaged blue jeans...

By the time abduction researcher Budd Hopkins had finished regressing her, Horton told an elaborate narrative of how, in the summer of 1950, multiple short, hairless beings with bulbous heads and large eyes had taken her to a domed, brightly lit room. Once inside, one of the entities engaged in pleasant telepathic conversation before requesting they "take a piece of her" from her leg. The room, she claimed, had "an ozone smell... Kind of a clean smell, but nothing very specific."[425]

Ozone is the second most common smell in UFO encounters, albeit a distant one. With the exception of séances and exorcisms, it is exclusive to UFO lore. It is not uncommon to encounter reports of ozone during abduction examinations like Horton's—in fact, one of the earliest abductions of the modern era, the 1951 Fred Reagan case, featured entities like "huge stalks of metallic asparagus" who exuded a smell of "ozone or sulphur."[426]

Grey aliens may be more common today than metal vegetable monsters, but the smells coming from extraterrestrial visitors have remained consistent. The 1967 Bob Luca abduction featured an examination by Grey aliens in a white, sterile room smelling of ozone;[427] on January 17, 1970, a pregnant woman recalled smelling ozone when she was taken from her New York home, returning with skin marks and a bloodied nightgown;[428] a female patient claimed in May 1976 to have been cured of her cancer by two short, slant-eyed beings who took her aboard a craft that smelled similarly.[429]

When not present in abductions, witnesses almost always report the scent in conjunction with structured craft.

- Marion Smith of Levelland, Texas, described a curious "dirigible" in 1957 that disabled his car and some 12 others. "It was gun-metal in color but when it took off it turned into a ball of fire. Some of us went over where it had rested and could feel the ground was warm. There was a smell of ozone in the area."[430]

- Iowa farmer Ronald E. Johnson was awakened at 2:10 a.m. on April 23, 1966, by a loud roar coming from a 60-foot-long cigar-shaped object that landed in a field near his house. The object, with red lights on one end and blue lights on the other, gave off a series of loud reports and was accompanied by a smell similar to ozone.[431]

- A witness recalled an evening in October 1966, when she saw a "large, flaming object" hover over her New Boston, Michigan home. Her entire body felt electrified and she noted a strong ozone smell. Later, the witness tried to rouse her family members, to no avail. She later experienced nightmares of strange, gray entities.[432]

- On November 19, 1980, an object hovering at ground level was witnessed in Longmont, Colorado. The witness's car levitated briefly, and an ozone odor prevailed.[433]

- A hunter near Peppertown, Indiana, noticed a strange electrical hum and the smell of ozone at 6:30 p.m. on September 27, 1999. Upon reaching a shallow valley, the witness saw three beings huddled around a deer carcass, with a large, circular object just behind them. When the beings started approaching him, the hunter fired three shots and retreated, noticing a strange sound as he fled.[434]

Just enough sightings have featured ozone through the years to make the odor a minor meme in UFOlogy. No doubt this is due to the fact that, like SO_2, ozone fits with preconceived notions about extraterrestrial spaceships (after all, ozone is created through the release of energy). For this reason, some of UFOlogy's old guard were quick to seize upon ozone as the primary smell in UFO cases. Recall Olsen's dismissal of sulfur smells—Edward J. Ruppelt similarly speculated that the odor in DesVergers' case might have indicated ozone, despite any strong support for the theory.[435]

Science and history

The manner in which ozone is generated has already been discussed. The gas's creation is *photochemical*, meaning that it can be created not only by atmospheric electrical discharges, but also by ultraviolet (UV) light. In the modern era, ozone is yet another pollutant derived from fossil fuels, albeit indirectly—hydrocarbons and nitrogen oxides from emissions are converted to ozone via sunlight.[436] There is evidence to suggest that, at ground level, prolonged exposure to ozone can cause respiratory distress, damaging lung function and irritating the respiratory system,[437] as well as having detrimental effects upon the cardiopulmonary system.[438] For this reason, we are sensitive to ozone (threshold detection 0.01-0.05 ppm), although not as highly as sulfur.[439]

Despite these health risks, ozone is essential to life on the surface of this planet. High concentrations of ozone in our atmosphere simultaneously protect us from and are created by the sun's UV rays, which would irradiate every living thing if unfiltered.[440] To put this in perspective, sunburns are caused by what few UV-B rays reach the surface. What does this mean for UFO cases where witnesses receive sunburn-like effects? Perhaps, as in our atmosphere, UFO radiation not only burns witnesses but simultaneously creates ozone, protecting them from far more dangerous UV emissions.

In addition to its helpful atmospheric role, ozone is also a popular antimicrobial agent, used to negate unpleasant smells and sterilize air or water sources—many municipal drinking water systems employ the gas.[441] For this reason, it seems feasible that UFOs (or USOs, Unidentified Submersible Objects) could be deliberately producing ozone to sterilize their surroundings, both for their benefit and ours—extraterrestrial diseases would no doubt be devastating for all parties.

Because he was the first to isolate the gas in 1839, Christian Friedrich Schönbein is credited with ozone's discovery, though it was inferred much earlier from its odor, which was detected after electrical discharges.[442] The distinctive aroma can be described as akin to diluted chlorine, pungent, peppery even, easily noted following lightning strikes or the burnout of electrical equipment.

As already addressed, the confusion between ozone and sulfur compounds is ancient, dating back to the Greek classicists. In 1638, a violent storm hit Widecombe-in-the Moore, England, an event one witness described as "a fearful flash of lightning accompanied by a ball of fire, with deafening thunder… and a loathsome smell like that of brimstone."[443] This conflation persisted until relatively recently, with such luminaries as American polymath Benjamin Franklin[444] and Spanish physiologist Santiago Ramón y

Cajal[445] perpetuating the myth—both made references to sulfur's generation during electrical storms in the mid-eighteenth century.

Further confusing and complicating the matter is the work of Immanuel Velikovsky, who in 1940 wrote (but never published) *In the Beginning*, a book that has gained increasing popularity among alternative cosmologists. The manuscript, which describes Velikovsky's controversial theory of the formation of the universe, perpetuates the notion that sulfur can be generated from pure air via electrical discharge (which, if possible at all, would require power in excess of that utilized by modern particle accelerators—not out of the realm of possibility for extraterrestrial technology, but enormous nonetheless).[446]

Not only was ozone mistaken for sulfur, but sulfur was mistaken for ozone as well. Widespread Victorian belief held that the seaside's ability to promote health came from the sea air, which was full of ozone. This is a misnomer, of course. In reality, the distinctive aroma of ocean air comes from dimethyl sulfide, a compound produced mostly by seaborne bacteria consuming dying phytoplankton.[447]

Given this fact, we would be remiss to not point out the longstanding connection between UFOs and bodies of water: "50% of UFO encounters are connected with oceans and 15% more with lakes," said UFOlogist Vladimir Azhazha.[448] UFOs might simply smell like the sea.

Tip-of-the-nose

Given the longstanding conflation with the seaside and ozone, we must entertain the frustrating possibility that smells compared to seawater might indicate the presence of ozone, sulfur, or both. On July 28, 1975, five police officers in Salisbury, Rhodesia (modern Harare, Zimbabwe), saw an object hovering above the ground, an event followed by a motorist's midnight sighting of a large, orange light that filled his car with the smell of "foul sea water."[449]

Since it is rarely encountered in our daily lives, it is unsurprising that ozone is difficult to identify for some. It therefore stands to reason that a majority of witness testimony suffers from the tip-of-the-nose effect, where ozone is compared to something else.

In *Confrontations*, Vallee suggested that electrical and ozone odors could be one-and-the-same.[450] Descriptions of burning cable, wiring, and electronics are quite common in UFO reports—for example, witnesses in the aforementioned 1980 Colorado case alternately described the accompanying ozone smell as "a strong electrical odor."[451]

- In February 1957, a South African witness saw the "moon" zigzag toward her window before morphing into a elliptical shape and departing, leaving behind "an odor like that of an overheated radio."[452]

- Alice and Carol, two of Budd Hopkins' abduction subjects, recalled under hypnosis that they had encountered "a rubber, acrid smell of burnt wiring," another likely attempt to describe ozone.[453]

- On March 12, 1967, witnesses in Las Cruces, New Mexico, observed a UFO that smelled similar to burning electrical insulation.[454]

- In 1975, observers in San Antonio, Texas, described a flying saucer that smelled like "burning wires or metal," an odor researcher Richard Hall compared to a 1959 New Zealand case where "an odor like pepper" was reported (both conform to ozone's olfactory profile).[455]

The theme of burning, persistent throughout all types of unexplained phenomena, raises its head once more. We will return to other UFO burning smells in due course.

Given its association with thunderstorms, ozone may alternately be described as smelling "like rain," the phrase Meagan

Elliott used to describe the room her car was pulled into during her 1980 abduction. Elliott, who was with her 18-month-old daughter, felt as though her Grey captors kept them for two weeks, though in reality the experience lasted just five hours.[456] A similar pong was smelled in 1971 by an engaged couple who followed a UFO with their car to a farm near Evan City, Pennsylvania. They watched the object for several minutes while noting a "sweet and clean smell" like that following a rainstorm.[457]

Less intuitively connected to ozone are descriptions of pine tree smells. The "peppery" component of ozone has been compared to pine scent, and for good reason—volatile organic compounds released by the trees can, at significant altitudes, react with UV levels and increase ambient ozone (hence the refreshing smell of "mountain air").[458] At least two UFO witnesses, both from Spain, have reported pine smells: Miguel Sierra was hauled aboard a craft that smelled like pine in 1977,[459] while the following year Julio Fernandez's car was overtaken by blue-skinned humanoids who dragged him to a hovering disk that smelled like "pine or ozone."[460]

Photochemistry

Because ozone has a photochemical nature, its presence in UFO cases supports Rullán's Hypothesis EO, i.e. energy from the object reacts with environmental sources to produce the odor. Such conjecture is well founded, as coronal discharges in our atmosphere have been proven to react with oxygen to generate ozone.

Beyond this basic logic, there is further evidence suggesting ozone as a UFO byproduct. When we view arcing electricity, more often than not we are actually seeing a blue/purple ionized-air glow rather than the electricity itself.[461] Ergo, it stands to reason that UFO sightings where ozone is noted should predominantly appear in conjunction with blue or purple lights. Returning once more to the 1980 Colorado case, the beam that lifted the witnesses' car from the road was blue; recall also the 1966 Iowa case, where one side of the craft featured blue lights.

There is no shortage of ozone smelled in conjunction with blue/purple lights.

- In May 1946, Gösta Carlsson witnessed a landed craft in a Swedish forest surrounded by a purple light. Circling the craft were 11 helmeted individuals in short black boots and gloves, appearing to finish some sort of repairs. Carlsson was halted from entering the purple light by one of the entities. When he returned to the site 30 minutes later, he noted the odor of ozone.[462]

- Two soldiers in Kazakhstan reported a 1976 encounter with a pair of short humanoids who were caught taking plant samples from the railroad track, accompanied by the odor of ozone. The beings, whose appearance had been preceded by a blue luminosity with red highlights, disappeared into the bushes. Moments later an elliptical UFO emerged from the woods.[463]

- On May 20, 1988, a husband and wife were allegedly abducted from their mountain home in Townshend, Vermont. Under regression Jack, the husband, recalled seeing a bright blue light shining through the window. Shortly thereafter, several Grey aliens manifested by the bedside and levitated the couple into the yard, where they stood in front of "a huge, house-sized glowing object sitting on a blue light that enveloped its underside." They recalled that "The air was filled with the acrid smell of ozone."[464]

- Researcher Peter Davenport reported that at 3:00 a.m. on June 2, 2003, an Ohio witness awoke to find his power out. He looked outside and observed an oval-shaped craft with a deep blue underside, accompanied by an ozone odor and an eerie silence.[465]

The smell of ozone and blue light in these cases immediately conjures ball lightning, the rare, spherical atmospheric phenomenon so evocative of UFO accounts (and undoubtedly responsible for some sightings). Ball lightning, which finishes its brief existence with a pungent-smelling explosion, is discussed in depth later.

Rarely are entities ever cited as the source of ozone smells, a logical assumption given the gas's absence in biology (this being said, one wonders if the luminous beings sometimes described in sightings would be capable of producing ozone directly). One of the rare cases to explicitly associate ozone with extraterrestrial entities is the alleged Aztec, New Mexico, UFO crash. According to 1987's *UFO Crash at Aztec: A Well Kept Secret*, a series of bodies were recovered from the crash site, each conforming to the typical Grey alien description: large head, slanted eyes, short, small mouth, etc. These entities were supposedly filled with a colorless liquid that smelled of ozone. This direct association of entities with an ozone smell—an extreme outlier in accounts—further reinforces Aztec's widely held reputation as a hoax.[466]

Sulfur and ozone

Stefan Michalak, a prospector from Winnipeg, Canada, was working near Manitoba's Falcon Lake in May 1967 when he saw a pair of cigar-shaped UFOs, the furthest of which alit around 150 feet away. He cautiously approached the craft and glanced inside an opening, hearing voices but seeing no one. Without warning, the portal slid shut and the entire object rotated, angling what Michalak assumed was an "exhaust vent" at him. He was instantly hit by a blast of scalding hot air that set his clothing and the surrounding debris on fire.

Feeling ill and badly burned, Michalak stumbled out of the woods and into the company of a Royal Canadian Mounted Police officer, who took him to a hospital. For the next several days, Michalak endured headaches, nausea, vomiting, weight loss, and a drop in lymphocytes, the apparent consequences of radiation poisoning.

Michalak's testimony is credible for the extensive paper trail left in the wake of his injuries, including test results, hospital paperwork, etc. Canadian UFOlogist Chris Rutkowski feels it is one of the finest sightings his country has to offer. The case is notable in our discussion for the manner in which the craft (and afterwards, Michalak) smelled... "like rotten eggs and burned electrical circuits."[467]

Though rare, reports of sulfur and ozone do occur together. For instance, consider Fred Reagan's aforementioned abduction, or the 1950 Argentina case investigated by Leonard Stringfield and Jose Escobar Faria where ozone and garlic were smelled together (as noted, garlic's high sulfur content contributes greatly to its odor).[468]

Such pairings imply that the presence of H_2S and ozone in UFO sightings is not an "either-or" scenario, but may well be "both-and." Lending credence to this possibility is the relationship between sulfur compounds and ozone: when ozone is introduced to H_2S, the resulting reaction yields water and SO_2. Expressed as an equation:

$$H_2S + O_3 \rightarrow H_2O + SO_2$$

If more energy is involved the reaction unfolds as $H_2S + O_3 \rightarrow S + H_2O + O_2$.[469]

The three most common smells encountered in UFO cases (H_2S, SO_2, and ozone) can all be found in one tidy equation. It seems feasible that this reaction is taking place whenever H_2S, SO_2, or ozone is noticed during sightings. Perhaps the predominant odor smelled by witnesses corresponds to where in this process the UFO is seen—in other words, those smelling H_2S may be encountering UFOs before O_3 is introduced, or vice versa. Similarly, those describing SO_2 (or nothing at all, in the case of the second equation) may be seeing UFOs after the reaction has completed.

Unfortunately, this is entirely speculative, and the equation yields more questions than answers. Regardless of the deeper meaning of this equation—if any—it is another compelling clue in the vast, interconnected web of UFO smells.

Chapter 14
UFO Smells: Chemicals

While it may seem farfetched to inquire whether UFOs have any odor, it would be particularly significant if witnesses have detected those very gasses that are produced in electrical discharges in direct association with them.

—James McCampbell,
UFOlogy: A Major Breakthrough in the Scientific Understanding of Unidentified Flying Objects

In March 1995, a young Canadian boy confided to his incredulous mother that a short spaceman with pointed ears, almond-shaped eyes, and three fingers had taken him in the middle of the night from his second story bedroom. The boy claimed he had miraculously levitated through the window to an awaiting flying saucer whose interior was covered in "pinky, orange cushioned walls that smelled similar to paint." After a brief medical examination, the beings returned the boy to his room.[470]

Though it is correct to argue that every smell is technically a chemical smell, UFO witnesses describe caustic, artificial odors with regularity. Unsurprisingly, these are often generic, like the "chemical smell" Bob Taylor remembered after being dragged aboard a silver-colored spacecraft in 1979 by "wheels with arms,"[471] or the "polish remover" smell recalled by one of Karla Turner's subjects.[472] There is little consistency between these reports—it is equally likely that a UFO might smell of turpentine or menthol (both have been reported) or something else entirely, and multiple odors present themselves at once.

More than perhaps any other olfactory category, these caustic chemical scents trigger physical reactions in witnesses. In 1966, Leonard Stringfield interviewed a woman who sighted a UFO out her bedroom window, accompanied by "an ill-smelling chemical odor" that made her dizzy. That evening, when the witness's daughter arrived home from a date, her first remark was, "Mom, what did you spray in the house?"[473]

Miscellany

All this said, chemical smells in UFO sightings do follow a few minor trends. Medicinal smells—disinfectants, hospital odors, etc.—are well represented in the literature, especially in abductions. According to South African media, farmer Jan Pienaar nearly ran his truck into a large object sitting in the road on March 30, 1995. The metallic craft was shaped like "two inverted soup plates with a pudding bowl on top" and had a visible gash in its side. His engine disabled, Pienaar stepped outside and stared at the object for three minutes before it ascended, leaving "a strange lingering odor in the air—almost like chloroform."[474]

In June 1964, Beauford E. Parham reported an object that spun like a top in the Georgia sky and left "a strong odor like embalming fluid" in his car. The UFO also produced "a very gaseous vapor" that congealed into viscous oil on the vehicle.[475] The following month, not 40 miles from Parham's sighting, a similar odor was noted coming from an unidentified craft in Tallulah Falls.[476] The second witness elaborated on the odor, further comparing it to "brake liquid."[477]

Ether and ammonia allegedly pervaded the UFO crash site of the 1996 Varginha case, according to eyewitness Carlos da Souza.[478] Ammonia is one of the more common chemical smells, as evidenced by three representative cases:

- A Pennsylvania witness had stopped to change a flat tire in the summer of 1933 when he noted a curious violet glow in a nearby field. The illumination was coming from a landed, spherical craft approximately ten feet long by six feet high. The curious motorist reached the object and peeked inside its slightly ajar opening, but all he saw was a windowless room, a console, dials, and tubes. The interior had a pervasive ammonia-like odor. After around ten minutes, he returned to his vehicle and left the scene.[479]

- At 7:30 p.m. on October 18, 1968, the McMullen family claimed to have seen a transparent, purplish-red object levitating outside their Florida home. Inside were two men "pumping a horizontal bar," releasing "a strong odor of ammonia" as the craft ascended.[480]

- Around 3:00 a.m. on January 18, 1978, military personnel stationed at New Jersey's McGuire Air Force Base observed 12 lights in the sky performing incredible acrobatics. Around the same time, a military police officer claimed a blue-green glowing oval object had buzzed his automobile, after which a short, thin, large-headed entity appeared in his headlights. Frightened, the MP allegedly shot and killed the creature. When Air Force Sergeant Jeff Morse (pseudonym) arrived on scene, he noted that the body was accompanied by "a bad stench coming from it… Like ammonia smelling but it wasn't constant in the air." As happens so often in such tales, higher authorities arrived and crated up the body, where it was allegedly placed on a flight to Wright Patterson Air Force Base.[481]

Odors of ammonia, nonexistent in spirit cases, are quite common in Sasquatch tales as well. There may be some significance to the fact that ammonia shares many qualities with sulfur, including a historical use as a fertilizer, cleanser, and antimicrobial (the same can be said for ozone, with the exception of the agricultural applications). Having said that, its detection threshold is much higher than either sulfur or ozone, at 5 ppm.[482] Ammonia is also reactive with SO_2.[483]

Another fumigant noted in UFO sightings is phosphine. On August 19, 1965, a young man was running his milking machine in Cherry Creek, New York, when its motor died. The nearby radio simultaneously screamed static, and a strange beeping noise filled the air. Over the tree line, he spotted an elliptical UFO emitting red vapor, agitating the livestock. When law enforcement arrived on the scene, they detected the distinctive garlic, rotting fish odor of phosphine, and saw an unidentified purple substance in the singed grass.[484]

Botanical odors, though rare, are also reported. The fragrance of camphor, an aromatic compound found in the camphor laurel and dried rosemary leaves, emanated from "angel hair" found near a Selkirk, Manitoba, sighting on October 8, 1980 (angel hair is a wispy, rapidly-evaporating material occasionally found at UFO sites).[485] The odor was also smelled during a sighting on April 5, 1967, in Jonestown, Pennsylvania (accompanied by sulfur, of course).[486]

Arnica, a medicinal perennial, was described in the sighting of Buenos Aires resident Ventura Maceiras. The elderly gaucho was sitting in his home on December 30, 1972, when his radio failed and he noticed a strange buzzing noise. Looking outside, Maceiras saw a purplish wheel spinning in the sky, complete with a spherical cabin housing a slant-eyed being in an astronaut suit. The craft moved away, leaving an odor like "sulfur or arnica" in its wake. Arnica is often considered to have a pine-sage olfactory profile that, coupled with the purple light, suggests ozone. Nearby trees were burned as a result of the event, and Maceiras suffered from diarrhea, nausea, hair loss, severe headaches, and watering eyes.[487]

The Cash-Landrum Incident

The most famous UFO sighting involving a chemical odor is the Cash Landrum Incident of 1980. On December 29, Betty Cash, Vickie Landrum, and her seven-year-old grandson, Colby, were returning home from dinner to Dayton, Texas, when they noticed a light in the distance. The object soon came closer, revealing itself as a flaming diamond shape.

Both women stepped outside for a closer look, finding that the car had become hot to the touch; Landrum's hand actually left an indentation in the melting vinyl of the dashboard. Eventually, the light ascended, escorted by more than 20 helicopters. The witnesses resumed driving, putting the experience behind them—they would live with the after effects for years, however. Medical evaluation determined that all three suffered symptoms consistent with radiation poisoning: nausea, vomiting, diarrhea, weakness, burning of the eyes and skin, sores, and hair loss. Cash, having stood outside longest, received the brunt of the effects.[488]

Much thought and debate surround the exact nature of what Cash and the Landrums saw that evening, including theories of extraterrestrial visitation, misidentified helicopters, and experimental terrestrial aircraft. Each notion has its own strengths and weaknesses.

Comparatively little attention, however, has been given to the fact that the incident was accompanied by the smell of lighter fluid.[489] Perhaps this is because the witnesses recalled this detail under hypnosis, which we have already established as problematic—in any case, the smell raises questions. If indeed it was present during the event, was the odor fueling the craft's flames? Was it an exhaust of some kind?

This lighter fluid smell has prompted some to question the fundamental nature of the sighting. Researchers Brad Sparks and Dr. Richard Niemtzow contend that the witnesses' symptoms and the timeline of their manifestation were more consistent with a volatile aerosol agent than radiation exposure, a theory supported by the chemical odor.[490] Similarly, natural science professor Michael D. Swords suggested that the lighter fluid smell was indicative of liquid hydrocarbons, gasoline, or rocket fuel, implying that the craft was of terrestrial origin.[491]

Given the physical effects of the UFO on the automobile (i.e. heating), Cash-Landrum raises the question of whether the *object* was smelled, or the object's *affect on the environment* was smelled. If fuel could have somehow been mistaken for lighter fluid, the odor needn't have come from the craft—perhaps the object heated the automobile's petroleum, or its synthetic interior, thus producing the "lighter fluid" odor. This line of thought is pursued to its logical conclusion in the next chapter.

Regardless of the origins of the Cash-Landrum craft, it is interesting to compare it to an Argentinean case from 1963. On October 21, three women left the Moreno farmhouse to investigate strange lights along the railroad tracks, only to discover a flying saucer hovering above the ground.[492] Like in Cash-Landrum, the craft emitted flames, burned the witnesses, and exuded an unpleasant odor (a smell of sulfur). Six balls of light accompanied the craft and, like the helicopters reported by Cash-Landrum, escorted the vehicle into the sky. Multiple residual effects included a lingering smell and heat at the site, withered trees, and half-inch balls of calcium carbonate (chalk) strewn across the ground.[493]

Metallic odors

On June 30, 1966, a middle-aged Canadian couple took a trip with their teenage son to Onion Lake, Ontario. Upon arriving at their campsite around 11:00 p.m., they noticed an unsettling, "total, complete darkness and stillness," and the unpleasant odor of "carborundum [silicon carbide, an industrial-strength abrasive] rubbing on steel." The son suddenly disappeared, returning after what felt like an interminable amount of time to tell them about a saucer-shaped plane he had approached before losing consciousness. The boy was shaken and had a strange vaccination-like mark the size of a dime on his ankle. The family tried to leave, but the car initially refused to start—once they finally returned, the son was committed to a mental hospital, where he remained ever since.[494]

Metallic odors were one of the three main categories Ivan Sanderson ascribed to UFOs, alongside aromatic and sulfurous smells. Within this subset, witnesses have described UFOs as exuding the odor of brass, carbide, copper, and iron, often accompanied by the descriptor "hot" or "melted." These smells, which Sanderson equated with hot hydrocarbon oils, naturally imply structured, nuts-and-bolts spacecraft.

- Alicia Rivas Aguilar was turning in for the night on September 8, 1967, when she noticed a peculiar figure outside her bedroom window in Caracas, Venezuela. The creature was repelled by her screams and began floating above homes, encircled by a bluish-yellow glow. Several family members also saw the being, which they described as clad in a metal suit that left the odor of "melted iron" in the air.[495]

- Tatyana Goloveshko was battling insomnia during her 1989 vacation to Sochi, Russia, when she saw two short, greenish-gray humanoids approach her bedside. The entities stared into her face, revealing a frightening visage: pear-shaped heads with hollow eye sockets and, oddly enough, beards. After a moment, these "ancient gnomes" stepped back from the bed and disappeared, their presence replaced by a glowing, crackling orb of light that flew through the open window. At last able to move again, Goloveshko ran to shut the door. The experience fried the television, stopped all the clocks, and left an odor like hot iron in the room.[496]

- A family in Tasmania's Huon Valley had a series of unsettling encounters in early 1996. The encounters began with strange airborne lights, sightings of a tall, thin entity in the garden, and shorter entities with "dark round eyes, round bodies and small arms and legs." Each incident agitated the livestock on the farm and was accompanied by a metallic smell (since the description also included the odor of "burnt wiring," ozone may have been involved).[497]

Other cases combine metallic smells with the odor of burning wiring, frustratingly blurring the line with ozone smells. For example, a witness of the aforementioned 1975 San Antonio sighting later elaborated on the "burned electrical wiring smell" he described, adding it was a "very severe odor, like burning copper"[498] (recall how Credo Mutwa described the aliens he encountered: "like hot copper").

Metallic smells overlap with metallic tastes, a common symptom reported by abductees. Occasionally both are reported in tandem. On December 14, 1975, three witnesses— Eugene Bell, Ray Lanier, and Iris Brenner—claimed they were searching for a lost dog northeast of Salt Springs, Florida, when they spotted a saucer-shaped object hovering among the power lines. Encircling the craft were red, white, and blue flashing lights. The closest it came during the 30-minute affair was 10 feet from the ground. All three witnesses noted a humming noise, a metallic smell in the air, and "a funny metallic taste" in their mouths.[499]

Benzene

In addition to citing SO_2 as a common UFO odor, James McCampbell voiced the opinion that benzene was commonly reported in sightings. "A pulsed source of microwaves in air can generate nitric oxide and, in subsequent reactions, the benzene family that has been detected near UFOs," McCampbell wrote in 1976's *UFOlogy: A Major Breakthrough in the Scientific Understanding of Unidentified Flying Objects*. "As benzene is not decomposed by the field, any formed would tend to accumulate to detectable concentrations."[500] The presence of benzene, a carcinogenic hydrocarbon and natural constituent of crude oil, also supports Ivan T. Sanderson's conclusion that "hot hydrocarbon oils" were responsible for reports of metallic smells in conjunction with UFOs.

The central problem with Sanderson and McCampbell's logic is that explicit descriptions of benzene are minimal in the literature, the few extant examples largely confined to a French UFO flap from 1954. In October of that year, two saucers in the sky near Clermont paralyzed witnesses and released "an odor of nitro-benzene,"[501] while a landing site the following month in Maubeuge exuded "an odor like benzene."[502] One of the few cases outside the 1954 French flap is the March 18, 1950 sighting by Argentinean rancher Wilfredo H. Arévalo, who watched two metallic craft in the sky emit a blue-green vapor and "an intense smell of burning benzine [sic]." The craft appeared to be piloted by "four tall men" dressed in a cellophane-like material.[503]

In spite of the infrequency of these odors, McCampbell's research is not without merit—it is entirely possible that individuals smell benzene, yet suffer from the tip-of-the-nose phenomenon. Moreover, McCampbell astutely wrote:

> Electrical discharges in the atmosphere initiate some important chemical changes. Energy states of atoms are modified and numerous chemical compounds are formed from the constituent gases. In a high-voltage spark, nitrogen is elevated to a metastable state having several interesting properties. It produces a soft, white glow that continues for some time after the electric discharge has been stopped. Such excited nitrogen is known chemically as "activated" because it will readily combine with many other elements whereas ordinary nitrogen will not. It combines with hydrogen to form ammonia (NH_3) and with oxygen to form nitric oxide (NO). This oxide is quite stable at high temperatures but

below 150⁰ C it reacts with oxygen to form nitrogen dioxide (NO_2). The dioxide can react with still other atmospheric gases to form nitrobenzene, an oily substance that is highly poisonous and has a strong odor like oil of bitter almonds.[504]

Our thoughts naturally turn to cases where almond odors were reported, notably Cape Cod in 1975. McCampbell's chemical insights will be particularly useful to us when discussing ball lightning later.

Roswell

UFOlogy needs more commentary on Roswell like a submarine needs a screen door.

For anyone who has lived as a hermit for the past three decades, the Roswell UFO incident refers to the purported 1947 crash (and recovery) of an extraterrestrial spacecraft near Roswell, New Mexico. A press release from July 8 stated that the United States military had retrieved a "flying disc," a statement quickly rescinded—the recovered wreckage was, in actuality, a weather balloon.

Or so they claimed. The story remained dormant for 30 years until dogged UFOlogists like Stanton T. Friedman revived the case, speaking with hundreds of witnesses who not only undermined the weather balloon narrative but also lent credence to reports that the extraterrestrial wreckage had been taken to Ohio's Wright-Patterson Air Force Base. According to popular narratives that emerged during the 1990s, the crash would eventually fuel clandestine reverse-engineering efforts at Nevada's Groom Lake Air Force Base (aka "Area 51"). Since then, speculation has swirled around the Nevada facility, with rumors of experimental aircraft and alien bodies housed within.

Any perceived disdain for Roswell in this book comes not from a sense that the event is inauthentic, but rather from the fact that the subject has been given far too much focus. Books on Roswell are legion, nearly every facet has been scrutinized within an inch of its life, and practically all witnesses have passed on. While there may have once been a chance of learning some objective "truth" about UFOs from studying the incident, that window has long since closed.

Still, it would be an oversight to ignore the odors associated with the event. Curiously, few witnesses mentioned smells over the years, to the extent that Jacques Vallee wrote in 1991 that the lack of odors in eyewitness testimony undermined Roswell's credibility.[505] Explicit memories of odors associated with the crash did not receive much attention until the early 1990s, when the Area 51 craze reached its height.

In *Witness to Roswell: Unmasking the 60-Year Cover-Up*, Sergeant LeRoy Wallace's widow remembers how her husband was fetched one evening "to help load the bodies" from a secretive crash site.

> When [Wallace] returned home early the next morning, the first thing she noticed, besides his disheveled appearance, was the smell. "The stench on his clothes was the worst smell you'd ever want to smell. It was the worst combination of smells you could imagine. I had to strip off his clothes. We ultimately burned them and buried the ashes." She said that her husband bathed frequently with lye soap and an old Army scrub brush after that, and would wash his hands up to 10 times a day to the point of becoming raw. "He walked around for two days after he returned home and did not sleep, and for the next two weeks, when he ate, he wore gloves because the smell was still on his body."[506]

Recall when Lon Strickler's wife shunned his presence after encountering a ghost who smelled of sickly honeysuckle. An odor lingering on witnesses is a common motif in many unexplained phenomena.

Like testimony of the event, descriptions of smells associated with Roswell are varied and contradictory. Descriptions of acrid, foul, unpleasant odors prevail. But what exactly *was* this smell?

J. Bond Johnson, a photographer from the Fort Worth *Star-Telegram*, was dispatched to cover the capture of a flying disk in July 1947. Johnson was sent to Brigadier General Roger Ramey's office at Eight Army Air Forces Headquarters, where the New Mexico debris was initially taken. Upon entering the room, Johnson saw "a bunch of rather unimpressive debris." Much more striking to the reporter was "an acrid odor, something like burnt rubber, only there was no evidence of rubber in the room."[507]

Just what was this "unimpressive debris?" Shortly after the 1947 crash, Major Jesse Marcel returned home with a box of debris gathered from the site to share with his family. His son, Jesse Marcel, Jr. saw among the debris chunks of thin, broken material that he compared to Bakelite.

Bakelite is a brand of plastic first developed in the early twentieth century. For years the material saw a variety of molded applications, from telephone sets to radios, game tokens, machine parts, and even jewelry. When heated, Bakelite has a distinctive smell described by some as acrid, sickly-sweet, acidic, and almost icthyc (fishlike).[508]

There is historical precedent for the odor of Bakelite during UFO sightings. B.J. Colley (a pseudonym) was driving to work in the English countryside at 4:30 a.m. on October 26, 1967, when his vehicle abruptly stopped. He eventually got the engine restarted, only to have it fail once more a few hundred yards later. Exiting the car, he noted a dark, metallic craft glinting in the night sky, accompanied by "an all-pervading, quite powerful and rather oppressive smell" that he equated with "Bakelite and electrical sparking." The UFO soon departed and he resumed his journey.[509] Three months later, an Australian couple was stopped by four frantic individuals who had a light in the sky raise their car and drop it to the ground—inspection of the vehicle revealed a burst tire and a smell approximating Bakelite.[510]

This line of speculation is all fine-and-good—until one considers the fact that Marcel perceived no odor from the debris in 1947, and, having worked with Bakelite later in life, was adamant that the materials were not one-and-the-same.[511]

In spite of this fact, others present at the Roswell crash site did note an odor associated with Bakelite. Sergeant Frederick Benthal claimed he was deployed from Washington, D.C., to Roswell in July 1947. Benthal, who served as a photographic specialist in the United States Navy, was zipped in a protective rubber suit and sent to a crash site north of the town. A tent had been erected among the wreckage, housing several small, thin bodies with large heads, which he was instructed to photographically document. "There was a strange smell inside the tent that smelled something like formaldehyde," he later stated.[512]

Along with phenol, formaldehyde is the chief ingredient of Bakelite, and is commonly invoked in descriptions of the material's odor when heated.[513] Exposure to formaldehyde includes symptoms with which we are now familiar: nausea, mucous membrane irritation, respiratory problems, etc. Though drawing such connections conflates the smell of the *entity* with the smell of the *craft*, it is conceivable that bodies involved in an airborne disaster might become infused with the smell of the crash.

UFOlogist Stanton T. Friedman reached the conclusion that not one, but *two* crash sites were discovered in July 1947. In *Crash at Corona*, he reports the testimony of Gerald Anderson, who allegedly discovered the second crash location with his brother, father, uncle, and cousin. The men happened upon a blimp-like craft amongst a small grove of trees in the terminus of a dried-out riverbed, complete with small, strange bodies.

"There was a real strong smell, too," Anderson said. "Like, maybe, rubbing alcohol or acetone or something like that."[514] There is also a connection here to the smells from Roswell. Formaldehyde is the simplest of the organic compounds known as aldehydes, while acetone is the simplest of the ketones—both have similar structures, containing the carbonyl group, -C=O.[515]

In addition to its properties as an irritant, formaldehyde is also carcinogenic. So is asbestos, another ingredient often used to fill out the material in early Bakelite products.[516] Given this knowledge, what are we to make of years of allegations and lawsuits asserting that workers at Groom Lake Air Force Base—confirmed recently as Area 51—have been exposed to carcinogens during their tour of duty?

Chapter 15
UFO Smells: Burning Odors

Y'know, this was supposed to be my weekend off, but no. You got me out here dragging your heavy ass through the burning desert with your dreadlocks sticking out the back of my parachute. You gotta come down here with an attitude, acting all big and bad... and what the Hell is that smell?!?

— Captain Steven Hiller, *Independence Day*

Two witnesses in Mendoza, Argentina, had a peculiar encounter in the summer of 1982. Sitting at the dining table, they noticed a small, glowing figure among the branches of a nearby tree, vaguely triangular, luminous, and transparent. It had a small head and appeared to be dressed in some sort of robe. Fetching a broom, the pair stepped outside, noting how the branches seemed as if they were filled with "tiny stars." Without warning, a loud sizzling sound assailed their ears, the broom electrified, and the smell of smoke filled the air. The figure faded into nothing.[517]

Was it a ghost? An alien? The BVM?

By now, reportage of "burning odors" should not be surprising in UFO cases. The consistency of the combustion motif is striking: sulfur is odorless until burnt, ozone smells like burnt electrical wiring, Bakelite smells when heated. It is a mystery why such odors should prevail. Intuitively, combustion smells imply a release of energy or an effort to disinfect. Burning sulfur was used as a fumigant in antiquity, ozone is a modern antimicrobial, and, in general, combustion has historically been an excellent means of removing odors—consider how we light matches or candles to combat unpleasant odors.[518]

Classification of these odors in UFO cases is difficult, as burning smells often overlap with other categories. For instance, hypnotherapist Dolores Cannon devotes a great deal of writing in her book *The Custodians* to one client who experienced a series of dreamlike encounters with non-human entities. The witness obsesses over defining the horrid smell pervading these interactions, finally settling on a "burning metal" odor akin to zinc.[519] While such testimony should be viewed with *extreme* skepticism—some of Cannon's past life regression work strains credulity to the breaking point—it is nonetheless illustrative of the difficulty in separating these odors from one another.

Generic "burning" and smoke smells are most common in this category, and are more often associated with craft than their alleged occupants. If it is combustible, a witness somewhere has smelled it during an encounter: burning oil, metal, tires, insulation tape, even mesquite trees. The odor of cooking sausages has even been reported in conjunction with UFO sightings, both in Scandinavia in 1954 (Norway, a flying saucer that smelled of "fried sausages")[520] and 1958 (Sweden, a landed craft and short entities that left behind "a smell like 'ether' or 'burned sausage'").[521]

A handful of other representative cases:

- In 1939, a young boy and his mother were taking a walk through the English countryside when they detected an odd humming underfoot and smelled something on fire, similar to burnt paper. A bright ball of light appeared at a nearby hill, accompanied by tiny men who appeared, chattered excitedly, and then vanished. Note the visual similarities to Celtic faerie lore and olfactory similarities to Strieber's "burnt cardboard."[522]

- Candelaria Hernandez was washing her clothes in the river

one day in 1945 when she claimed to see a giant "burning bullet" crash into the Guatemalan jungle. Shortly thereafter, a neighbor entreated her to come see "the dummies that fell from Heaven," who were dead and "smelled like burned rubber." Hernandez declined the offer, later running into some foreign soldiers who, with the chief of police, allowed her to see three small, unrecognizable bodies.[523]

- On April 25, 1966, young John Howard Bloom saw a strange blue light, two feet wide, descend into the woods near Upland, Pennsylvania. Bloom claimed the light smelled of burning rubber and left his eyes irritated the following day.[524]

- During the Rhodesian UFO flap of the mid-1970s, farm laborers told investigators that the large, orange orb seen flying through the sky was not an extraterrestrial craft, but rather "a spirit from the dead" whom they had met in the past. The spirit, they said, "gave off a strange smell like two stones rubbed together."[525]

- In 1976 the Sunderland family of Wales experienced a series of odd UFOlogical incidents. In one encounter, young Gaynor was riding her bike along a lane when she spotted a silvery cigar-shaped object in a field. Hiding behind a hedge, the girl watched a being—pale, rigid, with a large head, dressed in a one-piece bubble suit—zap holes in the ground with some type of ray gun. After some time Gaynor fled, hearing a humming noise and smelling a burning odor as the craft ascended.[526]

- Two witnesses were allegedly roused from sleep in January 2006 when a humming noise pervaded their Canadian home. Stepping outside, the witnesses filmed several blue lights before they eventually descended in the distance. The rest of the evening they were plagued by strange howls, bangs on the outside of the house, and even a pale, human-like figure with glowing eyes that darted across the driveway. Before returning inside, the witnesses noted a strong, warm breeze that smelled like burning plastic.[527]

Perhaps the smell was heated Bakelite. It is worth noting—though tangential—that the powerful hallucinogen DMT, most commonly ingested via smoking, smells like burning plastic when lit.[528]

The Flatwoods Monster

It is a great disservice to cover the Flatwoods Monster of Braxton County in a few brief paragraphs. The story is famous in the annals of UFOlogy, as strange aerial lights were seen in conjunction with the creature; however, the details of the events, as well as the description of the entity, are more bizarre than usual.

Things began when young brothers Fred and Edward May, along with their pal Tommy Hyer, saw a bright object dart across the West Virginia sky around 7:15 p.m. on September 12, 1952. After watching the light disappear near a neighbor's land, the boys rounded up a party that included their mother, West Virginia National Guardsman Eugene Lemon, and friends Neil Nunley and Ronnie Shaver.

Upon arriving on the property where the light had landed, Lemon's dog bolted out of sight, only to return frightened with its tail between its legs. Shortly thereafter, the seven witnesses reached a hilltop where a 50-foot ball of fire pulsed in the forest. A noxious mist rolled out of the tree line to greet them, stinging their eyes and noses, and soon a 10-foot-tall figure emerged from the forest, hissing and bounding toward them. The entity was described as having a spade-shaped, blood red face, its body covered in a skirt of green armor. Naturally, the group fled, coughing and screaming all the way.

Shortly after the main sighting, George and Edith Snitowsky were traveling from Queens, New York, to Cincinnati, Ohio, on a route that took them through Braxton County. When their car stopped unexpectedly, George stepped outside to take a look and immediately noticed an odor like "ether and burnt sulfur." Within moments, the pungent mist rolled in, the forest lit up, and an entity strikingly similar to the one from Flatwoods arrived on-scene. George jumped back inside the car and grabbed a knife from the glove compartment, bracing himself for the worst; the entity dragged a hand across the windshield and hood before drifting away, leaving the car to start normally once again.[529]

Descriptions of the poisonous mist's smell in the initial encounter vary widely. Upon arriving at the site later that evening, Braxton County law enforcement noticed a "sickening, burnt, metallic odor" and an odd oil puddle (shades of the 1965 Cherry Creek case). The main witnesses to the event described the odor of the mist as similar to burning sulfur.[530] Visitors to the site, where the smell persisted for some time, would also compare it to "oil on hot metal."[531] In reality, it seems as though everyone was suffering from the tip-of-the-nose phenomenon, only able to agree that the odor was irritating.

Whatever the smell, the monster's mist had a detrimental effect on all involved. Eyes watered, throats tightened, and the witnesses vomited for hours afterward. Skeptics suspect the symptoms were the result of mass hysteria, an explanation hard to swallow when one learns that Lemon's dog was not only sick as well, but actually died.[532] Ivan T. Sanderson speculated that a species of ground vegetation, "tar-grass," could have produced the strange oil and sickening smell, but this seems unlikely given the severity of the symptoms.[533]

In Nick Redfern's 2013 book *Monster Files*, the author mentions a stunning possible connection between declassified World War II documents and the Flatwoods Monster. According to Redfern, British Army intelligence experimented with various forms of psychological warfare, including a 12-foot-tall "scarecrow" rigged to generate loud noises and flashing lights, designed to terrify the enemy. This device, if combined with some type of mild chemical warfare, would resemble the entity from 1952, raising the possibility that the Flatwoods Monster may have actually been a civilian field test of non-lethal military technology.[534]

Vehicular vapors

In none of these cases is there any assurance that witnesses are smelling UFOs or their occupants—any odors may well be caused by the phenomenon's effect upon the environment, especially if heat is involved. This subtle-yet-significant problem has run through our entire discussion of UFO odors, and nowhere is this issue more apparent than in reports of burning smells.

It is widely accepted that many UFOs generate some form of radiation, given how often witnesses report heat and post-sighting sunburns. Interestingly, a substantial portion of witnesses who report burning smells are in or near motor vehicles—recall the 1968 Dolomite Mountains case, where the witness was awoken by a burning odor in his automobile. It is reasonable to entertain the notion that, as recently suggested in our discussion of the Cash-Landrum Incident, vehicles produce odors as a result of the phenomenon's radiation.

Regardless of what UFOs may be, they often detrimentally affect internal combustion engines. The literature is rife with examples of cars malfunctioning when the phenomenon appears, as outlined by Joe Kirk Thomas in his excellent 1987 essay "The Vehicle Interference Effect."[535] It is a small leap in logic to conclude that similar interactions could heat the many synthetic materials used in the construction and operation of automobiles, thus releasing their odors.

Witnesses explicitly mention heating effects on their cars—in October 1973, a witness in Georgia reported that after her sighting, her hood was billowing smoke and had melted to the point that "it looked like you could poke your thumb through it,"[536] a description reminiscent of the dashboard in Cash-Landrum. Similarly, USAF missile engineer James Stokes observed a bright egg-shaped object in the sky near Orogrande, New Mexico, in 1957 that shut down his car and left its battery steaming.[537]

With this in mind, a whole subset of UFO smells reveals its likely source: the witness's vehicle. Any case seen from an automobile involving the odor of burning oil is certainly suspect. In 1962, a truck driver was traveling near Valparaiso, Chile, when he saw five humanoids loitering about a stand of trees, above which hovered a whistling disc. The witness noticed a powerful, burned oil smell, and felt an unbearable heat coming from the area (later investigation revealed the trees had withered). Was the smell from the UFO, or from its heat bombarding the truck's oil?[538]

Other possible culprits are irradiated car batteries. In March 1977, a peculiar airborne object with flashing lights drained a car's battery near Queensland, Australia, accompanied by "a very acrid smell, similar to that when a number of car batteries are being charged in a confined area."[539] Similarly, the Chiasson family was driving through the Quebec countryside in 1976 when a red light beam began pacing their car. After several miles, the beam was replaced by a bright white light that hovered over the road, emanating heat and shutting down the car's headlights and radio, all accompanied by an acrid smell that irritated the nose.[540]

Tires could be a source of odors as well. On March 10, 1969, Lavern Janzen, police chief of Westhope, North Dakota, had his car spotlighted by a bright white light just after 10:00 p.m. From his vehicle, Officer Janzen watched a disc with a turquoise dome and red lights around its edge hover in the sky. He stepped outside and, though he feared to come closer, detected an odor like burned rubber.[541]

It is interesting—albeit predictable, at this point—that the foul smell often associated with corroding car batteries is caused by an out-gassing of H_2S, and that some of the stench of burning tires is thanks to sulfur, which is added to rubber during the vulcanization process for durability (in fact, the odor of benzyl mercaptan, found in boxwood trees and coffee, has been described as smelling like "rotten burning rubber").⁵⁴² It is almost as if sulfur is deliberately sought out by the phenomenon.

A sinister suggestion

Carolyn Joyce and her daughters were returning home to Omaha, Nebraska, on August 16, 2004, when one of the girls spotted an airplane hovering above their neighborhood. Looking closer, they realized the "plane" was actually a dull gray flying saucer, complete with dome, multicolored lights, and a bright beam spotlighting the ground. Once they reached the driveway the family jumped out of the van, staring at the object hovering directly above them. As the UFO silently ascended into the heavens, one of the girls came down with a headache, while another noticed the pungent stench of burning hair.⁵⁴³

UFOlogical odors are compared to burning organic material with a minor degree of regularity, at least frequently enough to warrant mention within the larger scope of burning smells. Given their horrendous medical procedures, it is unsurprising that burning organic odors are found in abduction tales. In 1989, "Paul," an abductee from Portsmouth, England, recalled the horrifying stink of burning flesh during his experiences,⁵⁴⁴ an experience similar to one of John Mack's subjects. "Dave" (mentioned earlier) claimed aliens employed exotic technology to generate peculiar metaphysical encounters, noting a "smell like burning flesh when the beings attached him to the machine that separated the spirit from his body."⁵⁴⁵ Such reports agree with findings from a 1994 MUFON study claiming that, of those reporting an odor in their experiences, over 20% of abductees described the smell of their own hair burning.⁵⁴⁶

If UFOs can burn our cars, they can burn us, too, and certain entities may have similar powers. Patrick Webel encountered a short, glowing figure with a giant head and large eyes after suffering car trouble near Liège, Belgium, in 1995. Terrified, he ran home, where he noticed a burning odor clinging to his person: his portable cassette player and its batteries had melted.[547]

In light (pardon the pun) of the irradiating effect UFOs have upon their surroundings, the unsettlingly sinister question must be asked: are some witnesses describing the smell of their own flesh cooking? Stefan Michalak would certainly consider this a possibility. It is disturbing to ponder… but perhaps the Scandinavian reports of "burned sausages" should be reevaluated with this in mind. "Sonny" DesVergers, the Florida scoutmaster, later qualified the smell during his sighting as "a sickening, nauseating stench—worse than rotten eggs and more like burning flesh."[548] Similarly Carol, one of Budd Hopkins' subjects, recalled a room in one of her abductions "with a strong, unpleasant odor" like "burning meat" (this odor was later replaced with "a slight odor of vinegar").[549]

Heat need not be felt to smell the effects of radiation upon one's body, and such odors are often misidentified as something other than burning tissue. There is a tragic medical precedent for this fact in radiation therapy. One cancer patient remarked, "About two weeks in, you begin to identify this smell. It's the most bizarre thing. You realize that you're smelling yourself burning."[550]

Another radiation therapy patient remarked on her misidentification of this odor: "It's the most horrible experience ever… I don't like the smell of burning, and I could smell and feel my neck burn! [My doctor] says I smell the ozone, that I'm not burning, but ozone is produced from burn, so there's no difference to me."[551] It is sadly ironic that ozone and burning tissue odors are conflated—as noted, burning tissues, in particular hair, nails, and feathers, smell foul because of their sulfur content. The sulfur-ozone conflation obliquely raises its head again.

Could the same release of energy generating ozone in UFO cases generate smells of sulfur from our own bodies? The notion explains the overwhelming consistency of ozone, sulfur, and burning odors in encounters—after all, oxygen and human flesh are present in every sighting.

Chapter 16
UFO Smells: Misidentification and Speculation

FARNSWORTH: You'll find that every Heavenly body has its own particular scent. Here, I'll point [the Smell-o-scope] at Jupiter.
FRY: Smells like strawberries.
FARNSWORTH: Exactly. And now, Saturn.
FRY: Pine needles. Oh man, this is great… hey, as long as you don't make me smell Uranus!
FARNSWORTH: I'm sorry, Fry, but astronomers renamed Uranus in 2620 to end that stupid joke once and for all.
FRY: Oh. What's it called now?
FARNSWORTH: Urrectum.

— *Futurama*, "A Big Piece of Garbage"

Determining just what UFOs and their occupants might be is a difficult puzzle, perhaps more so than any other unexplained phenomena. Misidentifications of mundane activity are at least partially responsible for sightings, while other, more intimate encounters (including the abduction scenario) are more difficult to explain away. The Extraterrestrial Hypothesis remains quite popular for a great many researchers, but given the outright strangeness and absurdity of some accounts, activity that blurs the lines between reality and dreams, and conflation of the objective and subjective, this theory cannot be the sole answer. In truth, multiple types of activity are likely to blame for UFO sightings: natural phenomena, man-made craft, altered states of consciousness, psychological manifestations, and, yes, maybe even little green men.

Attempting to solve this riddle has baffled researchers for decades—perhaps the application of what we have learned regarding UFO smells can shed new light on the true nature of these bizarre sightings. What follows is *not* a conclusive list of theories. Rather, what follows examines which scenarios are best supported—and discredited—by our survey of UFO smells.

Misidentification: Conventional Aircraft

Skeptics love to suggest that those who see anomalous lights in the sky are simply mistaking conventional, terrestrial aircraft for something spooky. There is a great deal of strength in this argument, now that consumer-grade drones are flooding the air. This position is particularly potent when objects are observed at high altitude.

Most smells from UFOs, however, occur when the objects are much closer to witnesses, making misidentification harder to swallow. Even if we ignore the peculiar humanoids who frequently accompany close range sightings, the odors referenced by witnesses fail to support a case of mistaken identity.

The most common odors smelled by UFO witnesses—sulfur and ozone—do not conform to the way most laypeople would describe jet fuel, which is commonly compared to kerosene or diesel. It must be admitted that generic "chemical smells" or even benzene odors could refer to jet fuel, but such reports are less frequent in the literature. Similarly, rocket fuels, which contain ammonia-smelling hydrazines, would correspond with only a handful of reports.[552]

Conventional aircraft *do* produce emissions similar to automobile exhaust, such as SO_2 and, via the creation of nitrogen oxides, ozone.[553] However, the SO_2 generated rarely has the "fireworks" quality described in reports, and ozone is not created in close proximity to the craft (put another way, if airplanes are to blame, witnesses *should* describe the smell as similar to car or—for those of us who have flown—airplane exhaust).

No known aircraft smells of sulfur, and barring an external wiring malfunction, none really smell of ozone either. Of course, this doesn't rule out *unconventional* aircraft, which we will address shortly.

Misidentification: Natural phenomena

While it is common knowledge that lightning produces ozone, more obscure are reports of storms producing sulfur. In a *Weatherwise* article from 1997, Howard G. Altschule and Bernard Vonnegut—brother of author Kurt Vonnegut—list the vast amount of natural phenomena to which smells of sulfur have been ascribed throughout history: storms, meteors, and, most prominently, tornadoes.

While some of these are certainly explainable as sulfur-ozone conflation, it is more difficult to explain away the testimony of American founding father Alexander Hamilton, who described a hurricane at sea: "A strong smell of gunpowder added somewhat to the terrors of the night; and it was observed that the rain was surprisingly salt. Indeed, the water is so brackish and full of sulfur that there is hardly any drinking it."[554] No doubt Hamilton, who had a career in the military, was familiar with the smell of gunpowder, making confusion with ozone less likely.

Sulfurous smells present in meteorology should catch the attention of any UFOlogist, as weather is often another prosaic explanation for strange aerial sightings. Indeed, there are many accounts of falls of sulfur from above. In 1832, the *American Journal of Science* reported an apparent rain of sulfur powder in Kourianof, Russia, while on April 13, 1879, flammable yellow "snow" rained upon towns in Pennsylvania.[555]

Many anomalous falls from the sky are attributable to strong winds lifting surface deposits from earth; sulfur, however, is uncommon in surface deposits. While it is true that volcanoes and sea spray emit some particulate sulfates, it is not enough to generate sulfur precipitation.[556] Perhaps there is some unknown atmospheric means by which such deposits are generated, a notion which—given sulfur's odor and ability to luminesce (flammability)—should give UFO researchers pause. According to *Symons's Monthly Meteorological Magazine,* on October 18, 1867, inhabitants of Thames Ditton, England, witnessed a brilliant "shower of fire" which left behind a thick deposit of sulfur.[557] We must also wonder if these deposits are linked to sulfurous powders left at landing sites.

Most smells associated with UFOs occur in nature, and as such natural phenomena should be examined for possible explanations. In 1966, Project Blue Book deployed Dr. J. Allen Hynek to investigate a UFO flap in Michigan. After looking into the events, Hynek made the fatal mistake of telling the press that the sightings *could* have been the result of "swamp gas," an explanation that stuck and became a meme ironically referenced in perpetuity. In a December 17 follow up article in *The Saturday Evening Post,* Hynek wrote:

> Searching for a justifiable explanation of the sightings, I remembered a phone call from a botanist at the University of Michigan, who called to my attention the phenomenon of burning "swamp gas." This gas, caused by decaying vegetation, has been known to ignite spontaneously and to cast a flickering light. The glow is well-known in song and story as "jack-o'-lantern," "fox fire," and "wil-o'-the-wisp." After learning more about swamp gas from other Michigan scientists, I decided that it was a "possible" explanation that I would offer to the reporters.
>
> The press conference, however, turned out to be no place for scholarly discussion: it was a circus.[558]

It is true that odorless methane can phosphoresce, and theoretically possible that it could fully ignite in marshes to produce lights in the sky.[559] Once again, while useful in explaining anomalous lights, the theory does little to explain away appearances of structured craft. It *is* interesting to note, however, that the proximity of such phenomenon to marshes and swamps would no doubt feature an accompanying smell of decay, in particular H_2S.

The will-o'-the-wisp shares much in common with ball lightning. Regarded as a myth until the mid-twentieth century, this elusive atmospheric electrical phenomenon manifests glowing spheres during thunderstorms, ranging from the size of a pea to several feet across. Unlike its air-to-surface counterpart, ball lightning lasts several minutes, drifting in an almost lifelike manner before violently exploding. Numerous theories exist for how it is generated; none are conclusive.

It is plain to see why ball lightning is attractive to skeptics. It is almost certainly responsible for some UFO sightings throughout the years, and as such has become a secondary field of interest to many UFOlogists. Once again, however, we are left with unsatisfactory answers to why witnesses interpret orbs of electricity as flying discs and spacemen; some have proposed that the phenomenon can generate hallucinations when seen in close proximity, but this is quite speculative.

If accounts are to be believed, exploding ball lightning generates odors of ozone and sulfur with equal regularity. Unlike its linear cousin, however, scientists are less vocal about the likelihood of ozone/sulfur conflation, probably because the phenomenon is so poorly understood. James Dale Barry wrote in *Ball Lightning and Bead Lightning* that "the odor is described as sharp and repugnant, resembling ozone, burning sulfur, or nitric oxide."[560]

Suffice to say, the presence of both sulfur *and* ozone in these accounts is compelling, and further reinforces the probability that a portion of UFO witnesses see ball lightning. Barring misidentification, it is possible that both ball lightning and UFOs could be generating similar odors via the same means, as McCampbell proposed. These tantalizing clues led Rullán to write at the end of his study:

> If odors are generated by energy emission from UFOs, then why don't all UFOs (which presumably fly in the same polluted air and with similar propulsion systems) generate odors? Maybe the UFOs represent a multitude of phenomena that are not the same. Maybe there is more than one type of propulsion system. Maybe odors are all related to ball lightning and true UFOs don't smell?[561]

Ball lightning and a phenomenon known as "earthlights" may be one-and-the same. Also called "earthquake lights," these luminous orbs are believed to be the byproduct of seismic activity. Like ball lightning, this phenomenon is poorly understood, with multiple hypotheses proposed. Some speculate that the breaking of peroxy bonds in certain rocks ionizes subterranean oxygen, whose ions in turn travel through fissures and create glowing plasma in the air above.[562]

Regardless of the mechanism, such anomalies are frequently reported in proximity to earthquakes, most recently observed immediately following the August 24, 2014 earthquake that rocked Sonoma County, California.[563] While sometimes harbingers of doom, these glowing spheres also appear at sites that are tectonically active but mostly benign (the Brown Mountain Lights of western North Carolina, for example, sit along a mostly-dormant fault line).[564]

While earthlights may not necessarily exude an odor, tectonic activity certainly can. Fissures prior to earthquakes can release fumes of radon, methane, and nitrogen oxides, as well as sulfur compounds such as H_2S—many have cited the detection of these gases as a mechanism by which animals "predict" earthquakes.[565] Ancient man believed subterranean fires, whose fumes spread plague when the ground tore asunder, generated such miasmas.[566]

While radon and methane are odorless, nitrogen oxide is aromatic and, as mentioned, humans are highly sensitive to sulfur compounds. As such, impending earthquakes are associated with a rotten egg odor, particularly in low-lying areas.[567] Sulfurous smells were noted prior to Italy's 1857 Basilicata earthquake[568] and the 1868 earthquake of Darya-ya Namak, Iran.[569] Seismologists contend that these odors can function as an early warning system for seismic activity.[570]

Anomalous (albeit natural) light phenomenon often coincides with sulfurous odors. While not explanatory of all sightings, this overlap certainly grants new insight into some cases.

Misidentification: Neurology

Many of the volunteers in Michael Persinger's "God helmet" study experienced visions of the divine: Jesus, the Virgin Mary, Muhammad, even benevolent Native American spirits. Some, however, had more sinister visions. Imagine one subject's surprise when, hoping to see the Lord, he instead was greeted with "the sight of an enormous set of eyes and the smell of burning sulfur."[571]

It is tempting to suggest that UFO sightings, in particular alien abductions, are the result of the sort of temporal lobe stimulation Persinger's work focused on. After all, those afflicted with temporal lobe epilepsy report olfactory hallucinations—in one case study, camphor was the predominant odor, while a 2003 study found that "all odors were perceived as unpleasant—fetid, rotten, burning, charring or medicinal."[572] The parallels to UFO smells are obvious.

Still, only a paltry 6% of those involved in Persinger's experiments reported odors of any kind.[573] Is this the same percentage of UFO witnesses who report smell? While odors are not reported in a majority, or even a plurality of sightings, this number still feels low.

Consider also that, in Persinger's view, pleasant or unpleasant hallucinations correspond to which amygdala is more sensitive in an individual, the left or the right.[574] It strains credulity to assume that, in multiple-witness sightings where smells are reported, everyone has the same sensitivity, which in turn manifests itself in the exact same imagined odor.

Slightly more believable is the Birth Memories Hypothesis, put forth by professor Alvin Lawson, which postulates that abductees are recalling their own delivery. The theory is strikingly powerful in explaining the imagery and sensations of the abduction scenario: both infants and abductees are snatched from a dark, warm environment of comfort and thrust into a bright, sterile, setting full of frightening medical procedures. Lawson claims that the BMH can explain away "unpleasant tastes or odors" in such cases as well.

In his non-fiction article "Flying Saucers Stink: Alien Odors and Supernatural Smells," Dan Clore offers an incisive counter to such notions: "Perhaps hospitals should begin airing out their delivery rooms, which apparently must reek of sulphur, ammonia, benzene, ozone, or other noxious gases."[575]

Speculation: Unconventional aircraft

Secret, experimental aircraft are a go-to explanation for skeptics and UFOlogists alike. Like all possible explanations, it is a certainty some sightings can be blamed on classified aeronautical projects. Do UFO smells support theories surrounding unconventional aircraft?

In 2008, the experimental Zephyr-6 drone beat the unofficial world record for the longest flight by an unmanned aircraft, clocking in at 82 hours, 37 minutes. Through daylight, the craft was powered by solar paneling, while lithium-sulfur batteries, charged by the sunlight, sustained nighttime flight. "Lithium sulphur is more than double the energy density of the best alternative technology which is lithium polymer batteries," said representative Chris Kelleher. "They are an exceptional performer... We're actually the first application in the world for them."[576]

The Zephyr-6's endurance, coupled with its ability to perform

UFO Smells: Misidentification and Speculation 177

maneuvers that manned aircraft would be unable to execute, makes it noteworthy to UFOlogists. While the lithium-sulfur batteries are a compelling connection, it is unlikely they would outgas detectable sulfur, and the craft certainly strikes a mundane, airplane-shaped silhouette.

In 2001, Terry Melanson penned an excellent essay on his blog entitled "UFOs, Do They Smell? The Sulphur Enigma of Paranormal Visitation." In it, he tracks the development of the sulfur lamp, first developed in the mid-1990s. The device, which creates light by stimulating sulfur plasma with microwave radiation, was a pet project of the United States Department of Energy and, by some accounts, the Department of Defense (DoD). The resultant illumination has more in common with the quality of natural light than conventional options. After briefly falling out of favor following their inception, sulfur lamp production is once more on the rise.[577]

Melanson, citing the thoughts of Australian researcher Simon Harvey-Wilson, outlines the similarities between sulfur lamps and the UFO phenomenon: blindingly bright lights of a different quality than typical artificial illumination; microwave emissions; and, of course, the possibility of sulfurous odors. Could unconventional aircraft somehow employ similar technology, perhaps for propulsion or illumination? Throw in the possible DoD involvement, as well as the fact that sulfur lamps can produce electromagnetic interference, and the entire affair becomes quite compelling.[578]

It is also worth noting that in late summer 2015 German scientists determined that, at record high temperatures, H_2S functions as a superconductor. "When solidified, the compound conducts electricity without resistance at 203.5 K," wrote Adrian Cho, staff writer for *Science* magazine, published by the American Association for the Advancement of Science. "That's still cold—about 70°C below the freezing point of water. But it's far higher than anything ever achieved before and a big step closer to the lofty goal of achieving superconductivity at room temperature."[579]

Could there possibly be a secret government program—

or breakaway civilization—utilizing this technology aboard unconventional aircraft?

Speculation: The Extraterrestrial Hypothesis

If—and it is a cosmic-sized if—UFOs do indeed represent extraterrestrial visitation, perhaps there is supporting evidence in the types of odors noticed by witnesses. Does space have a smell?

Astronauts returning from spacewalks often describe a faint scent lingering on their equipment. Generally referred to as "acrid," descriptions of the odor vary, including the smell of seared steak or hot metal.[580]

"The best description I can come up with is metallic; a rather pleasant sweet metallic sensation," wrote International Space Station Science Officer Don Pettit. "It reminded me of my college summers where I labored for many hours with an arc welding torch repairing heavy equipment for a small logging outfit."[581] According to researcher Jeff Oishi of the New York's Museum of Natural History, this is likely due to polycyclic aromatic hydrocarbons, which are produced when planets and stars form—or when grilling meat.[582]

There certainly is some overlap here, given how often the theme of combustion appears in UFO odors. If astronauts returning from space walks smell like hot metal, then it stands to reason that extraterrestrial craft may exude a comparable smell (although surely atmospheric reentry would contribute to the odor as well).

Celestial bodies have unique odors too. Retired aerospace engineer Robert Verish described the smell of a meteorite:

> The smell that is being given off by this meteorite is hard to describe. When I first smelt it, I tried to think of the proper words to describe the odor. I tried to think of things that had a similar smell: like hot metal, or like a cast-iron skillet that has overheated, or like the metal filaments when you first

turn on an electric heater.

Also, a lot like when you make sparks by striking two flint-rocks against each other. Maybe a little like ozone, but with a more smoky, sulfurous aroma.

That's when the phrase "burnt gunpowder" came into my mind.[583]

Literally every descriptor has appeared in UFO accounts.

Apollo astronauts claim that Moon dust also smells "like spent gunpowder," a reliable description since all were familiar with firearms.

"It is really a strong smell," said Charlie Duke, pilot for Apollo 16. "It has that taste—to me, gunpowder—and the smell of gunpowder, too." Gene Cernan remarked on the following mission that, inside the capsule, it smelled "like someone just fired a carbine in here." In spite of its sulfurous smell, Moon dust is composed of silicon dioxide glass, iron, calcium, magnesium, olivine, and pyroxene.[584]

Sulfur is likely a common smell on other planets. It is estimated as the tenth most abundant element in the universe—fifth by weight[585]—and Europa, Jupiter's sixth-closest moon, has yielded evidence to suggest that it is abundant in sulfuric acid hydrate.[586]

It is conceivable (as most things are when speculating interplanetary life forms) that sulfur is linked to extraterrestrial biology. Alternative biochemists have suggested that, though all terrestrial life forms are carbon-based, sulfur could make a viable substitute, due to its ability to form long-chain molecules.[587] After all, plenty of bacteria subside on sulfur, and some of the oldest geologic formations on earth indicate activity of sulfate-reducing bacteria as early as 3.47 *billion* years ago.[588] If life had decided to take a different fork in the road eons ago, we may well have evolved into sulfur-based organisms. In fact, researchers from the

Massachusetts Institute of Technology speculate that the presence of sulfur in an atmosphere may be an important biomarker for alien life—if life evolved from anaerobic bacteria, it would emit H_2S as a waste product.[589]

This scenario might be playing out in our own neighborhood. The thick cloud layer of Venus is filled with large amounts of H_2S and SO_2, despite the fact that these gases shouldn't coexist—the two compounds are reactive ($2H_2S + SO_2 \rightarrow 3S + 2H_2O$). Ergo, some scientists speculate that *something* on Venus is generating these gases faster than they can react. Other researchers have theorized this layer of sulfur compounds serves a role similar to Earth's ozone layer, absorbing harmful UV rays bombarding the planet—but what on Venus needs protecting?[590]

Regardless of what lies behind the UFO phenomenon, its mystery will endure after a consensus "solution" is reached. Even if the ETH, the most fanciful of the above explanations, is proven true, there will remain a justifiably dissatisfied contingent of researchers. They will point out that the scenario of little green scientists on interplanetary expeditions fails to answer all cases, and they will be right. Those few who readily embrace the reality-warping High Strangeness of UFO sightings will be even further marginalized, their quest for answers even farther out of reach than it is today.

Our concluding chapters feature further musings on the possible significance of smells from spirits, UFOs, and Sasquatch, examined from a panparanormal perspective. We now shift our focus even closer to home than Venus, to examine what strange creatures might lurk in our own backyard.

Part IV: Sasquatch Smells

Chapter 17
Sasquatch Smells: A History

For now we can only conclude that the Abominable Snowman is using the wrong kind of soap.

— John Keel

In July 1984, three passengers were traveling along the eastern side of Prince of Wales Island with their car windows down, enjoying the cool breeze of an Alaskan summer. Around 11:00 p.m., the witnesses were less than 10 miles from their destination and heading up a rise when the driver "caught a whiff of some awful smell." Rolling up her window, she simultaneously saw a tall shape keeping pace alongside the vehicle, which was traveling 35 miles-per-hour.

"In the edge of the headlights just fifteen feet to my side, we could see a creature about seven feet tall and covered all over with dark hair," the driver later recalled. "It was swinging its arms like a man but was a lot heavier built… We sped up and it seemed to veer off as we left it behind."[591]

This case carries many of the hallmarks of encounters with the entity known as Bigfoot or Sasquatch: a fleeting glimpse in the wilderness of something extremely large, manlike yet imbued with a decidedly animalistic demeanor, vaguely aggressive yet quick to retire, all preceded by a rancid stench. Exactly what people see remains uncertain; some have theorized that, in remote locations, populations of relict hominids such as *Gigantopithecus blacki* yet cling to existence, while many in the scientific establishment relegate accounts to the realm of mistakes, archetypes, and lies. Others feel the reports represent a truly anomalous *cryptid*, or undiscovered animal.

What *is* certain is that people the world over tell legends of giant, smelly, hirsute wildmen, fond of abducting women and devouring human flesh. This phenomenon is both international and strikingly consistent. The Japanese tell of the *hibagon*, a foul-smelling man-sized brute who stalks the forests around Mount Hiba.[592] In the Amazon rainforest, tribes speak of the *mapinguari*, alternately described as a tall man-monkey hybrid or gigantic sloth; either way, it purportedly hypnotizes its victims and leaves a disgusting stench in its wake.[593] Pakistani villagers fear the repugnant-smelling *barmanu* ("Big Hairy One"),[594] while Cambodian legends warn of the *tek tek*, who surprises campers with its horrid stench.[595] Local folklore in Central Asia's Pamir Mountains holds that a hunter wrestled with a *Gul-Biavan* in 1939, describing the beast as a "wooly" wildman who exuded "a terrible odor."[596] Hikers in the deep bush of Australia still encounter the *Yowie*, a creature whose odor makes an impression equal to its imposing, shaggy presence.[597]

Though present throughout the lore of most indigenous North American peoples, such tales are particularly common in the Pacific Northwest, where the entities have become renowned for their 24-inch humanlike footprints. Such prodigious tracks earned them the moniker "Bigfoot," although in our discussion we will utilize the more dignified name *Sasquatch*, a term derived largely from the Halkomelem word *ses'quac*. All Native American tribal lore agrees that the beasts are tall (generally six to ten feet), covered in thick hair, and smell deplorably.

In 1856, indigenous people in Oregon told ethnologist George Gibbs of hairy beings called the *tsiatko*, tall and long of foot, who were "said to live in the mountains, in holes underground, and to smell badly."[598] In Washington, the Spokane were often alerted by the "most intolerable" stench of tall, hairy giants who stole their salmon in the night[599]—similarly, the Tolowa of Northern California claim "your nose would tell you that they were near, as they smelled like rotten meat."[600] Meanwhile, in the American southeast, the Choctaw and Chickasaw spoke of debilitating odors from the *shampe*[601] and the *lofa*.[602] In an ironic inversion of these legends, some native peoples contend, "the reason white men are unable to approach them is because 'Sasquatch does not like the white man's smell.'"[603]

More than any other unexplained phenomenon, Sasquatch are renowned for their foul odor. We have an embarrassment of riches from which to choose when selecting representative cases. The association between rancid smells and Sasquatch is so strong that, like unexplained wood knocks, howls, and "stick structures," just about any stench in the forest is seized upon as a sign by overeager "'squatchers" that the creature is nearby (without visual confirmation, Sasquatch behavior is just as accurately described as that of a wilderness poltergeist).

Setting aside the veracity of every whiff in the woods, witnesses are indeed often alerted to the entity by the presence of an unpleasant smell. Sasquatch odors suffer from the usual tip-of-the-nose frustrations common to the unexplained: the beasts smell "foul, rank, terrible, powerful," etc. in ways that are not always clearly defined. This tendency has generated a wide array of descriptions, and as such it is even less possible than usual to comprehensively address every odor.

In his book *Raincoast Sasquatch*, researcher J. Robert Alley lists dozens of encounters ranging from northwest Washington through southeast Alaska. Many witnesses describe the smell in vague terms, such as smelling "animalistic," while others qualify the odor by what it did *not* evoke (e.g. "a real rank odor" *unlike* the musk of a bear).[604]

The literature is replete with generic approximations.

- Frank Dan, a Canadian medicine man, told Ivan T. Sanderson of his July 1936 encounter with a large, hairy creature who began throwing boulders at his canoe. The beast, enraged at Dan entering its territory, emitted "a repugnant odor; that was carried down to the canoe by a wisp of wind. The smell made Frank dizzy and his eyes began to smart and pop. Frank never smelt anything in his whole medicine career like it. It was more repelling than the stench of moccasin oil gone rotten." Dan claimed that the stench even drove the fishes from their hiding places to flee to the main body of the river, a course of action Dan himself adopted.[605]

- Four young people parked in a Decatur, Illinois, "lover's lane" were startled to see an enormous, black humanoid "monster" approach their vehicle in September 1965. The couples fled the scene, but, after dropping their dates off, the men returned to the site. The beast reappeared, this time curiously inspecting the vehicle. Even though the windows were up and the doors shut, they could still smell its fetid stench.[606]

- In spring 1968, Brenda Ann Adkins had stopped to take some pictures at Monteagle Mountain in Tennessee when she detected a "nauseating" odor and heard rustling in the woods behind her. She turned and saw a seven-foot-tall creature staggering toward her, covered in blackish-red hair and looking like a mixture of an ape and a human. The beast stopped six feet away, snarled, and retreated into the forest.[607]

- On September 20, 1985, four witnesses in west Rutland, Vermont, were alerted by a bad odor. Their attention was drawn to a large, hairy figure walking underneath a nearby streetlight.[608] That same year, two teenage witnesses skinny-dipping in a pond in Gavleborg County, Sweden, swore they had been stalked by a large ape with a terrible stench.[609]

Malodorous mixes

Though outliers certainly exist, the stench of Sasquatch is usually compared to wet dog, urine, skunk, feces/manure, garbage, cabbage, musk, sweat, body odor, and, naturally, sulfur. Icthyc (fishy) smells are reported occasionally, though with no real regularity.

It is an understatement to say the hedonic associations are not pleasant. A majority of these smells fall under the larger umbrella of "decaying odors," though one could argue that the true unifying factor is the presence of sulfur—while we have established how some of these, like skunk smell, are connected to the element, we will investigate sulfur's connections to other odors in short order.

These noxious scents tend to mingle and form uniquely rank bouquets, with witnesses often identifying several odiferous components. For example, BFRO investigator Stan Courtney spoke with an Illinois witness who saw a nine-foot-tall, hairy figure scratching its back on a clothesline pole in the wee hours of the morning on December 3, 2012. The shadowy figure was accompanied by an odor of cow manure and skunk.[610] In another case from 1982, a Pennsylvania man was walking through the woods when he detected a "mixture of rotten eggs, spoiled potatoes, and urine," a smell presaging an encounter with an eight-foot-tall Sasquatch further down the trail.[611]

Such combinations make it impossible to fit Sasquatch odors into discrete categories. In the late 1990s, a hunting trip in Alberta, Canada, was plagued by strange bipedal figures rustling through the bush, blood-curdling screams, wood knocks, and an odor of rotten fish and human feces, "but a lot worse." A follow-up interview with investigator Tyler Huggins added wolverine musk, body odor, and decaying garbage to the mix.[612]

Equally revolting was the smell described by a witness in Washington in 2005, who detected "a foul odor resembling vomit, feces, sweat and rotted meat" after stumbling upon anomalous footprints and strange noises.[613] Witnesses with farming experience often invoke the smell of pigs, but with a little something extra: in

2013, a Florida woman startled a six-foot-tall, dark blond figure that smelled like a "wet dog that had rolled in a pig sty."[614]

These descriptions are often darkly humorous in their inventiveness—one is reminded of the ever-escalating descriptions attributed to a revolting cologne in the 2004 comedy *Anchorman*, which culminated in an unfavorable comparison to Sasquatch's genitalia. In a direct parallel, researcher Dr. W.H. Fahrenbach of the Oregon Regional Primate Research Center compared the smell of a suspected Sasquatch bedding site to the aroma of human preputial glands, found underneath foreskin.[615]

On September 17, 2005, a man bow-hunting deer in rural Maryland had his kill stolen, heard strange vocalizations, and was hit with the stench of "wet musty roadkill with dirty diapers."[616] One of the more evocative accounts comes from an Idaho man who, while cutting firewood near Oakley on July 15, 1999, noticed a foul stench and looked up to see a hairy, bipedal form shambling away from him; upon asking him to elaborate, investigators were told "the smell reminded him of when he had been 'lambing,' and the smell when a sheep gave birth to a dead lamb, one which had died days before the birth." The Sasquatch odor "was so foul it made him feel like vomiting."[617]

A peculiar outlier comes from outspoken Sasquatch enthusiast Bob Garrett, who claimed multiple encounters while prospecting gold on Colorado's Spanish Peaks. On one occasion, he allegedly observed multiple female Sasquatch holding their young, an activity accompanied by the smell of "spiced honey, but stronger." Garrett postulated that the odor was deliberately released to soothe the infants.[618] If sweet smells were reported with any regularity, Garrett's testimony would be compelling—however, unlike spirit and UFO odors, Sasquatch *never* smell pleasant. It is possible the mothers had discovered a beehive and were sharing high-calorie honey with their young… still, it seems unlikely the smell would be strong enough to waft to a secluded observation point. In any event, Garrett's may well be the *only* account where a fragrance is noted and, as such, it should be taken with the proverbial grain of salt.

Discrepancies

With so many scents intermingling, it is only natural for interpretations to vary between witnesses. During the Missouri Monster ("Momo") flap of 1971-72, a tall, smelly, large-headed beast covered in black hair harassed citizens near Louisiana, Missouri. The creature was allegedly responsible for the death of at least one dog. Witness Edgar Harrison equated Momo's odor to "a moldy, horse smell or a strong garbage smell,"[619] saying "it stank so bad you would have thought you were walking in horse manure."[620]

After his sighting, Harrison accompanied reporter Richard Crowe to an abandoned shack thought to be the creature's refuge. Inside, Crowe noted "an overwhelming stench that could only be described as resembling rotten flesh or foul, stagnant water." Curiously, Harrison confirmed this smell as that of Momo, even though the description is quite different from his initial impression.[621]

Contradictory descriptions can even originate from a single sighting. In 1967, Roger Patterson and Robert Gimlin filmed the most famous footage of what appears to be a female Sasquatch near Bluff Creek, California. The film's veracity remains in a constant state of flux; while many have sought to discredit the film, even today's advanced analytical tools fall short of confirming or denying whether or not an actual creature was filmed that day.

Patterson and Gimlin had set out with the express purpose of filming a Sasquatch in the wilds of northern California on October 20. Around 1:30 p.m., the duo rounded a turn in a creek bed and came face-to-face with a creature crouched by the water. According to Gimlin, Patterson dismounted his bucking horse, grabbed his camera from the saddlebag and began filming the Sasquatch, which by now had turned to leave. The entire encounter lasted less than two minutes, with just under a minute of footage shot.

Patterson claimed to have caught a whiff akin to "a wet dog rolling in cow manure" during the encounter.[622] Gimlin, on the other hand, disagreed. "I thought it had kind of a... musty, skunky type of smell," he said in a 2014 interview. "Pretty stinky, but with a must to it."[623] While some might feel this inconsistency implies outright fabrication, it seems equally likely that the tip-of-the-nose phenomenon was at play, especially considering how Gimlin has failed to shy away from the discrepancy in recent years.[624]

Effects

Perhaps more so than with any other phenomenon, the putrid scents of Sasquatch physically affect witnesses in an immediate and intense manner. The stench makes eyes water, triggers gag reflexes, and even induces vomiting.

On May 16, 2008, at around 11:30 p.m., a woman in northwestern Pennsylvania heard her Labrador growling at the patio door, alerted by the sound of breaking and crashing. Something was scrambling up the lattice to her second floor deck and, after hearing a loud thud, the witness gathered the courage to peek outside. Staring back was the flat, humanlike face of a hairy figure, towering seven feet over her. Even through the closed door she could smell "a very foul odor," and watched the creature for several seconds before flicking on the outdoor light. The beast bailed over the side of the deck, and the witness ran downstairs to catch a better look; cracking the door, she was hit again with the overwhelming stench, which very nearly made her vomit.[625]

A National Parks worker in Australia was less resilient. While cutting timber near Springbrook in early 1978, the witness heard what he thought was a grunting pig and decided to investigate. Stepping further into the forest, he was startled to behold a "big black hairy man-thing" no more than a dozen feet away. "It looked more like a gorilla than anything," he said. "It had a flat, black shiny face, with two big yellow eyes and a hole for a mouth... We seemed to stand there staring at each other for about 10 minutes before it suddenly gave off a foul smell that made me vomit—then it just made off sideways and disappeared."[626]

Tigers utilize low-frequency vocalizations known as infrasound to repel rivals and stun prey, an ability hairy hominids may also employ. Some researchers speculate this biological adaptation would not only allow Sasquatch to disorient large mammals and satisfy their high caloric needs, but would also handily explain why many witnesses feel unease and nausea during sightings.[627] However, it seems equally feasible—in light of cases like the ones above—that witnesses react not to infrasound, but to the beast's smell. If not solely the case, perhaps Sasquatch employ a one-two punch, using both infrasound *and* their stench to cripple potential threats (the implications of this, namely the possibility of a scent gland, are addressed later).

The odor has staying power. In his 1998 book *North America's Great Ape: The Sasquatch*, wildlife biologist John Bindernagel takes particular note of how Sasquatch's stench clings to footprints and bedding sites long after the creature has disappeared. He draws comparisons to the observations made by anthropologist Birutė Galdikas following a fight between two orangutans, who noted "the smell of their pungent perspiration lingered on the ground even after they were back in the canopy."[628]

According to family legend, one William Hall was hunting in British Columbia in 1918 when he happened upon a gang of four *bogwish*, the Kitimaat term for Sasquatch. Terrified, he ran for his life and somehow passed out, regaining consciousness later atop a large boulder. Below, the angry *bogwish* reached and clamored, only to depart after he begged them for peace. Hall dismounted the rock and made his way back to the canoe, tailed by the creatures the entire time. According to his grandson, he "had the same rancid odor [as the *bogwish*] permeating from his body until the day of his death, eight years later." The odor was so bad he sequestered himself in a separate hut "so as not to offend his family." As a compelling coda to the tale, the encounter left

Hall clairvoyant—an ability also reported by some modern alien abductees.⁶²⁹

Anthropologist Ed Fusch collected legends of the *S'cwene'y'ti*, an entity whose name translates in Spokane as "tall, hairy, smells like burnt hair." In one tale, a young girl was taken from her village by *S'cwene'y'ti*. Search parties returned empty handed, and the girl was deemed lost. After several years, the girl returned, but smelled so strongly of the beast's stench that no man wanted her. She was forced to live outdoors and, though the tribe saw to her needs, slowly descended into madness.⁶³⁰ The girl was a virgin when she was abducted; we are left to wonder whether or not she actually smelled, or if potential suitors simply proclaimed her spoiled by the experience. Human beings can unfairly apply hedonic associations based on assumed indiscretions (e.g. two women equally perfumed might "smell pretty" or "smell like a whore," depending on their perceived moral laxity).⁶³¹

Sasquatch analogues have equally persistent olfactory effects across the globe. In 1975, a man in Brazil saw a *mapinguari* and claimed that the stench made him dizzy, such that he was "not right for two months."⁶³² A Mrs. Reiko Harada of Japan told Janet and Colin Bord that, after spotting a *hibagon* in the woods, searchers found no trace of the creature save its stench: "the place smelled like a dead body after it starts decomposing."⁶³³

By now, the scenario wherein a witness is "infected" by the stench of a spirit, UFO, or Sasquatch is familiar (recall the Strickler case, as well as the smell that clung to LeRoy Wallace for two weeks). There is actually a grim scientific precedent for affliction by an ineradicable odor. Scientists working in laboratories with hydrogen telluride (H_2Te) are advised to handle the compound with extreme care, as even small exposures can infuse the body with an overpowering stench of rotten garlic, or rancid leeks. According to chemist Linus Pauling, those few reckless lab workers unfortunate enough to develop "tellurium breath" have been ostracized or, worse, committed suicide due to the lingering smell.⁶³⁴

What's in a name?

With so many worldwide reports of stinking ape-men, it is natural to assume that Nepal's famous *yeti* derives its pop-culture nickname "Abominable Snowman" from its smell. This is not the case, though the myth is quite common (Keel himself was under the assumption that the name referred to the beast's odor).[635] In reality, *Calcutta Statesman* columnist Henry Newman coined the phrase in 1921 as a mistranslation. Newman reported that, while making their way up the Tibetan side of the Himalayas, C.K. Howard-Bury and company spied several distant, dark shapes moving up the mountain. Upon reaching their location, Howard-Bury found tracks "three times those of normal humans."

The Sherpas in the company claimed the footprints came from the *met-teh kang-mi*, or "man-sized wild snow creature," and Howard-Bury recorded the term as *metoh-kangmi*. Newman in turn corrupted the term into *metch kangmi*, loosely meaning "filthy snowman," which evolved into "Abominable Snowman."[636] Smell never entered the equation—actually, odors are less common in yeti sightings, perhaps as a result of the colder climate.

On the other hand, the Skunk Ape of the American southeast solely has odor to blame for its unfortunate moniker. Nearly every encounter with the beast, which is said to stalk the humid Florida everglades, details its stench. By most accounts, the skunk ape seems more simian than its northwestern counterpart, leaving behind knuckle prints and apelike tracks, with a large toe branching from the side of the foot. According to cryptozoologist Loren Coleman, Skunk Apes come in a variety of scents but most commonly smell like rotten eggs, manure, or, obviously, skunk spray.

Though tales of hairy hominids in the everglades stretch back into native Seminole legend, the origin of the term "Skunk Ape" is lost to time. As can be best discerned, the name dates back to the early 1970s, possibly coined by the father of David Shealy, who now runs the Skunk-Ape Research Headquarters in Ochopee,

Florida. Shealy recalls a local man named Raymond Wooten who would visit his home for dinner in the early 1970s, engaging in long conversations with his father on the topic and using the term freely. The earliest printed reference seems to come from *The National Observer*, a Silver Springs, Maryland, publication that ran a story on August 16, 1971, when sightings caught the entire country's attention.[637]

Existing Research

There is some contention regarding just how often odors are reported in hairy hominid encounters. Researcher John Green, one of the fathers of modern Sasquatch study, told Janet and Colin Bord in 1984 that only 5.6% of reports contained a reference to smell;[638] eleven years later he revised that figure, writing, "In British Columbia and Alberta strong smells are mentioned in only 4.5% of reports."[639]

Green's statement has misled some researchers into claiming that reports of odors are overemphasized. This is simply not the reality. A cursory look at the Bigfoot Field Researchers Organization (BFRO) website yields hundreds of sightings where smells are recorded. In 1999, Loren Coleman and Jerome Clark wrote of the wave of hairy biped encounters that rocked Florida in the 1970s, "almost all [sightings] mentioned the creature's strong, unpleasant odor."[640] Meanwhile, MUFON investigator Sharon Cornet contended in a 2005 essay that smell featured in 30%-50% of Sasquatch encounters.[641]

Green's 4.5% figure is grossly conservative in a global context, with recent reports suggesting the trend is becoming more common—for example, in Janet and Colin Bord's updated edition of *Bigfoot Casebook: Sightings and Encounters from 1818 to 2004*, there is a marked increase in the number of witnesses noting smells post-1960.[642] Perhaps expectations affect observation, as asserted with spirits.

This is not to say that Green was incorrect, rather that his assertion must be interpreted carefully. During his career, he focused almost exclusively on the Pacific Northwest; large, hairy hominids, on the other hand, are spotted throughout the United States, to say nothing of international sightings. Ergo, we might infer that—if sighting distances are comparable worldwide, and witnesses elsewhere aren't simply beyond the "scent zone"— Sasquatch outside British Columbia and Alberta are more odiferous than their Canadian cousins.

Research into Sasquatch smells beyond Green has been feeble at best, with nothing approaching the level of excellence attained by Antonio F. Rullán with UFO odors. While both Fahrenbach and Cornet have published theories relevant to later discussion, the field has by-and-large failed to produce any in-depth commentary.

Explanations for the odor's source are as varied as the smells themselves. Cryptozoologist Dale Drinnon posited that the smell was from intestinal venting and sweat/feces clinging to the fur, while Colorado researcher Leon Drew contended that the odor was a function of environmental heat and humidity.[643]

To fill in this research gap, perhaps it would be helpful to posit a categorization system of hypotheses, à la Rullán. We can roughly divide all proposed theories into origin and intent, rendering four possibilities:

- **Exogenous Unintentional** – the odor is produced outside the body and is beyond the creature's control (e.g. foul debris clinging to Sasquatch fur);

- **Exogenous Intentional** – the odor is produced outside the body, but is applied for a specific reason (e.g. the way dogs are fond of rolling in feces and dead animals);

- **Endogenous Unintentional** – the odor is produced inside the body, and is beyond the creature's control (e.g. sweat, oils, etc.);

- **Endogenous Intentional** – the odor is produced inside the body, and is released for a specific reason (i.e. a deliberately activated scent gland).

Sufficient evidence exists in favor of each hypothesis, and all are addressed in the following chapters.

Before we proceed, a note on sources: while many of the following accounts come from the existing literature, they are heavily supplemented by reports from the Bigfoot Field Researchers Organization's online database. Internet sources should normally be viewed with great caution. However, each case in this book was subjected to follow-up investigation by BFRO representatives, who spoke directly with witnesses to corroborate their sightings and gauge their sincerity. This vetting process naturally gives such claims greater weight than random accounts posted to the internet without follow-up.

But it does not make them infallible. As ever in Forteana—*caveat emptor*.

Chapter 18
Sasquatch Smells: Animal Odors and Scent Glands

If it looks like a skunk and smells like a skunk, it is most assuredly a skunk.

— John Keel

In the heart of Singapore lies Bukit Timah, the highest point of the bustling city-state and home to the Bukit Timah Nature Reserve, a 410-acre island of trees surrounded by a sea of urbanity. Its small size lies in stark contrast to the vast swathes of Canadian wilderness, yet, like the Pacific Northwest, it is allegedly home to a large, hairy hominid: the Bukit Timah Monkey Man (BTMM). Witnesses claim that the beast is the size of a man, bipedal, and covered in shaggy gray hair.

In ages past, sightings of BTMM were more common. Malay folklore references the being, and reliable accounts exist from Japanese soldiers during World War II. A 65-year-old man from the Bukit Panjang district recalled the warnings of adults during his youth. "We were always told as children when in the Kampung not to go near the forest at night due to the Monkey Man," he said. "Once we were shown these footprints near the forest road, and I remember the strong urine smell. Whenever we heard shrieks coming from the jungle we would tell each other—don't disturb the Monkey Man."[644]

Urine

It only makes sense that Sasquatch and its ilk reek of animal smells—after all, most accounts appear to depict a biological, flesh-and-blood creature. Of these odors, urine is quite common.

- In 1966, a man in Elfers, Florida, saw a hairy figure walking near the Anclote River. "The thing had a rancid, putrid odor like stale urine," he said. He returned later with his dog, which refused to follow the scent. The beast, he said, was at least seven feet tall with a four-foot wide chest.[645]

- A cyclist traveling Alaska's North Tongass Highway in August 1998 was alarmed to see a Sasquatch in a roadside ditch, digging at something in the dirt. The creature didn't seem to notice or care about the man's presence as he began peddling faster. "I got a lungful of the most awful gagging smell, like a combination of rotten meat, urine and damp earth," he told J. Robert Alley. "It smelled so bad it made me want to throw up." He also remarked that the creature was surrounded by a swarm of flies.[646]

- On November 16, 2004, a hunter in Passaic County, New Jersey, was approaching his tree stand when a "very potent, strong, harsh smell" reminiscent of deer urine, except "much stronger and more intense," washed over him. The odor came and went for the next two hours, intensifying when he decided to try a different tree stand. While walking the trail, a tall, broad-shouldered shape stepped into the path and stared at him for several seconds before vanishing into the forest.[647]

- When researcher Linda Godfrey knocked on a tree while hiking in Wisconsin's Kettle Moraine region on July 8, 2012, she did not expect to receive a response. However, the ensuing wood knocks, clatter of something running through the forest, and giant tree limb tossed in her direction confirmed that she had indeed gotten something's attention. She returned shortly thereafter with a friend and her daughter, who caught a glimpse of a gray-beige biped retreating into the foliage. The trio examined the felled tree limb and found it infused with "a very strong, musky, somewhat skunk-like odor" that Godfrey likened to urine.[648]

- A couple traveling through New Mexico stopped for a bathroom break around 1:00 a.m. in the town of Las Vegas on October 18, 2013. To the husband's dismay, the service station they chose was closed, and he was forced to relieve himself behind the building. While urinating, he began to feel as though he was being watched; looking over his shoulder he saw an eight-to-ten-foot-tall shape covered in dark brown, matted hair, crouched in the sparse vegetation. The creature started and retreated into the shadows, away from the light of the parking lot. "He remembers the area smelling like cat urine," wrote investigator Boyd Omer after the follow-up interview. "It reminded him of a mountain lion's urine, a smell that he is familiar with in the past." The witness, a scientist and self-professed skeptic, found the experience life changing.[649]

Ammonia is also invoked in Sasquatch cases, a refined description of the urine odor. BFRO investigator R. Monteith recalled a tale when his uncle, a police officer, was dispatched to a Florida trailer park during the prominent Skunk Ape flap of the early 1970s. Residents claimed a prowler had been lurking about their neighborhood.

"He and his partner arrived to see a very large, muscular, hairy bipedal shape looking into the window of a trailer," Monteith wrote. "It ran away as they approached it, leaving behind a very strong 'pungent, ammonia, horrible B.O.' smell."[650] Years later, witnesses dredging for gold in a creek in Tennessee's Cherokee National Forest were visited by a Sasquatch that smelled strongly of ammonia or insecticide, "like a bear, only worse, like it had urine and feces in its hair."[651]

It is an interesting correlation that ammonia is an effective dog repellant, and dogs are often terrified when confronted by Sasquatch. There may well be a connection here; for example, one sighting of a freezer-robbing Sasquatch in Twisp, Washington, was accompanied by the intense smell of ammonia, which aggravated nearby dogs.[652] Eager canine trackers will stalwartly refuse to follow a Sasquatch's trail—perhaps ammonia, whose strong odor is like an olfactory punch to a dog's face, plays a role in this behavior.

Some speculate urine smells might be linked to territory marking, a habit found in a variety of mammals, including some primates. Indeed, researchers have postulated that aggressive Sasquatch behavior could be the result of a perceived territorial threat—for example, in 2015 a truck driver claimed that, after urinating in the woods, he was roused from a nap by something violently rocking his cab.[653] Scent-based territorial behavior, however, is largely limited to monkeys and prosimians (lemurs and the like), rather than apes;[654] this may lend credence to the notion that Sasquatch are closely related to lemurs, as proposed by some researchers.[655]

Seth Breedlove, a documentarian who focuses on small town monster legends, obliquely proposed the notion that this ammonia smell may be the product of diet or environment rather than urine. While filming *Minerva Monster*, which chronicles sightings from the eponymous Ohio town, Breedlove noted than many of the encounters included an ammonia smell. Breedlove also remarked how hair was collected from a chicken coop during the 1978 flap; raw, rotting chicken can produce an ammonia-like odor, as can filthy coops.[656]

Sasquatch are often accused of poultry theft—could too much time in coops, or bits of raw chicken clinging to fur, cause an accompanying ammonia odor? Perhaps that was the case for the "big hairy man" spotted on September 12, 1992, by two boys near Klamath, California. The creature had been lurking in the bushes, accompanied by the strong stench of rotting chicken.[657]

Gulf Coast Bigfoot Research Organization founder Bobby Hamilton recalled an expedition in Louisiana where he noted strange hoots, crashing in the woods, and an unpleasant odor similar to an "extremely strong urine or ammonia smell."

> It was just like you walk into a brick wall… It caught me where I was actually inhaling at the time, you know, breathing in, and I got a whole set of lungs full of this stuff… Like it's been peeing in a fold of skin or something for twenty or thirty years and it's just sitting there just fermenting and getting real rancid and rank. But you take that smell and you combine it with a… if you have a raccoon that won't tree, you know, he'll live in a creek bank or something… they stink… they just have a nasty, wild animal smell to them. You put that smell with that real strong urine-ammonia scent, and that's pretty close to what this thing put out there.[658]

Hamilton speculated that the stench came from a scent gland, a possibility investigated at the end of this chapter. His description of the damp raccoon odor is also reminiscent of one of the more common animal smells: wet dog.

Wet dog

A man from Pekin, Illinois, saw something large and hairy swimming the Illinois River on July 25, 1972, an image bearing a strong similarity to the 10-foot-tall white ape seen that evening in Cairo. Two days later, two witnesses told police they ran into "a cross between an ape and a cave-man" that smelled like a "musky, wet-down dog." By the end of the following day, the East Peoria

Police Department had received more than 200 calls concerning the beast.[659]

So many different odors have been attributed to Sasquatch that it is difficult to determine which prevails. That said, a strong case could be made that the odor of "wet dog," alongside sulfur, is most common. The description is curious, as Sasquatch usually appears dry and appears to lack canine heritage.

- In October 1979, a man from northern California noticed enormous tracks, excessively large humanlike droppings, and the odor of a "very filthy wet dog" near his logging site. Some time later he returned to the location to hunt and observed a Sasquatch through the scope of his rifle.[660]

- An elderly couple living in Allegheny County, Pennsylvania, started hearing strange sounds near the dumpsters of their trailer park beginning in the late 1970s. Thinking a vagrant was to blame, the husband kept a cautious eye on the area. The summer was replete with a host of odd activity including strange howls and "a terrible stench, like a skunk and a wet dog combined." Events escalated until the couple caught a large beast covered in white hair rummaging through the dumpster one evening.[661]

- The Sasquatch around Ketchikan, Alaska, seem to effuse "eau de wet dog" regularly. In June 2001, a serene, man-sized figure approached two witnesses, its black hair visible in the light of a bonfire. Before jumping in their car and leaving, the witnesses noted the smell of "wet dog and garbage mixed." Seven months prior, a couple parked off Revilla Road saw a *kushtakaa*, or land-otter man, from their car. They were alerted to its presence by "a real rank odor, kind of like the smell of wet dog hair."[662]

- Stan Gordon reported a November 17, 2003, sighting of

a Sasquatch in rural Pennsylvania. Around 6:30 p.m., two witnesses saw an eight-foot-tall creature standing by the side of the road. "They reported a wet dog smell at the time of the observation."[663]

- In 2008 a witness biking in the Huron-Manistee National Forest saw a furry head appear in the window of a burned-out camper, prompting him to ride off quickly. Simultaneously, he noted the revolting odor of "a wet dog that just emerged from the swamp mixed with skunk."[664]

Researchers Loren Coleman and Mark Hall have noted that a subset of ape-men, collectively dubbed "marked hominids" for their piebald appearance, are more likely to exhibit this wet dog odor. Skunk apes also commonly smell like wet dogs; of the creature witness Charlie Stoeckman saw in the Florida Keys in 1977, he said "it stunk awful, like a dog that hasn't been bathed in a year and suddenly gets rained on."[665]

Other "wet animal" smells have been referenced. Witnesses report the generic smell of wet fur, or equate the odor to an animal scent with which they are equally familiar—for example, multiple witnesses at a campground in Molalla, Oregon, saw a nine-foot Sasquatch in 1993 which they said smelled like a "wet ferret."[666] When hunter Bob Snyder caught an unpleasant whiff during autumn 1984, he thought the odor came from a wet elk, an assumption reinforced when he saw a large, hairy figure cross the swamp. After several steps, however, Snyder realized this was no elk: it walked on two legs, stood over eight feet tall, and was covered in gray hair.[667]

One of the more popular explanations for why Sasquatch smells is that it takes on attributes of its environment (Exogenous Unintentional). Many researchers, including Linda Godfrey, have endorsed the possibility. "Maybe it's the state's swamp water combined with heat and high humidity that intensifies the scent," she wrote of Florida's Skunk Ape.[668]

Climate may indeed play a role. Starting with John Green, many researchers have noted "where the annual rainfall is under 20 inches a year there are hardly any Sasquatch reports."[669] By contrast, the rainforests and jungles of the world are much more likely to harbor tales of large, hairy hominids. The propensity for Sasquatch to both inhabit damper climates and smell like a wet dog should not be ignored; odiferous compounds of any sort are released through evaporation, which requires water. In addition to rainfall keeping the beast's coat wet, heat and humidity could perhaps contribute to other factors like sweat and mold. Anomalous hairy hominids also seem to display an affinity for water not shared by other apes, using waterways as means of travel.

It is peculiar that, given their antagonistic relationship, Sasquatch should smell like dogs. Why do wet dogs stink anyway? Yeast and bacteria in canine fur excrete odiferous volatile compounds, which are displaced and freed by the presence (and evaporation) of water.[670] Additionally, sebaceous glands in canine skin produce an oil known as sebum, which collects in hair follicles and coats each strand. The oil assists in waterproofing a dog's coat, but also contributes to a dog's characteristic pong when wet.[671]

Human beings, however, have denser clusters of sebaceous glands than nearly any other mammal. "In terms of the numbers and sizes of sebaceous and apocrine glands, man has to be considered as quite by far the most highly scented ape of all," writes David Michael Stoddart in *The Scented Ape: The Biology and Culture of Human Odour*. Put simply, if apes and humans bathed with equal frequency, we might well be the stinkiest of the lot. Stoddart further contends that different hair colors produce sebum of varying quality: sebum from red-haired follicles tends to be sweeter, fair-haired follicles produce sour odors, and the axillary sebum of dark-haired subjects smells akin to "rancid fat."[672]

Such research raises obvious questions for those interested in Sasquatch. Do different odors correspond with different hair colors? Could Sasquatch, who is almost always accompanied by an odor, steal the title of "most highly scented ape" from humans?

If so, does this imply that the creatures are apelike humans, rather than humanlike apes?

Skunk

An outdoorsman in Jasper County, Iowa, had risen early one morning in October 2012 to go hunting. Around 3:15 a.m. he was walking along a tree line when he heard a strange whistling noise, following by a revolting stench akin to "a combination of dead skunk and wet dog." Plugging his nose, the witness soldiered on until he saw the outline of two figures in the field, each appearing "like a perfect linebacker." In the early morning moonlight he was able to discern a reddish-tinted hair covering their bodies, and in short order the figure on the left tossed something at the hunter. He fled for his life.[673]

The connection between skunk spray and sulfur has been established. The substance's chief malodorous compounds are thiols, simple chemical structures generated by joining a single sulfur atom to a single hydrogen atom. These odors are quite common in Sasquatch encounters—for example, Joan Mills and Mary Ryan, two witnesses during the Momo flap, compared the beast's smell to "a whole family of skunks."[674]

- Two boys were bicycling near Rutherford, New Jersey, in July 1975 when a nine-foot-tall creature "covered in brown, gray-tinged, shaggy hair came from the lake and stepped across the path in front of them." The beast left a skunk-like odor in its wake.[675]

- A witness in Missouri was bow hunting in October 1991, when he heard the rustling of leaves by Sni-A-Bar Creek. Turning in the direction of the sound, the hunter saw a seven-foot-tall figure covered in black, matted hair ascend the far side of the creek dike. The being stood at the peak for several seconds before descending in the witness's direction, bringing with it a "wet, thick smell" similar to "a very pungent skunk." The witness, who had been hiding in the brush, fled once the beast was out of sight.[676]

- In November 1994, a witness in Wilton, Arkansas (32 miles from Fouke, home of the "Boggy Creek" sightings of the 1970s), encountered a Sasquatch on a railway at twilight. It acted aggressively, "growled and had an odor worse than a skunk."[677]

- Residents living in the shadow of Carpenters Knob, a mountain in Cleveland County, North Carolina, have whispered for years about "Knobby," an apelike beast featured in over a dozen sightings from the late 1970s. More recently, Thomas Byers and Carolina Wright were traveling nearby when a large animal crossed the road on March 22, 2011. The bipedal figure was covered in brown fur and "had an odor that smelled something like a cross between a skunk and sewage."[678]

- On December 4, 2012, a woman near Kamiah, Idaho, was roused from sleep by her dogs barking in the outdoor kennel. Having noted the odor of skunk earlier, she cautiously opened the back door in the hope of intervening before her pets got sprayed. Imagine her surprise when she saw a silvery-gray Sasquatch darting uphill in the moonlight.[679]

Skunk apes, of course, exude their namesake stench on occasion as well. In July 1997, six British tourists north of Ochopee, Florida, saw an entity they described as "flat-faced, broad-shouldered, covered with long brown hair or fur and reeking of skunk."[680]

It is interesting to note that in significant concentrations skunk spray is much like tear gas and can actually induce vomiting—a reaction of many Sasquatch witnesses. It is also fascinating that skunk spray is highly flammable when ignited, a tidy link to our combustion odor motif.[681] Suffice to say, the presence of skunklike odors in Sasquatch encounters is highly suggestive that the creatures might possess a scent gland.

Researcher J.C. Johnson suggests that perhaps the Sasquatch odor comes from *literal* skunk spray. In 2010, Johnson and fellow investigators from New Mexico discovered a curiously ruptured irrigation pipe, its interior slick with blood. The pipe had been carried from its point of installation by some unseen force, which left behind two enormous holes in its PVC exterior in addition to fingerprints and tooth marks. Nearby lay the corpse of a skunk.

The suggested narrative was that a Sasquatch on the hunt drove the skunk into the pipe, which it then carried into a nearby field. In an effort to capture its prey, the Sasquatch punched holes on either side of the skunk, effectively trapping it inside the pipe for extraction.

The most interesting detail was the manner in which the dead skunk was deprived of its internal organs and scent gland. Crypto 4 Corners, Johnson's organization which investigates unexplained phenomena in the American southwest, released a video in which he said:

> [Sasquatch] do have an odor all their own, the wet dog mixed with horse pee or something, I've heard it described a lot of different ways. But when you add the skunk scent on top of it, then you've got something I think most people have encountered, the complete smell, the smelly wet dog with the skunk blended in. We've often wondered if these creatures had the ability to make the smell themselves, if they were under duress or stress, all the sudden you would smell something like that, but I have been in stressful situations and didn't get that particular smell. That day a few yards away from the area we were investigating… I got a whiff of something that was the smell of the animal by

itself, mixed with the skunk....[682]

The implication is that Sasquatch deliberately "harvest" skunk scent glands to augment their natural stench (hypothesis Exogenous Intentional). Johnson went on to speculate that perhaps this was a means of protecting their young, deterring predation from other large carnivores. The idea is reminiscent of theories that Sasquatch apply animal fat to keep biting insects away (though one would think such behavior would only exacerbate the problem).

"Skunk harvests" seem far-fetched, and Johnson has a reputation for telling stories that push the boundaries of credulity... yet perhaps there is some germ of truth to the idea. After all, nearly all dog owners have recoiled in horror as their pet rolls in roadkill or a pile of manure. This tendency is poorly understood; some theorize it is a vestigial behavior from when wolves needed to mask their scent on the hunt, while alternate ideas hold that it is a communication medium between dogs ("Smell where I've been and what I found!").[683] In any event, this utilization of scent is much less sophisticated than the targeting of skunks for a specific organ.

Musk or must?

It was a sunny morning in May 1981, and Lon Strickler—who would encounter a ghost smelling of honeysuckle years later—was fly-fishing in Maryland's Patapsco River. Around 10:00 a.m., he noticed a stray dog on the opposite bank. After a few minutes, the mutt disappeared into the brush and began to bark and growl.

> Suddenly, I heard a loud yelp from the dog and the creature stood up. The best I could tell is that this "thing" was about 7-8 ft. tall and had dark matted hair. I could only see the body from the chest up because the rest of the body was obscured by the

Sasquatch Smells: Animal Odors and Scent Glands 209

weeds and thickets. I stood completely still and could hear a series of "tick" sounds while observing this creature walk slowly through the thickets towards the woods. I started to follow it and in the meantime I noticed a strong musky scent that reminded me of fox urine.

Strickler jumped in his car and drove to a payphone, where he contacted the authorities. They told him to meet by the river. Upon returning, Strickler was startled to see a Maryland State Policeman already on-scene. The officer instructed him to leave, despite the fact that he was the one who had placed the call. An hour later he drove back by the site, "and the place was crawling with people and many state and other official vehicles."[684]

Many witnesses describe Sasquatch as smelling of "musk," a frustratingly vague term that could mean any number of aromas—the word applies to an entire class of odorous substances, usually mammalian in nature. Musk is also present in several species of crocodilians, turtles, beetles, and even a handful of plants. On occasion, witnesses will be a bit more descriptive, invoking the musk of a specific animal in their accounts.

- One of the first modern accounts of a Sasquatch comes from the 1892 book *Wilderness Hunter: Outdoor Pastimes of an American Hunter*, written by future President Theodore Roosevelt. Roosevelt detailed the harrowing tale of a trapper named Bauman who, in the wilds of Montana, encountered a beast with a "strong, wild-beast odor." The shaggy, bipedal creature faded back into the forest after being shot; two days later, Bauman returned to his camp to find his partner slain.[685]

- A Modoc man recalled a story from his grandfather, who lived near Tule Lake in northern California. One evening in the summer of 1897, his grandfather encountered a hairy "man of the mountain" along a deer trail and, as a gesture of friendship, offered the beast a string of fish he had caught. This began a relationship between the grandfather and the *matah kagmi* (recall the Tibetan *met-teh kang-mi*). The grandfather said the creatures smelled strong and musky.[686]

- Campers near Seneca, Illinois, heard something walking towards their campfire one summer night in 1983. The footfalls continued to circle them for several hours until they caught a glimpse of an eight-foot-tall, hairy figure in the firelight. The two men fled, later noting they had detected "a very musky smell. It smelled a little bit like garbage, a little bit like musky cologne… It had a little bit of a weird smell, one that I won't forget."[687]

- The Fouke Monster of Arkansas is often described as smelling like a mix of animal musk and death. In winter 2000, a raccoon hunter's dogs were spooked by something on two legs that moaned and smelled putrid, "like when you kill a wild hog." Similar reports have described the odor like "somebody had killed a deer or walked off the road and dumped some hog guts or something."[688]

- On October 19, 2009, a father and son were traveling to the store after hunting in Florida's Richloam Wildlife Management Area when a skunk ape crossed the road. The beast was eight-foot-tall, covered in brown-red hair, with dark eyes and a wide nose and mouth. It carried a unique odor. "I can't describe it," the father wrote. "It's got a smell all of its own. If I had to try to describe it, I would say that it was something like a cross between a skunk, a boar looking for a sow, and something else that I just can't describe. It's nasty."[689]

Sasquatch Smells: Animal Odors and Scent Glands 211

If there is any chance that sightings of Sasquatch are simple misidentification, witnesses are likely seeing bears walking on their hind legs. While all ursine species *can* stand on two legs, it isn't particularly common for them to travel great distances bipedally, unless an injury forces the issue. This being said, bears do have a distinctive odor consistent with the odor found in some Sasquatch reports, characterized by one biologist as "musky and musty."[690]

This description highlights another problem: as if the term wasn't ambiguous enough, witnesses confuse "musky" smells with "musty" smells. For example, activity around a camp in New York's Adirondack Mountains featured a "strong and *musty* smell," according to the witness, yet a follow up report by BFRO investigator D.A. Brake revealed the presence of an "unusual, strong *musky* odor that the witness described as a wet dog smell."[691]

This conflation is quite common. The two words are often used interchangeably, a difficulty further compounded by the fact that large male mammals during rutting season are said to be *in must*, during which they often release *musk*. We are left to wonder, in an era where so many people use "literally" figuratively and nuance is a lost art, how much language misapprehension skews our data.

It is easy to write off all "musty" descriptions as verbal slips, yet some witnesses evoke the term quite specifically. At 11:30 p.m. on May 17, 1988, Sam Sherry was preparing for some nighttime fishing in Pennsylvania when he saw a bedraggled Sasquatch standing in the woods 25 feet away. The accompanying smell, described specifically as "musty," may have been related to the fact that the creature appeared on the verge of death, covered in mange.[692]

Six years prior, another group of fisherman were pelted with large rocks on Washington's Duckabush River, at a location where a "wet dog/cardboard/sourish" smell was often noted.[693] How many witnesses smelling musk actually smell must, and vice versa? If we are to gain any headway in parsing out the meaning of different smells, it is imperative researchers solicit more specific descriptions differentiating the two.

Feces

In 2001, researcher Tony Healy presented a paper at Australia's Myths & Monsters conference on "'High Strangeness' in Yowie Reports." The term refers to the more fanciful aspects reported in some hairy hominid sightings, such as glowing eyes, resistance to gunfire, sightings alongside UFOs, etc.

"In about 10% of Yowie cases the creatures have exuded a mind-bogglingly foul stench. It can be bad enough to make a person vomit and the pongy pongids seem to be able to release the choking miasma at will," Healy said. "Usually the smell is compared to that of rotting meat, bat droppings or a 'badly kept country dunny [outhouse]' but occasionally witnesses say the creatures left a distinct electrical smell 'like burnt electrical wiring,' 'burnt bakelite,' 'a sulphury stink.'"[694]

Hairy hominids the world over exude the stench of feces. Such reports beg the question why dogs seem so afraid of the beast; surely the fecal odor would draw them in like moths to a flame. In any case, comparisons are both direct ("we smelled a smell similar to dog poop," said one Californian witness in 1979)[695] and oblique: comparisons to outhouses, sewers, and septic tanks abound (since the latter two derive their distinctive rotten egg odor from H_2S rather than indole and skatole, they are mostly saved for discussion later).

- A young witness was playing hide and seek near Gettysburg, Pennsylvania, in July 1971 when he ran into a hairy, man-sized animal with a distinctive "cow manure and deer musk" smell. "Whatever it was, it came almost like a ghost and left the same way," he wrote years later.[696]

- A Yowie peered into the window of a Spinbrook, Queensland, home on January 29, 1978. The eyewitness said it was covered in black hair, with a small, flat nose on its egg-shaped head, and smelled like "a badly kept public lavatory."⁶⁹⁷

- In July 1978 Lavena Kline of Ohio spotted a Sasquatch with glowing eyes hunched along a railroad crossing. A few days later, her sister Theresa saw the creature and described it as smelling like cow manure.⁶⁹⁸

- Albert Kubo saw Japan's *hibagon* while working in a rice field. "I was petrified," he said, "but the stench was what really got to me. He must have bathed in a septic tank and dried off with cow dung. I nearly passed out." Instead, the terrified Kubo ran five miles straight home.⁶⁹⁹

- In March 2008, a Florida woman was walking her dogs before daybreak when she caught sight of something odd sitting in the street. "I initially thought it was a truck because it was so big," she said. "At the time I really couldn't get my mind around it being anything else." Within moments, she realized she was looking at an enormous Skunk Ape, which followed her as she walked home, closing the distance between them whenever she looked away. Eventually she reached her driveway and bolted inside. "The odd thing was that for the next three mornings there was a very strong musty or poopy odor outside the front door that hung like a wet blanket in the air," she said. "As soon as I opened the door and smelled it I shut the door because I felt it was in the yard."⁷⁰⁰

Sulfur's link to feces has already been firmly established, particularly in the form of H_2S. Animals also excrete methanethiol— the "natural gas" odor— in feces. The compound is detectable at just 1 ppb.⁷⁰¹

A number of explanations could account for fecal odors, spanning each of our proposed endogenous/exogenous intentional/unintentional categories. Could their feces be deliberately used as a deterrent (Endogenous Intentional), or could the feces of *other* animals be deliberately applied as a deterrent (Exogenous Intentional)?

Perhaps the most likely answer—as posited by Dale Drinnon—is that the odor comes from feces clinging to the animal's coat (Endogenous Unintentional).[702] It is worth noting that, according to researchers Vaughn Bryant, Jr., and Burleigh Trevor-Deutsch, "most non-human coprolites generally emit a musty odor during rehydration. Human coprolites, on the other hand, produce an intense fecal odor."[703] Recall how hairy hominids appear in conjunction with rainfall, which would provide ample rehydration to any clinging feces. Perhaps musty-smelling Sasquatch are more closely related to apes, while fecal-smelling Sasquatch are closer to humans.

Scent glands

Musky smells in Sasquatch reports raise the question of whether or not large hairy hominids might possess scent glands, organs which secrete pheromones and other odiferous compounds. Without a doubt they do—most mammals have scent glands of some sort, including human beings (our apocrine sweat glands respond to stress and sexual stimulation, though the resultant odor isn't always consciously noticeable to us).[704] Rather, the question should be, "Does Sasquatch possess *strong smelling* scent glands?"

Odors in the animal kingdom are most commonly used to communicate warnings, identify members of a species, mark territory, and influence courtship, regulated by special glands. Such glands are common in carnivores—bears, cats, dogs, hyenas, opossums—which possess an anal gland that, depending on the species, may be expelled via defecation, seepage, or oozing. In the mustelids (skunks, wolverines, weasels, otters, badgers, etc.), these glands are particularly prominent.

Apes, however, are not of the order carnivora. Is there any evidence for particularly pungent scent glands in primates?

It has been long established that the armpits of male mountain gorillas house well-developed axillary organs comprised of apocrine sweat glands. When agitated, these glands release an odor that mammalogist George Schaller compared to pungent human sweat, manure, and distant burning rubber.[705] Renowned primatologist Dian Fossey similarly detailed males reflexively producing an "overpowering, gagging odor" when fleeing poachers.[706] John MacKinnon described the smell as "powerful, musty," while Geoffrey Bourne and Maury Cohen called it "very strong and acrid."[707]

There may be an additional malodorous component. W.H. Fahrenbach noted that gorillas will occasionally release diarrhea under these agitated conditions, similar to the manner in which dogs, cats, and humans will defecate themselves when frightened.[708]

In July 2011, a woman and her dog fell asleep while stargazing near Pennsylvania's Allegheny River. The next thing she noticed was something furry—her pet, she presumed—pawing her hand. Annoyed, she opened her eyes only to see her dog wounded and an enormous Sasquatch towering over her. The beast promptly fled the scene, releasing an odor like "rotten egg with a hint of animal kill." The abrupt departure of the Sasquatch implies surprise or fright, which in turn suggests that sudden defecation may have played a role (though no physical evidence was left behind).[709]

We are left to wonder whether every smelly Sasquatch is secretly afraid. An April 17, 2014, article from *Cryptozoology News* claimed that witnesses who have not been noticed by the creature are less likely to report an odor, a fact that would conform nicely to the notion of a fear response/deterrent.[710]

Until recently, it was assumed that all ape axillary glands were reflexive in nature, responding unconsciously to stress. In 2014, University of Stirling researchers Michelle Klailova and Phyllis C. Lee questioned that assumption by publishing their 12-month study of Makumba, a wild male silverback gorilla in the Central African Republic. They discovered that Makumba could activate his scent at will. In the presence of allies, the silverback would release an odor declaring his dominance; when unfamiliar (and therefore threatening) rivals appeared, the odor would disappear. "Our results suggest that silverback odor strength can be 'turned up' or 'turned down' as well as 'turned on' or 'turned off' as a function of the context and relationship between the emitter and perceivers," Klailova and Lee wrote.[711]

Might Sasquatch possess control over their stench as well?

"These things had to have a scent gland, to release this smell on will, because it wasn't there all the time," researcher Bobby Hamilton said. "They had to be able to release this scent... If it smelled that way all the time, it'd starve to death, because it couldn't sneak up on anything—it'd smell it."[712]

Setting aside the specious logic that the stench would undermine hunting—as we have noted, some scientists suspect canines employ foul odor to aid, not hinder, catching a meal—the literature certainly suggests Sasquatch can regulate their smell. Many witnesses report a sudden onset of odors, as if deliberately released (recall the 1978 Australian who watched a Yowie for an extended period of time before a sudden wave of stench made him vomit).

The odor's abrupt appearance calls to mind the experience of a British Columbia elk hunter who in 2007 noticed an awful smell, "worse than any bear... worse than any skunk, and [which] was almost a cross between a wet dog/dead animal." He looked up and saw a Sasquatch, which disappeared as he reached for his rifle. The odor arrived and left as if someone had "turned it on and off," BFRO investigator Blaine McMillan wrote in the follow-up report. "It did not come slowly, wafting up the valley."[713]

No one has produced a Sasquatch body to determine the prominence of these scent glands. Rumors to the contrary persist, however. A curious document—allegedly penned by a forensic expert and anatomist for the United States Department of Agriculture named "Dr. H.A. Miller"—appeared on the internet sometime after 2010. Dubbed the "Miller Document," the message claimed that Miller, under governmental supervision, extensively catalogued several species of large North American apes. Naturally, a conspiracy prevented his findings from reaching the public.

Any record whose provenance is as spotty as the Miller Document raises dozens of red flags. Veracity aside, our interest lies in a single line of text, where the purported doctor writes, "This Pacific Northwest (PNW) creature found in 1962-63 also had scent glands on her forearms. This is more evidence that *C. nerteros pacificus* is arboreal to some extent, leaving scent marks up and down the tree while climbing."[714]

If the Miller Document is indeed a hoax, the author knew enough about primate anatomy to place scent glands in the correct general area (if not the armpits themselves). It is also interesting to note that the author does not mention scent glands on southerly Sasquatch, yet Skunk Apes usually smell the worst of the lot. Such discrepancies remind us that multiple factors may be at play; to engage in reckless speculation (a favorite pastime), perhaps Pacific Northwest Sasquatch smell because of scent glands, but Skunk Apes are simply victims of their swampy environs.

If Sasquatch do have scent glands, they are presumably obscured by the creature's thick hair. Few if any sightings describe anything resembling a scent gland, though some native lore does hold that odors originate from specific areas. Amazonian natives claim that the *mapinguari* derives its foul stench from its torso, which houses a peculiar "third eye" (perhaps in actuality a scent gland).[715] Not coincidentally, a stab to the belly button is the only way to defeat the hairy giant.[716]

The 1900 testimony of Harry Colp tells of a gold prospector who encountered a troop of hideous creatures near Thomas Bay, Alaska, and may describe scent glands. "I couldn't call them anything but devils, as they were neither men nor monkeys—yet looked like both... their bodies covered with long, coarse hair, except where the scabs and running sores had replaced it... The air was full of their cries and the stench from their sores and bodies made me faint."[717] The prospector escaped the beasts in his canoe, but we are left to wonder whether the sores were actually scent glands, possibly exposed by an outbreak of mange.

With so many different smells reported in Sasquatch encounters, some have proposed that their scent gland control may not be limited to *when* they smell, but *how* they smell, drawing from a broad repertoire of odors. While on its face far-fetched, the notion would explain the vast array of smells claimed by witnesses, and there is precedent for species exuding varying scents according to different emotional states (humans, for example, release separate odors when aroused and when afraid).

In his book *Our Life with Bigfoot*, Christopher Noël shares the story of a Texas resident who, tired of the Sasquatch activity around her home, vented while mowing her lawn one day:

> All of a sudden I had this unexplainable fear, and I yelled out, "You bastards, you are *not* taking over my property!" And my heart's still pounding… So then I'm going in the back, and I haven't mowed way back by the goat house yet, I'm getting there, but the whole time I am mowing I get hit with like "Essence of Gym Locker #3," and "ode to Skunk," and the third time it smelled like dead body. And after the third time I said, "Look, I know you've got all these acres of woods, all I'm asking for is my *yard*." And I said, "Whether you like it or not, I'm mowing." And the smells quit.[718]

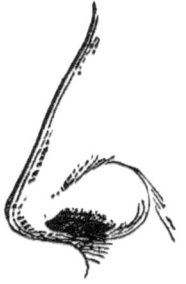

Chapter 19
Sasquatch Smells: Garbage, Decay, B.O., and Burning

About 50 yards past the footbridge, I began to smell a nauseating stench. The odor was a locker-room effluvium; a thick, noxious stench like an overweight lineman's armpit after late-summer drills.
— Bob Nelson, *Camping Out in Bigfoot's Backyard*

It almost seems—if we could ascribe an agenda to large, hairy hominids—that they wish to fill witnesses with revulsion. What could be more revolting than the stench of that which we throw away?

Garbage

A variety of accounts include descriptions of garbage-like odors coming from Sasquatch. Occasionally, the comparison is explicit—one Pennsylvania bow hunter saw what appeared to be an entire family of Sasquatch tromping through the woods of Adams County in 1997, leaving "a foul, garbage-like odor behind"[719]— but just as often, the stench of trash is implied. A camper in the eastern Sierra Nevada Mountains shone his flashlight on a huge, hairy, bipedal figure one night in June 1988, and for several hours smelled "what I thought were rotten oranges. At times it smelled very strong, like when you have a bag of fruit in your refrigerator and open it to find them green and moldy."[720]

- A farmer from Sharpsville, Indiana, went to check on his dogs one night in summer 1971, only to find them harassed by a nine-foot-tall man-beast covered in stringy hair. The creature was awkwardly taking swipes at one of the dogs, and "the smell of it almost made you want to barf, like a decaying meat and vegetable combination."[721]

- Two separate vehicles narrowly avoided hitting a Sasquatch along a rural road in Clinton County, Pennsylvania, in 1990. The driver of one vehicle stopped within 10 feet of the large brown beast, which they did not smell until it left the scene. The witnesses compared the odor to "the stench of rotting garbage."[722]

- In 2006, a Wisconsin witness biking to a friend's house near Eau Galle passed through a swamp and noticed the sound of sticks breaking. Looking in the direction of the noise, the witness saw a broadly built, seven-to-eight-foot-tall figure covered in matted hair. It screamed as he drove off, and smelled like a combination of a rotten wet dog, fish, and garbage.[723]

Numerous witnesses have described Sasquatch caught in the act of "dumpster diving," digging through human refuse ostensibly in the hope of finding edible scraps. Any creatures smelling of garbage spotted near civilization may have been soiled in the act of finding dinner (another candidate for hypothesis Exogenous Unintentional).

Decay

Perhaps the greatest missed opportunity in anomalous research is the loss of the "Minnesota Iceman," an alleged relict hominid trapped in a block of ice displayed by exhibitor Frank Hansen. When it arrived in Milwaukee, Wisconsin in autumn 1967, college

Sasquatch Smells: Garbage, Decay, B.O., and Burning 221

zoology major Terry Cullen alerted investigator Ivan T. Sanderson to the specimen. Shortly thereafter Sanderson, alongside zoologist Bernard Heuvelmans, was permitted to examine the hirsute corpse from outside its ice box. They determined it was genuine.

The body disappeared after this startling conclusion. Hansen claimed to have switched out the real exhibit for a model after a run-in with U.S. Customs officials, and that the original was in the hands of "a millionaire" (rumored to be Jimmy Stewart, who allegedly sought to suppress the evolutionary/religious implications the specimen raised). Today, all we have of the original are a series of photographs and Heuvelmans' book on the affair entitled *Neanderthal: The Strange Saga of the Minnesota Iceman*, recently translated into English by Paul LeBlond.[724]

The Iceman differed from other roadside attractions because of its apparent veracity: if a hoax, it was exceptional, seemingly covered in lice, with plant matter in its teeth. "This was no phony Chinese trick, or 'art' work," Sanderson said. "If nothing else confirmed this, the appalling stench of rotting flesh exuding from a point in the insulation of the coffin would have been enough." Apparently while inspecting the corpse, Heuvelmans had touched a hot lamp to the glass encasement, cracking it and releasing the smell of decay.[725]

Garbage odors are inextricably tied to smells of decay. Although the odor of the Minnesota Iceman was attributed to its putrefaction, it is unclear whether the beast would have smelled any better alive. Alongside wet dog and sulfur, rotting meat is described in Sasquatch encounters with great regularity. Witnesses often find themselves under the false assumption that they have stumbled upon a dead animal, or driven over some particularly rank roadkill, just prior to seeing Sasquatch.

- On August 27, 1966, Jerri Mendenhall was grabbed through her car window by a Sasquatch covered in matted, slimy hair in Fontana, California. The creature fled when she hit the accelerator but left a smell "like a dead animal."[726]

- Roachdale, Indiana, residents Randy Rogers and his sister Lou began hearing something banging on their walls and windows at night in 1972. For several weeks thereafter, a curious Sasquatch would show up each evening, stinking of "dead animal or rotting garbage."[727] It should be noted this particular case features quite a few strange happenings in addition to the hairy hominid: events began with a UFO sighting, and Lou seemed able to intuit when the beast would appear. It occasionally appeared semi-transparent, and when it ran, the creature made no sound, nor left any tracks—even when passing over mud.[728]

- On October 25, 1975, a witness in Applegate, Oregon, was sitting in a pickup truck on a logging road when his dog became agitated. A seven-foot-tall Sasquatch stepped into the open for 30 seconds, accompanied by a "dead animal" smell.[729]

- Workers set to demolish an abandoned farmstead in Florida noticed a foul odor coming from the cellar in August 1979, and assumed an animal had died in the building. To their surprise, a red-haired Skunk Ape emerged two hours later and bolted for the forest.[730]

- A large, shaggy figure startled two snowmobilers around Christmas 1980 in British Columbia, according to BFRO investigator Blaine McMillan. The shape crossed the snowy trail in a flash, leaving a smell of rotting meat and large, barefoot tracks.[731]

- In November 1987 a turkey hunter outside Meyersdale, Pennsylvania, heard trees cracking and detected a stench like "decomposed meat or seafood." Shortly thereafter, he spied a large, dark creature on the hillside above. It roared for a few moments before running away, taking the stench with it but leaving behind 19-inch footprints.[732]

- A pair of wildmen, male and child, allegedly snuck into an army barracks in Kargopol, Russia, in early 1992. A soldier on duty spotted the duo and alerted his comrades. The adult creature tried to communicate before the child became frightened, and the two fled. The soldiers described the adult as eight-feet tall, covered in light hair, and smelling of rotten meat.[733]

Many have attempted to explain why a very alive entity might smell so very dead. One witness suggested to John Green that Sasquatch roll around on rotting animal carcasses in a manner similar to canids.[734] The late Sasquatch enthusiast Datus Perry, who claimed a dozen sightings of the beast in his lifetime, naively contended that reports of Sasquatch odor were "nonsense… If bigfoot smells, it's because of rotten meat on the animal hides that it wears."[735] Never mind the fact that sightings rarely mention such couture.

More compelling are suggestions that the stench of decay is a result of bad breath. There is ample evidence that Sasquatch, like chimpanzees and humans, prefers an omnivorous diet. It seems possible that more carnivorous individuals might generate an abundance of the malodorous compounds that make both corpses and halitosis smell foul: cadaverine, putrescine, and sulfur compounds. While this may be a satisfactory explanation for odors in close-range encounters, it is a laughable suggestion in most sightings.

Still, there is at least one case providing oblique support to this theory. In September 1976, the dog of a farmer attacked a tall, hairy figure in Wisconsin, protecting its owner. The farmer noted that the beast's saliva had dripped onto his pet during the scuffle, imparting an unpleasant odor.[736]

In 1989 two newspapermen traveling near Oak Hill, Florida, caught an apelike being in their headlights around 3:30 a.m., accompanied by a gag-inducing odor similar to cabbage.[737] While not immediately apparent, the odor of cabbage could be perceived as a subset of the "garbage" or "decay" categories—the odor of dimethyl sulfide, a common compound released during composting, has an olfactory profile universally compared to that of cabbage.[738] Another sulfur connection emerges.

Like rotten meat and garbage smells, this cabbage stink may be related to diet. "Skunk cabbage and devil's club stems and roots have been noted in partially consumed states in association with Sasquatch sightings and tracks, forcibly pulled from the ground at their stem bases," wrote author J. Robert Alley.[739] Indeed, a hunter in Washington in 1984 observed a Sasquatch obliviously munching away in a cluster of skunk cabbage.[740] It takes little deduction to see where the plant gets its name—skunk cabbage smells like a skunk or rotting meat (recall that it was also once believed that witches gained their foul odor from a diet of cabbage).

Earth

The presence of dimethyl sulfide in composting naturally calls to mind the odor of earth, also described in some encounters. These smells are usually combined in the now familiar manner: "a smell like rotten meat, urine, and damp earth," "musty and earthy," etc. For example, on April 16, 1981, an Indiana witness was trudging through the snow to an outhouse when he noticed an eight-foot-tall, dark-haired form exuding a moldy, dirty smell.[741]

Such descriptions again suggest hypothesis Exogenous Unintentional, that an external, unintentional source may contribute to Sasquatch's stench. Whereas climate was a proposed factor earlier in our discussion, living quarters (i.e. dens) are also another candidate. Though Green was skeptical of the notion,[742]

Sasquatch has long been suspected of avoiding detection by holing up deep in caves and caverns, and these environs would certainly impart an earthy dampness to their fur.

"According to some of its pursuers, the creature lives in muddy and abandoned alligator caves deep in the steamy Everglades swamp," wrote Brad Steiger of the perennially foul Skunk Ape. "The gators leave the rotting remains of their kills behind to putrefy in the heat of their hideaway, and the Skunk Apes absorb the stench into their hair, thus accounting for their awful smell."[743] There is ample testimony that suspected bedding sites smell foul—a Texas witness, involved in ongoing activity, noted an abandoned building on her property was full of hay that smelled incredibly rank[744]—but it remains uncertain in these cases whether the home is fouling the sleeper, or vice versa.

A Missouri witness checked his deer lick late one evening and saw what he thought was a poacher in a ghillie suit lurking at the forest's edge; turning on his high beams, he saw a tall, muscular Sasquatch and was hit with the odor of mildew.[745] In addition to the mildew smell, the witness also noted a more familiar tone underlying the stench: human body odor.

Body Odor and Sweat

Fred Nicholas was hiking the Pennsylvanian portion of the Appalachian Trail with several friends when he felt the sudden urge to relieve himself. Stepping just off the path and behind a tree, he was instantly hit with a memorable miasma.

"It smelled like latrines and stale sweat and something left dead for a week in the summer sun," he said. "I could barely control my gag reflex." The brush all around him started rustling, and out stepped something tall, dark, and hairy. He quickly returned to his friends, who chided him for being so afraid and suggested that he had seen a tall, bearded hiker who hadn't bathed for a while.[746]

As usual, these descriptions are often inventively evocative. One West Virginia witness compared the smell to "a dirty, sweaty man who hadn't had a bath in a few years,"[747] while another likened the stench to "burning rubbish and the sweat of a hundred high-school football teams."[748] Though not as commonly reported as other odors, some researchers contend that foul body odor is the primary reason for Sasquatch's stench. These descriptions naturally overlap with much of our earlier discussion regarding scent and sebaceous glands.

- A man changing a tire on his truck near Satus Pass, Washington, in 1989 noted the "most god-awful smell… like someone with a terrible case of B.O." Afterward he spotted a Sasquatch and fled the scene. Curiously, he was plagued in the coming months by nightmares not of Sasquatch, but of alien abduction.[749]

- On December 17, 1997, two friends were sky watching from their car in Sevier County, Tennessee, when a black bear on its hind legs wandered from the woods into their headlights. Flicking on the high beams, the driver saw the "bear" turn… and shield its eyes with a humanlike hand. It was covered in dark brown hair, approximately four feet wide and eight feet tall, and watched them for several moments before rushing up the mountainside. The witnesses left and turned on their heater, filling the car with "something like strong urine and an odor of mixed sweat, and strong body odor." The stench made both witnesses gag and could not be vented by rolling down the windows.[750]

- Following a sunset picnic alongside north Georgia's Minnehaha Falls on May 23, 1998, a hiker noticed a figure squatting in the darkness. Deciding to display southern hospitality, the witness moved to greet the person when it stood, revealing a nine-to-ten-foot-tall frame outfitted in dark brown, matted hair. Wheezing, the creature took several steps before the witness fled. Prior to the sighting, he had noticed "a whiff of something smelly in the area. Not quite the smell of a dead animal, but the smell of something very musty and almost sweaty." Once the figure was sighted, the smell had become "almost overpowering" and pungent, like a "body odor and fecal smell" mix.[751]

- A Florida man literally ran into a 7-foot tall, mangy Skunk Ape in the darkness outside his home in early 2000. The creature stared at him for several moments before fleeing into the swamp, but left behind an eye-watering stench that clung to the witness. The smell was described as a mixture of a septic system, sweet garbage, and "bad body odor, like someone had never used deodorant and was out sweating for days on end." Even after an hour-long shower, the smell still persisted on his person for three days.[752]

- Officer Brandon Ware (pseudonym), a Ute Indian, saw a Sasquatch stalking Fort Duchesne, Utah's Bottle Hollow neighborhood, while on early morning guard duty. Ware spoke of his tribe's lore about the beast: "Sasquatch, he's an old man… that lives on a mountain… never takes care of himself, and just smells real bad." In his experience, Ware described it as a "dirty human being smell… like dirty bad underarms."[753]

Attributing Sasquatch's odor to sweat suggests hypothesis Endogenous Unintentional. "Hair-covered monsters … develop gaseous auras as a result of dried sweat, natural body odor, wet hair, and a high-fiber diet," author W. Haden Blackman cheekily wrote in *The Field Guide to North American Monsters*.[754] There is a primatological precedent for such scents—excited male chimpanzees have been known to exude an odor like "rancid human sweat."[755]

There is also a tantalizing medical connection. Sufferers of acromegaly, a condition of the pituitary gland, receive too much growth hormone and as a result experience excessive development, particularly in height, hand, and foot size. Acromegaly also affects the skin, causing excessive coarse hair growth, greater sebum production, increased sweating, and very offensive body odor.[756] Could similar hormonal imbalances be the reason behind the foot size, height, hair, and body odor of Sasquatch?

Finally, note that sulfur plays a role in body odor. Sweat is actually odorless; rather, bacteria produce its unpleasant odor, in the form of androstenone and androstenol (which smell musky or ammonia like) and 3-methyl-2-hexenoic acid (described as acrid or pungent). Since the 1990s, several other malodorous contributors have been isolated, including 3-hydroxy-3-methylhexanoic acid (cheesy, rancid) and, germane to the discussion at hand, 3-methyl-3-sulfanylhexan-1-ol, which contains sulfur.[757] MSH, as it is known, is one of multiple volatile sulfur compounds just recently gaining scientific attention.

The connection of sulfur to body odor can be easily demonstrated. The sweaty armpits of many individuals have undertones of onion, a vegetable whose primary flavor compounds are sulfur-containing S-alk(en)yl-L-cyestine sulfoxides. These sulfoxides produce volatile sulfur compounds not unlike body odor, as well as ammonia.[758]

Burning smells

Our theme of combustion, noted at length in spirit and UFO cases, surprisingly carries into Sasquatch accounts as well. Although there is precedent for this odor in primates—we have already noted how gorilla axillary glands smell similar to "distant burning rubber"—burning odors usually appear in more unusual Sasquatch cases. For example, initial witnesses to Stan Gordon's infamous 1973 sighting detected "a smell of burning rubber similar to that of a tire burnout on hot asphalt" when they first spotted a glowing UFO in a nearby field—recall how the case ended in a confrontation with two bulletproof Sasquatch.[759]

Similarly impervious were the Sasquatch which allegedly attacked an Oklahoma family in 2000. Dubbed the "Siege of Honobia," the events began when venison started disappearing from an outside shed. Over the course of two years, the family was plagued nightly by tall, hairy hominids with a "musky urine, burned hair type odor" prowling their property.[760] After one tried to enter the house, the women and children relocated, leaving the men behind. Following extensive phone and email conversations, BFRO investigators learned of even more activity, including an incident where a Sasquatch ran undaunted into the woods after being shot. Investigators were baffled to hear that the creatures seemed fearless in the face of gunfire, despite multiple incidents where firearms were discharged in their direction. "They'd pull back a bit in the trees, then move to a different part of the hillside and could be seen through the brush when the spotlights reflected off their eyes," one investigator noted—but they held their ground.[761]

From 1970-73, a farm in Derry Township, Pennsylvania, was regularly visited by UFOs and Sasquatch with glowing red eyes. The hairy creatures were attributed a variety of odors by various family members: most compared the smell to burning chicken feathers, though others invoked rotten meat, "chemical-like" odors, and smells similar to "when you scald a chicken or a pig." Notably, the father of the farm experienced extrasensory perception and precognition throughout the years as well.[762]

Sulfur's presence contributes to the offensive smells of burning rubber (which requires the element to be vulcanized), hair, and feathers (which use it to create strengthening keratin). Such connections may admittedly seem tenuous. The association with sulfur is much more overt, however, when witnesses describe the stench of brimstone itself.

Chapter 20
Sasquatch Smells: Sulfur, Strangeness, and Screen Memories

In many close encounters with Bigfoot, witnesses report a strong obnoxious odor which some have described as smelling similar to rotten eggs, sulphur, rotten meat, etc. Such accompanying smells are not reported in all Bigfoot incidents.

— Stan Gordon

"I noticed what I thought was a bear sitting down under a huge pecan tree on the right," the North Carolina witness said of his July 1999 sighting. "I decided to pull off to the side of the road and watch him for a minute."

The man was sitting at the intersection of NC-172 and US-17 near the Camp Lejeune Marine Corps Base, waiting to take the same turn he made every morning on his daily commute. The "bear" was sitting about 55 feet away, its back to the car.

"It was a warm July morning," he reported later. "I had the windows of my truck rolled down as usual and noticed the most ungodly smell I had ever experienced. It was kinda like rotten eggs mixed with sewage and sulfur."

The witness watched in horror as the shape rose on two feet and reached out to shake the tree. Hoping for a better look, he honked the car horn, freezing the figure until he honked again. The beast then turned, revealing a manlike countenance covered in reddish brown hair and towering nearly 10 feet tall. The Sasquatch shrieked and covered the distance to the woods in a split second. "On my way home that day I decided to stop again, and though the creature was gone I could still smell that ungodly mix of stench," the witness said. "To this day when I pass by that pecan tree my heart races."[763]

If his memory was accurate, there is no question that the witness smelled something sulfurous that summer morning. It comes as a surprise—not in the context of this book, where sulfur smells abound, but rather in the context of mammalian biology—that Sasquatch are often reported smelling of sulfur. It is important, however, to stop just short of the claim that a *majority* of Sasquatch smells are described in this fashion. Sulfur smells may only represent a plurality, equal in number to "wet dog" descriptions.

As in other anomalous cases, this stench is frequently evoked in a generic way. These vague odors are commonly just another symptom among many suggesting (but not confirming) Sasquatch's presence: cries in the night, rocks tossed into campsites, and eerie feelings of being watched. For instance, a couple summering in Charlevoix, Michigan, was surprised to find their 2008 vacation interrupted by deep moans, animalistic screams, and an extremely strong smell combining sulfur and human waste "mixed with the strongest male body odor I have ever encountered." BFRO investigator T.L. Kimball interviewed the wife, stating, "The witness cannot stress enough how powerful and overwhelming the first occurrence of the odor was."[764]

Other encounters with the sulfur stench are more tolerable. Several friends staying in a cabin just north of Grantsburg, Wisconsin, in the autumn of 1985 heard strange rustling noises on an evening walk and were hit with a foul mixture of "rotten meat, sulfur, and musk all rolled into one." Notably, the odor "didn't quite smell as bad as a skunk." The witnesses also heard snaps and splashes as though they were being followed.

Everyone was awoken early the following morning by "the silhouette of a head and large broad shoulders" in one of the windows. "It looked like a guy with a really big head wearing a furry hood" with forward-set eyes that "were lightly glowing orange-red." One of the party shut the shades and, with a peculiar nonchalance, simply fell back to sleep.[765]

This seeming disinterest in astounding events occurs in UFO sightings as well, particularly abductee and contactee encounters. That, coupled with the glowing eyes—a feature nonexistent in nature, not to mention primates—should give any intellectually honest researcher pause.

The theory that Sasquatch is an undiscovered ape suffers from the same problems of the Extraterrestrial Hypothesis in UFOlogy: it is a tidy explanation for an extremely untidy phenomenon. It is something of a dirty secret in the Sasquatch community that no small number of sightings include supernatural details. While some seek to downplay the frequency of these reports, strange things happen all the time: Sasquatch vanish, leave three-toed footprints, appear in conjunction with strange lights and UFOs, and, as mentioned earlier, are apparently bulletproof. Like UFOs, there are even examples of Sasquatch's presence stalling car engines[766] and damaging electrical components.[767] Less dramatic but equally strange are Sasquatch footprints whose trail suddenly stops cold in the middle of open fields, or the glaring fact that the corpses of gigantic apes are somehow very, very hard, if not impossible, to find.

The mental gymnastics Sasquatch researchers engage in to explain away such discrepancies are legion. Glowing eyes are eye shine (even in cases where no light source is present), disappearing Sasquatch are just fast (despite their literal evaporation in front of some witnesses), and the ability to shrug off gunfire is thanks to their robust build.

Smells appear in these High Strangeness cases with regularity. In his seminal work *Silent Invasion*, which covers the Pennsylvania UFO/Sasquatch flap of the early 1970s, Stan Gordon listed more than a dozen Sasquatch cases where the smell of sulfur or sulfur compounds was noted; while not always connected with anomalous lights, there is certainly an implied link, given the region's concurrent UFO activity.[768]

Most of Gordon's cases involve the perplexing detail of self-illuminating eyes. On July 31, 1973, a figure with red glowing eyes peeked in a window eight feet off the ground in Greensburg. The witness, who had just finished his evening shave, noticed "a foul odor of cucumber or something" and looked outside to see the prowler. Other witnesses in the house compared the odor to sulfur. Sulfurous beasts with glowing red eyes were also spotted that year in Merrittstown (July), Kingston (August), and Alverton (September).[769]

This stench had a profound effect upon witnesses during the flap. The hairy thing that ran atop the roof of a Monongahela witness in August had a sulfurous odor so strong the witness "could hardly breathe. Her eyes were watering and her nose seemed to become dry."[770] The next month, residents of Jeannette's Silver Dolphin Mobile Home Court noticed strange footprints and a strange sulfur stench—one woman walked outside and promptly vomited.[771]

Much more explicit High Strangeness was reported by a group of young boys on January 10, 1980, in—you guessed it—Pennsylvania. The youths were walking outside one evening when a tall, hairy figure with reddish brown hair and luminescent red eyes appeared before them, accompanied by a strong sulfur stench and a strange white light. The creature tossed rocks at the boys before disappearing.[772]

Lest it seem like just a local phenomenon, sulfurous Sasquatch with odd characteristics have been spotted outside Pennsylvania. Recall the bulletproof beasts of Honobia and Noxie, Oklahoma, or the famed Beast of Whitehall, New York. Usually described as having glowing eyes, the monster appeared in October 1987 to a security guard who said that the creature smelled sulfurous and vanished once he shouted a prayer.[773]

The September 28, 1975, edition of the *Cincinnati Enquirer* ran a story on an "ape" terrorizing the citizens of Joplin, Missouri—it also sported "red glowing eyes" and smelled of sulfur.[774] Two years later, a pair of boys near Eaton, Ohio, was pursued by a tall, hairy hominid smelling like rotten eggs with glowing eyes. The beast disappeared as they reached their home.[775]

A good example of the manner in which Sasquatch, poltergeist, and UFO pageantry blend together comes from a 1976 Spanish case collected by Manuel Ramírez and translated by Scott Corrales. Early in the morning on July 10, several young photography enthusiasts reached a vacation house in Fuengirola, a location that had allegedly experienced livestock mutilation and flying saucer activity in the days prior. Shortly after their arrival, the witnesses noticed a heavy, raspy breathing outside the home, which disappeared when they went to investigate. The noises resumed shortly before dawn, and the group stealthily crept to the window nearest its source.

Outside, they saw the outline of a "man," extremely tall with two glowing eyes. Panicking, the group gained enough composure to grab fighting implements and charged outside. The figure was gone, but a curious heat and powerful sulfur odor lingered. Returning indoors, the remaining hours of darkness were filled with strange shadows, sounds on the roof, and unidentified rapping[776] (it is ironic—damning, some might say—that a group of photographers failed to document the activity).

We would be remiss in failing to acknowledge the curious "sulfur name game" that follows Sasquatch. In his book *The Beast of Boggy Creek: The True Story of the Fouke Monster*, author Lyle Blackburn emphasizes the staggering number of sightings along the Sulphur River between Arkansas and Texas, going so far as to suggest that the inaccessible river bottoms are the creature's home.[777] In neighboring Oklahoma, the town of Sulphur boasts local legends of a large, hairy hominid.[778] The BFRO has catalogued sightings near Sulphur Creek (Alabama),[779] Sulphur Creek Camp (Washington),[780] White Sulphur Springs (Montana),[781] and Sulphur Spring Road (California).[782] No other anomalous activity seems quite as tied to the word as Sasquatch.

None of this is to suggest that Sasquatch is deliberately choosing to appear in locales with sulfurous monikers. Rather, it is to shed light on the possibility that—like the weirdness associated with UFOs—some aspect of the Sasquatch phenomenon operates in a much weirder, twilight realm, a space where modern science is unable or afraid to go, where something tugs at frayed strings from the fabric of reality.

Sulfur dioxide and hydrogen sulfide

If sulfur-exuding primates seem counterintuitive, apes reeking of SO_2 sound downright fanciful. Indeed, the few accounts involving the smell of burning sulfur contain similar High Strangeness. A letter written by Nathaniel G. Squire and published in a Bracken County, Kentucky, newspaper in February 1866 told of a bright burst of light that shook the community, accompanied by "a smell of burning sulfur." The light manifested "a creature of gigantic stature, and the most horrifying appearance. It was nearly as high as the comb of the cabin, and had a monstrous head not similar [sic] in shape to that of an ape; two very short white horns appeared above each eye, and its arms were long, covered with shaggy hair of an ashen hue, and terminated with huge paws, not unlike those of a cat, and armed with huge and hooked claws." After three seconds, the creature vanished in a burst of flame.[783]

H_2S, on the other hand, appears in cases a bit more mundane (well, at least as mundane as seeing a giant apeman can be). The odor is one of the most commonly noted smells in Sasquatch encounters. Though often reported with the familiar "rotten egg" description, comparisons to flatus, natural gas, and sewage all describe H_2S (sewage smells are quite suggestive of the compound, since it is generated in great concentrations where feces is decomposed in oxygen's absence).

As with UFO cases, it is impossible to tell how many individuals describing "sulfur" actually mean H_2S. It remains possible that other descriptions, like "garbage" and "rotten meat," are the result

Sasquatch Smells: Sulfur, Strangeness, and Screen Memories   237

of H$_2$S as well. This succinct list should help emphasize how often the stench appears.

- **Marshall, Michigan: May 1956.** A huge, black, hairy creature snatches up two workers. It drops them after a friend turns on the headlights of his nearby automobile and grabs his gun.[784] The clothes of all three are permanently imbued with a rotten egg odor.[785]

- **Ojai, California: August 1964.** A witness sees a Sasquatch emerge from a thicket, accompanied by a smell like "a horrendous fart." He cocks the hammer of his carbine but has a change of heart. The creature crosses the firebreak and returns to the forest.[786]

- **British Columbia, Canada: October 1965.** A family traveling to Fort St. John watches a large hairy figure cross the Alaska Highway. "A lingering smell of egg" is noted.[787]

- **Myrtle Point, Oregon: Autumn 1971.** A Sasquatch walks by a glass door, causing the witness to faint. The sighting was preceded by the smell of a septic tank.[788]

- **Youngstown, Pennsylvania: September 1, 1973.** A young lady visiting a cemetery detects the "strong stench of rotten eggs," only to look up and see a "large, hairy apelike creature walking out of the nearby woods."[789]

- **Northwest River Park, Virginia: June 1981.** A crash rouses camper Sherry Davis, who turns on her headlights. She sees a seven-foot-tall hairy creature for 15 seconds, accompanied by the smell of "an uncovered septic tank."[790]

- **York County, Maine: September 15, 1988.** A group of Boy Scouts and six campers see a red-haired creature digging at the ground on Katahdin Mountain. It stinks of rotten eggs, an odor that lingers after it walks into the trees.[791]

- **Byng, Oklahoma: October 1992.** A youth playing in her parents' camper sees a fawn rush out of the forest, pursued by a red-haired Sasquatch that smells like sewage.[792]

- **Clackamas County, Oregon: January 1996.** A couple out hiking discovers an abandoned mineshaft. Upon entering, the wife notes a "dead smell, combined with sewer" inside. Her flashlight falls upon a silver-grey haired figure sitting against the wall, its arms around its knees. She flees.[793]

- **Muscle Shoals, Alabama: January 12, 2005.** Two witnesses run home after a Sasquatch steps out the trees during their deer hunt. The duo describes the smell of something "deader than dead… similar to rotten eggs and earthy, as well as smelling like the creature hadn't bathed ever."[794]

- **East Canton, Ohio: September 9, 2011.** A father and son smell an "odor of rotten eggs and rotted flesh" in the woods. Shortly thereafter they spy a tall, hairy bipedal figure and observe it for several minutes before leaving in fear.[795]

- **Ruskin, Florida: March 29, 2012.** A motorist sees a man-like, hairy creature in broad daylight on I-75. Her window, which is cracked open on the passenger side, lets in "a terrible odor like rotten eggs, sulphur, or something bad" that takes 10 minutes to dissipate.[796]

- **Ludowici, Georgia: May 30, 2014.** Owners of a property plagued by shrieks, howls, anomalous footfalls, and the smell of rotten eggs see a Sasquatch run across their lawn.[797]

Sasquatch Smells: Sulfur, Strangeness, and Screen Memories 239

What causes such a consistent H_2S presence? When challenged on Sasquatch's odor, Datus Perry not only proffered the "rotten animal hide" explanation, but also suggested "maybe Bigfoot is farting."[798] This attitude was mirrored in the speculation of Dale Drinnon, who similarly suggested that "sulfurous fumes... can come from the small intestine" of the creatures.[799]

In her 2005 essay on High Strangeness Sasquatch cases, MUFON investigator Sharon Cornet noted that "people who lack an adequate amount of certain enzymes may excrete more H_2S from their sweat glands, bowels, and skin," suggesting large hairy hominids may be similarly afflicted. Additionally, a diet high in sulfur-rich foods would contribute to Sasquatch flatus.[800]

While it is true that the compound is produced in all mammalian digestive tracts, it seems an unlikely cause for the presence of H_2S in so many cases, unless it is some sort of defense reflex akin to gorilla diarrhea. In spite of her dietary hypothesis, Cornet counters this argument by noting how few (if any) cases offer visual or auditory support for the flatus theory (i.e. no one sees diarrhea after, nor hears flatus during, encounters where H_2S is detected).[801] Overall, using hypothesis Endogenous Unintentional to explain H_2S does not seem a particularly rich vein of speculation.

Taking a different approach, Cornet put forth the possibility that the H_2S smell could be environment related (Exogenous Unintentional). The odor occurs "near areas of geothermal activity, volcanism, active plate tectonics, and fault lines," as well as around "exposed or subsurface granitic plutons (areas with granite rock), mines (open pit quarries or shafts), water wells, underground streams, underground caverns or caves (karst caves or igneous rock caves, sandstone, and gypsum caves as well), forested and mountainous locations, etc."—all, of course, locations where Sasquatch is seen. It is possible such miasmas are infusing Sasquatch with this stench, or (more coincidentally and less likely) that witness are conflating geographic odors with the smell of the creature.

In his book *Bigfoot Film Journal*, Christopher L. Murphy went so far as to wonder if Sasquatch "might bath [sic] in hot springs and thereby retain a 'rotten egg' smell (which truly takes one aback) caused by the sulphur in the water." While most primates eschew water, Sasquatch has an established affinity of lakes, rivers, and damp climes. Murphy also astutely points out how "some monkeys in Asia… are known to bathe in hot springs."[802] The idea may have some merit—after all, Harrison Hot Springs in British Columbia is reputedly a hotbed of sightings.[803]

Such speculation falls apart, however, when one considers the manner in which Sasquatch's stench seems to come and go as it pleases. As already noted, the literature is full of sightings where the odor seems under the entity's control, a fact hypothesis Exogenous Unintentional fails to take into consideration.

What if the answer to why Sasquatch smells lies not in one explanation, but rather two separate notions—are we erroneously lumping two separate phenomena together?

High Strangeness and Screen Memory Sasquatch

On November 30, 1966, a young lady was changing her flat tire near Brooksville, Florida, when she heard a rustling in the woods and was hit with a disgusting odor. From the side of the road rose a huge, hairy beast that was, for no apparent reason, glowing green. The creature watched the terrified witness for a moment before casually sauntering into the brush. In January of the following year, the beast appeared again to frighten four other girls near Elfers, Florida, who reported a nauseating-smelling "chimpanzee" that stood on the hood of their car. "It was greenish in color, with glowing green eyes," a witness confirmed.[804]

Needless to say, there are no examples of glowing primates in modern mammalogy.

Western society is obsessed with absolutes. The dictatorship of empiricism demands that things are or aren't, with little room for the excluded middle. One simply needs to observe the ebb and flow of left-right politics in America to see how little tolerance we have for ideas in the center.

Most explanations of Sasquatch fall into similar traps. Either it is real or it isn't. If it is real, Sasquatch is either an undiscovered primate, or something far stranger; if the former, it's either man or beast, and if the latter, either a spirit or an alien.

It is disingenuous to suggest that all Sasquatch sightings can be answered by conventional biology. It is equally disingenuous to ignore the fact that a great many sightings exhibit typical primate behavior and physiology: hooting, piloerection (hair standing on end), conical heads, bluff charging, etc.

But there is a moderate approach by which we can reconcile mundane and bizarre sightings. Consider the possibility that some witnesses see undiscovered primates, while others see something far stranger *that is utilizing the imagery* of an undiscovered primate.

The notion has precedent in esoteric thought. Mike Clelland, experiencer and author of *The Messengers: Owls, Synchronicity and the UFO Abductee*, has long noted how owls gravitate toward those experiencing psychic phenomena and UFO activity. Clelland doesn't deny that, to borrow from Freud, an owl is sometimes just an owl. There are flesh-and-blood birds that fly through the forests on whispery wings, eat, drink, breathe, and defecate (to put it politely).

But occasionally the owls are stranger. For some, they appear when speaking about UFOs. Others note how owls accompany synchronicities, those deeply profound coincidences we all experience in our lives. In some instances, it is owl imagery, rather than the birds themselves, which intrudes on the daily lives of those thinking and writing about the occult (synchronistically enough, the writing of this particular passage was interrupted by an individual wearing an owl-emblazoned sweater).

Most blatantly, owls seem to be employed as "screen memories," a term UFOlogists use to describe false recollections projected into the minds of abductees. A motorist's waking memory of three owls in the road, for example, may reveal itself under hypnotic regression to be a repressed memory of three Grey aliens in the road. The owl's defining features—its large ocular sockets and small beak—make a clear analogue for the large eyes and small mouth abductees attribute to their captors.

What if—not unlike Clelland's owls—there is an actual, biological Sasquatch roaming the woods, whose imagery is sometimes employed by anomalous forces as a screen memory?

Differentiating between the two is not an original idea. Keel, for example, used glowing eyes as a signifier to separate biological Sasquatch from their paranormal brethren. This isn't necessarily claiming that "supernatural" Sasquatch are aliens or spirits—we may never divine their true origins—only to suggest that they be studied separately from more orthodox sightings.

What *is* original is the idea that odor could provide a clue as to which Sasquatch are biological and which are paranormal. It seems that burning odors, along with sulfurous smells, are more common in High Strangeness Sasquatch sightings. By contrast, more animalistic odors—smells of ammonia, feces, wet dog—are detected when Sasquatch exhibit more traditionally primatological behavior.

As bizarre as tales of Sasquatch may be, the concept of a large, hairy hominid is easy to comprehend. There is historical precedent for such animals in the fossil record—and it is a small leap in logic to postulate their survival into the modern era. More difficult to conceive are the truly bizarre creatures that lurk in the shadows of reality, beasts defying modern science by their very presence. These are the misfits of Forteana, the half-human horrors and malevolent monsters whose existence seems impossible.

Part V: Other Anomalous Smells

Chapter 21
Other Anomalous Smells:
Various Entity and Monster Odors

Research records show again and again, when humanoids are near, so is an odor.

— Leonard Stringfield

The Chilean newspaper *El Constituyente* published a letter from the directors of a Copiapó copper mine on March 18, 1868. The fantastic story, as translated by Spain-based UFOlogist Christopher Aubeck, tells of a strange unidentified creature that flew over the work site one evening:

> It passed over just above our heads and we could see the strange structure of its body. Its great wings were covered in brownish feathers; the head of the monster looked like that of a lobster and its eyes open wide and bright like embers, and it seemed to be covered in something resembling thick hair, like a sow. Its body was long like a snake's and only bright scales could be seen on it, which sounded like metallic pieces when the strange animal moved them… Some claim they detected a terrible smell in those moments, a smell similar to arsenic when it is burnt. Others say their senses were not so injured in such an odd manner. The superstitious be-

lieve it was the devil himself who they saw pass over, while others remember having witnessed, in that city, years ago, the passing of a similar monstrous bird.[805]

Though technically unidentified, flying, and an object, the 1868 Copiapó creature fails to adhere to traditional UFOlogical lore. The best researchers can do is heap the sighting onto the cryptid pile as an unexplained airborne animal.

There is a plethora of unexplained phenomena defying categorization, and as usual, it is impossible to be comprehensive. Our survey of smells draws to a close with a whirlwind tour of the truly weird.

Star jelly

One of Forteana's more confounding marvels is the appearance of "star jelly," a gelatinous substance of unknown origin found on grass and in trees. In Welsh, the substance was called *pwdr sêr* (pronounced "pie-dre-th ser,"[806] meaning "star rot"), while more modern names include astral jelly, star shot, or the clinical designation *astromyxin*. Usually translucent or dingy white, the stinky goo was said to fall to earth during meteor showers[807] (ancient man held that meteors could spread miasmas and plagues with their passing).[808]

In addition to the aforementioned rains of sulfur, appearances of star jelly are loosely connected to other anomalous falls from the sky, such as rotten meat. In 1841, a Tennessee tobacco field was showered with foul-smelling blood, fat, and tissue from a red cloud.[809] Over the centuries a number of explanations have been proposed to answer such riddles, evolving over time to include everything from vulture vomit to faulty airline toilet systems, all failing to provide a satisfactory explanation.

By all accounts, star jelly smells awful. Professor Rufus Graves published an article in the *American Journal of Science* on an August 13, 1819, glob of star jelly he had the privilege of examining; the material had fallen to earth in a "brilliant white light" and exuded an "offensive, suffocating smell…producing nausea and dizziness."[810] On October 26, 1846, a four-foot lump of star jelly landed in Lowell, Massachusetts; it was by all accounts "extremely odiferous."[811] More recently, two women driving near Sturgis, Michigan, felt their car stall at 3:00 a.m. on June 10, 1982, when strange lights appeared in the sky above them, raining brown slime smelling of rotten eggs.[812]

The sulfur connection is compelling, echoed in an experience relayed by occultist Austin Osman Spare. Spare, who worked with famed magician Aleister Crowley, claimed in his last year of life to have given a magical talisman to fellow occultist Gerald B. Gardner. "Clanda," an associate of Gardner's, employed the talisman at a magic rite, where she suffered visions of "a huge bird that gripped her in its talons and carried her off into the night." Though no one at the ceremony saw the entity, they did experience a cold chill and discover claw marks on a window frame. The sill was smeared with a gelatinous material that pulsed as if breathing, creating "a strong odor of the sea" that "permeated the temple for days"—recall how the seaside derives its odor from dimethyl sulfide.[813]

Water monsters

If spirits haunt our homes, UFOs fill our skies, and Sasquatch patrol our forests, it seems equally likely that monsters swim in our lakes, rivers, and oceans. Cultures worldwide hold that creatures of varying description lurk beneath the waves, and at least some of them stink.

Smells among water monsters are not altogether common for several reasons. First, like UFOs, sightings of these creatures tend to take place at great distances. Second, it seems that water dilutes or dampens any odor not noticed in extreme proximity.

One exception to this rule are stinky "globsters," massive lumps of gelatinous organic material found on beaches the world over.

Such finds stretch into antiquity; for example, a Norwegian folktale describes the remains of a sea serpent on the shores of Helgöy (Helgøy) Island, which had to be hauled out to sea to rid the isle of its putrid stench.[814] In the modern era, most globsters appear to be hunks of whale blubber, deriving their stench from decay—as such, we focus our attention on what appear to be living, genuinely anomalous specimens.

Odors from living water monsters do exist, though most are vague. On July 24, 1923, J.A. Johnson described a horned, alligator-like beast that rose from Alkali Lake, Nebraska. Keeping with native lore, it produced "a very distinctive and somewhat unpleasant odor noticeable for several moments before the beast had vanished into the water."[815] W. Haden Blackman chalks the Alkali Lake Monster's odor up to "the result of rotting plant or animal matter, which attaches to the hides of these creatures."[816]

Other cultures describe equally awful odors, but are no more explicit. Amazonian natives are wary of both of the "tapir nymph" and the "water jaguar" when traversing the river; while the former is simply smelly, the latter's oily odor renders prey unconscious.[817] Similar legends from Japan warn of the *akkorokamui*, a large cephalopod whose ink smells unbearably awful.[818]

When specified, water monster odors are often icthyc in nature. Edward Brian McCleary's fantastic testimony claimed he evaded a sea serpent while diving in Pensacola Bay, Florida, on March 24, 1962. The beast smelled like dead fish and allegedly claimed the lives of four friends.[819] A similar stench was recorded in 1830 by Captain Stockdale of the HMS *Rob Roy*, who saw an enormous, 129-foot long "sea snake" that came "so close I could even smell his nasty fishy smell."[820]

Crew aboard another sailing vessel, the *Fort Salisbury*, beheld a glowing, scaled "monster" riding alongside the ship on October 28, 1902. Witness A.H. Raymer wrote: "a strong odor like that of a low-tide beach on a summer day pervaded the air." The odor was likely dimethyl sulfide, though it is debatable whether the "monster" was a living creature, or some submersible machine.[821]

On June 22, 1902, the *Duluth News Tribune* published an article about a monster in Lake Superior. Dubbed a "huge fish of the 'electrical' variety," the creature interfered with compasses between Knife Island and Devil's Island (shades of UFO interference). According to the story, watchmen aboard the ship alerted their captain to a smell of musk, "as though we had a cargo of muskrats aboard." At that moment, an unseen, bellowing beast began circling the boat, covering the ship (and its captain) in "some sort of oily substance having a most disagreeable odor."[822]

Musky smells are also associated with North America's lake monster celebrity, Champ. For centuries, residents along Lake Champlain have spotted the creature from the shores of New York, Vermont, and Quebec. Many researchers hold that the lake may host a relict aquatic species—popular candidates are the long-necked *plesiosaur* or *tanystropheus*—capable of navigating both land and water.

The evening after her first water sighting, researcher Katy Elizabeth claimed to detect a distinct smell on the shore, accompanied by the sound of a heavy animal running into the lake. Elizabeth described the odor as "musky," a scent confirmed by fellow researcher Dennis Hall.

"It smelled like a snake," Hall said of the smell he noticed just prior to seeing Champ. "Strong, snaky, skunky, musky… wicked strong, sickening strong, heavy."[823] Anyone entering a pet store specializing in reptiles can attest to this odor. Depending on the species, the smell of snakes is compared to skunk spray, mouse droppings, garlic, wet dog, or billy goat musk (more on that later), augmented with a healthy dose of feces released when the animals are handled roughly.[824]

Winged things

Admittedly, the existence of water monsters—obscured by waves and tide, lurking in hidden depths—is a greater possibility than the notion of dragons among the clouds or patrolling the countryside. So it may come as a surprise to learn that people have claimed such sightings.

These accounts are dubious. For example, a short entry in the April 21, 1895 edition of San Francisco's *The Call* mentions a group of children frightened by an aggressive red dragon dwelling in an abandoned mine behind Old Sausalito. Reading between the lines, the likelihood increases that the anonymous author—who wrote that the children were gathering poppies when they smelled the beast's "musky" odor—may have been chasing a different kind of "dragon."[825] A similarly described (and equally fanciful) creature was supposedly encountered near Bakersfield nine years prior: pungent, red, and angry.[826]

Reports from other countries are marginally more believable, if only because their heritage references such creatures. Chinese legend is replete with depictions of flying (though wingless) dragons; in August 1944, a black dragon supposedly fell from the sky along the shores of the Mudan River in Heilongjiang province. Once it reached the ground, the creature was on the verge of death and covered in flies, attracted by its strong icthyc smell.[827] Around the same time, Marjorie Courtenay-Latimer interviewed a Namibian boy who saw a huge flying "snake" that smelled like burning brass and landed with a loud noise, knocking him out.[828] The sighting resonates with African legends of the *kikiyaon*, a flying creature whose smell is "said to resemble a dead serpent that has been lying in the sun," with a cry "likened to the sound of a person being strangled to death."[829]

The UFO community invariably seizes upon such cases and labels them spacecraft. They are equally apt to adopt tales of flying humanoids, like the "flying mummy" whose presence created the smell of ozone in an Ohio motorist's car in May 2014.[830] Perhaps UFOlogy is justified in taking such orphan cases, as they are usually too odd to fit into any other category.

In *The Mothman Prophecies*, John Keel postulated that the lack of sickly sweet or sulfurous odors in most flying humanoid cases "could indicate some subtle difference in the basic structure of

Other Anomalous Smells: Various Entity and Monster Odors 251

these creatures" as compared to more odiferous entities.[831] Indeed, many flying humanoids seem devoid of odor (likely because of their distance from the witness). Notable exceptions are the *aswang*, a vampire of the Philippines with lethal flatulence,[832] and its analogue of the Zanzibar Islands, *popo bawa*.[833] When modern sightings of flying humanoids include odors, they are described generically (e.g. unpleasant, foul, etc.).

One smelly flying humanoid of note was the Van Meter Visitor. When the gargoyle-like fiend descended upon the eponymous Iowa town in autumn 1903, it caused quite a ruckus. Over the course of several evenings, multiple townspeople saw the entity, which was soon joined by a second—on one occasion, the town doctor even opened fire upon the horned, winged creature at point blank range, to no effect. Events came to a close when a posse allegedly drove the entities down an abandoned mineshaft.

All encounters with the Visitors made note of their putrid, stupefying, overpowering odor. As in most flying humanoid cases, descriptions of this odor were vague, and its origin remains unknown.[834]

El chupacabras

In the spring of 1995, Puerto Rican farmers began reporting the unexplained deaths of their livestock. Animals were found exsanguinated across the island; what few witnesses caught the perpetrators in the act reported a short, impish figure, sometimes winged, akin to a Grey alien with a row of spikes down its spine.

Locals dubbed the beast *el chupacabras*, "the sucker of goats," globally Anglicanized in popular culture as "chupacabra." There is strong evidence suggesting the entity's description was based upon the alien from the 1995 film *Species*[835]—pop-culture inspiration aside, livestock were (and are still) dying mysteriously in Puerto Rico.

Those who claim to have spotted the creature report the stench of brimstone. One terrified witness told author Benjamin Radford that she inferred the chupacabra's presence by its sulfurous odor.[836] In his book *Chupacabras and Other Mysteries*, Scott Corrales recorded multiple cases where sulfur was noted in conjunction with chupacabra attacks.

Not only do the beasts smell of brimstone themselves, but the sulfur stench clings to mutilation sites,[837] as evidenced by the slaughtered pigs of farmer Heítor Paniago (though Paniago's livestock were completely exsanguinated, it should be noted their intestines were also exposed, and any gastrointestinal tract fissure would naturally vent H_2S).[838] In another instance, the creature left behind a sulfurous "yellow goo" after draining a colt of blood. Other witnesses likened the smell to battery acid or paint thinner.[839]

In recent years, many witnesses started applying the term "chupacabra" to hairless dogs preying upon livestock in the American southwest. It is unclear why the name took hold so strongly. What *is* clear is that the animals are *not* the same things seen in Puerto Rico—most seem to be coyotes (or coyote-dog hybrids) with a case of mange. It should be noted that an infection of scabies could also result in hair loss and would be accompanied by a putrid smell.[840]

Some contend that these "Texas Blue Dogs" have abnormal features pointing to more mysterious origins. For example, even mangy animals will display patches from their once-thick coat, yet the blue dogs have skin similar to an elephant's. They also have blue eyes, strange nodules near the tail, shorter forelimbs, and two nipples rather than the usual ten. Their skulls are also inconsistent with those of coyotes.[841]

Researchers Ken Gerhard and Jon Downes have suggested that the blue dogs display genetic mutations from environmental pollution. Gerhard and Downes noted that sightings of the animals in south Texas are generally in the vicinity of coal burning plants, which release immense amounts of SO_2. While we have discussed this sulfur compound at length, we have not addressed the fact that it is a mutagen, affecting mammalian development in the womb—this could, at least conceptually, contribute to the creatures' appearance.[842]

Black cats and dogs

Unlike the other subjects in this book, we know that large black cats and dogs exist. We can go to the zoo and watch a panther, or adopt a black Labrador from the animal shelter. They seem mundane.

Fortean interest piques when large black cats are seen darting across the British Isles, which boast no large native feline species, or when black dogs with eyes like glowing embers blink into existence at lonely crossroads. Even when panthers are seen in upper North America, they pose a conundrum: while cougars are native to the United States, there are no confirmed examples of melanistic (all-black) individuals.

Such felines are referred to as Alien Black Cats (ABCs)—"alien" in the strange, rather than extraterrestrial, sense—and can sometimes be smelled. Witnesses at Bushylease Farm in Surrey, England, saw an ABC throughout the winter of 1962-63, accompanied by howls and the odor of ammonia.[843]

On April 10, 1970, a truck driven by Mike Busby of Cairo, Illinois, stopped without warning. Stepping outside to examine the problem, Busby noticed two eyes glowing in the forest. Whatever it was leapt upon Busby, shredding his torso with its claws. Though it seemed bipedal, Busby had a feline impression of his attacker, which smelled like wet hair.[844]

Again, we see the electronic difficulties common in unexplained events, something unexpected in tales of flesh-and-blood felines. Some sightings are even more bizarre—ABCs regularly fraternize with the most extreme phenomena, appearing in areas beset by UFO sightings and other strange events. For example, in a February 2016 interview on the *SasWhat* podcast, cryptozoologist Loren Coleman said that it was "very easy" to find overlaps between ABC reports and Sasquatch flaps.[845]

When the town was in the midst of its 1978 Sasquatch flap, multiple Minerva, Ohio, residents watched two cougars from Evelyn Clayton's front porch. According to researcher Ron Schaffner, a large, hairy biped stepped out of the brush and in front of the cats, seemingly as a protective gesture. After about 10 minutes, all three creatures quietly walked away, leaving a lingering odor of ammonia and sulfur.[846]

Typically, large cats—like their pint-sized brethren—are fastidious groomers, removing any strong odors that might tip off prey.[847] In Greek mythology, on the other hand, the panther has a naturally pleasing fragrance, which it uses to ensnare its dinner. "The beast's delightful smell is involved in the arts of venery, magic, and amorous seduction," writes Annick Le Guérer in *Scent: The Essential and Mysterious Powers of Smell*. "It has also, in an odd transmutation, become a motif in Christian symbolism, the panther's capture representing the effect of Christ's words upon the soul."[848] The only beast able to resist this aroma was the dragon.[849] We will return to the panther's beguiling scent and symbolism later.

If the panther traditionally represents Christ, the black dog represents Satan. The hellhound is a worldwide motif dating back to Cerberus, multi-headed dog of the Greek Underworld. The iconography is particularly prevalent in the British Isles, where it is called a variety of names: Barghest, Bargtjest, Black Shuck, Old Shuck, etc.

The mysterious canid appears in sightings alongside deserted country lanes, frequently with glowing eyes and a build as large as a small horse. In one famous tale, Old Shuck appeared in churches in Bungay and Blythburgh, England, where it killed congregants, ruined the church clock (mechanical interference again), and left claw marks on the door that can be seen to this day.

Naturally, these black dogs were accompanied by the strong smell of brimstone. One story tells of a farmer in Dartmoor, England, who heard animal footsteps behind him, only to turn and see a large black dog. He tried to pet it, but his hand passed through the creature, which issued "a stream of sulphurous vapor" and ran to a crossroads, disappearing in a flash.[850]

In his 1890 *English Fairy and Other Folk Tales*, Edwin Sidney

Hartland wrote:

> In Norfolk, and in some parts of Cambridgeshire, the same kind of apparition is well known to the peasantry by the name of "Shuck," the provincial word for shag. Here he is said chiefly to haunt churchyards, but other lonesome places are not secure from his visitations. Thus a dreary lane, in the parish of Overstrand, is called, from his frequent visits there, Shuck's Lane. The spot on which he has been seen, if examined soon after his disappearance, is found to be scorched, and strongly impregnated with the smell of brimstone![851]

Note the curious "shag/shuck" connection, which etymologically ties black dogs to the famous Shag Harbour UFO incident.

Modern sightings persist in the most unlikely of places. For instance, rumors in San Antonio, Texas, whisper of a large black dog smelling of sulfur that prowls San Jose Mission.[852] In December 1991, a witness near the Cannock Chase—an English forest renowned for its peculiar happenings—was drawn to an odd patch of fog. Stepping closer, he was hit with the stench of brimstone, setting his hair on end. From the mist appeared a dog the size of "a young horse," a mix of German Shepherd and Pit Bull. The apparition prepared to charge the witness, causing him to back away; the dog followed suit, and the two lost sight of one another. The witness then watched as a luminous orb hovered over the patch of fog as it dissipated.[853]

Once more, High Strangeness enters the picture: like Sasquatch, black dogs are sometimes seen in conjunction with UFOs. Alan Godfrey, whose abduction we have mentioned before, recalled interacting with an entity named "Joseph," who, along with his large black dog, smelled foul.[854]

An especially vague-yet-intriguing tale related by—of all people—abductee Betty Hill describes a group of friends out UFO hunting in Eliot, Maine, in 1966. The friends had pulled into a gravel pit to skywatch when an unnaturally large dog ran past their cars. The party took chase except for the last friend in line, who was stopped by an odd, unplaceable odor. After a moment, he perceived an ominous figure in the pit, the apparent source of the smell, and was compelled to follow it as it glided away. He barely managed to exert enough willpower to remain behind.[855]

Man-things

During the 1760s, the Gevaudan region of southern France found itself under siege by a large, peculiar wolf. The enormous beast killed hundreds of men, women, and children, and those few who managed to survive spoke of its "evil smell." After much effort, hunter Jean Chastel at last felled the beast with bullets fashioned from a silver chalice, which had also been blessed by a priest. The corpse was taken to Versailles for display, but the bearers were forced to bury it along the way due to its horrible stench of decay.[856]

The Beast of Gevaudan is reminiscent of the Werewolf of Flixton, a similarly odiferous monster that stalked England in the late tenth century.[857] By the time adulthood is reached, most have set aside the notion of such creatures—but imagine having that certainty challenged. Though it may seem just as impossible as sightings of dragons, witnesses report werewolves—anthropomorphic canines—with startling regularity. To avoid the built-in ridicule factor, researchers like Linda Godfrey prefers to call this entity "Dogman."

The Dogman appears much like Sasquatch, albeit with three major deviations: backwards-hinged canid legs, claws, and a wolfen head. Sightings of such entities were relatively overlooked until Godfrey's seminal 2003 work *The Beast of Bray Road*, which chronicled not only the Dogman sightings of Elkhorn, Wisconsin, but also the American Midwest's rich history of such encounters. Since then, she has been inundated with firsthand accounts.

As with any other unexplained entity, these testimonies involve odors. The level with which these correspond to Sasquatch smells is interesting (to reconcile such correlations, some researchers laughably suggest the Dogman is a baboon-headed Sasquatch). One case even encapsulates the manner in which Sasquatch smells intermingle. In June 2005, an arrowhead collector ran into a six-foot-tall bipedal figure with the head of a wolf in south Georgia. The creature left behind paw prints the size of the witness's hand, and smelled like "a combination of the worst possible wet dog smell, musky urine, and excrement."[858]

Unsurprisingly, sulfur plays a role in these interactions. One High Strangeness tale from November 1974 involved six teens UFO hunting in California's Texas Canyon. Though no flying saucers were seen, the youths were terrified when tall, hairy, dog-faced entities threw stones at their car and left a stench of rotten eggs. After looking into the incident, researcher Adele Childress claimed a member of military intelligence confided to her that the beings were from a crashed flying saucer.[859] More recently, entities with a similarly sulfurous smell were spotted in July 2008 near Taua, Brazil. The half-man, half-dog creatures were accused of absconding with sheep, and were only sighted during the new moon.[860]

In 1936 Mark Schackelman, a night watchman at St. Coletta convent in Racine, Wisconsin, saw a manlike wolf creature skulking about the property's Native American burial grounds, smelling "like long-dead meat" and uttering the arcane word "gadarrah" (which, it might be added, bears a striking resemblance to *garra*, the Spanish word for "claw;" or, more relevant to our discussion, "Gehenna," the Jewish Hell).[861] Livingston County, Kentucky, boasts the Beast of Land Between Lakes, a wolf-faced monster whose odor one sickened witness described as "rank... [yet] unlike the smell of rotting animals."[862]

Another frightening manimal is the Goatman, who appears in urban legends throughout the United States. While most Goatman sightings seem to be the product of rumor, reality and fantasy sometimes bleed together in surprising ways. On July 26, 1974, a family in Mariemont, Ohio, noticed an odor of "something like gas in the house," and looked outside, where neighbors had gathered together to discuss the strange smell. To escape the stench, the family went for a drive, during which they spotted a half-man, half-goat satyr, akin to Pan from Greek mythology.[863]

In Kewaskum, Wisconsin—80 miles north of the Bray Road Dogman sightings in Elkhorn—Jason Miller claimed to see a creature in 2003 with "the head and arms of a human, a long gray beard, and two goatlike legs" in the woods off South Mill Road. Local lore also calls the route Goatman's Road. According to Miller, the creature was "muttering obscenities and had a powerful, nauseating odor… like rotting flesh and garbage mixed into one."[864]

The following year, Ed Rollins claimed to have observed a horned, goat-man hybrid along a creek near Point Pleasant, West Virginia's Bethel Church Road. The beast smelled of sulfur, he said, though Rollins attributed the odor to residue in the water from the nearby abandoned TNT plant, rather than the creature itself. A similarly sulfurous Goatman is said to inhabit a cave near Parker, Arizona; its hindquarters smell like "garlic and putrid water."[865]

It is unsurprising that these creatures should smell unpleasant, as bucks are renowned for having a strong, distinctive—though not sulfurous—odor. This pungent mix comes from a combination of sebaceous scent glands near their horns and copious amounts of urine deliberately sprayed on their faces during rut.[866] One reporter described the resultant stench like "musky patchouli gone bad."[867]

In spite of the Goatman's apocryphal status, one individual achieved national notoriety in the summer of 1969, when residents of Fort Worth, Texas, began crossing paths with a scaly, furry, horned beast. The Lake Worth Monster was first spotted on July 10 by three couples who claimed it leapt from a tree onto the car of John Reichart. The creature appeared to be a white-haired "cross between a man and a goat." Twenty-four hours later, nearly 40 witnesses had spotted it, including, in the most dramatic encounter, three law enforcement officers who were forced to dodge a spare tire thrown their way.[868]

The Lake Worth Monster smelled atrocious by all accounts. Many witnesses spoke in vague terms about the beast's stench, though Charles Buchanan had the opportunity to experience it up-close and personal. At 2:00 a.m. on November 7, Buchanan was camping by the lake in the bed of his pickup truck when he was jerked to the ground. Startled, he opened his eyes to see a tall, shaggy humanoid with a stench that made him gag. Buchanan grabbed a nearby bag of leftover chicken and shoved it in the monster's face, causing it to flee, either in satisfaction or revulsion.[869]

Like UFOlogists adopting dragons, Sasquatch researchers are quick to seize upon anything tall and hairy as one of their own, conveniently ignoring descriptions of the Lake Worth Monster's horns (to be fair, some testimony describes a more apelike creature). Less likely to enter their fold are sightings of Frogmen.

In 1976, a young engaged couple were sitting in their car by Michigan's Williams Lake when something reached through the open window and grabbed the driver. He managed to break free, but the entity ran to the opposite side and seized the woman. While beating at the creature's arms with a soda bottle, the driver caught a glimpse of a wide-mouthed, froglike face and flipper-like hands. In the moments before the monster released its grip, he got an up-close look: "As I leaned across its arm or tentacle, I could tell it was slick or slimy. It had no strong odor except for a dank or musty smell like stagnant water."[870]

Ohio's famous "Loveland frogs" apparently smell much better. Since 1955, several witnesses have seen the diminutive creatures, starting with Robert Hunnicutt. Sometime that spring, the short-order cook was heading home around 3:30 a.m. when he spotted three short men huddled by the Madeira-Loveland Pike. Curious, he stopped his car and stepped out to investigate, only to see that the figures had froglike faces: gray skin, large, lipless mouths, and bald heads, plopped atop a lopsided body. He watched a few minutes as one of the creatures raised a sort of rod into the air before fastening it to its ankles. Hunnicutt jumped back in the car to fetch witnesses, noting the odor of "fresh-cut alfalfa and almonds" (recall UFO sightings involving an almond-like odor). By the time he brought the Loveland chief of police to the site, the entities had disappeared.[871]

This pleasant odor testimony is in direct contradiction with a contemporary report of similar creatures collected by investigator Ted Bloecher. That summer, another driver told Bloecher he saw four squat figures from his truck as he crossed a river near Loveland. The beings were huddled beneath the bridge, and a foul stench permeated the air.[872] Whatever they were (and whatever they smelled like), the creatures would return in March of 1972, where they earned the "Loveland Frogmen" moniker.

The Mad Gasser of Mattoon

Perhaps no unexplained event has featured smell as prominently as the bizarre happenings in Mattoon, Illinois, beginning late in the summer of 1944. For two months, more than 20 people fell victim to the "Mad Gasser of Mattoon," a tall, spectral individual dressed in dark clothing with a tight-fitting cap.

The first of the victims, Urban Raef, was awoken the night of August 31 by an odd odor that made him nauseous and weak. After a fit of vomiting, Raef's wife suspected a malfunction with the pilot light on the kitchen stove, but when she decided to get up and check, she found herself paralyzed. Neighbors experienced similar problems.[873]

The gasser himself was first spotted the following evening, after the experience of a Mrs. Kearney around 11:00 p.m. "I first noticed a sickening sweet odor in the bedroom, but at the time I thought that it might be from flowers outside the window," she said. "But the odor grew stronger, and I began to feel a paralysis of my legs and lower body." Mr. Kearney arrived home after midnight, and saw the gasser lurking outside his home. Like later victims, Mrs. Kearney suffered from a burning sensation in her mouth and throat.[874]

Mass hysteria is likely to blame for at least some sightings of the Mad Gasser of Mattoon. Similar events a decade earlier in Botetourt County, Virginia, have been cited as possible inspiration, but it seems far-fetched that events so distant (both geographically and temporally) are to blame. In addition to the mass hysteria solution, others have suggested environmental pollution, a mentally disturbed assailant, and even paranormal activity.

Little in the way of evidence was discovered during this period, with one exception: a man's handkerchief on the porch of Carl and Beulah Cordes. Even though it is speculated his work was carried out with an aerosol gun, most presumed the handkerchief belonged to the gasser—Beulah became violently ill after smelling it, including the typical symptoms of nausea and paralysis.[875]

In addition to describing it as "sweet" and "sickly," witnesses also called the gas's odor "musty," akin to cheap perfume or gardenias.[876] To this day, no one has satisfactorily answered what gas was utilized; FBI analysis of the Cordes handkerchief was inconclusive.[877] In spite of this lack of answers, an article published in the September 12, 1944, edition of the Mattoon *Journal-Gazette* featured a proclamation from chief of police C.E. Cole that the attacks were caused by "large quantities of carbon tetrachloride" leaking from a nearby diesel engine plant. The effects of the compound corresponded with witnesses' symptoms, which seemed good enough for the Mattoon Police Department.[878]

An alternate gas is just as possible. Recall the odor and effects of H_2S above 30 ppm: a sickeningly sweet smell and mucous membrane irritation. Granted, the fact that no one died during the 1944 attacks may preclude this explanation—H_2S is lethal—but the connection is compelling nonetheless. H_2S possesses another quality that resonates with the Mattoon events; this attribute is central to our conclusions, and will be discussed shortly.

MIB & BEK

Long before their ascent to pop-culture stardom, the Men-in-Black (MIB) were appearing on American doorsteps, intimidating UFO witnesses and making vague threats if any shared their stories. Generally described as pale with thin lips and slightly slanted eyes, the MIB showcase an affinity for black suits, black fedoras, and anachronistic black Cadillacs far too new for their make and model.

While many have speculated ties to the government, the reality of the MIB seems to have less in common with clandestine intelligence organizations and more in common with the flying saucer occupants they so desperately attempt to cover-up. Interactions with them are universally bizarre. The entities exhibit preternatural abilities to instill fear and vanish at will, yet are woefully lacking in a basic knowledge of culture and customs (perhaps the most famous example is the tale of a MIB who, when served Jell-O in a witness's home, attempted to drink it). Tales abound where witnesses spot imperfectly applied makeup, as if to hide their true appearance. There is even anecdotal evidence that the MIB may be a form of artificial intelligence—one witness was told as a MIB left, "My energy is running low—must go now—goodbye."[879]

Suffice to say, most are not human beings. As such, one would expect them to have an odor akin to other unexplained phenomena.

Some of the first MIB encounters of the modern era come from UFOlogist Albert K. Bender. Bender had just founded the International Flying Saucer Bureau when he started interacting with three intimidating men in dark suits. In early August 1952, a rattled Bender could not shake the sensation of being followed as he returned home late from the cinema. Ascending the stairs to his attic apartment, he was startled to see a blue light emanating from beneath the door.

> I unlocked the door and pushed it open. A large

object of undefinable outline was aglow in the center of the room. It looked like a bright, shimmering mirage. As I switched on the room light the strange effect disappeared and everything seemed to be normal… I then noted another peculiar thing. A strange odor filled the room. It smelled like burning sulphur, and was so strong it irritated my eyes. I opened a window to let in fresh air and began a quick examination of the room because I had noted that several files of IFSB records were disturbed. I was startled to find my radio was on, but without any sound coming from it….[880]

After this event, Bender began receiving regular visits from three MIB, always accompanied by the strong odor of sulfur or decomposing eggs. Interactions with these entities eventually convinced Bender to disband the IFSB.[881]

In his book *The Real Men in Black*, author Nick Redfern suggests that Bender's experiences—ill defined bright lights, sulfurous smells—could have actually been the product of migraines and phantosmia (olfactory hallucination), respectively. Bender was apparently migraine-prone and, as Redfern astutely points out, many epileptics suffer both from migraines and phantosmia. Perhaps Bender was indeed an epileptic and was simply noting one of the most common phantosmic smells: sulfur.[882]

Another common smell reported by phantosmia sufferers is burning rubber, which appeared in a story related to Redfern in 1994 by a lady living in the Cannock Chase. Shortly after spotting a UFO, the witness was visited by a "horrible little man about 5 feet tall," dressed all in black with an ill-fitting black wig. He looked emaciated and frightfully pale, with the exception of his "lips," which seemed covered in lipstick.

The figure advised the witness to "cease her studies" of "the sky lights," then told her to "dream easy." He walked down her drive and the witness, now feeling ill, retreated to bed. After a three-hour nap she awoke to a "horrible smell like burning rubber all through the house" that she hadn't previously noticed. "We had to have the windows open for days and get the carpets cleaned to get rid of [the smell]," she said.[883]

Another MIB case with a delayed odor comes from John Keel's *The Mothman Prophecies*. In 1968, Long Island, New York, resident "Jane" witnessed a strange bright light in the night sky, and shortly thereafter was approached by a MIB who introduced himself as "Mr. Apol." On their first encounter, Apol gave Jane a small metallic disc wrapped in parchment.

"Wear this always," he instructed, "so they will know who you are." Afterwards, Jane felt extremely dizzy yet promptly mailed the disc to Keel. Keel found the bauble unremarkable and carefully sent the parcel back as it had arrived. The following day, Keel received a phone call from Jane, who chastised him for bending the disc and tearing up the paper, further complaining that the disc was now black and smelled like rotten eggs.[884]

There is a compelling sulfurous coda to Jane's story. On one occasion, Mr. Apol requested a glass of water at her house so that he might take some pills. She obliged, and Apol gave her three of the pills as well, instructing her to take one immediately and one the following day. The third, he said, "was for her to have analyzed to assure herself it was harmless."

After taking the first pill, Jane experienced an intense headache and her eyes became bloodshot. Her parents said her eyes glazed over as well. She presented the spare pill to Keel, who had it analyzed: it was a sulfa drug, used to treat urinary tract infections (sulfonamides, which contain sulfur, were the first antibiotics to see widespread use). Convinced of its benign nature, Jane took her second pill as instructed.[885]

Keel also told the story of Shirley Cromartie, part-time housekeeper for the Key Biscayne, Florida, retreat of President Richard Nixon. In 1971, Cromartie claimed to have met a bizarre *woman* in a store parking lot who demanded she shoplift several items on her behalf. Cromartie, who pled *nolo contendere* to the subsequent charges, claimed to have fallen into a sort of daze after the mysterious woman "released a jasmine-like scent from her left hand," which compelled her to steal. Cromartie said the lady had been dressed entirely in black and was wearing a wig—traits shared with MIB.[886]

"Almost certainly, 'the jasmine-like scent' was a substance that is known officially as scopolamine," Redfern wrote in his 2016 book *Women in Black: The Creepy Companions of the Mysterious M.I.B.* "It is synthesized from the Borrachero Tree, which grows widely in Colombia. Aside from its jasmine-like odor, scopolamine is a powerful drug, exposure to which can almost instantaneously take away a person's free-will, self-preservation, and self-control." We would be remiss to not point out the recurrence of jasmine in spirit encounters, or scopolamine's nickname "the Devil's breath." [887]

Though not nearly as common as the MIB, there is no shortage of tales featuring ladies whose countenance and demeanor mirrors Keel's black-suited intimidators. On occasion, the entities appear as a couple, as they did in Tampa, Florida, in late 2008. Just before closing up around 3:00 a.m., a bar manager was startled to find a man and a woman, both dressed in black, walk in and ask for a pair of non-alcoholic beers. Pale and gaunt, the two patrons stood for a moment before the woman cleared her throat, as if to get the witness's attention.

"That's when I noticed the stench emanating from this woman," she later wrote. "Not only did she smell like she hadn't bathed in a month, she also smelled like chemicals. I used to apprentice as an embalmer, and I swear that woman smelled just like formalin." Formalin, of course, is an aqueous solution of formaldehyde, a common odor in UFO sightings.

The man pulled several photographs from his black leather satchel. He then asked the witness if she knew any of the individuals in the pictures; though several were her friends, she lied and denied. The duo grinned as if calling her bluff, then left without drinking a drop of their beers.[888]

Like the MIB and WIB, no one wants to see the Black Eyed

Kids (BEKs) on their doorstep. Often appearing as youths aged 9-12 and wearing dark clothes, these entities ask homeowners to let them inside for some mundane reason, such as using the telephone. Witnesses report intense feelings of unease and fear, irrational until the children reveal their faces: jet-black eyes set in clammy, dead skin. Their motivations are unclear, as very few have ever given in to their requests for entry.

BEKs are arguably a variation on the MIB trope. In addition to their dark garb, they seemingly materialize out of thin air and have great difficulty interpreting normal social cues, often repeating the same phrase over-and-over. Some paranormally inclined researchers have gone so far as to suggest that they may in fact be adolescent MIB.

There is some difficulty, however, in parsing out just how *real* the BEK phenomenon is. Although there are a handful of similar stories from centuries past, most BEK tales did not surface until relatively recently, well within the internet era, where individuals can spin a yarn and send it all the way around the world within an hour.

The veracity of encounters aside, BEK smells show consistency with other anomalous phenomenon. Researcher David Weatherly has done a great deal to legitimize the BEK phenomenon, meeting with witnesses and vetting their claims thoroughly. On the subject of odors in BEK cases, Weatherly said:

> In the accounts that I've collected, maybe somewhere between 20-30% of the cases [include smells]. It's reported as being the most foul odor that you could ever imagine. People report it as being something akin to sulfur, which we know is often associated with demonic activity, people report it as being the smell of something rotting, of decay... There are some strange things that occur with that. There are people who have encountered these kids, been in close proximity, and found that the

odor has permeated their clothing… and they have an extremely difficult time getting that smell out.[889]

Smells of mold and earth occur as well. One witness claimed that, before answering a long knock at his door, he was hit with a sense of dread. Opening the door, he saw two boys on his porch, aged 10-12. One was astride a bike, the other, taller boy simply standing; both kept their faces down. The witness greeted the children, who told him that they "just needed to come in for a minute, and it wouldn't take long."

It was at this moment the witness noticed their eyes: jet black, no iris, no sclera. He also claimed that their skin "looked like the belly of a fish, and they smelled kind of like sulfur or dirt, and death." The witness wisely denied their request for entry and was notably disturbed by the encounter for years afterward.[890]

Faeries

Contrary to effete Victorian depictions, the faeries of yore were powerful entities to be feared. These imposing elementals came in a wide array of shapes and sizes, from tiny *brownies* to the tall, shaggy *woodwose*. The fae folk were forces for both good and evil—leaving food offerings for them could enlist their help in keeping a tidy household or, at worst, simply prevented them from wreaking havoc in one's life.

While the richest faerie traditions come from Europe, the entities are found in every pre-Christian culture across the globe. Their characteristic odors are familiar to us at this point. The *kataw*, which inhabited waters off the Visayan Islands in the Philippines, looked much like mermaids, yet their beauty was offset by their icthyc stench. Another Filipino faerie, the *dwende*, was an import from the islands' Spanish colonists; it smelled either of damp earth or dried feces.[891]

Overtly sulfurous descriptions are found in European tales. A race of Italian giants known as the *orculli* smelled of rotting corpses, and their very touch could kill livestock. Far to the north, the *drakes* of British folklore were invisible household spirits who kept the hearth burning, yet could foul homes with their characteristic rotten egg odor (their name was synonymous with dragons). The Irish *pooka*, notorious for its pranks and shapeshifting abilities, was fond of appearing as a demonic horse with glowing eyes and flaming nostrils, exuding the smell of sulfur.[892]

Folktales are intriguing, but first-hand accounts are something else entirely. In one wonderful account from the late nineteenth century, a Yorkshire man reminisced about the area's pervasive faerie beliefs during his youth. Reverend M.C.F. Morris elaborated on one of his tales:

> … a young woman, into whose house this same gentleman once went, told him that she had never seen fairies (though her relations often had) but she had smelt them. On his asking what sort of odour he was to expect so that he might be similarly favoured, she went on to enquire if he had ever been in a very crowded 'place of worship' wherein the people had been congregated for a length of time. Such was the description; a very different one had been looked for; but it is the unexpected which happens.[893]

Such testimony conjures up numerous possibilities: incense, mustiness, body odor. Morris offered a strange interpretation of this description; he claimed the lady was "trying to give an idea of the gushes of hot air one sometimes comes across on broken ground." Such a description sounds startlingly like the release of volcanic gases like SO_2.[894]

Another oblique sulfur connection comes from the native tribes of New York State. Early folklorists reported that factions within the Iroquois confederation believed in little people who helped protect and nurture fruits and grains. Supposedly, these elves were poor hunters because the fauna had grown wary of their scent—to combat this shortcoming, they sought the fingernails of humans, which they would tie in tiny sachets and toss into their baths, thus masking their odor. In addition to the sulfur-keratin connection, this resonates vaguely with African folklore, which, as it will be recalled, holds that spirits' fingernails smell.[895]

Sightings of little people continue into the present day, sometimes accompanied by odors. The rich *duende* tradition of Latin America yields modern reports with regularity. On May 22, 2003, five young farmers near Calama, Chile, claimed to have watched six hairless, gray creatures, no more than two feet tall, emerge from some nearby bushes. The air was filled with the odor of sulfur as they studied the entities: oval heads, almond eyes, pointed ears, large "deformed" noses, and giant mouths full of yellowed teeth. Despite this frightening countenance, they began to roughhouse amongst themselves in a playful manner.

Once they noticed the men, however, things took a more sinister turn. The creatures approached a nearby pen, where they began violently "playing" with a sheep, inflicting mortal wounds. After several minutes of throwing rocks at the beasts, the witnesses were able to drive off the attackers and attend to the sheep. It died, having been exsanguinated during the attack (shades of chupacabra activity).[896]

Faerie scents are not universally unpleasant, however. In some traditions, the entities were responsible for the fragrance of flowers.[897] The *pukwudgies*, a species of faerie in North American legend, had a disposition that varied from tribe to tribe—while often sinister, some held that the entities were associated with flowers and exhibited a sweet fragrance.[898]

Marjorie Johnson, late collector of faerie encounters and former head of Britain's Fairy Investigation Society, once related the experience of American witness Martha C. Smith. Smith was praying for serenity and peace just before bedtime when she claimed to see five short entities in her bedroom, enveloped in a blue haze and engaged in some sort of conference. Through several bits of conversation, she determined they were speaking about her. Within moments the diminutive council vanished and somehow Smith was able to go to sleep, noting the "faint odour of medicine or herbs" as she dozed off.[899]

Given their longstanding association with the wilderness—and, by extension, gardens—herbal, floral odors make perfect sense in faerie lore. William Thornber wrote of a boggart, an elemental spirit tied to a specific location, in 1837's *The History of Blackpool and its Neighbourhood*:

> The registers of Poulton Church testify the respectability and numerous offspring of the Singletons of Staining; and within its walls many of them lie interred, without a single monument to record the spot. Staining, in old writings, is termed a lordship, and at this day pays a dutchy rent. Its hall has a 'Boggart,' according to tradition, the wandering ghost of a Scotchman, murdered near a tree, which has since recorded the deed by perfuming the ground around with a sweet odour of thyme.[900]

Such an account underscores the manner in which faeries have been identified not only as their own discrete race, but also as having a close association with the souls of the dead. Use of the term *boggart*, from which we get today's *bogeyman*, finds use in a variety of applications. An 1886 glossary of words and phrases from East Lancashire describes "the white quartz nodules found in gravel" as "boggard [sic] stones." The entry reads: "When rubbed together, these are supposed to emit a brimstone-like odor."[901] Folklore has commonly called such minerals "stink stones," "devil stones," or "fairy stones," which, when ground together, not only release a sulfurous stench but also phosphoresce. Strange illuminations and the odor of sulfur immediately reminds one of the Rhodesian UFO sightings of the 1970s, wherein witnesses described the craft as smelling like "two stones rubbed together."

Returning to the broader theme of faeries and nature smells, odors of dirt and earth are quite common in fae folk encounters. The *Dames Vertes* were said to be tall, seductive entities dwelling in the woods of eastern France—though they embodied springtime and the life of the forest, they nonetheless smelled of earth, mold, and death.[902]

The Fairy Investigation Society also received correspondence from a woman who experienced a faerie vision in 1996, during a particularly rough period of her life. The witness claimed to have been lying awake in bed one morning when she saw a cloaked, one-foot-tall figure dart across her lawn. At the same time, she heard a small voice whisper, "Please don't cry; we'll look after you." The sighting culminated in "a strange earthy smell" from her pillow, which quickly dissipated after she sat up.[903] It is worth comparing this bedside smell to the musty odors reported by victims of the Old Hag.

Some descriptions of faeries compare their smell to mushrooms, certainly consistent with descriptions of earthen odors.[904] For example, another witness studied by Johnson claimed to have been followed during her childhood by a gnome smelling of fungus. She identified it as a troll, though an African cook attached to her family said it was a bogeyman. Johnson had encounters with similar-smelling gnomes in her childhood as well.[905]

Perhaps this fungal odor is the "overpowering" stench smelled by Richard O'Donnell during his 1982 standoff with a troll in northern Minnesota. O'Donnell was walking home on a warm July day when he took a shortcut through a neighbor's farmland. After some time, he spied a grotesque figure waddling down the path toward him: short, with "coarse black hair, deep-set black eyes, and an enormous honker." The troll stood around five feet tall, sporting a dirty shirt and oversized overalls, but was barefoot.

O'Donnell claimed the entity tackled him and, after he struggled free, began to grow before his very eyes, gaining eight inches and fifty pounds in a matter of moments. Simultaneously, he noticed a foul odor. "The smell of him became almost overpowering," he said. "He stank bad enough when he was a short bugger, but now he could win a fall by his smell alone." Taking advantage of his well-earned freedom, O'Donnell ran off as fast as he could, not stopping until he reached town.[906]

Another odiferous fae encounter happened on a lonely stretch of road near Wortley, England. In 1987, Graham Brooke and his son had set out for a jog when they ran into a figure clad in a hooded brown cape. The being seemed to be somehow walking a path lower than the existing road, a fact which set their hair on end. Soon, they were close enough to smell "something really musty" and see that the figure had no face before it vanished.[907]

Some may counter—and rightly so—that this experience seems more akin to a ghost encounter than a run-in with a faerie. In truth, the lines between the fae folk and all unexplained phenomena blend and blur; faeries, after all, were long held to be the souls of the dead in Celtic lore. The smell of earth also provides a subtle connection to those we have buried. As such, faerie accounts are difficult to categorize.

Jacques Vallee was one of the first to point out the similarities between yesterday's faerie tales and today's UFO stories. In both phenomena, accounts frequently feature short entities led by a taller supervising figure, missing fetuses/infants, strange circular impressions in fields, and large swaths of missing time. Even more confounding are the commonalities across faerie-UFO-Sasquatch lore: strange lights during encounters, elaborate taxonomies proposed by researchers, purported underground dwellings, interbreeding with humans, accusations of livestock mutilation, witness paralysis, and the conspicuous offering of food and drink.

Consider the following two cases, and make up your mind accordingly: faerie, ghost, or alien?

The Brazilian UFO investigatory group CICOANI reported that, in the summer of 1972, Joao Alves Sobrinho was traveling near Jequitiba, Brazil, when he happened upon a strange "boat" by the side of the road, busily circled by two short figures. Though he never saw their faces, Sobrinho could tell that the duo wore light colored capes and sported waist-length hair. Sobrinho went to fetch two friends to corroborate the event, but the boat was now airborne; in its wake, it left a strong stench of "gas and burnt gunpowder."[908]

Vallee himself recorded a peculiar case blurring the alien-faerie lines. In his book *Confrontations*, Vallee interviewed one of the few remaining Cortina Indians, who told him that each summer he would watch as a strange being floated from a landed "airplane" and into his cabin. The entity smelled foul, was approximately 3.5 feet tall, always dressed in a brown jumpsuit, and had a large nose and long hair (a composite of the aforementioned encounters from Chile and Brazil). The being would simply float through the cabin's walls, unperturbed.

"Ten years before Whitley Strieber's blockbuster books became national nonfiction best-sellers," Vallee wrote, "a Cortina Indian in California had described in poor English a small being who glided along the ground and came into his home by going through the walls."[909]

Pushing the boundaries

The Sherman Ranch sits on an unassuming parcel of land in Uintah County, Utah. In 1994, the eponymous family purchased the 480-acre parcel without any idea of the area's history or reputation.

Everyone, from previous owners to the Ute tribal elders, held that the land was cursed. The Shermans soon discovered this for themselves: cattle died mysterious deaths, strange hairy hominids prowled the countryside, gigantic canids terrorized their livestock, strange lights manifested in the tree line, poltergeist activity moved objects, and, perhaps most surprisingly, structured UFOs were seen arriving and leaving through bizarre portals in the sky.

In short, the area was, and remains, a locus for the unexplained.

The ranch's reputation was further fortified when biochemist Colm Kelleher and journalist George Knapp chronicled billionaire Robert Bigelow's extensive scientific efforts at the site in their 2005 book *Hunt for the Skinwalker*. The accounts the duo collected are astounding, and their personal experiences are equally harrowing. In one instance, Kelleher and Knapp were surveying the property with researchers when they discerned odd depressions in the ground. "The tracks were perfectly round and appeared to be from some mechanical object rather than from a known animal," they wrote.

While following the trail, "an overpowering stench of musk assailed" the authors' nostrils. They noted the peculiar localization and strength of the odor, as well as the sensation of being watched. Though nothing was seen, Bigelow's researchers "swore that the smell was associated with the 'phenomenon,' whatever it was." Kelleher and Knapp were haunted by the odor throughout their time at "Skinwalker Ranch," and later described the stench as "sulfur-laden."[910]

UFO? Sasquatch? The jury is still out. Beyond such quaint categories, things stranger still lurk at the edges of perception.

Part VI: Speculation

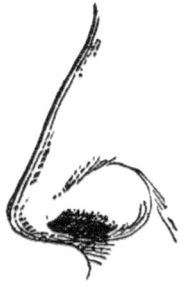

Chapter 22
Speculation: Observations

So what are the "aliens" trying to tell us? We're told they extract ova and semen; that they're keen on "punch biopsies" and nasal implants. Is there an intelligible symbolism at work behind the forever-rippling veil of sensationalism? If so, can we even hope to decode it?
— Mac Tonnies

Science is quick to trot out the adage of Occam's Razor: that, "among competing hypotheses, the one with the fewest assumptions should be selected." Such incisive logic has been used to argue against a host of Fortean phenomena, with justifiably powerful efficacy.

What no one wants to speak of is the fact that Occam was William of Ockham, an English Franciscan friar who applied this logic to spirituality. Put bluntly, the progenitor of the scientifically lauded principle of Occam's Razor lived his entire life in the service of unseen supernatural forces.

Using Occam's Razor, we must consider the following questions, regardless of how they may challenge our perceptions. Do demons smell of Hell's brimstone? Do UFOs have sulfurous exhaust? Do Sasquatch constantly exude flatus? Do falls of star jelly represent airline toilet waste? Do chupacabra attacks expose intestinal gases? Do black dogs explode into our reality in a cloud of H_2S? Does the Goatman bathe in sulfurous creeks? Do Men in Black and Black Eyed Children carry rotten eggs in their pockets?

Do faeries stink of subterranean sulfur deposits? Do all such phenomenon *just so happen* to manifest at sites like Skinwalker Ranch?

As the villainous Auric Goldfinger once told fictional superspy James Bond, "Once is happenstance. Twice is coincidence. Three times, it's enemy action." Is it possible there is a singular reason for sulfur's prevalence in these widely disparate sightings?

"What, it will surely be asked, are we to make of all this?" wrote author Dan Clore of such olfactory consistencies in the paranormal. "The data are, undoubtedly, reasonably uniform, and gain in uniformity when we take into account the nature of the data... Surely such a set of data must conclusively support *some* theory or other. But *which* theory?—that is the question."[911]

If not a common source, the similarities are certainly suggestive of a common mechanism or motivation. To that end, let us set aside the theories proposed in previous chapters and audaciously speculate on what this cross-phenomenal commonality could be.

At the macro level, there are two distinct possibilities: these smells are either unintentional or intentional. We have addressed the former at great length throughout previous chapters; the remainder of our discussion focuses upon the latter.

Few have ever fully engaged with the possibility that supernatural smells are intentionally produced, instead assuming that the odors noticed by witnesses are mere by-products, an unfortunate stink generated when strange phenomena manifest in our reality. This seems a grave miscalculation. Whatever is behind spirits, UFOs, Sasquatch, MIB, etc.—be it a single actor or multiple sources—it is certainly calculating and deliberate. In each instance, the phenomena appear wholly in control of their presentation. They rarely, if ever, make mistakes, are seldom caught on film, and have evaded widespread cultural acceptance for centuries, if not millennia. Given the omnipotence with which the supernatural behaves, we may find more answers when we work from the assumption that the odors noticed in encounters *serve a purpose*. Therefore, let us address a handful of observations in a manner that, if not exhaustive, is at least thoughtful.

If nothing else, the past 76,000 words have certainly driven home the prevalence of sulfurous odors in anomalous encounters. The element's odor is shockingly pervasive; even when not directly identified by witnesses, its presence contributes to the detectability of other odors on a molecular level. Smells of rotten eggs, fireworks, natural gas, flatulence, gunpowder, skunk, onions, garlic, cabbage, decay, body odor, burning hair, burning rubber… all derive at least part of their overall revulsive nature from sulfur, to say nothing of witnesses who describe "putrid, foul, awful, or disgusting" odors. Such consistency certainly implies that sulfur lies at the heart of these mysteries.

If scientists were tasked with designing an odor to grab the attention of human beings, they would be hard-pressed to find a more appropriate candidate than sulfur compounds. We detect these scents at smaller amounts more consistently than any other family of odors. Even in infinitesimal amounts, they are profoundly noticeable—recall how mercaptans are actually added to natural gas to warn of leaks.

This property is illustrated clearly in the number of reports where witnesses notice the phenomenon's stench before the phenomenon itself. If supernatural forces wish to remain undetected, sulfur compounds are a poor choice; ergo, if these odors are deliberately chosen, such forces *wish to be noticed*. An equally poor choice is the smell of burning, which also gets our attention—from an instinctive standpoint, the smell of combustion sets humans on high alert, warning of fire or, more insidiously, toxic smoke.

"Consciously experienced striking smells generally have a warning function," wrote olfactory psychologist Piet Vroon. "Ask someone to list smells, and he or she will think mainly of unpleasant and penetrating smells. Pleasant or neutral smells are anchored less well in consciousness and memory." What is more, in odor mixtures "unpleasant smells are generally better spotted and recognized than pleasant ones"—such is the power of foul odors to capture our attention.[912]

In addition to alerting witnesses, the choice of noticeable odors reinforces the reality of the apparition. Our eyes play tricks upon us, but our noses are much more faithful. In fact, French philosopher Gaston Bachelard felt that scents played too great a role in "substantialist belief"—they tend to usurp critical thinking and endow apparitions with substantiality. "He considered the action of odors to be particularly pernicious in that, owing to their direct and intimate quality, 'they appear to be bringing us a certain message from a material reality,'" wrote Annick Le Guérer.[913]

This not only implies that supernatural phenomena wish to be noticed, but that they wish to be *believed and remembered*. We have belabored the important relationship between smell and memory. In 2009, Swedish researchers determined conclusively that "retention of odors that were perceived as unpleasant was higher than that for olfactory information perceived as pleasant."[914] Such findings resonate with the words of Sasquatch witness and retired Pike County, Georgia, deputy James P. Akin: "This had… a rotten trash, dead animal smell that was mixed in with a sour, pig pen smell. It was startling, and if you ever encounter this smell, you'll never forget the smell. The smell is overwhelming, it's pungent."[915]

To what end do these phenomena wish to be noticed? Who knows. It certainly supports what many have suspected: the supernatural regularly engages in manipulation and theater to achieve its ends, whatever those may be. Perhaps the event itself is more important that the entity; the *sighting* is the focal point, not the spirit, the UFO, the Sasquatch. Attention is drawn to these events because the instigator wishes to create a reaction in the witness, be it terror or awe. Researchers have speculated that certain entities may "feed" upon strong emotions such as fear… what better way to ramp up anxiety than to introduce smells human beings are hedonically hard-wired to avoid?

The phenomena may wish to impart a message of some kind. Author and psychonaut Terence McKenna frequently spoke at length about the inefficiency of verbal communication:

> We use rapidly modulated small mouth noises. As primates we have incredible ability to make small mouth noises. We can do this for up to six hours at a stretch without tiring. No other thing we can do approaches the level of variation with low energy investment that the small mouth noises do. A person using a deaf-and-dumb language is exhausted after forty-five minutes. But a problem with the small mouth noises mode of communication is: I have a thought, I look in a dictionary that I have created out of my life experience, I map the thought onto the dictionary, I make the requisite small mouth noises, they cross physical space, they enter your ear, you look in your dictionary, which is different from my dictionary, but if we speak what we call "the same language" it will be close enough that you will "sort of" understand what I mean. Now if I don't say to you, "What do I mean?" you and I will go gaily off in the assumption that we understand each other.[916]

As a counter to this flawed system, McKenna proposed that the ultimate form of communication would be telepathy, the ability to instantaneously grasp the thoughts of others. The closest approximation to this on Earth, he held, were the visual communication systems of cephalopods, in particular octopi. By changing the texture and color of its skin, an octopus can unambiguously convey a great deal of information to other members of its species within milliseconds.

McKenna was incorrect, however, about the supremacy of visual communication—olfactory communication would trump the ocular. Communicating through smell would instantaneously trigger memories, superseding normal language perception with hard-wired responses, bypassing cognition via the direct evocation of emotion.

The tip-of-the-nose sensation is a perfect illustration of how olfaction conveys more subtleties than language. "Whether or not a person can generate an odor's name, or even an idiosyncratic verbal response to the odor, does not capture the complete spectrum of semantic odor identifications," wrote psychologist Frank Schab. "Thus, an odor may evoke semantic as well as perceptual associations, but these may not lend themselves to overt verbalization."[917]

If this is an attempt at communication, what is the message? "Stay away" is certainly a possibility, given how foul these phenomena stink. It seems equally likely that the stench is designed to communicate a sense of revulsion to the witness. Other aspects of the paranormal seem engineered to do just that—the medical procedures of alien abductions, for example, seem more concerned with terrifying subjects than performing efficient surgery (human beings may not have mastered interstellar travel yet, but we have technology far less invasive than the drills and probes favored by the Greys). Unpleasant odors would certainly augment the experience.

In 2013, researchers at Rutgers University determined that sensory nerves in the mammalian nose actually adapt when a smell is associated with fear, making the individual hypersensitive to the related odor. While it has long been held that associative learning changes *processing* in the brain, it is now apparent that the neurons *themselves* actually resensitize in response to fear-associated scents. In mice, this can result in a fourfold increase in sensitivity, to say nothing of the possible epigenetic implications wherein this trait might be passed to successive generations.[918]

According to these findings, frightened supernatural witnesses become hypersensitive to smells noticed during their encounters. But again, we must ask—to what end? It is obvious how a mouse might benefit by increasing its detection of cat scent, but how is a heightened sensitivity to rotten eggs beneficial to a poltergeist witness? What evolutionary advantage is there to an abductee who can detect minute amounts of ozone? How is a newfound aversion to wet dogs of any consequence to someone who smelled a

Sasquatch?

Consider another, more intriguing possibility. If there is one central theme uniting a majority of the smells surveyed, it is entropy. A vast majority of the odors evoke decomposition in some sense: rotten eggs, decaying meat, dead animals. In addition to these explicit themes of rot and decay, musty smells call to mind the presence of fungus and mold, essential players in the breakdown of biological material.

Combustion is another strong trend, exemplified by smells of burning material. Both combustion and decomposition are fundamental chemical reactions, and to the ancient alchemists—predecessors to modern chemists—the two were identical: dissolution of the extant, a transformational breakdown of the complex into simpler components. The same could be said of digestion, which produces other smells noted in supernatural cases: feces, urine, ammonia, etc. These are the odors of deconstruction—deconstruction that breaks apart our notions of reality.

From a psychological standpoint, these odors all point to the Jungian concept of the *shadow*, the unconscious aspect we all carry inside of us, eclipsed by our conscious ego. "We may interpret the smell of sulfur in paranormal cases as denoting the presence of a 'rotting substrata' left neglected," writes Fortean blogger Red Pill Junkie. "Kind of like the Jungian concept of the shadow, and the part of our personality which we shove deep into our subconscious... until it finally seeps through...."[919]

Unexplained phenomena have much in common with this psychological construct. Both remain "hidden in plain sight," as it were, both represent the more mysterious, untamed, primal side of existence. The odors in paranormal encounters may subtly imply that these events are external projections of our internal nature.

Alternatively—if these forces are indeed external—could they wish to impart a message of impermanence, a reminder of our own mortality? It seems possible. Perhaps these entities seek to "scare us straight," à la when convicts frighten juvenile delinquents into giving up their destructive tendencies. To cite one common odor, scientists have implicated H_2S in several mass extinctions throughout our planet's history—the purpose of entropic smells in supernatural events could be to obliquely convey a warning about the fragility of our existence.

UFO abductees often emerge from their experiences with a newfound regard for the environment, warning against mankind's destructive tendencies. Residents of haunted homes find their spirituality rekindled in the face of frightening activity. Sasquatch witnesses view the woodlands with greater respect than they once did, realizing that the world is a more dangerous place than previously suspected.

All are reminded of how tenuous our existence is, how we are all battling entropy yet doomed to succumb to it. Could odors play a reinforcing role in these expanded perspectives?

As lofty as these propositions may be, none resonate with the data in any profound way. They seem inefficient and mundane, their motivations obscure. Moreover, while most smells in the supernatural do have an entropic connotation, it seems a bit too reductive to lump all of them together.

How do we explain the more common outliers? While ozone's electric origins do vaguely fit the combustion theme, it isn't particularly entropic in the same sense that other common odors are.

There is another comprehensive explanation for why specific odors appear in conjunction with unexplained phenomena, one that encompasses *a majority* of odors, not just the sulfurous. While more complete and internally consistent than notions of communication, this alternate explanation requires an open-minded approach.

Indeed, that phrase is key… the supernatural may employ odors to *open minds*.

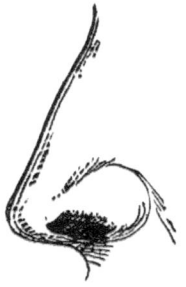

Chapter 23
Speculation: Altered States

You know, people tend to complain there's no adventure left in the world, the world is devoid of challenge. I say to you: five grams [of dried mushrooms] in silent darkness in the confines of your own apartment on a rainy Sunday evening and you'll feel that Ferdinand Magellan should take a back seat.

— Terence McKenna

Following an argument with his family in 1973, Zenon Carlos Rios was drifting to sleep on the roof of his apartment building in Divinópolis, Brazil, when he saw a blue, egg-shaped craft hovering close overhead. Through a window, he could make out two humanoids inside, dressed in black with white hair. After a moment, he found himself sucked into the object through a portal. He was soon hit with "a strong odor of kitchen gas, only the smell was much more penetrating… It was the most horrible, the strongest, I have ever smelled!" The gas rendered him unconscious. His next memory was his body hitting the roof, from which he had disappeared three days earlier.[920]

* * *

Yelena, a 25-year-old sufferer of sleep paralysis from Moscow, Russia, recalled one particularly frightening bout after the condition developed eight years prior. "I felt like I couldn't breathe, but suddenly I felt the most horrible and terrifying smell in my life," she wrote. "Then I felt someone's arms around me... The smell was so intensive [sic] that I thought, 'That's how people smell when they are dead.'" The ordeal concluded when she grabbed her attacker's fingers, one of which she felt detach and land in her hand before she finally awoke."[921]

* * *

In September 2008, a Sasquatch enthusiast from Kentucky was checking his Adair County game cameras when he "noted a strong smell that reminded him of a wet dog." Moments later, he was startled to see an incredibly muscular, tall, hairy figure staring at him, no less than 80 feet from his parked car. As he slowly walked toward the driver's side, the witness was hit with an earth-shaking bellow from the beast, accompanied by a new smell: rotting meat.

"That really ramped up my anxiety level," he told researchers from the Kentucky Bigfoot Research Organization. "The combination of the yelling and odor and adrenaline was disorienting for a few moments and I felt the strong and nonsensical urge to just sit or lie down on the ground on the driver's side of the car." Thankfully, the witness pushed through the impulse and managed to escape.[922]

* * *

In each of these three examples witnesses experienced some type of physiological affect in conjunction with their assailant's odor, namely an impairment of (or, in the last example, a strong desire to forfeit) motor control. This reaction is not uncommon in paranormal encounters—in fact, paralysis is frequently described in such cases.

Could the smell of sulfur, another common attribute of supernatural interactions, provide an insight into this shared symptom? If so, would it in turn shed light on *why* these paralytic episodes take place?

Suspended animation

In 2005, researchers from the University of Washington and the Fred Hutchinson Cancer Research Center successfully induced suspended animation—the "reversible cessation of all visible life processes in an organism"—in laboratory mice.

To accomplish this astounding feat, they employed H_2S.[923]

Mark Roth, director of the Roth Lab at the Hutchinson Center, spoke at a February 2010 TED conference:

> I was watching a television show... about caves in Mexico. And this particular cave was Lechuguilla, and this cave is incredibly toxic to humans, researchers had to suit up just to enter it. It's filled with this toxic gas, hydrogen sulfide. Now, hydrogen sulfide is, curiously, present in us. We make it ourselves. The highest concentration is in our brains... Yet it was used as a chemical warfare agent in World War I. It's an extraordinarily toxic thing. In fact, in chemical accidents, hydrogen sulfide is known to—if you breathe too much of it—you collapse to the ground, you appear dead, but if you are brought out to room air, you can be reanimated without harm... So I thought, "Wow, I have to get some of this!"... It binds to the very place inside of your cells where oxygen binds, and where you burn it, and you do this burning to live... Might we be able to give a person some hydrogen sulfide, and might it be able to occupy that place—like in a game of musical chairs—where oxygen might bind, and because you can't bind the oxygen, maybe you wouldn't consume it, and then maybe it would reduce your demand for oxygen....[924]

The mice lost consciousness within minutes of breathing a carefully regulated mixture of 80 ppm H_2S. During the six hours they were under, their respiration dropped to just ten breaths per minute (from a baseline of 120) and their body temperature plummeted an astounding 46.8 degrees Fahrenheit, from 98.6°F to 51.8°F. They were essentially rendered cold-blooded. All recovered without negative side effects, simply by removing the H_2S.[925] At his TED conference talk, Roth announced that Phase I clinical trials had been completed in humans, although it appears (for reasons unknown) that this research has since ground to a halt.[926]

History has hinted at such findings. In Athanasius Kircher's 1664 *Mundus Subterraneus*, he mentions a trip to the Italian cave known as the *Grotta de Cani*, "The Cave of Dogs." While some went in to die, many canines seemed impervious to the miasma of the cave.

> On the shore there is a farm cottage, where the owner breeds a large number of Dogs to use for tests in the cave. As soon as we arrived at the spot, he took a Dog and tied it to a long stick, whereupon a man who knew about these things pushed the beast into the deadly Flue of the Cave. When the Dog entered the Flue he could not bear the acidity of the toxic vapours that arose from it, and appeared to suffocate and be completely unable to move. The Dog was pulled out of the Hole and submerged in the waters of the Lake and, after a short time, as though he had been roused from a deep sleep, he started to walk again. After he had been refreshed with a little food, he was returned to his Master.[927]

This isn't to imply H_2S is benign—it is still a lethal gas. But, in a monitored setting, it has the incredible potential to induce stasis in the mammalian body. The scientific possibilities are astounding;

suspended animation could render tolerable the daunting travel time required for interstellar travel, or extend the window during which trauma victims could reach the emergency room.

The implications regarding paranormal reports—where H_2S is far and away the most consistently noted odor, and likely appears more often than is explicitly reported—are equally significant. The compound's presence provides a possible explanation for the sensations of paralysis and lethargy frequently described by witnesses. For example, consider the effects of the Mad Gasser of Mattoon, whose sweet gas (like H_2S in higher concentrations) caused unpleasant physical symptoms (like high quantities of H_2S) and induced paralysis, the obvious first symptom of a suspended animation scenario.

Given the prevalence of H_2S in the unexplained, it should be considered a likely candidate for such effects. Moreover, subsequent research has shown H_2S-induced suspended animation results in a lower lymphocyte count,[928] a side effect many attribute to the UFO abduction experience as well.

Accounts persist where anomalies—spirits, UFOs, Sasquatch, etc.—simply vanish into thin air before the eyes of witnesses. It is feasible that the H_2S noted in cases is actually deployed as an escape mechanism, akin to the cloud of ink left by a frightened squid. By slipping witnesses into a light state of suspended animation—perhaps so mild they remain upright—these entities might cloud minds just enough to facilitate a getaway, thus presenting the illusion they have "disappeared." Sharon Cornet suggested this very possibility in her 2005 essay, "Vanishing Bigfoot and Anecdotal Accounts."[929]

Suspended animation research also provides a convenient explanation for accounts of missing time, wherein witnesses to the supernatural cannot account for large periods of their waking hours. These realizations often occur after checking a clock, only to discover that the time is hours later than expected. Such activity is commonly noticed by alien abductees, though witnesses to other paranormal phenomena experience variations of the syndrome as well—travelers to the faerie land of yore return years later, witnesses feel as though time slows when staring down Sasquatch, some note time dilation in sleep paralysis, etc. What better way to immobilize a victim than to physically shut them down?

Given such evidence... yes, perhaps the negative spiritual entities associated with sleep paralysis render victims helpless by releasing H_2S. It seems equally possible that flesh-and-blood Sasquatch utilize H_2S to stun witnesses. And who is to say that alien astronauts, descending to Earth in nuts-and-bolts-craft, do not spray abductees with H_2S to sedate them for their obtuse experiments?

And yet paralysis is not noted in *every* case, nor is the rotten egg odor. As common as the symptoms may be, the literature is replete with witnesses who report no drowsiness, no lethargy. Maybe H_2S plays an additional role, one parallel to—or at least subtler than—the suspended animation effect, a role somehow supplemented by other odors. Perhaps the chemical's importance is not only physical, but mental as well.

With this in mind, we should explore other scenarios, theories that may challenge our commonly held notions of ghosts as dead spirits, UFOs as aliens, and Sasquatch as apes. There could well be another reason H_2S is implemented, a deeper motivation beyond simple immobilization, one that accounts for the broad spectrum of entities seen during supernatural events.

Consider the possibility that one singular phenomenon, wearing many hats, wishes to put us into an altered state of consciousness to facilitate interaction with it—an interaction accomplished by inducing suspended animation.

Altered states of consciousness

There are many forms of consciousness we experience during our lives. While most individuals spend a majority of their time in waking consciousness, others engage in altered states of consciousness for both recreational and spiritual reasons.

Speculation: Altered States

For eons, shamans have consumed *entheogens*, psychedelic substances which "release the god" and facilitate contact with the spirit realm, granting the ability to divine the future, right karmic wrongdoing, and show others the path to enlightenment. These elements were eaten, drunk, or—in a nice parallel to our discussion of respiration and combustion—inhaled. The oracles of Delphi once breathed laurel smoke to induce their visions,[930] ancient Scythians inhaled hemp in sweat lodges,[931] and the Amazonian *Araweté* still puff large tobacco cigars until they are "translucent enough to experience shamanic visions."[932]

In eastern traditions, monks strive for ever more focused meditation, hoping to achieve similar altered states. Today, intrepid psychonauts seeking deeper truths about reality ingest a variety of substances, some benign, some less so.

Altering one's consciousness has a certain pejorative connotation in western thought. In the American zeitgeist, such activity is largely associated with drug users wishing to escape reality by slipping into a fantasy realm. While there is a robust history of recreational use of hallucinogenic compounds, there is an equally populous faction using such substances for more lofty aims: treating post-traumatic stress disorder, curing addiction, easing anxiety in terminal patients, and learning profound life lessons about compassion and selflessness. LSD, psilocybin mushrooms, Amazonian *ayahuasca*—all have been implemented in these endeavors to great effect.

Even if you have never taken such substances, you have entered an altered state of consciousness. Each time we dream, we slip into a different reality. Ergo, it stands to reason that H_2S-induced suspended animation would be an altered state of consciousness as well.

This is germane to our discussion because, frankly, it seems that hallucinations are not always *just* hallucinations. While the materialist dictatorship of modern science is quick to write off things seen and heard in altered states as outright fabrications of an overexcited brain, there is a vast body of anecdotal evidence to suggest that these stimuli are not entirely subjective. It is not uncommon for psychedelic users to experience temporary psychic powers; in one famous tale, six *ayahuasca* drinkers told an anthropologist in the Amazon that his grandmother had died, a fact that reached him via radio two days later.[933]

Equally compelling are stories where multiple individuals take a single substance together and share visions. One young lady from Atlanta, Georgia, had taken psilocybin mushrooms with her boyfriend before fetching some water. While inside, she looked into the garden and saw a bright light in the sky shoot a beam at her boyfriend, a classic pop-culture representation of a UFO abduction. Equally curious and frightened, she ran out the door to find her boyfriend looking back in shock.

"You wouldn't believe it," he said breathlessly before she could speak. "I was about to be taken by a bright light in the sky."[934]

While anecdotal, such stories certainly imply that an external reality is acting upon both users. Some have gone so far as to suggest that the human mind is akin to a radio, with the ability to tune itself into different realities.

Anyone seeking to tear down the validity of altered states of consciousness by emphasizing their subjectivity will be disappointed to learn that even our sober, alert, waking consciousness is subjective as well. According to Carnegie Mellon University assistant professor of psychology and neuroscience Timothy Verstynen, much of our waking life is generated from subjective mental models.

"That's a much more efficient way to get around in the world than to try to process every single bit of sensory data that your senses collect," Verstynen said in 2015. "Rather than trying to process all these tsunamis of incoming information, it's probably more important to have this simulation of the world and just randomly and sparsely check your senses to see if your model is correct and if it's not, fix it." Verstynen posited that perhaps as much as 90% of our perception of reality is a mental construct, filling in gaps in perception.[935]

What do people experience in these altered states? Individual experiences vary, as do sensations from substance to substance. Many users report visions strikingly similar to paranormal encounters: anomalous lights, buzzing noises, out-of-body experiences, and telepathy. Those who ingest DMT also report time dilation—while the experience is complete in 15 minutes, psychonauts often feel as if they have been away for much, much longer.

Some users of psychedelics are even approached by short entities resembling yesterday's faeries (or today's Grey aliens). These beings dismember the experiencer, then piece them back together again, all while making claims that they have been somehow rendered "better" or "fixed."

Many suggest that some type of intelligence uses altered states to manifest and manipulate witnesses, resulting in the bulk of what we call paranormal phenomena. This possibility is most obvious in European fae lore, where anyone in a trance was said to be astrally lost in faerie land, or in modern UFO abductions, which nearly always take place during altered states of consciousness (sleep, in the case of bedroom invaders, or road hypnosis in the case of highway interceptions). Perhaps this dissociative state is the reason so many witnesses absent-mindedly forget to use their cameras or firearms when encountering the unknown.

It is up for debate whether one entity or multiple forces are at play, or whether its origins are extraterrestrial, spiritual, interdimensional, or something more peculiar. Such points are irrelevant. What is important is to recognize that similar methods are utilized across all phenomena.

The altered state model answers many questions asked through the years. Why do UFOs come in so many shapes, with so many varying occupants? Why has no hunter ever bagged a Sasquatch? Why is it so difficult to catch a spirit on film?

Perchance these things are not "real," in the sense that materialism demands they be defined. They interact with this world, yet inhabit a dominion of shadows, only seen when they enter our mental realm.

As such, we engage in an act of co-creation with these entities, our expectations of smoking ghosts, little green men, and hairy monsters overlaying a *subjective* cultural interpretation over fundamental interactions with an *objective* intelligence.

Examining witness testimony from this approach could help researchers make sense of details that are nonsensical, or conflict with other witnesses. "Many of us would be tempted to say that these accounts are either faulty recollections or screen memories imposed by aliens," said author and researcher Greg Bishop of the abduction phenomenon. "I am not so sure that any extra-human consciousness needs to impose any mind control on us. I think that we have our own built-in screen memories that function quite well in earthly situations such as childhood trauma. So one of my questions is, 'How much do we bring to the dance?' Meaning, how much of the UFO encounter is our minds trying to make sense of unexpected, startling, and frightening input?"[936]

It is a small leap of logic to extrapolate Bishop's well-articulated notion of co-creation in the UFO field to other anomalies, including Sasquatch, spirits, MIB, etc.

There are examples in the literature of entities utilizing odors to slip witnesses into altered states. One overt example comes from Budd Hopkins' *Sight Unseen*, which tells the unsettling story of Ohio abductee "Sally." During her youth, a professional woman contacted Sally about coming in for a job interview. Upon arrival, the office building was completely empty, save for a single desk and an ominous male interviewer.

> He starts talking to me, and there's one chair and I sit down in it. I think I saw a flash of light in the corner of the office... There are no windows in this office. He tells me about my salary, how high it is, and I think it's a joke. He says they sell perfumes, and shows me a little bottle. He says, "Would you like to try it on?" and I say no. He put it underneath my nose. The chair begins to spin and I fall... and I

keep looking at this light. I'm standing up and he's shaking my hand and telling me the interview was very good. And I go home.

Sally recalled that the perfume "had a strong smell," later telling Hopkins that the missing time between smelling it and leaving the building was filled with medical procedures conducted by Grey aliens. While it is possible mundane (albeit nefarious) human beings instigated this insidious act, Sally's other experiences suggest this was part of her ongoing abduction narrative.[937]

So—to circuitously bring this conversation back to H_2S and suspended animation—what are we to make of the fact that the most consistent smell noted by paranormal witnesses is associated with a compound known to cause an altered state of consciousness?

Perhaps this aforementioned objective intelligence facilitates interaction with humans by placing them into an altered state of consciousness via H_2S. How the gas is generated in this scenario is unclear, although there is no shortage of sulfur or hydrogen in our reality. As noted, the former is the tenth most abundant element in the universe, while the latter is literally *the* most abundant.[938]

This is not to suggest H_2S is a hallucinogen. It is assuredly not, nor does it need be: even if the H_2S-induced altered state is not enough to facilitate extrasensory interactions on its own, our bodies produce DMT, widely regarded as the strongest hallucinogen on the planet. Rather, the central point is that we may enter a dreamlike consciousness (i.e. an altered state) when interacting with these entities. H_2S sets a stage for our consciousness to interface with the other.

Even if most witnesses don't seem fully immersed in a state of suspended animation, it does not mean that some quasi-hypnotic affect isn't achieved. Perhaps the resultant state is liminal, somewhere between consciousness and unconsciousness. Science acknowledges the existence of such states, during which apparitions are commonly seen—sleep paralysis, for example, is a hypnagogic state between sleep and wakefulness accompanied by terrifying visions.

Critics of this idea will accurately point out that not every witness to the supernatural notes anomalous odors. Recall, however, that H_2S becomes undetectable at higher concentrations. Granted, such doses are higher (100-150 ppm)[939] than the amount needed to place mice into hibernation (80 ppm)—but almost certainly the threshold for H_2S-induced suspended animation in humans is higher than in rodents.

It would be exceedingly important for any intelligence utilizing H_2S to carefully regulate witness doses, lest its subjects perish outright. This level of finesse is currently out of the realm of human control but is conceivable in the hands of a supernatural entity. The pieces of the puzzle are all there—how they fit together is a subject for another day.

As compelling as the suspended animation angle may be, it is still only a partial answer. After all, while H_2S and sulfur are certainly the most common smells in paranormal encounters, dozens of other odors appear with a frequency too consistent to ignore. Is there an overarching commonality to these varied outliers beyond sulfur?

Though not immediately apparent, many of the other smells in paranormal encounters do share a common trait: nearly all are strong stimulants of the trigeminal nerve.

Trigeminal stimulation

Though few laypersons are aware of it, the trigeminal nerve is the largest cranial nerve in the human body.[940] Its three parts serve the forehead, middle face between the eyes and mouth, and the lower portion of the face, giving the nerve its name.[941] The primary function of the trigeminal nerve is to provide sensation to the face, as well as communicate motor function like jaw movement to facial musculature.[942]

Certain foods assert their characteristic sensations by stimulating the trigeminal nerve; without it, mint would lack its distinctive coolness and hot peppers would be rendered mild. In some ways, trigeminal stimulation functions as a sixth sense. These sensations are neither touch nor taste, but something different altogether. [943]

With taste and smell so closely related, it comes as little surprise that odors affect the trigeminal nerve. Anyone seeking to test this concept should take a large whiff of vinegar—that tickling sensation is a reaction of the trigeminal nerve. This attribute makes vinegar and ammonia, two strongly irritating odors, effective dog repellents: the noses of mutts are so sensitive that the trigeminal overload is unbearable.

"Irritants or stimuli for the trigeminal nerve induce violent reflexes, respiratory and the like," wrote Harvard University professor of zoology G.H. Parker in his book *Smell, Taste, and the Allied Senses in Vertebrates*. "True odors are much milder than stimulants for the trigeminal nerve, and seldom call forth strong responses."[944]

This "true odor" distinction is important. Just as the sensations of heat, coolness, tingliness, etc. are decoupled from taste, so trigeminal stimulation is a separate sensation from olfaction. For this reason, even sufferers of anosmia, who lack the ability to smell, react to trigeminal stimulation[945] (recall the anosmic ghost hunter on Mackinac Island).

Most odors stimulate the trigeminal nerve in some capacity. A handful do not. Among these few are vanilla and, interestingly, H_2S[946] (this being said, recent research suggests endogenous H_2S might increase the excitability of trigeminal nerve bundles).[947]

"Odors with strong trigeminal stimulation (for example, ammonia) are often immediately repelling," wrote Rachel Herz, one of the leading psychologists of olfaction. "The irritation caused by trigeminal nerve activity when we are exposed to the odor produces an avoidance response. So it may well be that when an odor is automatically repelling, with no prior exposure to it, we are avoiding the unpleasant trigeminal aspect, not the olfactory aspect per se."[948]

The question, therefore, is not whether non-sulfurous smells in paranormal encounters stimulate the trigeminal nerve—they most certainly do. The question, rather, is *how strongly* they stimulate the trigeminal nerve.

There is a wealth of evidence suggesting most paranormal odors are strong trigeminal stimulants. Even when a smell is poorly defined, clues suggest its stimulative quality—any case describing a physical smell sensation (tingling, burning, etc.) or a "sharp" odor is likely the cause of strong trigeminal stimulation.

Even the term "pungent," which commonly appears in encounters, refers to trigeminal stimulation. In a clear example of this observation, consider the testimony of a man in South Dade, Florida, who in May 1992 ran across a Skunk Ape smelling like "a combination of sulfuric acid and formaldehyde mixed together. The smell was so pungent, it actually burned the inside of my nostrils."[949]

Consider the conclusion reached by Antonio F. Rullán in his "Odors from UFOs" essay: "Of all the symptoms described in the UFO odor cases, the ones that stand out are nausea, watering eyes, burning nostrils/throat, and dizziness." Irritation of mucous membranes is certainly consistent with strong trigeminal stimulation.

Even more compelling, a list of the strongest trigeminal irritants reads like a synopsis of this book:

- Nitrobenzene, James McCampbell's contender for the most common UFO odor;[950]

- Ammonia, one of the contributors to the odor of urine and described in Sasquatch and UFO cases alike;[951]

- Camphor, noticed in the 1980 Manitoba and 1967 Jonestown UFO sightings;[952]

- Butyric acid, which imparts the stench of vomit, sometimes noted in Sasquatch reports;[953]

Speculation: Altered States 299

- Diethylamine, a component in urine, has a fishy smell like that of lake monsters;[954]

- Benzaldehyde, whose almond-like smell calls to mind the Loveland frogs;[955]

- Vinegar, the odor reported by Budd Hopkins' subject Carol;[956]

- Benzyl acetate, a component in jasmine, a staple of ghost perfumes;[957]

- Valeric acid, which is not only used in fragrances, but also imparts a cheesy, musty, footy odor in significant amounts, not unlike Whitley Strieber's visitors;[958]

- Formic acid, whose pungent, vinegar/urine-like odor appears in any number of cases;[959]

- Limonene, a citrus-like odor that recalls the possible 2010 abduction of a George Fox University security guard;[960]

- Toluene, a "paint thinner odor" similar to that described in some chupacabra reports;[961]

- Piperidine, alternately described as musty or peppery, a smell noticed by New Zealand UFO witnesses in 1959;[962]

- Formaldehyde, famously noted after the alleged Roswell UFO crash;[963]

- Cinnamaldehyde, which creates the distinctive odor of both cinnamon and Strieber's visitors;[964]

- The odor of onions, referenced in reports both directly and obliquely, in the form of body odors (watery eyes are a sure sign of trigeminal irritation);[965]

- And, lastly, ozone, reported in countless UFO cases.[966]

The list continues. Recall how frequently perfume appears in hauntings—some of us sneeze when exposed to these fragrances, a reaction to their stimulating effect upon our trigeminal nerve.[967] Heptanol, hexanol, and terpineol, all components used in perfumes and colognes, are potent trigeminal irritants[968] (peculiarly enough geraniol, found in roses, is only a mild stimulant).[969]

The burning motif is also representative of trigeminal stimulation. Nicotine is an oft-cited trigeminal stimulant,[970] as are many other chemicals released during combustion, depending on what is burned. Wood smoke, for example, can contain formaldehyde.[971]

Ozone's reputation as a strong trigeminal irritant is noteworthy. Interestingly, it is also gaining traction as a therapy for sufferers of trigeminal neuralgia. This extremely painful condition causes sharp, stabbing pain throughout the face lasting from a few seconds to a full minute.[972] Some patients have found relief in the injection of ozone directly over the affected nerve area.[973]

Although H_2S is a "true odor" as Parker would call it, the second most-common sulfur compound, SO_2, is not. It causes acute stimulation of the trigeminal nerve.[974]

In short, paranormal encounters feature two types of odors: H_2S and trigeminal stimulants. The question naturally arises as to what this trend means.

The trigeminal nerve is "part of a protective mechanism that helps us sneeze and clear irritants and toxins before they harm us," wrote Alan. R. Hirsch, neurological director of the Smell & Taste Treatment and Research Foundation. "Think of it as a backup system designed to protect against various toxic substances."[975]

This role—that of alerting the body—is precisely why

smelling salts work so effectively. "Smelling salts, which have a strong ammonia odor, provide another example of the way the trigeminal nerve is 'irritated,' thereby activating the part of the brain responsible for keeping us awake and alert," Hirsch adds. "Exposure to smelling salts… results in burning eyes and difficulty breathing, a response that was initiated with an odor stimulating the olfactory nerve."[976] This ability to foster an alert mental state is the reason why, in a 2008 pilot study, sufferers of epilepsy enjoyed a 50% reduction in the frequency of seizures after three months of consistent trigeminal stimulation.[977]

In case the implications are not clear: of the two odor types reported by witnesses, one can render human beings unconscious, while the other can render human beings conscious. They sit at opposite ends of a process, with H_2S putting witnesses into an altered state of consciousness (suspended animation), and trigeminal stimulants bringing witnesses out of an altered state of consciousness (à la smelling salts).

A theoretical picture begins to form. Consider the following hypothesis:

1. **An Intelligence of unknown origin wishes to establish contact with a witness.**

2. **The Intelligence, by means unknown, releases H_2S.**

3. **An altered state of consciousness is induced in the witness, during which the Intelligence is able to interact.**

4. **The Intelligence and witness act together to co-create a culturally appropriate, albeit anomalous, appearance: in a historical home, the Intelligence is a spirit, in the sky a UFO, in the woods a Sasquatch.**

5. **To fully rouse the witness out of this altered state, the Intelligence—by means again unclear—releases a tri-**

geminal stimulant, perhaps one that has a special psychological connotation for the subject.

The witness—paying more attention just prior to or just after the event—then associates the corresponding odor with the entity. If the start of the event is clearest in their memory, they remember sulfur. If the conclusion is clearest, they remember the trigeminal stimulant.

It should be noted that trigeminal stimulation is not needed to rouse subjects out of H_2S-induced suspended animation. In Mark Roth's original studies, the mere cessation of the gas was enough to bring the mice back to their natural state. What to make of this? Perhaps the trigeminal irritant is used to accelerate the recovery process, or is employed to keep the altered state from becoming too deep. Such efforts would approximate the hypnagogia experienced by sleep paralysis victims, avoiding a complete suspended animation scenario.

Before addressing the weaknesses in this theory—it is far, far from perfect—let us first look to the literature for support of the notion. Are there instances where trigeminal stimulation seems to remediate or combat an altered state of consciousness?

One of the earliest accounts suggesting this scenario comes from Irish faerie lore. A fae musician of the Tuatha Dé Danann named Aillen Mac Midhna came each Halloween (Samhain Eve) to play his *timpan*—a belled tambourine—at Tara, the king's palace. Each year he played so marvelously that all who heard him fell into a deep slumber, during which Midhna would set the palace ablaze with "three blasts of fire out of his nostrils." After 23 years of rebuilding Tara each Samhain, Finn of the Fianna finally defeated Midhna. He accomplished this goal by inhaling the venomous fumes of his magic spear, which was so pungent that "no one who smelled it could sleep, however lulling the music."[978]

An account related to John Keel by Jaye P. Paro, who entertained the enigmatic Princess Moon Owl, is also suggestive. While out for a walk one evening, Paro was approached by a well-dressed man in a black Cadillac, who demanded that she get into the car. Paro foolishly obliged, and the vehicle took off for Mount Misery, a Long Island UFO hotspot. Keel relays the events:

> "There was a funny smell inside," she reported. "Antiseptic… like a hospital. And there were flashing lights on the dashboard. I couldn't take my eyes off them. I felt like they were hypnotizing me." The car traveled isolated back roads until it reached a crossroads where another vehicle was waiting. A man holding something like a doctor's bag was standing there. He got into the Cadillac and waved a small object in Jaye's face, like a bottle of smelling salts. She felt her willpower drift away and sat there helplessly while the men asked her questions which didn't make any sense to her. Finally they returned her to the spot where they had picked her up.[979]

Note how the "smelling salts" were administered prior to Jaye's release, toward the end of the encounter.

As attractive as the concept of odors ushering in altered states of consciousness may be, it is not without weaknesses. One would expect that, if H_2S were employed, it would be quite common for witnesses to collapse during encounters as they slip into a state of suspended animation. Witnesses rarely lose motor function to such extreme degrees—even when paralyzed they remain upright. Additionally, even though smells are strikingly consistent in paranormal encounters (either H_2S or a strong trigeminal stimulant), not every case involves a smell.

Moreover, while plenty of cases exist that are too strange to be easily explained, there is no shortage of accounts that seem to support the traditionally-held notions that ghosts are spirits of the dead, UFOs are alien craft, and Sasquatch are anomalous primates. Like every paranormal hypothesis, the one-size-fits-all approach fails to account for the nuances inherent in every case.

Then again, every witness is different, so why should there be a singular answer?

Terence McKenna was fond of telling an anecdote wherein biochemist Alexander Shulgin exposed his Berkeley classroom to a vial of some undefined chemical. Of the 200 students in the room, all but two failed to detect any odor; the two who could became physically ill. McKenna explained:

> And then [Shulgin] explained to us that these people were probably up to 50,000 times more sensitive to this chemical than most people, and that this is a gene you carry for sensitivity to this thing. Well, those kinds of compounds—aromatic compounds, compounds with an electronically active ring structure—are the very nearest relatives to drugs, and so it's reasonable to suppose that there are genetic differences in the way we relate to drugs, which doesn't mean racial differences, it means from person-to-person.[980]

The possibility for odors to induce altered states of consciousness is compelling, and perhaps the best scientific explanation for why witnesses report the same odors time after time in their sightings.

The motivations for interactions are murky at best, however. Though this is likely to remain an unanswered question for the foreseeable future, perhaps we can gain insight—if not a clear solution—from the symbolic interpretation of McKenna's other great interest: alchemy.

Epilogue:
An Alchemical Answer

[Scientists] no longer believe they're giving a complete explanation of a phenomena, they just say, "Well, here's a model"... but they will never be more than crude approximations to an unspeakable mystery... Part of the ego-dominator pathology is to demand closure out of everything. There is no closure; you have to learn to sit with the messiness of the mystery.

— Terence McKenna

For millennia mankind has sought to bend reality to its will. Contemporary society has made a valiant effort, with its endless parade of gadgetry, yet there are some in the distant past who exercised even greater control on existence, if ancient accounts are to be believed. Their goals were to unlock the secrets of the universe and cure diseases, fashion elixirs of immortality, and, most famously, perfect chrysopoeia: the transmutation of base metals such as lead into noble metals, like gold.

These were the alchemists, precursors to modern chemists, whose journey winds through protoscience, philosophy, magic, mysticism, and spirituality. Attempts to discern their esoteric texts are filled with vagaries and contradictions; this confusion was deliberate, designed to foil the uninitiated.

The efficacy of alchemists' arcane efforts is less important to the matter at hand than their symbolism. The objective reality of transmutation is sketchy at best. Rather, it is hoped that a semiotic examination of alchemical thought may yield simple truths, stripped of over-complicated modern thought.

Though a significant detour is required to provide a thorough "crash course" in alchemy, it is well-worth pursuing. After all, at the heart of the discipline's robust symbolic vocabulary lie three simple, basic elements: salt, mercury, and sulfur.

Origin and concepts

The etymology of the word *alchemy* reveals its ancient origins. Though the discipline's origins include several cultural paths, the term is taken from the Arabic *Al-Khemia*, "from the land of Khem," referring to the fertile black soil on the banks of the Nile river. Legend holds that godlike beings came to live among the Egyptians eons ago, and wished to breed with the daughters of men (this narrative is found in multiple religious traditions, including the Old Testament).[981]

In exchange for breeding rights, these visitors shared their knowledge of magic and metallurgy. One particularly influential god, Thoth (depicted in Egyptian iconography as a man with the head of an ibis) was responsible for the creation of language, mathematics, music, magic, religion, science, and, naturally, alchemy, the ability to manipulate nature. The knowledge of Thoth was recorded on scrolls and slabs, including an emerald tablet, kept inside two great pillars.[982]

When Alexander the Great became pharaoh in 332 B.C., he took the pillars and their contents to the Library of Alexandria, the greatest repository of knowledge in the world. The diffusion of Egyptian culture led to new identities for Thoth: in Rome, he was synonymous with the god Mercury, while in Greek tradition he became Hermes Trismegistus, a priest and contemporary of the Jewish prophet Moses. This is the reason why the term *hermeticism* is synonymous with *alchemy*.[983]

Alexandria became the center for the discipline, producing influential alchemists like Bolos, Zosimus, and Monetho. It was here that the concept of the *Prima Materia* (First Matter) was codified, a vague concept of the bedrock of reality and alternately identified as imagination, consciousness, quintessence, etc. Alexandrian alchemists eventually seized upon the thoughts of Aristotle to define the *Prima Materia* as four primary elements: fire, air, water, and earth (recall the manner in which Aristotle paired these elements with each of the senses—notably, fire was paired with smell).[984]

Contained within this fundamental concept were the Two Contraries. Originating in Egyptian myths of Isis and Osiris, this concept of two opposites forming one cohesive whole diffused across the globe, appearing in the alchemical traditions of Asia (reflected in the Taoist *yin-yang* symbol) and India (where Agni, the god of fire, created metals using the semen of Hara).[985]

The eventual destruction of the Library of Alexandria scattered alchemists to the four corners of the globe. In addition to texts that had already been translated in Baghdad, Christian mystics brought alchemical traditions to Persia and Arabia, where it took root. The greatest of Arabian alchemists, Jabir, penned texts so arcane they became known as "gibberish"; more importantly, he was the first to introduce the key concepts of the Philosopher's Stone (the means by which lead could be turned to gold) and elaborated on the concept of the Two Contraries, identifying Sulfur and Mercury as the primeval forces (the capitalization is deliberate).[986]

Author and alchemist Dennis William Hauck described the dichotomy of the Two Contraries in 1998:

> The most basic tenet of alchemy is that there are two primary ways of knowing reality... The first way of knowing is rational deductive, argumentative, intellectual thinking that is the hallmark of science... The alchemists called this solar consciousness, and assigned it many code words, such as the King, the Sun, Sulphur, Spirit, the Father, and ultimately the One Mind of the universe... The alchemists called

the other way of knowing lunar consciousness. This intelligence of the heart is a non-linear, image-driven intuitive way of thinking that is an accepted tool of the arts and religion. Among its many symbols are the Queen, the Moon, the metal Mercury, the Soul, the Holy Ghost, and ultimately the One Thing of the universe.[987]

Interestingly, there is a chemical reality to this pairing of mercury and sulfur. It may be recalled that organosulfur compounds known as thiols are also called mercaptans. William Christopher Zeise coined this term in 1832 as a portmanteau of *mercurium captans* ("capturing mercury"), a word meant to depict how readily and strongly thiols bind to mercury.[988]

This purely chemical interpretation belies the complexity of the Sulfur-Mercury dichotomy, however. The Two Contraries, though in contradiction with one another, were inseparably enmeshed in alchemical philosophy, and emerged more as philosophical concepts, rather than literal elements. "Sulfur and Mercury are like two dancers who change into one another as they spin around the dance floor," wrote Hauck. "These two volatile principles are sometimes so hard to distinguish from one another that alchemists believed they were actually two faces of the same thing."[989]

Of this contradiction, Jungian scholar James Hillman wrote: "Sulfur has affinities with the Devil—as corrupter and compeller—and with Christ, giver of warmth and life. Though it is the urgent agent of change, sulfur at the same time not only resists sublimation but is that very component of the psyche, as Jung said, 'responsible for our resistance to psychology in general.'"[990] We shall return to the symbolism of Sulfur and Mercury shortly.

The eventual fall of Spain to Muslim forces in the eighth century brought alchemy to the heart of Europe. Though opposed by the Christian church, the tradition flourished in the hands of luminaries such as Albertus Magnus and Roger Bacon, who further defined the Sulfur-Mercury dichotomy as *sophic*, or metaphoric.[991]

Sophic Sulfur, sharing an affinity with heat, became associated with the sun god Apollo, masculine "superiority," consciousness, height, spirit, fire, and fixity; Sophic Mercury was assigned to Hermes, representing Earth, feminine "inferiority," unconsciousness, depths, soul, water, and mutability. Both could be found in all things.[992]

This interpretation gained further traction when European alchemists defined the Great Work—the transmutation of the *Prima Materia* into the Philosopher's Stone—as a spiritual, as well as literal, process (Nicolas Flamel, for example, supposedly achieved the alchemical goal of turning lead into gold, but was so spiritually changed by the process that he donated it all).[993] The Stone itself represented perfection and immortality, and naturally gained a Christ-like significance to alchemists.

In this sense, our very lives are alchemy. We strive towards a goal of "spirit redeemed from matter," as McKenna said.[994] Because of this, alchemy has become a metaphor favored by some in the psychedelic community. Those interested in achieving altered states of consciousness have two choices: the slow, steady, methodical discipline of meditation or the rapid, haphazard choice of taking psychedelics. Alchemists believed in similar means of attaining their goals, speaking of a "Wet Way" technique that required months of patience, or a treacherous "Dry Way" which, according to Hauck, was very dangerous for unprepared initiates and could result in madness or a loss of personal identity."[995]

In the sixteenth century, Paracelsus turned the notion of the Two Contraries on its head. The Swiss German philosopher restructured Jabir's model into the *Tria Prima*, which included Sophic Sulfur, Sophic Mercury, and a new aspect, Sophic Salt.[996]

"The three principles were assigned qualities that made it possible to identify their presence through normal chemical operations," wrote science historian Allen G. Debus. "With few exceptions this meant the application of heat either through decomposition (simple combustion) or through distillation. Sulfur was considered to be the cause of combustibility, structure, and substance. Solidity and often color were due to salt, and the vaporous quality was always assigned to mercury."[997]

The *Tria Prima* remained the dominant model of alchemy from that point forward. In essence, the model could be reduced to consciousness (Sophic Sulfur), fluidity (Sophic Mercury), and physicality (Sophic Salt).[998] To symbolize this trifecta, students of Paracelsus adopted the emblem of the three-headed dragon.

The fundamental importance of sulfur—symbolic and literal—in alchemy draws a striking parallel to the prevalence of sulfurous odors in paranormal events. Perhaps this is an indicator that we should look to alchemy as a way of understanding the unexplained.

Alchemy and the unexplained

To encode their techniques and impart deeper meaning to their discipline, alchemists made extensive use of symbolism. As with all other aspects of alchemy, these were varied, obscure, and often contradictory. Not only was the *tria prima* a three-headed dragon, but individuals, materials, and techniques could be represented by a variety of signs and symbols, especially animals.

Each stage of the Great Work, for example, was represented by a specific bird, culminating in the representation of the Philosopher's Stone as a Phoenix or, according to chemistry professor Arthur Greenberg, a circle representative of perfection and the separation of Heaven and earth.[999] Winged dragons often depicted Mercury, while wingless dragons were sulfur. Other, less important elements were assigned imagery as well: a dead king sometimes meant that gold was impure, while a wolf could represent antimony.[1000]

One of the more famous alien abduction tales seems to directly invoke this alchemical imagery. In January 1967, Betty Andreasson and her family claimed to have observed a large craft descend from the sky and land upon their lawn in South Ashburnham, Massachusetts. Small Grey aliens—similar to the ones reported six years earlier in Betty and Barney Hill's abduction—then escorted Andreasson to the craft, where an entity identifying itself as "Quazgaa" showed her a variety of symbolic tableau.

After seeing a variety of alien iconography and structures, which she described as vaguely Egyptian (the birthplace of alchemy, you may recall), Andreasson was escorted to a chamber housing an immense bird that erupted into flame before her eyes, leaving behind a small pile of gray ash. This is obviously evocative of the Phoenix, a potent alchemical symbol. The parallels grew deeper when, instead of being reborn once more as a bird, the ashes yielded a plump, gray worm.[1001] The Germanic word for dragon—particularly the wingless variety, which doubles as an alchemical symbol for sulfur—is *worm*, derived from the Old English *wyrm*.

The notion of utilizing alchemy's extensive symbolic language to gain insight into other disciplines is not a new idea. Perhaps the most famous person to do so was Carl Jung, who used its imagery to form his hypothesis of the collective unconsciousness. This construct holds that all mankind shares an unconscious mind—not unlike the "Intelligence" proposed in the last chapter—populated by consistent, timeless archetypes and instincts. To Jung, the Great Work could be applied to the manner in which the human psyche reasserts order from chaos.[1002]

Jung also compared alchemical symbolism to the paranormal, specifically anomalous aerial phenomena. In his seminal *Flying Saucers: A Modern Myth of Things Seen in the Skies*, Jung suggested that the circular shape of the flying saucer was representative of a *mandala*, a circular eastern religious symbol that represented the universe and, thusly, wholeness. UFOs were a projection of mankind's collective unconscious, expressing a psychological desire for wholeness.[1003]

The mandala itself is also a variation on alchemical iconography. To Jung, the *ourobouros*—a common depiction in alchemical texts of a serpent eating its own tail—was a mandala, again representative of the Two Contraries.

> The Ouroboros is a dramatic symbol for the integration and assimilation of the opposite, i.e. of the shadow. This 'feed-back' process is at the same

time a symbol of immortality, since it is said of the Ouroboros that he slays himself and brings himself to life, fertilizes himself and gives birth to himself. He symbolizes the One, who proceeds from the clash of opposites, and he therefore constitutes the secret of the *prima materia* which... unquestionably stems from man›s unconscious.[1004]

In a charming synchronicity, the chemist Auguste Kekulé wrote that on one night in the late nineteenth century he had a dream of serpents, one of which "had seized hold of its own tail." The image roused Kekulé immediately and he instantly began jotting down his ideas on the chemical structure of benzene—a ring.[1005] The inspiration proved correct. (This circular compound has, as mentioned earlier, featured in a great deal of UFO speculation.)

Jung's embrace of alchemical thought meant he was comfortable with the idea that the very reality of UFOs might be akin to the paradox of the Two Contraries. In a February 1951 letter, he wrote, "I'm puzzled to death about these phenomena, because I haven't been able yet to make out with sufficient certainty whether the whole thing is a rumour with concomitant singular and mass hallucination, or a downright fact... The phenomenon of the saucers might well be both, rumour as well as fact."[1006]

Besides UFOs, other supernatural phenomenon can be seen as representations of the alchemical ideal, opposites made one. Ghosts are somehow both alive and dead, Sasquatch is both man and beast. In *Daimonic Reality*, author Patrick Harpur writes about ancient perceptions of the supernatural's binary nature, which held they were "neither spiritual nor physical, but both. Neither were they, as Jung discovered, wholly inner nor wholly outer, but both. They were paradoxical beings, both good and bad, benign and frightening, guiding and warning, protecting and maddening."[1007]

Put another way, all Fortean phenomena are *liminal*, representing neither one thing nor another. This is why, as Harpur points out, such phenomena manifest at places of transition—trolls

Epilogue: An Alchemical Answer

live under bridges, black dogs appear at crossroads, mysterious beasts emerge at twilight. Liminality is about transition; transition is about transformation; transformation is alchemy.

We can also perceive alchemy as a microcosm of reality, of the supernatural versus the natural. Jung compared the UFO in modern consciousness to the ideal of Sophic Mercury: like its alchemical counterpart, UFOs are ever changing, appearing in a variety of configurations. They are elusive and vaporous, like smoke in the *tria prima* metaphor, and speak to our unconscious side, residing in a peculiar dream realm.[1008]

The idea is echoed in the writings of Harpur, who contends that the supernatural represents reality's mercurial Hermetic side. By contrast, what most call the natural—modern society's preoccupation with scientism, rationality, and technology—is representative of the Apollonic ideal, of Sophic Sulfur. The Hermetic draws mankind back toward mystery, intuition, earth, and emotion.[1009] Is it any wonder that inhabitants of the "uncivilized" world, more in touch with the Hermetic aspect of existence, experience more supernatural events in their lives?

And yet we see the odor of sulfur appearing in anomalous encounters time and again, undermining this otherwise elegant metaphor. If Sophic Mercury symbolizes the unexplained, why the smell of sulfur? Most drawing comparisons to alchemy have overlooked this contradiction in paranormal phenomena, a peculiar habit given how the central tenets of alchemy stress the union of opposites. It is obvious that, if we indulge in an alchemical interpretation of the supernatural, this inconsistency must be explored and reconciled.

Supernatural smells and Sophic Sulfur symbolism

One of the primary guiding principles of alchemy is the axiom, "As above, so below." Everything in the microcosm mirrors the macrocosm, and vice versa. Sulfur certainly follows this concept, a fragment of the Two Contraries that somehow embodies the conflicting ideals of the Two Contraries within itself: it is at once the tool of the divine and the demonic. In magic, it can be used to summon or repel entities, depending upon intent.

If nothing else, applying the symbolism of Sophic Sulfur to the unexplained helps explain two common odor motifs reported by witnesses. We have belabored the presence of burning odors in a wide variety of paranormal cases; Sophic Sulfur was synonymous with combustion, a vital aspect of the alchemical process.

"In the literature of the period the importance of fire as a means of analysis is everywhere stressed," wrote Debus. "Chemical processes in the laboratory were almost exclusively carried out with the aid of heat, and alchemical tradition affirmed that fire caused a separation, not generation... The belief that analysis by fire would duplicate the separation obtained by a slow natural putrefaction was widespread."[1010]

In 1660, Nicholas Lefevre wrote that natural putrefaction released "sulfureous and mercurial vapors after their binding salt had been dissolved."[1011] Ergo—in the eyes of ancient alchemists—decomposition, another common supernatural smell, accomplished the same goals as combustion. Alchemists perceived that both processes could separate matter into its consistent elements. They were transformative processes, with Sulfur acting as the guiding force.

The most commonly used alchemical symbol for Sulfur is a Greek cross surmounted by a prominent triangle.[1012] This simple icon and its variations are used in a number of alchemical and tarot traditions. Because of the Church's anti-alchemy stance and the longstanding association of sulfur with Satan, triangular symbolism was thus grafted onto demonic activity. This relationship extends to depictions of the number three: 3:00 a.m. is the witching hour when paranormal activity peaks (an inversion of the hour of Christ's death at 3:00 p.m.), demons supposedly leave scratches on their victims in threes, entities often appear as a trio, etc.

It seems not inconsequential that the craft reported in some of the most prominent UFO landing cases—the 1980 Rendlesham

Forest[1013] and 1964 Socorro cases spring to mind—featured markings with prominent triangular shapes. In the latter event, some researchers contend the logo bore a resemblance to the Arabic symbol for Venus—the goddess who gave her namesake to a planet choked in sulfurous gases.[1014] Consider also that the skeletal formulae for SO_2 and H_2S—the three-dimensional representation of their molecular shapes—are triangular. These are striking coincidences, but no less striking than the fact that UFOs sometimes appear as literal black triangles in the sky, or that anomalies tend to manifest in zones defined as triangles (e.g. the Bridgewater Triangle of New England or, more famously, the Bermuda Triangle).

In addition to the triangular symbol, specific animals also represented Sophic Sulfur in alchemical tradition. We already mentioned the use of dragons to portray Sophic elements in ancient texts. Lions were depicted commonly as well.[1015]

"The cipher alchemists used to designate putrefaction was the astrological Fire sign of Leo, which the Egyptians associated with the lion-headed god Sekhmet," Hauck writes.[1016] Similarly, Sophic Sulfur was sometimes depicted as a red lion, or as a lion eating a snake, like in the work of alchemist Basil Valentine.[1017]

"The lion is a well-known symbol of the solstice of the sun, when the sun is at its highest, speaking astrologically, but it is also a symbol of resurrection," wrote Swiss Jungian psychologist Marie-Louise von Franz. "It is also a symbol of passionate devouring, the power drive, not only in the narrow sense of the word, but generally the drive to possess. The outstretched paws and wide open jaw illustrate the lion, the powerful, passionate hot nature."[1018]

This resurrection imagery naturally ties large feline iconography to Christ, a connection mentioned in an earlier chapter (note how the rebirth motif is also echoed in post-experiential changes in the lives of witnesses, who often find renewed meaning after encountering the paranormal). The mythological panther possessed the ability to lure prey with its captivating scent, an attribute early Christians compared to the alluring words of Christ's Gospel. In modern times, Alien Big Cats seem almost like a pan-paranormal avatar for the unknown, appearing during Sasquatch and UFO flaps alike.

The panther's fragrant ability to draw in prey was referred to by ancient Greeks as *iunx*, a word with a variety of meanings. The term—anglicanized as *jynx*—had many meanings: a frantic species of bird, a sorceress, or a special tool used in love magic. Belgian historian Marcel Detienne defines the Grecian jynx tool as such:

> In women's hands it becomes an instrument of seduction to be used in love magic... The *iunx* takes the form of a wheel pierced by two holes, one on either side of its centre; this wheel is held by a cord passed through first one end and then the other hole with quite a long piece left over at either end. The wheel is set in motion by pulling on both ends of the cord and, as it turns, it makes a strange whirring noise or whistling sound... When sorceresses manipulate a *iunx* it emits deep notes which provoke the same fascination as the movements of the [eponymous] "bird of frenzy."[1019]

It is interesting how the object's description—that of a rounded disc using a buzzing sound to hypnotize a subject for the purpose of lovemaking—could be used to describe the narrative of modern day alien abductions.

The use of the Grecian jynx to bewilder is where the term *jinx* originated, the notion of a curse placed on a victim. A jinx, therefore, is not only the scent released by the mythical panther—representative of Sophic Sulfur—it is also a sort of bewitchment or trance. This resonates as a strong parallel to modern supernatural encounters: H_2S, a sulfur compound, can cause an altered state of consciousness and is the odor most often associated with unexplained phenomena. In terms of symbolism, it is equally significant that women were the primary users of the ancient jinx tool, as both Hermetic thought and felines are emblematic of femininity.

Perhaps unexplained phenomena—associated by Jung and his disciples with Sophic Mercury—utilize Sophic Sulfur as a tool. Mercury is too passive, too subtle to accomplish its goals and, as von Franz wrote, "Sulphur is the active part of the psyche, the part which has a definite goal."[1020] In this sense, Sulfur and Mercury, the Two Contraries, unite towards a single goal: the transformation of the witness.

A hidden world

Psychiatrist and UFO abduction researcher John Mack often invoked the concept of the "reified metaphor," that perhaps the phenomenon uses symbolic manifestations to convey its true intentions in our reality.

"There may be no flesh-and-blood hybrid fetuses sulking in vials of synthesized amniotic fluid," wrote the late Mac Tonnies of the idea. "But the implications they conjure—the joining of two worlds, the intimate juxtaposition of the alien and the familiar—achieve the desired end nonetheless."[1021]

Perhaps the reified metaphor Mack proposed is the alchemical ideal, the Two Contraries joined as one in balance. It seems to extend to all things anomalous, and maybe the point of spotting spirits, UFOs, and Sasquatch is to simply inject a little uncertainty into our lives, to reinforce the notion that we, as a species, are not masters of all we survey; our existence is far stranger than mainstream science would have us believe.

One would be hard pressed to find a more fitting metaphor for the paranormal than smells. Like the forces behind paranormal encounters, scents are invisible-yet-undeniable, constantly surrounding us yet unseen. Odors are part of a hidden world that manipulates us, that we respond to in subtle ways that even we do not realize. They influence every aspect of our lives: our decisions, our reactions, our perceptions.

The profound effect of supernatural sightings on witnesses is well documented. In extreme examples, some live the rest of their lives in fear, while others have their faith in mystery rekindled and are set anew on a spiritual path.

Most of us, however, simply notice a tiny, hairline fracture in our worldview, letting in the thinnest sliver of light from the room beyond—a room whose existence many abandoned during adolescence, ascribing it to fairytales from their youth. It is Shangri-La, it is Fairyland, it is Venus, Oz, Middle-Earth, Heaven or Hell. As we peer through this crack, we cannot make out much, save vague shapes and the sense that something *must* be on the other side.

We glimpse, as Terence McKenna put it, "the burning, primary reality that lies behind the dross of appearances."[1022] For some of us this paradigmatic fissure weathers and expands with time.

As we stare transfixed at the crack, we see things. Some turn away, saying, "I cannot believe my eyes."

Others hear things yet deny them as well. "I cannot believe my ears."

But none of us ever say we cannot believe our nose.

Acknowledgments

I can scarcely believe that another book is out, but here we are. I would be remiss without acknowledging the help of several very important people. If I forget anyone, please attribute my *faux pas* to an overstuffed mind, rather than malice or a lack of appreciation.

First and foremost, thanks to both you, the reader, and the Fortean community at large, for its continued support.

Specific appreciation goes to my fellow podcasters at *Where Did the Road Go?*—Seriah Azkath, Michael M. Hughes, and Red Pill Junkie—for their continued encouragement. A huge debt of gratitude in particular to RPJ, who provided the most thoughtful, insightful edits an author could hope for—in his second language, no less!

This book owes a huge debt to the outstanding work of Albert Rosales, Antonio F. Rullán, and Dan Clore. Everyone should treat their research as essential companion pieces to the book in your hands.

I am indebted to a few subject matter experts as well: Curt Coman, for helping me understand several chemical equations; Melanie Zimmer, for her knowledge of New York First Nations lore; and Greg Bishop, for his contributions on the odor of jet fuel.

Thanks to everyone who passed along leads, stories, and research, in particular Dr. Beachcombing (if you aren't reading his Bizarre History Blog, you should be ashamed), Tim Swartz, and Dan Bailey.

All the love and support in the world to my ParaManiacs.

Of course, continued thanks to Micah Hanks, for pushing this little baby bird out of the nest in the first place. Thanks also to Patrick Huyghe, who has the patience of a saint with me.

And speaking of people who have an abundance of patience: my wife, Sarah. I couldn't do this without you. Nor could I without the continued love, support, and prayers from my mother, father, sister, brother-in-law, and dearest nephews. Each of you is the world to me.

Endnotes

1   Kroeber, A.L. (1976). *Handbook of the Indians of California*. New York, NY: Dover Publications, Inc.

2   Guiley, R.E. (2007). *The Encyclopedia of Ghosts and Spirits* (3rd ed.). New York, NY: Facts On File, Inc. (Original work published 1992)

3   Pratt, B. (2004, February). UFOs still haunting Brazil's Valley of the Old Women. *MUFON UFO Journal 430*, pp. 3-8.

4   No author. (1973, June 26). Big, muddy 'critter' sighted at Big Muddy. *Southern Illinoisan*, p. 3.

5   Knol, A. S. (1985, December 7). Reliving the tale of the Big Muddy Monster. *Southern Illinoisan*, retrieved from http://www.bfro.net

6   Coleman, C.K. (1999). *Ghosts and Haunts of the Civil War*. Nashville, TN: Thomas Nelson.

7   Lewis, C.S. (1964). *The Discarded Image: An Introduction to Medieval and Renaissance Literature*. Cambridge, UK: Cambridge University Press.

8   Keel, J.A. (2002). *The Complete Guide to Mysterious Beings*. New York, NY: Tom Doherty Associates, LLC. (Original work published 1970 as *Strange Creatures from Time and Space*)

9   Keel, J.A. (2015). Savage Little Men From Outer Space – *Saga* Magazine – March 1969. In A. B. Colvin (Ed.), *The Book of Mothman: Everything You Wanted to Know About Reality Distortion But Were Afraid to Ask* (Kindle Location 1745-1971). Point Pleasant, WV: New Saucerian Books [Kindle Edition].

10   Guiley 2007.

11   Cheremisinoff, P.N., Morresi, A. C., & Young, R.A. (1975). Human Response and Effects of Odors. In Cheremisinoff, P.N. & Young, R.A. (Eds.), *Industrial Odor Technology Assessment* (pp. 1-25). Ann Arbor, MI: Ann Arbor Science Publishers Inc.

12   Hucklebridge, R. (2004, March 23). Report #8345 (Class A): Truck driver has a short but memorable encounter. Retrieved September 16, 2015 from http://www.bfro.net/

13   Freud, S. *Civilization and Its Discontents*. (2005). New York, NY: W.W. Norton & Company, Inc. (Original work published 1930 as *Das Unbehagen in der Kultur*)

14   Vroon, P. A., van Amerongen, A., & de Vries, H. (1997). *Smell: The Secret Seducer*. (P. Vincent, Trans.). New York, NY: Farrar, Straus and Giroux. (Original work published 1994 as *Verborgen verleider)*.

15   Le Guérer, A. (1994). *Scent: The Essential and Mysterious Powers of Smell.* (R. Miller, Trans.). New York, NY: Kodansha International. (Original Work published 1988 as *Les Pouvoirs de L'Odeur*)

16   Le Guérer 1994.

17   Vroon 1997.

18   Satti, J. (n.d.). *Miasma Analysis.* Retrieved September 15, 2015 from http://www.nanopathy.com/Miasma%20Analysis.pdf

19   Le Guérer 1994.

20   Cusik, D. (1828). *David Cusik's Sketches of Ancient History of the Six Nations (1828).* P. Royster (Ed.). Lincoln, NE: Faculty Publications, UNL Libraries.

21   Native Languages of the Americas. (n.d.). Legendary Native American Figures: Oniare (Oniont). Retrieved September 15, 2015 from http://www.native-languages.org

22   Bildhauer, B. (2003). Blood, Jews and Monsters in Medieval Culture. In B. Bildhauer & R. Mills (Eds.), *The Monstrous Middle Ages* (pp. 75-96). Bodmin, UK: MPG Books Ltd.

23   Le Guérer 1994.

24   Vroon 1997.

25   Le Guérer 1994.

26   Allan, W.K. (n.d.). Case 100. In A. Rosales (Ed.), *1969 Humanoid Sighting Reports.* Retrieved September 15, 2015 from http://www.ufoinfo.com/humanoid/humanoid-1969.pdf

27   Musgrave, J.B. (1979). *UFO Occupants & Critters.* Amherst, WI: Amherst Press.

28   Schacter, D., Gilbert, D., & Wegner, D. (2011). *Psychology* (2nd ed.). New York, NY: Worth Publishers.

29   Winter, R. (1976). *The Smell Book: Scents, Sex, and Society.* New York, NY: J.B. Lippincott Company.

30   Cheremisinoff 1975.

31   Moravec, M. (1980). *The UFO Anthropoid Catalogue.* Australia: Australian Center for UFO Studies.

32   Chaloupek, H. (n.d.). Case 159. In A. Rosales (Ed.), *1987 Humanoid Sighting Reports.* Retrieved September 15, 2015 from http://www.ufoinfo.com/humanoid/humanoid-1987.pdf

33 Trainor, J. (Ed.). (2000, July 13). UFO Roundup Volume 5, Number 28. Retrieved September 15, 2015 from http://ufoupdateslist.com/2000/jul/m13-012.shtml

34 Herz, R. (2011, January 6). Smell Manipulation: The subliminal power of scent. Retrieved September 15, 2015 from https://www.psychologytoday.com/blog/smell-life/201101/smell-manipulation

35 Vroon 1997.

36 Mitzman, D. (2014, May 28). Do people experience smell in their dreams? Retrieved September 15, 2015 from http://www.bbc.com/news/magazine-27590756

37 Spengler, J. D., McCarthy, J. F., Samet, J.M. (2000). *Indoor Air Quality Handbook*. New York, NY, USA: McGraw-Hill Professional Publishing.

38 Engen, T. (1982). *The Perception of Odors*. London, UK: Academic Press.

39 Engen, T. (1991). *Odor Sensation and Memory*. New York, NY: Praeger Publishers.

40 Dilks, D.D., Dalton, P., & Beauchamp, G.K. (1999) Cross-cultural variation in responses to malodors. *Chemical Senses 24*, 599.

41 Zaleski, C. (1987). *Otherworld Journeys: Accounts of Near-Death Experience in Medieval and Modern Times*. Oxford, UK: Oxford University Press.

42 Carter, C. (2010). *Science and the Near-Death Experience: How Consciousness Survives Death*. Rochester, VT: Inner Traditions.

43 Winter 1976.

44 Engen 1991.

45 Young, K. (2003, February). The Last Deed. *MUFON UFO Journal 418*, pp. 3-4.

46 Herriot, J. (1976). *All Things Wise and Wonderful*. New York, NY: St. Martin's Paperbacks.

47 Engen 1991.

48 Fields, H. (2012, April 12). Fragrant Flashbacks: Smells rouse early memories. Retrieved September 15, 2015 from http://www.psychologicalscience.org/index.php/publications/observer/2012/april-12/fragrant-flashbacks.html

49 Schab, F.R. (1995). *Memory for Odors*. Mahwah, NJ: Lawrence Erlbaum Associates.

50 Engen 1991.

51 Mitzman 2014.

52   Turner, K. (1994). *Taken: Inside the Alien-Human Abduction Agenda.* Tallahassee, FL: Rose Printing Company, Inc.

53   Jastrow, Jr., M., McCurdy, J.F., Kohler, K., & Ginzberg, L. (1906). Burnt offering. In *Jewish Encyclopedia*. Retrieved September 21, 2015 from http://www.jewishencyclopedia.com

54   Lis-Balchin, M. (2006). *Aromatherapy Science: A Guide for Healthcare Professionals.* London, UK: Pharmaceutical Press.

55   Le Guérer 1994.

56   Lis-Balchin 2006.

57   Le Guérer 1994.

58   Cunningham, S. (1989). *The Complete Book of Incense, Oils & Brews.* St. Paul. MN: Llewellyn Publications.

59   Le Guérer 1994.

60   Le Guérer 1994.

61   Foster, M.D. (2015). *The Book of Yokai: Mysterious Creatures of Japanese Folklore.* Oakland, CA: University of California Press.

62   Castillo, L.N. (n.d.). Case 83. In A. Rosales (Ed.), *1987 Humanoid Sighting Reports.* Retrieved September 15, 2015 from http://www.ufoinfo.com/humanoid/humanoid-1987.pdf

63   Guiley 2007.

64   Glanvil, J. (1689). *Sadiucismus Triumphatus: Full and Plain Evidence Concerning Witches and Apparitions.* London, UK: James Collins. (Original work published 1661)

65   Keel, J. A. (1976). *The Eighth Tower: On Ultraterrestrials and the Superspectrum.* New York, NY: E.P. Dutton & Co. Inc.

66   Vroon 1997.

67   Charles, R.H. (Trans.). (2013). *The Book of Enoch.* London, UK: Society for Promoting Christian Knowledge Classics. (Original work published 1917).

68   Rémy, N. (2008). *Demonolatry: An Account of the Historical Practice of Witchcraft.* M. Summers (Ed.). Mineola, NY: Dover Publications, Inc. (Original work published 1930).

69   Hall, M.A., & Coleman, L. (2010). *True Giants: Is* Gigantopithecus *Still Alive?* San Antonio, TX: Anomalist Books.

70   Meyer, B. (1977). *Sulfur, Energy, and Environment.* Amsterdam, Netherlands: Elsevier Scientific Publishing Company.

71   Vroon 1997.

72   Kroonenberg, S. (2013). *Why Hell Stinks of Sulfur: Mythology and Geology of the Underworld.* (A. Brown, Trans.). London, UK: Reaktion Books Ltd. (Original work published 2011 as *Waarom de hel naar zwavel stinkt*)

73   Glassé, C. (2008). *The New Encyclopedia of Islam* (3rd ed.). Lanham, MD: Rowman & Littlefield Publishers, Inc.

74   Fox, R.L. (2008). *Travelling Heroes: Greeks and their Myths in the Epic Age of Homer.* London, UK: Penguin Books Ltd.

75   Graves, K. (1999). *The Biography of Satan: Exposing the Origins of the Devil* (5th ed.). Escondido, CA: The Book Tree. (Original work published 1865)

76   Willison, J. (1820). *A Treatise Concerning the Sanctification of the Lord's Day.* Albany, NY: J. Boardman.

77   Hood, R.E. (1994). *Begrimed and Black: Christian Traditions on Blacks and Blackness.* Minneapolis, MN: Augsburg Fortress.

78   Gardenour Walter, B.S. (2015). *Our Old Monsters Witches, Werewolves, and Vampires from Medieval Theology to Horror Cinema.* Jefferson, NC: McFarland & Company, Inc.

79   Guiley, R.E. (2009). *The Encyclopedia of Demons and Demonology.* New York, NY: Facts On File, Inc.

80   Sharpless, B., & Doghramji, K. (2015). *Sleep Paralysis: Historical, Psychological, and Medical Perspectives.* Oxford, UK: Oxford University Press.

81   Le Guérer 1994.

82   Ruickbie, L. (2013). *Ghost Hunting: How to Identify and Investigate Spirits, Poltergeists and Hauntings.* London, UK: Constable & Robinson, Ltd.

83   Faust, J.G. (1993). *The Black Raven.* (K.H. Welz, Trans.). Decatur, GA: Knights of Runes. (Original date unknown, alleged 1500s, published as *D.I. Fausti Schwartzer Rabe*)

84   Warwick, T. (Ed.). *The Grand Grimoire: The Red Dragon.* (2015). US: CreateSpace Independent Publishing Platform. (Original date unknown, alleged 1750)

85   Bane, T. (2012). *Encyclopedia of Demons in World Religions and Cultures.* Jefferson, NC: McFarland & Company, Inc.

86   Hardtke, T. (2015). Deaths resulting from exorcism. In J.P. Laycock (Ed.), *Spirit Possession Around the World: Possession, Communion, and Demon Expulsion Across Cultures* (pp. 99-104). Santa Barbara, CA: ABC-CLIO, LLC.

87   Guiley 2009.

88   Guiley 2009.

89 Monahan, B. (Ed.). (1997). *An American Haunting: The Bell Witch.* New York, NY: St. Martin's Griffin.

90 Kroonenberg 2013.

91 Krebs, R.E. (2006). *The History and Use of Our Earth's Chemical Elements: A Reference Guide.* Westport, CT: Greenwood Press.

92 Sulfur (n.d.). *University of Minnesota's Mineral Pages.* Retrieved September 24, 2015 from https://www.esci.umn.edu/courses/1001/minerals/sulfur.shtml

93 Krebs 2006.

94 Wolchover, N. (2011, February 2). What are the ingredients of life? Retrieved September 24, 2015 from http://www.livescience.com/32983-what-are-ingredients-life.html

95 Meyer, O. (1994). Functional Groups of Microorganisms. In E.-D. Schulze & H.A. Mooney (Eds.), *Biodiversity and Ecosystem Function* (pp. 67-96). Berlin, Germany: Springer-Verlag.

96 Tangerman, A. (2009). Measurement and biological significance of the volatile sulfur compounds hydrogen sulfide, methanethiol and dimethyl sulfide in various biological matrices. *Journal of Chromatography B, Analytical technologies in the biomedical and life science 877*, 28.

97 Winter 1976.

98 Maynard, D.G. (1998). *Sulfur in the Environment.* New York, NY Marcel Dekker, Inc.

99 Meyer 1977.

100 Krebs 2006.

101 Habib, Y. (1975). Odor emission sources in the chemical and petroleum industries. In Cheremisinoff, P.N. & Young, R.A. (Eds.), *Industrial Odor Technology Assessment* (pp. 189-201). Ann Arbor, MI: Ann Arbor Science Publishers Inc.

102 Vroon 1997.

103 National Research Council of the National Academies. (2009). *Emergency and Continuous Exposure Guidance Levels for Selected Submarine Contaminants* (Vol. 3). Washington, DC: The National Academies Press.

104 Satterfield, Z. (2004, Fall). What does ppm or ppb mean? *On Tap*, pp. 38-40.

105 Engen 1982.

106   Duke Medicine News and Communications. (2012, February 6). Copper + Love Chemical = Big Sulfur Stink. Retrieved September 25, 2015 from http://corporate.dukemedicine.org/news_and_publications/news_office/news/copper-love-chemical-big-sulfur-stink

107   Brunvand, J.H. (2001). *Too Good to Be True: The Colossal Book of Urban Legends*. New York, NY: W.W. Norton & Company.

108   Coleman, L., & Clark, J. (1999). *Cryptozoology A to Z: The Encyclopedia of Loch Monsters, Sasquatch, Chupacabras, and Other Authentic Mysteries of Nature*. New York, NY: Fireside.

109   Pratt, B., & Luce, C. (1998, August). Varginha, Brazil ET crash, capture? *MUFON UFO Journal 364*, pp. 3-6.

110   Druffel, A., & Sider, J. (2000, July). Onomastic research. *MUFON UFO Journal 387*, pp. 3-10.

111   Clark, J. (2013). *Unexplained! Strange Sightings, Incredible Occurrences, and Puzzling Physical Phenomena* (3rd ed.). Canton, MI: Visible Ink Press.

112   Gater, P. (2003). *Living with Ghosts: An Investigation*. Staffordshire, UK: Anecdotes.

113   Guiley 2007.

114   Hiatt, L. (1975). *Australian Aboriginal Mythology: Essays in Honour of W.E.H. Stanner*. Canberra, AU: Australian Institute of Aboriginal Studies.

115   Meyer, M. (2013). Yokai.com: An online database of Japanese ghosts and monsters. Retrieved October 13, 2015 from http://yokai.com

116   Knappert, J. (1995). *African Mythology: An Encyclopedia of Myth and Legend*. London, UK: Diamond Books.

117   Haughton, B. (2012). *Famous Ghost Stories: Legends and Lore*. New York, NY: The Rosen Publishing Group, Inc.

118   Haughton 2012.

119   Catholic Insight. (2008). Our Lady of Laus. Retrieved September 29, 2015 from http://www.thefreelibrary.com/Our+Lady+of+Laus.-a0180277206

120   CatholicTradition.org. (n.d.). Our Lady of Laus: Adapted from *Magnificat* Vol. XL, No. 5 and Vol. XXXVI. Retrieved September 29, 2015 from http://www.catholictradition.org/Mary/laus.htm

121   Cook, K.A. (2010). *Marian Apparitions Are Real: Visits of Jesus and Mary*. US: CreateSpace Independent Publishing Platform.

122   Mann, S.A. (2014, March 28). Our Sunday Visitor: Who is Our Lady of Laus? Retrieved September 29, 2015 from https://www.osv.com

123   Sanctuaire Notre-Dame du Laus. (2015). Retrieved September 29, 2015 from http://www.sanctuaire-notredamedulaus.com/

124   Guiley 2007.

125   Anderson, C., & Chavez, E. (2009). *Our Lady of Guadalupe: Mother of the Civilization of Love*. New York, NY: Doubleday Religion.

126   Academy of the Immaculate. (2008). *Mary at the Foot of the Cross, VII: Coredemptrix, Therefore Mediatrix of All Graces. Act of the Seventh International Symposium on Marian Coredemption*. New Bedford, MA: Franciscans of the Immaculate.

127   Le Guérer 1994.

128   Aftel, M. (2001). *Essence and Alchemy: A Natural History of Perfume*. New York, NY: North Point Press.

129   Le Guérer 1994.

130   Rimmel, E. (2005). *The Book of Perfumes*. Boston, MA: Adamant Media Corporation-Elibron Classics Series. (Original work published 1865)

131   Aftel 2001.

132   Aftel 2001.

133   Rimmel 2005.

134   Peterson, J.H. (Ed.). (2001). *The Lesser Key of Solomon: Detailing the Ceremonial Art of Commanding Spirits Both Good and Evil*. York Beach, ME: Weiser Books.

135   Jung, C.G. (1989). *Memories, Dreams, Reflections*. (R. Winston & C. Winston, Trans.). A. Jaffé (Ed.). New York, NY: Random House. (Original work published 1961 as *Erinnerungen Träume Gedanken*)

136   Le Guérer 1994.

137   Cook 2010.

138   Kvideland, R., & Sehmsdorf, H.K. (Eds.). *Scandinavian Folk Belief and Legend*. (1988). Minneapolis, MN: University of Minnesota Press.

139   Ivanits, L.J. (1989). *Russian Folk Belief*. Armonk, NY: M.E. Sharpe.

140   Haughton 2012.

141   Burchum, J.R., & Rosenthal, L.D. (2016). *Lehne's Pharmacology for Nursing Care*

(9th ed.). St. Louis, MO: Elsevier Saunders.

142   Hagerty, B.B. (2009). *Fingerprints of God: The Search for the Science of Spirituality.* New York, NY: Riverhead Books.

143   Le Guérer 1994.

144   Rickard, B., & Michell, J. (2000). *Unexplained Phenomena: A Rough Guide Special.* London, UK: Rough Guides, Ltd.

145   Harpur, P. (2003). *Daimonic Reality: A Field Guide to the Otherworld.* Enumclaw, WA: Pine Winds Press. (Original work published 1994).

146   Hesemann, M. (2000). *The Fatima Secret.* W. Strieber (Ed.). New York, NY: Dell Publishing.

147   Windeatt, M.F. (1945). *The Children of Fatima and Our Lady's Message to the World.* St. Meinrad, IN: St. Meinrad's Abbey, Inc.

148   Hesemann 2000.

149   Harpur 2003.

150   Hauck, D.W. (2000). *The International Directory of Haunted Places.* New York, NY: Penguin Books.

151   Guiley 2007.

152   Verga, M. (2008). *When Flying Saucers Came to Earth: The Story of the Italian UFO Landings in the Golden Era of the Flying Saucers.* US: CreateSpace Independent Publishing Platform.

153   Lane, S. (2005). Ohio State Reformatory A.K.A. Mansfield Reformatory. In J. Belanger (Ed.), *Encyclopedia of Haunted Places* (pp. 126-127). Franklin Lakes, NJ: New Page Books.

154   Connally, K. (2005). The Baker Hotel. In J. Belanger (Ed.), *Encyclopedia of Haunted Places* (p. 183). Franklin Lakes, NJ: New Page Books.

155   Bailey, H. (2005). The Bush House. In J. Belanger (Ed.), *Encyclopedia of Haunted Places* (pp. 207-208). Franklin Lakes, NJ: New Page Books.

156   Guiley 2007.

157   Senate, R. (2005). Gold Hill Hotel. In J. Belanger (Ed.), *Encyclopedia of Haunted Places* (pp. 173-174). Franklin Lakes, NJ: New Page Books.

158   Guiley 2007.

159   Senate 2005.

160   Brown, A. (2012). *The Big Book of Texas Ghost Stories*. Mechanicsburg, PA: Stackpole Books.

161   Han, B. (2014). *The Ghost Files*. Bloomington, IN: Booktango.

162   Strickler, L., and Forker, S. (2015, October 12). *Arcane Radio Live Show Archive 10.12.2015: Mike Ricksecker* [Audio podcast]. Retrieved October 19, 2015 from http://www.arcaneradio.com/

163   Guiley 2007.

164   Taylor, T. (2007). Mineral Springs Hotel: The True Story of One of Alton's Most Haunted Locations. Retrieved September 29, 2015 from http://www.altonhauntings.com/mineral.html

165   Cadey, M. (2009). *Paranormal Bath*. Gloucestershire, UK: Amberley Publishing.

166   Vroon 1997.

167   Inglis-Arkell, E. (2015, July 15). Why is a Compound That Smells Like Feces Put in Perfume And Chocolate? Retrieved October 19, 2015, from http://io9.com/why-is-a-compound-that-smells-like-feces-put-in-perfume-1717903411

168   Belanger, J. (2007). *The Ghost Files*. Franklin Lakes, NJ: The Career Press, Inc.

169   Russell, R. (2008). *Ghost Cats of the South*. Winston-Salem, NC: John F. Blair.

170   Belanger 2007.

171   Dr. Beachcombing. (2013, October 10). Paranormal smells. Retrieved September 30, 2015 from http://www.strangehistory.net/2013/10/10/paranormal-smells/

172   Vosnaki, E. (2011, February 7). Mapping the vocabulary of scent: what smells like nail polish/metal/sweat/horses/hairspray/burnt toast/baby powder/dirty socks etc? Retrieved September 30, 2015 from http://perfumeshrine.blogspot.com/2011/02/mapping-vocabulary-of-scent-what-smells.html

173   Sloan, D.L. (1998). *Ghosts of Key West*. Key West, FL: Phantom Press.

174   Pattskyn, H. (2012). *Ghosthunting Michigan*. Covington, KY: Clerisy Press.

175   Hudnall, K. (2006). *Spirits of the Border: The History and Mystery of Tombstone*. Nashville, TN: Grave Distractions Publications.

176   Freeman, B. (2005). The Gravesite of James Dean. In J. Belanger (Ed.), *Encyclopedia of Haunted Places* (pp. 116-117). Franklin Lakes, NJ: New Page Books.

177   Revai, C. (2009). *The Big Book of New York Ghost Stories*. Mechanicsburg, PA: Stackpole Books.

178   Davis, J. (2005). Old New Castle. In J. Belanger (Ed.), *Encyclopedia of Haunted*

Places (p. 52). Franklin Lakes, NJ: New Page Books.

179   Belanger, J. (2005). *RMS Queen Mary*. In J. Belanger (Ed.), *Encyclopedia of Haunted Places* (p. 201). Franklin Lakes, NJ: New Page Books.

180   Coleman 1999.

181   Guiley 2007.

182   Guiley, R.E. (2014). *The Big Book of West Virginia Ghost Stories*. Mechanicsburg, PA: Stackpole Books.

183   Guiley 2007.

184   Tucker, E. (2007). *Haunted Halls: Ghostlore of American College Campuses*. Jackson, MS: University Press of Mississippi.

185   Price, H. (2012). *Poltergeist Over England: Three Centuries of Mischievous Ghosts*. Devon, UK: F&W Media.

186   Price 2012.

187   Hubbell, W. (1916). *The Great Amherst Mystery: A True Narrative of the Supernatural* (10th ed.). New York: Brentano's. (Original work published 1888)

188   Tyrrell, J. (2005). Market Square. In J. Belanger (Ed.), *Encyclopedia of Haunted Places* (p. 239). Franklin Lakes, NJ: New Page Books.

189   Legro, S. (2015, December 31). *Into the Fray: Haunted Las Vegas* [Audio podcast]. Retrieved January 12, 2016 from https://intothefrayradio.com

190   Gater 2003.

191   Deveraux, P. (2003). *Haunted Land: Investigations into Ancient Mysteries and Modern Day Phenomena*. London, UK: Piatkus Books.

192   Kennedy, R.C. (2005). *Coffin Nails: The Tobacco Controversy in the 19th Century – Cigarettes: Women*. Retrieved October 13, 2015 from http://tobacco.harpweek.com/

193   Keel 2002/1970.

194   Merry, A. (1908). Kilman Castle: The House of Horror. In R. Shirley (Ed.), *The Occult Review July-December 1908* (Vol. VIII, pp. 308-347). London, UK: William Rider & Son, Limited.

195   Coulombe, C.A. (2004). *Haunted Castles of the World: Ghostly Legends and Phenomena from Keeps and Fortresses Around the Globe*. Guilford, CT: The Lyons Press.

196   Hazelgrove, J. (2000). *Spiritualism and British Society Between the Wars*. Manchester, UK: Manchester University Press.

197 Playfair, G.L. (2011). *The Flying Cow: Exploring the Psychic World of Brazil*. Guildford, UK: White Crow Books.

198 Meyer 2013.

199 Hallenbeck, B.G. (2013). *Monsters of New York: Mysterious Creatures in the Empire State*. Mechanicsburg, PA: Stackpole Books.

200 Severus, S. (1894). Martin is tempted by the Wiles of the Devil. In P. Schaff (Ed.), *A Select Library of Nicene and Post-Nicene Fathers of the Christian Church, Second Series* (Vol. 11). (A. Roberts, Trans.). New York, NY.

201 Le Guérer 1994.

202 Iskander, A. (365). *Nicene and Post-Nicene Fathers of the Christian Church, Volume IV: St. Athanasius Select Works and Letters – Life of St. Antony* (P. Schaff & H. Wace, Eds.). OrthodoxEBooks.org.

203 Keel 2002/1970.

204 Ellwood, R.S. (1993). *Islands of the Dawn: The Story of Alternative Spirituality in New Zealand*. Honolulu, HI: University of Hawaii Press.

205 Machlin, M. & Beckley, T.G. (1981). *UFO*. Cape Town, South Africa: Quick Fox.

206 Finch, L.I. (Ed.). (1908, December). Haunted House near London. *The Annals of Psychical Science VII (41)*, pp. 258-260.

207 Chorvinsky, M. (1997, Summer). Encounters with the Grim Reaper. *Strange Magazine 18*, pp. 6-12.

208 Brunvand 2001.

209 Tucker 2007.

210 Coulombe 2004.

211 Baker, L. (2005). Port Arthur Historic Site. In J. Belanger (Ed.), *Encyclopedia of Haunted Places* (pp. 277-278). Franklin Lakes, NJ: New Page Books.

212 Coulombe 2004.

213 Swindell, B. (2005). Yorktown. In J. Belanger (Ed.), *Encyclopedia of Haunted Places* (pp. 102-103). Franklin Lakes, NJ: New Page Books.
214 Belanger, J. (2005). South Bridge Underground Vaults. In J. Belanger (Ed.), *Encyclopedia of Haunted Places* (pp. 303-304). Franklin Lakes, NJ: New Page Books.

215 Brunning, A. (2014, November 8). Why corpses stink – the science of smell. Retrieved October 1, 2015 from http://dyingwords.net/corpses-stink-science-smell/#sthash.qAkvGWFW.s6l5FMfq.dpbs

216   Revai, C. (2005). *Haunted New York: Ghosts and Strange Phenomena of the Empire State*. Mechanicsburg, PA: Stackpole Books.

217   Guiley 2009.

218   Sands, K.R. (2004). *Demonic Possession in Elizabethan England*. Westport, CT: Praeger Publishers.

219   Brown, A. (2006). *Ghost Hunters of the South*. Jackson, MS: University Press of Mississippi.

220   Cranmer, B., & Manfred, E. (2014). *The Demon of Brownsville Road: A Pittsburgh Family's Battle with Evil in Their Home*. New York, NY: The Berkley Publishing Group.

221   Maxwell-Stuart, P.G. (2011). *Poltergeists: A History of Violent Ghost Phenomena*. Gloucestershire, UK: Amberly Publishing.

222   Koch, K.E. (1986). *Occult ABC: Exposing Occult Practices and Ideologies*. Grand Rapids, MI: Kregel Publications (Original work published 1978 as *Satan's Devices*)

223   Bastien, J.L. (2008). *Ghosts of Mount Holly: A History of Haunted Happenings*. Charleston, SC: The History Press (Haunted America).

224   Kleen, M. (2010). *Haunting the Prairie: A Tourist's Guide to the Weird and Wild Places of Illinois*. Rockford, IL: Black Oak Press.

225   Brandon, T. (2002). *The Ghost Hunter's Bible*. Mansfield OH: Zerotime Publishing.

226   Guiley 2007.

227   Waters, S. (2011). *Haunted Manitou Springs*. Charleston, SC: The History Press (Haunted America).

228   Roth, J. (2014). *Ghost Soldiers of Gettysburg: Searching for Spirits on America's Most Famous Battlefield*. Woodbury, MN: Llewellyn Publications.

229   Ellis, M.M. (2014). *The Everything Ghost Hunting Book: Tips, Tools, and Techniques for Exploring the Supernatural World* (2nd ed.). Avon, MA: Adams Media.

230   Howard, R.A. (2006). Realities and Perceptions in the Evolution of Black Powder Making. In B.J. Buchanan (Ed.), *Gunpowder, Explosives, and the State: A Technological History* (pp. 21-41). Bodmin, UK: MPG Books Ltd.

231   Gamlin, L., & Price, B. (1988, November 5). Bonfires and Brimstone. *New Scientist 1637*, pp. 48-51.

232   Howard 2006.

233   Hunt, A. (2013). *Dictionary of Chemistry*. New York, NY: Routledge. (Original work published 1998)

234 Hall, W.J. (2014). *The World's Most Haunted House: The True Story of the Bridgeport Poltergeist on Lindley Street*. Pompton Plains, NJ: New Page Books.

235 Holzer, H. (2004). *Ghosts: True Encounters from the World Beyond*. New York, NY: Black Dog & Leventhal.

236 Meyer 1977.

237 Agency for Toxic Substances & Disease Registry. (2014, October 21). Toxic Substances Portal – Sulfur Dioxide. Retrieved October 19, 2015 from http://www.atsdr.cdc.gov/mmg/mmg.asp?id=249&tid=46

238 Baker, R.A., & Nickell, J. (1992). *Missing Pieces: How to Investigate Ghosts, UFOs, Psychics, and Other Mysteries*. Amherst, NY: Prometheus Books.

239 Guiley 2007.

240 Coleman 1999.

241 Zwicker, R.J. (2007). *Haunted Portsmouth: Spirits and Shadows of the Past*. Charleston, SC: The History Press (Haunted America).

242 Okonowicz, E. (2010). *The Big Book of Maryland Ghost Stories*. Mechanicsburg, PA: Stackpole Books.

243 Rodgman, A., & Perfetti, T.A. (2013). *The Chemical Components of Tobacco and Tobacco Smoke* (2nd ed.). Boca Raton, FL: CRC Press.

244 Chiras, D.D. (2015). *Human Biology*. Burlington, MA: Jones & Bartlett Learning.

245 Keritsis, G.D., Bokelman, G.H., & Gooden, III, D.T. (1982, December 7). Tobacco curing method - US 4362170 A. Retrieved October 19, 2015 from www.google.com/patents/US4362170

246 Lynch, G.J., Canwell, D., and Sutherland, J. (2012). *Famous Ghosts and Haunted Places*. New York, NY: The Rosen Publishing Group, Inc.

247 Bord, J., & Bord, C. (1989). *Unexplained Mysteries of the 20th Century*. Lincolnwood, IL: Contemporary Books.

248 Guiley 2007.

249 Dr. Beachcombing 2013.

250 Husak, R. (2005). The Emmitt House. In J. Belanger (Ed.), *Encyclopedia of Haunted Places* (pp. 124-125). Franklin Lakes, NJ: New Page Books.

251 Guiley 2007.

252 Guiley 2007.

253   Matthews, D. (2015, December 13). How a Weekend on Haunted Mackinac Island Resulted in Strange Insight Into the Nature of Ghosts. Retrieved January 15, 2016 from http://weekinweird.com/

254   Rainbolt, D. (2007). *Ghost Cats: Human Encounters with Feline Spirits*. Guilford, CT: The Lyons Press.

255   Guiley 2007.

256   Flanders, F.B. (2012). *Exploring Animal Science*. Clifton Park, NJ: Delmar.

257   Tyson, P. (2012, October 4). Dogs' Dazzling Sense of Smell. Retrieved January 13, 2016 from http://www.pbs.org/

258   Righi, B. (2008). *Ghosts, Apparitions, and Poltergeists*. Woodbury, MN: Llewellyn Publications.

259   Bord 1989.

260   Baker, L. (2005). Former Jasper County Care Facility. In J. Belanger (Ed.), *Encyclopedia of Haunted Places* (pp. 138-139). Franklin Lakes, NJ: New Page Books.

261   Guilet 2007.

262   Helmholtz Centre for Environmental Research. (2006, October 20). Money does not smell—until it is touched. Retrieved January 13, 2016 from https://www.ufz.de

263   Helmholtz Centre for Environmental Research 2006.

264   Schmit, S. (2005). Franek Kluski's Casts. In *The Perfect Medium: Photography and the Occult*. New Haven, CT: Yale University Press. (Original work published 2004)

265   Guiley 2007.

266   Jung, C.G. (1997). *Jung on Synchronicity and the Paranormal*. R. Main (Ed.). London, UK: Rutledge.

267   Winter 1976.

268   Guiley 2007.

269   Uhde, T.W., Cortese, B.M., & Vendeniapin, A. (2012). Sleep Disorders. In M. Hersen & D.C. Beidel (Eds.), *Adult Psychopathy and Diagnosis* (6th ed.) (pp. 717 - 747). Hoboken, NJ: John Wiley & Sons, Inc.

270   Siegel, R.K. (1992). *Fire in the Brain: Clinical Tales of Hallucination*. Westminster, UK: Penguin Books (Dutton Adult).

271   National UFO Reporting Center. (2003, March 4). Strange beam and apparition terrifies child. Retrieved October 13, 2015 from http://www.nuforc.org

272 Hamilton, W.F. (1993, August). Area 51 Encounter. *MUFON UFO Journal 304*, pp. 14-17.

273 Sharpless & Doghramji 2015.

274 Bruce, R. (2012). *Astral Dynamics: The Complete Book of Out-of-Body Experience* (2nd ed.). Charlottesville, VA: Hampton Roads Publishing Company.

275 Binnall, T. (2015, July 7). *Binnall of America Season IX: 7.7.15 – Carl DeMarco* [Audio podcast]. Retrieved October 19, 2015 from http://binnallofamerica.com/boaa070715.html

276 Heasmer, C. (2015, February 3). I'm stalked by a ghost which smells of FISH when something bad is about to happen. Retrieved October 13, 2015 from http://www.mirror.co.uk/news/real-life-stories/im-stalked-ghost-smells-fish-5098263

277 Gerhold, H.D. (2007). *A Century of Forest Resources Education at Penn State: Serving Our Forests, Waters, Wildlife, and Wood Industries*. University Park, PA: Pennsylvania State University Press.

278 Cooper, L.A. (2010). *Gothic Realities: The Impact of Horror Fiction on Modern Culture*. Jefferson, NC: McFarland & Company, Inc.

279 Paijmans, T. (2013, October 5). Spring-Heeled Jack in America. Retrieved April 20, 2016 from http://mysteriousuniverse.org/

280 Trench, B.L.P. (1966). *The Flying Saucer Story*. London, UK: Neville Spearman.

281 Orcutt, L. (2001). Catchpenny Mysteries: The Tulli Papyrus. Retrieved October 14, 2015 from http://www.catchpenny.org/tulli.html

282 Vallee, J., & Aubeck, C. (2010). *Wonders in the Sky: Unexplained Aerial Objects from Antiquity to Modern Times and Their Impact on Human Culture, History, and Beliefs*. New York, NY: Penguin Group (Jeremy P. Tarcher).

283 Woodward, J. (2005, November). Animal reactions to UFO encounters. *MUFON UFO Journal 451*, pp. 8-12.

284 Briazack, N.J., & Mennick, S. (1978). *The UFO Guidebook*. Secaucus N.J.: Citadel Press.

285 Keel 1976.

286 Sanderson, I.T. (1974). *Uninvited Visitors: A Biologist Looks at UFO's*. London, UK: Universal-Tandem Publishing Company Ltd.

287 McCampbell, J.M. (1973). *UFOlogy: New Insights from Science and Common Sense*. Belmont, CA: Jaymac-Hollman.

288 Bullard, T.E. (1987). *UFO Abductions: The Measure of a Mystery* (Vol. 1). Mount

Rainier, MD: Fund for UFO Research.

289   Olsen, T.M. (1980, November). UFO Odours and Origins. *Flying Saucer Review 26(4)*, pp. 12-13.

290   Durant, R.J. (1998, July). Buzzes and smells in Strieber's *Majestic. MUFON Journal 363*, pp. 7-9.

291   Rullán, A.F. (2000, July 2). Odors from UFOs: Deducing Odorant Chemistry and Causation from Available Data. Retrieved October 14, 2015 from http://www.ufoevidence.org

292   Rullán 2000.

293   Rullán 2000.

294   Vallee, J., & Vallee, J. (1966). *Challenge to Science: The UFO Enigma*. Chicago, IL: Henry Regnery Company.

295   Steinberg, G., & O'Brien, C. (2015, October 4). *The Paracast: October 4, 2015 – Stan Gordon* [Audio podcast]. Retrieved November 3, 2015 from http://www.theparacast.com/podcast/now-playing-october-4-2015-stan-gordon/

296   Vroon 1997.

297   Engen 1982.

298   Beckley, T.G. (1990). *The UFO Silencers*. New Brunswick, NJ: Inner Light Publications.

299   Clear, C. (1999). *Reaching for Reality: Seven Incredible True Stories of Alien Abduction*. San Antonio, TX: Consciousness Now.

300   Anfalov, A. & Crimean Anomalous Phenomena Research Group. (n.d.). Case 199. In A. Rosales (Ed.), *2002 Humanoid Sighting Reports*. Retrieved October 19, 2015 from http://www.ufoinfo.com/humanoid/humanoid-2002.pdf

301   Machlin & Beckley 1981.

302   Budden, A. (1999). *The UFO Files: Psychic Close Encounters*. London, UK: Cassell & Co.

303   Project Blue Book. (1952, August 25). DesVergers case file. College Park, MD: National Archives.

304   Project Blue Book 1952.

305   Conway, G. (2002, January 12). The Guardians. Retrieved October 15, 2015 from http://www.ufobc.com/Experiencer/guardians_v2.htm

306   Walton, T. (1997). *Fire in the Sky: The Walton Experience* (3rd ed.). New York, NY: Marlowe & Company. (Original work published 1979)

307   Mack, J. (1995). *Abduction: Human Encounters with Aliens.* New York, NY: Ballantine Books.

308   Thompson, J.C. (n.d.). Case 153. In A. Rosales (Ed.), *1973 Humanoid Sighting Reports.* Retrieved November 5, 2015 from http://www.ufoinfo.com/humanoid/humanoid-1973.pdf

309   Barnes, C. (1996, December 2). A Perth mother and son's bizarre encounter's with another world. Retrieved November 5, 2015 from http://www.auforn.com/Irenes_story.html

310   Turner, K. (1992). *Into the Fringe.* New York, NY: Berkley Books.

311   Steiger, B. (1988). *The UFO Abductors.* New York, NY: Berkley Books.

312   Miles, J. (2000). *Weird Georgia: Close Encounters, Strange Creatures, and Unexplained Phenomena.* Nashville, TN: Cumberland House Publishing.

313   Walters, E. (n.d.). Case 355. In A. Rosales (Ed.), *1990 Humanoid Sighting Reports.* Retrieved October 19, 2015 from http://www.ufoinfo.com/humanoid/humanoid-1990.pdf

314   Picknett, L. (2001). *The Mammoth Book of UFOs.* New York, NY: Carroll & Graf Publishers, Inc.

315   Lorgen, E. (1998, May 2). Common Symptoms of Abduction – Chart. Retrieved November 5, 2015 from http://evelorgen.com

316   Strieber, W. (1987). *Communion.* New York, NY: Avon Books.

317   Bryan 1995.

318   Schnabel, J. (1994). *Dark White: Aliens, Abductions, and the UFO Obsession.* London, UK: Penguin Books.

319   Thompson, J.C. (1998). The Enigmatic Troup-Heard Corridor. Retrieved November 5, 2015 from http://www.mufonga.org/article-troupheardcorridor.html

320   Moseley, J.W., & Pflock, K.T. (2002). *Shockingly Close to the Truth: Confessions of a Grave-Robbing Ufologist.* Amherst, NY: Prometheus Books.

321   Strieber, W. (1988, June). A Response to Critics. *MUFON UFO Journal 242*, pp. 7-8.

322   Moseley & Pflock 2002.

323   Strieber 1987.

324   Gilbert, A. (2009, March 15). Proust with an Anal Probe: The Smells of An Alien Abduction. Retrieved November 5, 2015 from http://www.firstnerve.com

325   Engen 1991.

326   Strieber 1987.

327   Strieber, W. (1997). *Transformation*. New York, NY: Avon Books. (Original work published 1988)

328   Casteel, S. (2012, January 20). A Conversation with Whitley Strieber. Retrieved November 5, 2015 from http://www.openminds.tv/a-conversation-with-whitley-strieber/14108

329   Cutchin, J. (2015). *A Trojan Feast*. San Antonio, TX: Anomalist Books.

330   Webb, D.F., and Bloecher, T. (n.d.). Case 254. In A. Rosales (Ed.), *1975 Humanoid Sighting Reports*. Retrieved October 19, 2015 from http://www.ufoinfo.com/humanoid/humanoid-1975.pdf

331   Schuessler, J. (1998, February). Physiological effects from abductions. *MUFON UFO Journal 358*, pp. 13-15.

332   Bullard, T.E. (1987). *UFO Abductions: The Measure of a Mystery* (Vol. 2). Mount Rainier, MD: Fund for UFO Research.

333   Melamed, A. (n.d.). Case 49. In A. Rosales (Ed.), *1990 Humanoid Sighting Reports*. Retrieved October 19, 2015 from http://www.ufoinfo.com/humanoid/humanoid-1990.pdf

334   UFOs Northwest. (2010, June). Security Guard Has Strange Encounter & Loses 3 Hours Time. Retrieved October 19, 2015 from http://www.ufosnw.com/sighting_reports/2010/newbergor06102010/newbergor06102010.htm

335   Martin, J. (n.d.). Case 161. In A. Rosales (Ed.), *1982 Humanoid Sighting Reports*. Retrieved October 19, 2015 from http://www.ufoinfo.com/humanoid/humanoid-1982.pdf

336   Angelucci, O. (1955). *The Secrets of the Saucers*. Amherst, MA: Amherst Press.

337   Girvin, C.C. (1958). *The Night Has a Thousand Saucers*. El Monte, CA: Understanding Publishing.

338   Clark, J. (2010). *Hidden Realms, Lost Civilizations, and Beings from Other Worlds*. Canton, MI: Visible Ink Press.

339   Moravec, M.l. (1980, August). Psiufological Phenomena: UFOs and the Paranormal. *MUFON UFO Journal 150*, pp. 13-15.

340   MacLaine, S. (2007). *Sage-Ing While Age-Ing*. New York, NY: Simon & Schuster, Inc. (Atria Books).

341   Owen, J. (2004, Spring). What Happened to That Hour? *Flying Saucer Review 49(1)*, pp. 6-7.

342   Rizzi, W. (1980, September). Close encounter in the Dolomites. *Flying Saucer Review 26(3)*, pp. 22-27.

343   Epperson, I., & Kahlert, C. (1973, December). California Man Has Good View of UFO—And Occupant! *Skylook Magazine 73*, pp. 4-5.

344   Rodriguez, L.F., & Pereira, M.J. (n.d.). Case 134. In A. Rosales (Ed.), *1979 Humanoid Sighting Reports*. Retrieved October 19, 2015 from http://www.ufoinfo.com/humanoid/humanoid-1979.pdf

345   Encarnacao, J. (2013, May 9). *The Patriot Ledger*: 'Unbearable' smell in Quincy a mystery. Retrieved October 21, 2015 from http://www.patriotledger.com/

346   Newkirk, G. (2013, May 15). Week in Weird: Unidentified Foul Objects: Quincy, Massachusetts Plagued by Odd Aircraft and Awful Smells. Retrieved October 21, 2015 from http://weekinweird.com/

347   Shields, B. (2013, May 9). WBZ-TV Boston: Mystery Aircraft Frightens Quincy Residents. Retrieved October 21, 2015 from http://boston.cbslocal.com/

348   Keel, J. (2002). *The Mothman Prophecies*. New York, NY: Tom Doherty Associates, LLC. (Original work published 1975)

349   Vallee, J. (2008). *Dimensions: A Casebook of Alien Contact*. San Antonio, TX: Anomalist Books. (Original work published 1988)

350   Vallee, J. (1990). *Confrontations: A Scientist's Search for Alien Contact*. New York, NY: Ballantine Books.

351   Braenne, O.J. (n.d.). Case 27. In A. Rosales (Ed.), *1936 Humanoid Sighting Reports*. Retrieved October 21, 2015 from http://www.ufoinfo.com/humanoid/humanoid-1936.pdf

352   Clore, D. (2015). Flying Saucers Stink: Alien Odors and Supernatural Smells. In D. Clore, *The Unspeakable and Others*. Odense, Denmark: H. Harksen Productions, pp. 293-309.

353   Worley, D. (2004, September). While Blue Book slept. *MUFON UFO Journal 436*, pp. 5-6.

354   Gribble, B. (1992, April). Looking Back. *MUFON UFO Journal 288*, pp. 17-19.

355   Mesnard, J., & Pavy, C. (1968, September). Encounter with "Devils": A strange account from the Cussac Plateau in France. *Flying Saucer Review 14(5)*, pp. 7-9.

Endnotes

356   Stringfield, L. (1976, January). Cincinnati area has variety of sightings. *MUFON UFO Journal 98*, pp. 5-6.

357   Hall, R. (1980, November). Italian UFO wave of 1978. *MUFON UFO Journal 153*, pp. 12-15.

358   Bullard 1987 Vol. 2.

359   Gordon, S. (1989, May). Pennsylvania Law Officer Reports CE2 Incident. *MUFON UFO Journal 253*, pp. 10-12, 23.

360   Wright, D. (1991, February). Current Case Log. *MUFON UFO Journal 274*, pp. 11-12.

361   Collins, A. (2012). *LightQuest: Your Guide to Seeing and Interacting with UFOs, Mystery Lights and Plasma Intelligences.* Memphis, TN: Eagle Wing Books.

362   Puckett, W. (2006, August). Sighting, odors, physical traces, and illness in Midwest encounter. *MUFON UFO Journal 460*, pp. 3-5.

363   Rosales, A. (2014). Case 84. In A. Rosales (Ed.), *2014 Humanoid Sighting Reports.* Retrieved October 21, 2015 from http://www.ufoinfo.com/humanoid/humanoid-2014.pdf

364   Gribble, B. (1989, September). Looking Back. *MUFON UFO Journal 257*, pp. 13-15.

365   Dains, D.K. (1974, December). Object in water checked in Pennsylvania. *MUFON UFO Journal 85*, p. 12.

366   Hall, R. (1988). *Uninvited Guests: A Documented History of UFO Sighting, Alien Encounters, & Coverups.* Santa Fe, NM: Aurora Press.

367   Hathaway, B.A. (2006). *Organic Chemistry the Easy Way.* Hauppauge, NY: Barron's Educational Series, Inc.

368   Bullard 1987 Vol. 2.

369   Sanchez-Ocejo, V. (n.d.). Case 42. In A. Rosales (Ed.), *1979 Humanoid Sighting Reports.* Retrieved October 21, 2015 from http://www.ufoinfo.com/humanoid/humanoid-1979.pdf

370   Smith, Y.R. (2014). *Coronado: The President, The Secret Service, and Alien Abductions* [Kindle Edition].

371   Chamish, B. (2000). *Return of the Giants.* Israel: Modiin House.

372   Freixedo, S. (1984). *¡Defendámonos de los Dioses!* Madrid, Spain: Editorial Posada, S.A.

373   Vallee 1990.

374   Collins, A. (2009). *The New Circlemakers: Insights Into the Crop Circle Mystery.* Virginia Beach, VA: 4th Dimension Press. (Original work published 1992)

375   Rutkowski, C., & Dittman, G. (2006). *The Canadian UFO Report: The Best Cases Revealed.* Toronto, ON: Dundurn Press.

376   Good, T. (2007). *Need to Know: UFOs, the Military, and Intelligence.* New York, NY: Pegasus Books LLC.

377   Feindt, C. W. (2010). *UFOs and Water: Physical Effects of UFOs on Water Through Accounts by Eyewitnesses.* Bloomington, IN: Xlibris Corporation.

378   Webb, D. (1980, January). The Middleton Humanoids Affair. *MUFON UFO Journal 143*, pp. 7-10.

379   Bloecher, T. (1978, February). CE-III Report from Montvale, N.J.: Preliminary Report. *MUFON UFO Journal 123*, pp. 4-7.

380   Smith 2014.

381   Keel 1976.

382   Agency for Toxic Substances & Disease Registry 2014.

383   Vallee 1990.

384   Fowler, R. & NICAP (n.d.). Case 81. In A. Rosales (Ed.), *1967 Humanoid Sighting Reports.* Retrieved October 21, 2015 from http://www.ufoinfo.com/humanoid/humanoid-1967.pdf

385   Randles, J. (1997). *UFOs & How to See Them.* New York, NY: Sterling Publishing Company, Inc.

386   Gribble, B. (1989, July). Looking Back. *MUFON UFO Journal 255*, pp. 19-21.

387   Rullán 2000.

388   Australian Government Department of the Environment. (2005). Sulfur Dioxide (SO_2). Retrieved October 22, 2015 from https://www.environment.gov.au

389   Gordon, S. (1999, January). Gordon reports on case that caused him to reconsider Bigfoot. *MUFON UFO Journal 369*, pp. 13-14.

390   Suttle, N.F. (2010). *Mineral Nutrition of Livestock.* Oxfordshire, UK: CABI.

391   Meyer 1994.

392   Shmueli, U. (2007). *Irritable Bowel Syndrome: Answers at Your Fingertips.* London,

UK: Class Publishing.

393   International Volcanic Health Hazard Network. (2015). Hydrogen Sulfide (H_2S). Retrieved October 23, 2015 from http://www.ivhhn.org

394   Rullán 2000.

395   Keel 1976.

396   Friedman, S.T., & Marden, K. (2007). *Captured! The Betty and Barney Hill UFO Experience*. Franklin Lakes, NJ: New Page Books.

397   Clean Diesel Fuel Alliance (n.d.). Guidance for Underground Storage Tank Management at ULSD Dispensing Facilities. Retrieved October 20, 2015 from http://www.clean-diesel.org/

398   Friedman & Marden 2007.

399   Martin, R. (1999, October 5). Great Zulu Shaman And Elder Credo Mutwa: A Rare, Astonishing Conversation. *The Spectrum, 1*(5), 1, 17- 32.

400   Mack, J. (1999). *Passport to the Cosmos*. New York, NY: Three Rivers Press.

401   Smith 2014.

402   Drake, R. (1977, July). Air Force Besieged by Saucers. *UFO Report*, p. 37.

403   Ribera, A. (1986, May). The Jinn and the Dolmen: The Most Amazing Case of Abduction Yet. *Flying Saucer Review 31(4)*, pp. 2-10.

404   Sochka, Y.V., Anfalov, A., & UFODOS. (n.d.). Case 62. In A. Rosales (Ed.), *1995 Humanoid Sighting Reports*. Retrieved October 23, 2015 from http://www.ufoinfo.com/humanoid/humanoid-1995.pdf

405   Lin, V.S., Lippert, A.R., & Chang, C.J. (2013, March 20). Cell-trappable fluorescent probes for endogenous hydrogen sulfide signaling and imaging H_2O_2-dependent H_2S production. *Proceedings of the National Academy of Sciences of the United States of America 110 (18)*, 7131-7135.

406   Kimura, H. (2002, August 26). Hydrogen sulfide as a neuromodulator. *Molecular Neurobiology 26*, 13-19.

407   Lefer, D.J. (2007, November). A new gaseous signaling molecule emerges: Cardioprotective role of hydrogen sulfide. *Proceedings of the National Academy of Sciences of the United States of America 104 (46)*, 17907-17908.

408   Benavides, G.A, Squadrito, G.L., Mills, R.W., Patel, H.D., Isbell, T.S, Patel, R.P., Darley-Usmar, V.M., Doeller, J.E., Kraus, D.W. (2007, November 13). Hydrogen sulfide mediates the vasoactivity of garlic. *Proceedings of the National Academy of Sciences of the United States of America 104 (46)*, 17977–17982.

409 Keel 2002/1975.

410 Keel 1976.

411 Iowa State University Extension. (2004, May). The Science of Smell Part 1: Odor perception and physiological response. Retrieved October 23, 2015 from https://store.extension.iastate.edu/Product/pm1963a-pdf

412 Vroon 1997.

413 United States Department of Labor. (n.d.). Occupational Safety & Health Administration: Hydrogen Sulfide. Retrieved October 23, 2015 from https://www.osha.gov

414 McCall, G.J.H., Laming, D.J.C., & Scott, S.C. (Eds.). (1992). *Geohazards: Natural and Man-Made*. London, UK: Chapman & Hall.

415 Greenburg, M.I., Hamilton, R.J., Phillips, S.D., and McCluskey, G.J. (Eds.). (2003). *Occupational, Industrial, and Environmental Toxicology* (2nd ed.). Philadelphia, PA: Mosby. (Original work published 1997)

416 Hemminki, K., & Niemi, M.L. (1982). Community study of spontaneous abortions: relation to occupation and air pollution by sulfur dioxide, hydrogen sulfide, and carbon disulfide. *International Archives of Occupational and Environmental Health 51(1)*, pp. 55-63.

417 Ward, P.D. (2006, October). Impact from the Deep. Retrieved October 24, 2015 from http://www.scientificamerican.com

418 Poulsen, K. (2009, March 13). Dangerous Japanese 'Detergent Suicide' Technique Creeps Into U.S. Retrieved October 23, 2015 from http://www.wired.com/2009/03/japanese-deterg/

419 Hall, A.H., & Rumack, B.H. (1997, June). Hydrogen sulfide poisoning: an antidotal role for sodium nitrite? *Veterinary and Human Toxicology 39(3)*, pp. 152-154.

420 Clark, J. (1967, November). Why UFOs Are Hostile. *Flying Saucer Review 13(6)*, pp. 18-20.

421 Lawson, H. (2013, August 4). The river UNDER the sea: Haunting images of scuba diver exploring mysterious channel flowing in water-filled cavern. Retrieved October 24, 2015 from http://www.dailymail.co.uk

422 Phillips, T. (2005, June). Physical Traces. *MUFON UFO Journal 446*, pp. 15-17.

423 Hanson, J., & Holloway, D. (2011). *Haunted Skies: The Encyclopaedia of British UFOs: 1960-1965* (Vol. 2). Woolsery, UK: Fortean Words.

424 Schwarz, B.E. (1971, May). The Port Monmouth Landing. *Flying Saucer Review 17(3)*, pp. 21-27.

Endnotes 345

425 Hopkins, B. (1981). *Missing Time*. New York, NY: Richard Marek Publishers.

426 Clore 2015.

427 Bullard 1987 Vol. 2.

428 Schuessler 1998, February.

429 Edwards, A. (1988). *On the (UFO) Road Again: Case Histories of Close Encounters of the Third Kind*. Seattle, WA: UFO Contact Center International.

430 Gribble, B. (1987, November). Looking Back. *MUFON UFO Journal 235*, pp. 20-21.

431 Keyhoe, D.E., & Lore, Jr., G.I.R. (Eds.). (1969). *UFOs: A New Look*. Washinton, D.C.: The National Investigations Committee on Aerial Phenomena.

432 UFOs Northwest. (2006, February 21). After 40 Years Woman Vividly Recalls Terrifying Encounter With Large UFO in Her Front Yard. Retrieved October 30, 2015 from http://www.ufosnw.com

433 Phillips, T. (2005, December). Physical Traces. *MUFON UFO Journal 452*, pp. 18-19.

434 Filer, G. (1999, November 4). Filer's Files #44-1999. Retrieved October 30, 2015 from http://www.ufoinfo.com/filer/1999/ff9944.shtml

435 Ruppelt, E.J. (2011). *The Report on Unidentified Flying Obects: The Original 1956 Edition*. C. Bennet (Ed.). New York, NY: Cosmo Classics. (Original work published 1956)

436 United States Environmental Protection Agency – Office of Mobile Sources. (n.d.). Automobiles and Ozone. Retrieved October 30, 2015 from http://www3.epa.gov/otaq/consumer/04-ozone.pdf

437 Horváth, M. Bilitzky, L., & Hüttner, J. (1985). *Ozone*. New York, NY: Elsevier Science Publishing Co., Inc.

438 Weinhold, B. (2008). Ozone nation: EPA standard panned by the people. *Environmental Health Perspectives 116 (7)*, pp. 302–305.

439 Centers for Disease Control. (n.d.). Occupational Health Guideline for Ozone. Retrievedd October 30, 2015 from http://www.cdc.gov/niosh/docs/81-123/pdfs/0476.pdf

440 Horváth, Bilitzky, & Hüttner 1985.

441 Rice, R.G., & Browning, M.E. (Eds.). (1976). *Ozone: Analytical Aspects & Odor Control*. New York, NY: Pan American Group/International Ozone Institute, Inc.

442   Rubin, M.B. (2001). The History of Ozone - The Schönbein Period, 1839–1868. *Bulletin for the History of Chemistry 26*, pp. 40-56.

443   Altschule, H.G., & Vonnegut, B. (1997, April/May). The Smell of Tornadoes. *Weatherwise 50 (2)*, pp. 24-25.

444   Franklin, B. (1882). *The Works of Benjamin Franklin* (Vol. V). J. Sparks (Ed.). London, UK: Benjamin Franklin Stevens.

445   Cohen, I.B. (1996). *Ben Franklin's Science*. Cambridge, MA: Harvard University Press. (Original work published 1990)

446   Melanson, T. (2001). UFOs, Do They Smell? The Sulphur Enigma of Paranormal Visitation. Retrieved November 13, 2015 from http://www.conspiracyarchive.com/

447   Kruszelnicki, K.S. (2007, June 27). Ozone Smell at the Seaside. Retrieved October 26, 2015 from http://www.abc.net.au

448   Strieber, A. (2013, July 10). Russian Documents Reveal Many Underwater UFO Events. Retrieved October 26, 2015 from http://www.unknowncountry.com/news/russian-documents-reveal-many-underwater-ufo-events

449   Hall, R. (1975, October). Southern Africa reports several UFO sightings. *MUFON UFO Journal 95*, pp. 14-15.

450   Vallee 1990.

451   Bullard 1987 Vol. 2.

452   Vallee, J. (1992). *Forbidden Science* (2nd ed.). Berkeley, CA: North Atlantic Books.

453   Bryan, C.B.D. (1995). *Close Encounters of the Fourth Kind*. New York, NY: Penguin Group (Arkana).

454   Rullán 2000.

455   Hall, R. (1976, April). Recapping and commenting. *MUFON UFO Journal 101*, p. 20.

456   Bullard 1987 Vol. 2.

457   Schmidt, R.A., Hillman, D., & UFORI. (n.d.). Case 79. In A. Rosales (Ed.), *1971 Humanoid Sighting Reports*. Retrieved October 30, 2015 from http://www.ufoinfo.com/humanoid/humanoid-1971.pdf

458   Wicks, Jr., ZW., Jones, F.N., Pappas, S.P., & Wicks, D.A. (2007). *Organic Coatings: Science and Technology*. Hoboken, NJ: Wiley Interscience.

459   Thomas, J. (n.d.). Case 379. In A. Rosales (Ed.), *1977 Humanoid Sighting Reports*. Retrieved October 30, 2015 from http://www.ufoinfo.com/humanoid/humanoid-1977.pdf

Endnotes 347

460   Bullard 1987 Vol. 2.

461   Holleman, A.F., & Wiberg, E. (2001). *Inorganic Chemistry*. (M. Eagleson & W. Brewer, Trans.). B.J. Aylett (Ed.). San Diego, CA: Academic Press.

462   Frederickson, S.V. (1972, March). The Ängelholm Landing Report. *Flying Saucer Review 18(2)*, pp. 15-17.

463   Degaudenzi, J.L. (1981). *Les OVNI en Union Soviétique*. Nice, FR: Alain Lefeuvre.

464   Fowler, R.E. (1993, April). The Allagash Abductions. *MUFON UFO Journal 300*, pp. 3-6.

465   Ridge, F. (2008, October 15). The 2003 UFO Chronology. Retrieved October 30, 2015 from http://www.nicap.org/waves/2003fullrep.htm

466   Steinman, W.S., & Stevens, W.C. (1987). *UFO Crash at Aztec: A Well Kept Secret*. Tucson, AZ: UFO Photo Archives.

467   Rutkowski & Dittman 2006.

468   Stringfield, L., & Faria, J.E. (n.d.). Case 55. In A. Rosales (Ed.), *1950 Humanoid Sighting Reports*. Retrieved October 30, 2015 from http://www.ufoinfo.com/humanoid/humanoid-1950.pdf

469   Rice & Browning 1976.

470   Rutkowski, C.R. (1999). *Abductions and Aliens: What's Really Going On?* Toronto, ON: Dundurn Press.

471   Gribble, B. (1989, November). Looking Back. *MUFON UFO Journal 259*, pp. 22-24.

472   Turner 1994.

473   Clore 2015.

474   Afrikaanse Sonntagzeitung Rapport - South Africa. (1995, April 2). Alien object lands to repair hole in its hull, says farmer. Retrieved November 3, 2015 from http://www.ufoevidence.org/cases/case713.htm

475   Gribble, B. (1989, June). Looking Back. *MUFON UFO Journal 254*, pp. 20-21, 23.

476   Rullán 2000.

477   Vallee & Vallee 1966.

478   Pratt, B., & Luce, C. (1998, September). Part Two: The Varginha ET Case. *MUFON UFO Journal 365*, pp. 8-13.

479   Clark, J. (1997). *The UFO Book: Encyclopedia of the Extraterrestrial*. Canton, MI: Visible Ink Press.

480   Keel, J.A. (1970). *UFOs: Operation Trojan Horse*. New York, NY: G.P. Putnam's Sons.

481   Citizens Against UFO Secrecy. (1986, January). Reported Killing of a UFO Entity. *Flying Saucer Review 31(2)*, pp. 25-26.

482   Centers for Disease Control. (n.d.). Occupational Health Guideline for Ammonia. Retrieved November 3, 2015 from http://www.cdc.gov/niosh/docs/81-123/pdfs/0028-rev.pdf

483   Meyer 1977.

484   Revai 2005.

485   Rutkowski & Dittman 2006.

486   Rullán 2000.

487   Romaniuk, P. (n.d.). Case 236. In A. Rosales (Ed.), *1972 Humanoid Sighting Reports*. Retrieved November 3, 2015 from http://www.ufoinfo.com/humanoid/humanoid-1972.pdf

488   Clark, J. (1998). *The UFO Encyclopedia: The Phenomenon from the Beginning* (Vol. 1: A-K, 2nd ed.). Detroit, MI: Omnigraphics, Inc.

489   Schuessler, J. (1983, September). Cash-Landrum Case: Investigation of Helicopter Activity. *MUFON UFO Journal 187*, pp. 3-6.

490   Van Utrecht, W. (2013, December 11). Cash-Landrum: The Light Pillar Theory Revisited by Wim VAN UTRECHT. Retrieved November 3, 2015 from http://www.blueblurrylines.com

491   Swords, M.D. (2013, November 21). Professor Michael D. Swords Reports of the Cash-Landrum UFO Investigation. Retrieved November 3, 2015 from http://www.blueblurrylines.com

492   Vallee, J. (1993). *Passport to Magonia*. Chicago, IL: Contemporary Books.

493   Lorenzen, C.E. (1966). *Flying Saucers: The Startling Evidence of the Invasion from Outer Space*. New York, NY: The New American Library – Signet Books. (Original work published 1962 as *The Great Flying Saucer Hoax: The UFO Facts and Their Interpretation*)

494   Colombo, J.R. (1992). *UFOs Over Canada: Personal Accounts of Sightings and Close Encounters*. Willowdale, ON: Hounslow Press (Anthony Hawke). (Original work published 1991)

495   Vallee 1993.

496 Bystrov, V. (1989, August 5). Case 234. In A. Rosales (Ed.), *1989 Humanoid Sighting Reports*. Retrieved November 5, 2015 from http://www.ufoinfo.com/humanoid/humanoid-1989.pdf

497 Tasmanian UFO Investigation Centre. (1997). Tasmanian UFO Report – 1997. Retrieved November 5, 2015 from http://tufoic.eu.pn/ar97.htm

498 Graber, G. (1976, February). Two occupants in craft. *MUFON Skylook: The UFO Monthly 99*, pp. 3-4.

499 Jones, J. (1976, January). Possible E-M Case in Florida. *The APRO Bulletin 24(7)*, p. 2, 5.

500 McCampbell, J. (1976). *UFOlogy: A Major Breakthrough in the Scientific Understanding of Unidentified Flying Objects*. Millbrae, CA: Celestial Arts.

501 Gross, P. (2014, October 2). The 1954 French Flap: October 2, 1954, Clermont-Ferrand, Puy-de-Dome. Retrieved November 5, 2015 from http://ufologie.patrickgross.org/1954/2oct1954clermont.htm

502 Phillips, T. (2005, September). Physical Traces. *MUFON UFO Journal 449*, pp. 18-19.

503 Vallee 1993.

504 McCampbell 1976.

505 Vallee, J. (1991). *Revelations: Alien Contact and Human Deception*. New York, NY: Ballantine Books.

506 Carey, T.J., & Schmitt, D.R. (2007). *Witness to Roswell: Unmasking the 60-Year Cover-Up*. Franklin Lakes, NJ: New Page Books.

507 Shandera, J.H., & Moore, W.L. (1990, September). 3 Hours That Shook the Press. *MUFON UFO Journal 269*, pp. 3-10.

508 Malanowski, G. (2011). *The Race for Wireless*. Bloomington, IN: AuthorHouse.

509 Winder, R.H.B. (1967, November). Vehicle Stoppage at Hook. *Flying Saucer Review 13(6)*, pp. 6-7.

510 Andrus, W. (1988, April). The Mundrabilla Incident – Part II. *MUFON UFO Journal 240*, pp. 14-17.

511 Durant, R.J. (1998, February). The Roswell debris testimony of Dr. Jesse Marcel, Jr. – Part 2: The I beam. *MUFON UFO Journal 358*, pp. 15-18.

512 Carey & Schmitt 2007.

513 Malanowski 2011.

514   Berliner, D., & Friedman, S.T. (2010). *Crash at Corona: The U.S. Military Retrieval and Cover-Up of a UFO—The Definitive Study of the Roswell Incident*. New York, NY: Cosimo Books. (Original work published 1992)

515   Gilette, M.L., & Gloffke, W. (2006). *General, Organic, and Biochemistry: Connecting Chemistry to Your Life*. New York, NY: W.H. Freeman and Company.

516   Meikle, J.L. (1997). *American Plastic: A Cultural History*. New Brunswick, NJ: Rutgers University Press. (Original work published 1995)

517   Barker, G. (1983). *The Year of the Saucer: Gray Barker's UFO Annual 1983*. Jane Lew, WV: New Age Press.

518   Olenik, T.J. (1975). Domestic Sewage and Refuse Odor Control. In Cheremisinoff, P.N. & Young, R.A. (Eds.), *Industrial Odor Technology Assessment* (pp. 117-146). Ann Arbor, MI: Ann Arbor Science Publishers Inc.

519   Cannon, D. (1999). *The Custodians: Beyond Abduction*. Huntsville, AR: Ozark Mountain Publishers.

520   Larsen, O.J. (n.d.). Case 288. In A. Rosales (Ed.), *1954 Humanoid Sighting Reports*. Retrieved November 9, 2015 from http://www.ufoinfo.com/humanoid/humanoid-1954.pdf

521   Gribble, B. (1988, December). Looking Back. *MUFON UFO Journal 248*, pp. 14-16.

522   Picknett 2001.

523   Lara, O.R.P. (n.d.). Case 14. In A. Rosales (Ed.), *1945 Humanoid Sighting Reports*. Retrieved November 9, 2015 from http://www.ufoinfo.com/humanoid/humanoid-1945.pdf

524   Clore 2015.

525   Hind, C.R. (1977, April). Orange UFO Over Rhodesia. *MUFON UFO Journal 113*, p. 18.

526   Randles, J., & Whetnall, P. (1979, May). The Sunderland Family Encounters – Part 1. *Flying Saucer Review 25(3)*, pp. 11-18.

527   National UFO Reporting Center. (2006, February 14). At about 2am, A friend [sic] and I were awoken in his country home south of Bragg Creek [sic]. Retrieved November 9, 2015 from http://www.nuforc.org

528   Strassman, R. (2000). *DMT: The Spirit Molecule*. Rochester, VT: Park Street Press.

529   Guiley, R.E. (2012). *Monsters of West Virginia: Mysterious Creatures in the Mountain State*. Mechanicsburg, PA: Stackpole Books.

530 Feschino, Jr., F. (2013). *The Braxton County Monster – Updated & Revised Edition: The Cover-Up of the "Flatwoods Monster" Revealed.* USA: Lulu Enterprises.

531 Coleman, L. (2002). *Mothman and Other Curious Encounters.* New York, NY: Paraview Press.

532 Feschino 2013.

533 Coleman 2002.

534 Redfern, N. (2013).*Monster Files: A Look Inside Government Secrets and Classified Documents on Bizarre Creature and Extraordinary Animals.* Pompton Plains, NJ: New Page Books.

535 Thomas, J.K. (1987, September). The Vehicle Interference Effect. *MUFON UFO Journal 233*, pp. 3-11.

536 Parker, B.R. (1973, December). Strange Creature Stalls Auto in Georgia – Car Intensely Hot. *Skylook Magazine 73*, pp. 7-8.

537 Gribble 1987, November.

538 Huneeus, J.A. (1987, June 26-28). Historical Survey of UFO Cases in Chile. In W.H. Andrus & R. Hall (Eds.), *MUFON 1987 International UFO Symposium Proceedings.* Seguin, TX: MUTUAL UFO Network, pp. 181-219.

539 Chalker, B. (1980, August). Australian "Interrupted Journeys." *MUFON UFO Journal 150*, pp. 3-8.

540 Ferguson, J. (1977). *Les humanoides.* Montreal, CAN: Lémeac.

541 Hall, R.H. (2001). *The UFO Evidence: A Thirty-Year Report* (Vol. 2). Lanham, MD: Scarecrow Press.

542 Stiles, D. (2007, April). Opinion: Bench Monkey. Retrieved January 5, 2016 from http://www.rsc.org/

543 Wheeldon, K. (2005, February). Family sights unusual object over home. *MUFON UFO Journal 442*, pp. 10-11.

544 Porter, H. (2006, Summer). Another Missing Week long Abduction, this time from Portsmouth England. *Flying Saucer Review 51(2)*, pp. 17-18.

545 Mack 1999.

546 Wright, D. (1994, February). The Entities: Initial Findings of the Abduction Transcription Project. *MUFON UFO Journal 310*, pp. 3-7.

547   Overmeire, G.V. (n.d.). Case 242. In A. Rosales (Ed.), *1995 Humanoid Sighting Reports*. Retrieved November 9, 2015 from http://www.ufoinfo.com/humanoid/humanoid-1995.pdf

548   Lorenzen 1966.

549   Clore 2015.

550   Nebraska Medical Center. (2010). Joann – Lung Cancer Patient: Fighting for Every Breath. Retrieved November 10, 2015 from http://www.nebraskamed.com/

551   MacPherson, M. (1999). *She Came to Live Out Loud: An Inspiring Family Journey Through Illness, Loss, and Grief*. New York, NY: Simon & Schuster (Scribner).

552   Davis, J.R., Johnson, R., Stepanek, J, & Fogarty, J.A. (Eds.) (2008). *Fundamentals of Aerospace Medicine* (4th ed.). Philadelphia, PA: Lippincott Williams & Wilkins. (Original work published 2002)

553   Inman, M. (2010, October 10). Plane Exhaust Kills More People Than Plane Crashes. Retrieved November 13, 2015 from http://news.nationalgeographic.com/

554   Altschule & Vonnegut 1997.

555   Clark 2013.

556   World Health Organization. (1979). *Environmental Health Criteria 8: Sulfur Oxides and Suspended Particulate Matter*. UK: WHO.

557   Clark 2013.

558   Hynek, J.A. (1966, December 17). Are Flying Saucers Real? *The Saturday Evening Post*, pp. 17-21.

559   Maunder, M. (2007). *Lights in the Sky: Identifying and Understanding Astronomical and Meteorological Phenomena*. London, UK: Springer-Verlag.

560   Barry, J.D. (1980). *Ball Lightning and Bead Lightning*. New York, NY: Plenum Press.

561   Rullán 2000.

562   Stromberg, J. (2014, January 2). Why Do Lights Sometimes Appear in the Sky During An Earthquake? Retrieved November 13, 2015 from http://www.smithsonianmag.com/

563   Carter, L.A. (2014, August 25). Did you see flashes? Yep, an earthquake can create 'em (w/video). Retrieved November 13, 2015 from http://www.pressdemocrat.com/

564   Williams, W.F. (Ed.). (2013). *Encyclopedia of Pseudoscience: From Alien Abductions to Zone Therapy*. New York, NY: Routledge. (Original work published 2000)

565 Ikeya, M. (2004). *Earthquakes and Animals: From Folk Legends to Science*. Singapore: World Scientific Publishing Co. Pte. Ltd.

566 Le Guérer 1994.

567 Marcuccio, P.R. (Ed.). (1992, August). *Federal Emergency Management Agency - Earthquakes: A Teacher's Package for K-6*. Washington, DC: The National Science Teachers Association.

568 Mallet, R. (1862). *Great Neapolitan Earthquake of 1857: The First Principles of Seismology* (Vol. 2). London, UK: Chapman and Hall.

569 Ambraseys, N.N., & Melville, C.P. (1982). *A History of Persian Earthquakes*. Cambridge, UK: Cambridge University Press.

570 Sit, J. (2010, October 14). Edmond Woman Says She Can Predict Earthquake Activity. Retrieved November 13, 2015 from http://m.newson6.com/

571 McTaggart, L. (2007). *The Intention Experiment: Using Your Thoughts to Change Your Life and the World*. New York, NY: Simon & Schuster, Inc. (Free Press).

572 Martin, G.N. (2013). *The Neuropsychology of Smell and Taste*. East Sussex, UK: Psychology Press.

573 Carter 2010.

574 McTaggart 2007.

575 Clore 2015.

576 Amos, J. (2008, August 24). Solar plane makes record flight. Retrieved November 13, 2015 from http://news.bbc.co.uk/

577 Melanson 2001.

578 Melanson 2001.

579 Cho, A. (2015, August 17). Stinky hydrogen sulfide smashes superconductivity record. Retrieved January 7, 2015 from http://news.sciencemag.org/

580 Live Science. (2012, July 20). What Does Space Smell Like? Retrieved November 13, 2015 from http://www.livescience.com/

581 Pettit, D. (2003, May 13). Expedition Six: Space Chronicles #4 – The Smell of Space. Retrieved November 13, 2015 from http://spaceflight.nasa.gov/

582 Hullinger, J. (2014, September). What Does Space Smell Like? *Mental Floss 13(6)*, p. 40.

583   Verish, R. (2010, September 1). Planetary Body Odors. Retrieved November 13, 2015 from http://www.meteorite-times.com/

584   Phillips, T. (2006, January 30). The Mysterious Smell of Moondust. Retrieved November 13, 2015 from http://science.nasa.gov/

585   Prieto, C.E.M.Y. (2006, December). *Distribution and Diversity of Sulfur-Reducing Prokaryotes in Sulfur-Rich Peat Soils* (Doctoral dissertation). The Pennsylvania State University: Department of Crop and Soil Sciences.

586   Carlson, R. W., Anderson, M. S., Mehlman, R., & Johnson, R. E. (2005). Distribution of hydrate on Europa: Further evidence for sulfuric acid hydrate. *Icarus 177 (2)*: 461.

587   Daily Galaxy. (2011, May 18). Stephen Hawking on Non-Carbon-Based Alien Life. Retrieved November 13, 2015.

588   Abe, S. (2011, December 17). The First Sulfur Eaters. Retrieved November 13, 2015 from https://astrobiology.nasa.gov

589   Seager, S., Bains, W., & Hu, R. (2013, October 1). A Biomass-Based Model to Estimate the Plausibility of Exoplanet Biosignature Gases. *The Astrophysical Journal 775*: 104 (28pp).

590   Hammonds, M. (2013, May 16). Does Alien Life Thrive in Venus' Mysterious Clouds? Retrieved November 13, 2015 from http://news.discovery.com/

591   Alley, J. R. (2007). *Raincoast Sasquatch: The Bigfoot/Sasquatch records of southeast Alaska, coastal British Columbia, & Northwest Washington from Puget Sound to Yakutat*. Blaine, WA: Hancock House. (Original work published 2003)

592   Swancer, B. (2008, November 20). Japan's Yeti: Hibagon. Retrieved November 17, 2015 from http://cryptomundo.com/

593   Steiger, B. (2011). *Real Monsters, Gruesome Critters, and Beasts from the Darkside*. Canton, MI: Visible Ink Press.
594   Coleman & Clark 1999.

595   Chapman, C. (2014, November 8). Tek tek, the yeti of Cambodia. Retrieved November 17, 2015 from http://www.phnompenhpost.com/

596   Keel 2002/1970.

597   Hamilton, S. (2008). *Monsters of Mystery*. Edina, MN: ABDO Publishing Company.

598   Varner, G.R. (2007). *Creatures in the Mist: Little People, Wild Men and Spirit Beings around the World – A Study in Comparative Mythology*. New York, NY: Algora Publishing.

599   Varner 2007.

600   Rawlings-Cody, A. (n.d.). Tolowa Indian stories... Del Norte County, California 1800's. Retrieved November 16, 2015 from http://www.bigfootencounters.com/

601   Mott, W.M. (2011). *Caverns, Cauldrons, and Concealed Creatures* (3rd ed.). Nashville, TN: Grave Distractions Publications.

602   Swanton, J.R. (1926). Social and Religious Beliefs of the Chicasaw Indians. *44th Annual Deport*. Washington, DC: Bureau of American Ethnology.

603   Wherry, J.H. (1969). *Indian Masks & Myths of the West*. New York, NY: Bonanza Books.

604   Alley 2007.

605   Sanderson, I.T. (2008). *Abominable Snowmen: Legend Come to Life*. New York, NY: Cosimo Classics. (Original work published 1961).

606   Coleman, L. (2003). *Bigfoot! The True Story of Apes in America*. New York, NY: Paraview Pocket Books.

607   Keel 2002/1970.

608   Bord & Bord 1989.

609   Eberhart, G.M. (2002). *Mysterious Creatures: A Guide to Cryptozoology*. Santa Barbara, CA: ABC-CLIO, Inc.

610   Courtney, S. (2012, December 17). Report #38337 (Class B): Possible nighttime sighting from a home by a young woman near Lake Lou Yaeger. Retrieved November 17, 2015 from http://www.bfro.net/

611   Rife, P.L. (2000). *Bigfoot Across America*. Lincoln, NE: Writers Club Press.

612   Huggins, T. (October 13, 2009). Report #26746 (Class B): Hunter recalls strange incidents while camping near Valleyview. Retrieved November 17, 2015 from http://www.bfro.net/

613   Illig, D. (2008, February 1). Report #23062 (Class B): Angler finds tracks, hears knocks and senses ominous presence east of North Bend. Retrieved November 17, 2015 from http://www.bfro.net/

614   Monteith, R. (2013, August 17). Report #41892 (Class A): Woman is startled to see a large hairy biped climbing her fence outside Clearwater. Retrieved November 17, 2015 from http://www.bfro.net/

615   Fahrenbach, W.H. (1997). Sasquatch Smell / Aroma / Odor / Scent. Retrieved November 30, 2015 from http://www.bigfootencounters.com/

616   Scott, B. (2005, September 18). Report #12601 (Class B): Bow hunter hears vocalizations, smells foul odor. Retrieved November 17, 2015 from http://www.bfro.net/

617 Bigfoot Field Researchers Organization. (2002, January 11). Report #3529 (Class A): Daylight sighting by a wood cutter on a logging road in the Mts. above Oakley. Retrieved November 17, 2015 from http://www.bfro.net/

618 Germer, W. (2015, August 2). *Sasquatch Chronicles Episode 132: A gold miners encounter* [Audio podcast]. Retrieved November 17, 2015 from https://www.sasquatchchronicles.com/

619 Coleman 2003.

620 Keel 1976.

621 Coleman 2003.

622 Long, G. (2004). *The Making of Bigfoot: The Inside Story*. Amherst, NY: Prometheus Books.

623 Cantrall, T. (2014, April 15). Candid Interview with Bob Gimlin by Thom Cantrall. Retrieved November 17, 2015 from http://bigfootevidence.blogspot.com/

624 Germer, W. (2015, March 29). *Sasquatch Chronicles Episode 90: Interview with Bob Gimlin* [Audio podcast]. Retrieved November 17, 2015 from https://www.sasquatchchronicles.com/

625 Steiger 2011.

626 Bord & Bord 1989.

627 Meldrum, J. (2006). *Sasquatch: Legend Meets Science*. New York, NY: Forge Books.

628 Bindernagel, J.A. (1998). *North America's Great Ape: the Sasquatch*. Courtenay, BC: Beachcomber Books.

629 Steiger 2011.

630 Fusch, E. (1992). S'cwene'y'ti and the Stick Indians of the Colvilles: The Interaction of Large Bipedal Hominids with American Indians. Retrieved November 17, 2015 from http://www.bigfootencounters.com/

631 Largey, G.P., & Watson, D.R. (1972, May). The Sociology of Odors. *American Journal of Sociology 77(6)*, pp. 1021-1034.

632 Townsend, J. (2004). *Out There? Mysterious Monsters*. Chicago, IL: Raintree.

633 Clore 2015.

634 Hargittai, I. (2011). *Drive and Curiosity: What Fuels the Passion for Science*. Amherst, NY: Prometheus Books.

635 Keel 2015.

636	Coleman & Clark 1999.

637	Coleman, L. (2006, December 13). Who Coined "Skunk Ape"? Retrieved November 19, 2015 from http://cryptomundo.com/

638	Bord, J., & Bord, C. (1984). *The Evidence for Bigfoot and Other Man-Beasts*. Wellingborough, UK: Aquarian Press.

639	Green, J. (1995). On the Scent of the Sasquatch. Retrieved November 16, 2015 from http://www.sasquatchdatabase.com/

640	Coleman & Clark 1999.

641	Cornet, S. (2005, May 22). Vanishing Bigfoot and Anecdotal Accounts: Implications and Challenges for Researchers. Retrieved November 30, 2015 from http://www.nabigfootsearch.com/

642	Bord, J., & Bord, C. (2006). *Bigfoot Casebook Updated: Sightings and Encounters from 1818 to 2004*. Enumclaw, WA: Pine Winds Press. (Original work published 1982)

643	Fisher, D. (2013, July 11). The Scent Of A Sasquatch: What's That Smell All About? Retrived November 30, 2015 from http://www.thecryptocrew.com/

644	Redfern, N. (2016). *The Bigfoot Book: The Encyclopedia of Sasquatch, Yeti and Cryptid Primates*. Canton, MI: Visible Ink Press.

645	Keel 2002/1970

646	Alley 2007.

647	Brake, D.A. (2005, March 11). Report #44837 (Class A): Hunter has early morning encounter 8 miles north of Riverdale. Retrieved November 19, 2015 from http://www.bfro.net/

648	Godfrey, L.S. (2014). *American Monsters: A History of Monster Lore, Legends, and Sightings in America*. New York, NY: The Penguin Group.

649	Omer, B. (2013, December 22). Report #43399 (Class A): Scientist skeptic has early morning encounter behind gas station near Las Vegas, NM. Retrieved November 19, 2015 from http://www.bfro.net/

650	Monteith, R. (2014, April 16). Report #44837 (Class A): Years of South Florida Skunk Ape stories supported by witness accounts and newspaper articles. Retrieved November 19, 2015 from http://www.bfro.net/

651	Gerard, T. (2001, August 17). Report #3008 (Class A): Gold dredgers have afternoon encounter in Cherokee National Forest. Retrieved November 19, 2015 from http://www.bfro.net/

652	Bindernagel 1998.

653 Germer, W. (2015, November 22). *Sasquatch Chronicles Episode 167: That is when the rock throwing started*. [Audio podcast]. Retrieved November 24, 2015 from https://www.sasquatchchronicles.com/

654 Swindler, D.R. (1998). *Introduction to Primates*. Seattle, WA: University of Washington Press.

655 BigfootEvidence [Screen name] (2011, July 10). *Melba Ketchum: Bigfoot is part lemur and part human* [Video file]. Retrieved March 7, 2016 from https://www.youtube.com/watch?v=nTRImzptOi4

656 Legro, S. (2013, March 1). *Into the Fray: Small Town Monsters* [Audio podcast]. Retrieved November 30, 2015 from https://intothefrayradio.com

657 Bord & Bord 2006.

658 Germer, W. (2015, July 7). *Sasquatch Chronicles Episode 122: Sasquatch at my window Part two*. [Audio podcast]. Retrieved November 17, 2015 from https://www.sasquatchchronicles.com/

659 Nunnelly, B.M. (2011). *The Inhumanoids: Real Encounters with Beings That Can't Exist*. Woolsery, UK: CFZ Press.

660 Hucklebridge, R. (2002, November 10). Report #5284 (Class A): Hunter/Logger has a sighting in a closed logging area near Hilt. Retrieved November 19, 2015 from http://www.bfro.net/

661 Wilson, P.A. (2010). *Monsters of Pennsylvania: Mysterious Creatures in the Keystone State*. Mechanicsburg, PA: Stackpole Books.

662 Alley 2007.

663 Filer, G.A. (2004, January). Filer's Files. *MUFON UFO Journal 429*, pp. 14-16.

664 Sherman, J. (2012, February 3). Report #32976 (Class B): Possible daylight sighting by a mountain biker in the Pere Marquette State Forest. Retrieved November 19, 2015 from http://www.bfro.net/

665 Coleman & Clark 1999.

666 Bord & Bord 2006.

667 Rife 2000.

668 Godfrey 2014.

669 Gill, G.W. (1980). Population Clines of the North American Sasquatch as Evidenced by Track Lengths and Estimated Statures. In M. Halpin & M.M. Ames (Eds.). *Manlike Monsters on Trial: Early Records and Modern Evidence* (pp. 265-273). Vancouver, CAN: University of British Columbia Press.

670   Woollaston, V. (2015, June 2). Why do wet dogs stink? Video reveals the chemistry behind your canine and how they're attracted to the smell of DEATH. Retrieved November 20, 2015 from http://www.dailymail.co.uk/

671   Eldredge, D.M., Carlson, L.D., Carlson, D.G., & Giffin, J.M. (2007). *Dog Owner's Home Veterinary Handbook* (4th ed.). B. Adelman (Ed.). Hoboken, NJ: Howell Book House (Wiley Publishing, Inc.).

672   Stoddart, D.M. (1990). *The Scented Ape: The Biology and Culture of Human Odour*. Cambridge, UK: Cambridge University Press.

673   Allen, S. (2012, November 12). Report #37336 (Class B): Unexplained activity around a farm near Bondurant. Retrieved November 20, 2015 from http://www.bfro.net/

674   Bord & Bord 2006.

675   Guttilla, P. (2003). *The Bigfoot Files*. Santa Barbara, CA: Timeless Voyager Press.

676   Driscoll, R. (2011, September 5). Report #30573 (Class A): Bowhunter recalls dusk encounter on creek dike near Oak Grove. Retrieved November 20, 2015 from http://www.bfro.net/

677   Blackburn, L. (2012). *The Beast of Boggy Creek: The True Story of the Fouke Monster*. San Antonio, TX: Anomalist Books.

678   Hairr, J. (2013). *Monsters of North Carolina: Mysterious Creatures in the Tar Heel State*. Mechanicsburg, PA: Stackpole Books.

679   Monteith, R. (2012, December 16). Report #38287 (Class A). Dogs alert homeowner to a late night visitor outside Kamiah. Retrieved November 20, 2015 from http://www.bfro.net/

680   Steiger 2011.

681   Rubin, J. (Writer), & Ohm, J. (Editor). (2009, January 24). Is That Skunk? [Television series episode]. In J. Donald (Producer), *Nature*. New York, NY: John Rubin Productions, Inc./Thirteen/WNET (Kravis Multimedia Education Center).

682   Johnson, J.C. (2010, August 31). The Harvest [Video file]. Retrieved November 30, 2015 from https://www.youtube.com/watch?v=_9oJxVZPhBs

683   Davis, T. (1998). *Why Dogs Do That*. Minocqua, WI: Willow Creek Press.

684   Strickler, L. (n.d.). 'Sykesville Monster' Encounter. Retrieved November 20, 2015 from http://www.phantomsandmonsters.com/

685   Bindernagel 1998.

686   Greyling, S. (1968, Fall). The Modoc Man and Sasquatch, The Tulelake Story. *Many Smokes National American Indian Magazine*.

687   Courtney, S. (2005, June 17). Report #11911 (Class A): Campers have lengthy nightime encounter near Seneca. Retrieved November 20, 2015 from http://www.bfro.net/

688   Blackburn 2012.

689   Betz, C. (2009, October 31). Report #26823 (Class A): Daylight sighting by hunter and son in Richloam Wildlife Management Area. Retrieved November 20, 2015 from http://www.bfro.net/

690   Brown, G. (2009). *The Bear Almanac: A Comprehensive Guide to the Bears of the World*. Guilford, CT: The Lyons Press.

691   Brake, D.A. (2005, June 24). Report #11956 (Class B): Unusual events at a remote family cabin near Keene Valley, NY. Retrieved November 20, 2015 from http://www.bfro.net/

692   Gordon, S. (2015). *Astonishing Encounters: Pennsylvania's Unknown Creatures – Casebook Three*. Greensburg, PA: Stan Gordon Productions.

693   Bouché, G. (2013, March 15). Report #40378 (Class B): Fishermen recount having large rocks thrown at them while fishing Steelhead on the Duckabush River. Retrieved November 24, 2015 from http://www.bfro.net/

694   Healy, T. (2001, October 20). "High Strangeness" in Yowie Reports. In P. Cropper (Ed.). *Myths & Monsters 2001 Conference Papers*. Paper presented at Myths & Monsters 2001, Sydney, Australia (pp. 64-72).

695   Bigfoot Field Researchers Organization. (2001, July 8). Report #2770 (Class B): Couple has frightening encounter near Lake Shasta. Retrieved December 9, 2015 from http://www.bfro.net/

696   Mateja, P.J. (2005, November 1). Report #12951 (Class A): Possible encounter between a juvenile and a human child, near Gettysburg. Retrieved December 9, 2015 from http://www.bfro.net/

697   Harpur 2003.

698   Bord & Bord 2006.

699   Redfern 2016 (*Bigfoot*).

700   Betz, C. (2011, June 10). Report #29414 (Class A): Woman walking her dogs has frighting early morning encounter near Charlotte Harbor. Retrieved December 9, 2015 from http://www.bfro.net/

701   Devos, M., Patte, F., Rouault, J., Lafort, P., & Van Gemert, L.J. (Eds.). (1990). *Standardized Human Olfactory Thresholds*. Oxford, UK: IRL Press.

702   Fisher 2013.

703   Bryant, Jr., V., & Trevor-Deutsch, B. (1980). Analysis of feces and hair suspected to be of Sasquatch origin. In M. Halpin & M.M. Ames (Eds.). *Manlike Monsters on Trial: Early Records and Modern Evidence* (pp. 291-300). Vancouver, CAN: University of British Columbia Press.

704   Saladin, K.S. (2013). *Human Anatomy* (4th ed.). New York, NY: McGraw-Hill Education.

705   Meldrum 2006.

706   Fahrenbach 1997.

707   Bindernagel 1998.

708   Hillix, W.A., & Rumbaugh, D. (2004). *Animal Bodies, Human Minds: Ape, Dolphin, and Parrot Language Skills*. New York, NY: Springer Science+Business Media.

709   Gordon 2015.

710   Cryptozoology News. (2014, April 17). The Science Behind Bigfoot Odor. Retrieved November 30, 2015 from http://cryptozoologynews.com/tsiatko-skunk-ape-bigfoot-odor/

711   Klailova, M, & Lee, P.C. (2014). Wild Western Lowland Gorillas Signal Selectively Using Odor. *PLOS ONE 9*(7): e99554. DOI: 10.1371/journal.pone.0099554.

712   Germer July 7, 2015.

713   McMillan, B. (2008, February 24). Report #23245 (Class A): Resting elk hunter smells and sees a Sasquatch near Whiteswan Lake. Retrieved November 30, 2015 from http://www.bfro.net/

714   Newton-Perry, L. (2015, September 22). The Original Post from Sophia about Dr. H.A. Miller. Retrieved December 1, 2015 from http://bigfootballyhoo.blogspot.com/

715   Ho, O. (2008). *Mutants and Monsters*. New York, NY: Sterling Publishing Co., Inc.

716   Smith, N.J.H. (1996). *The Enchanted Amazon Rain Forest: Stories from a Vanishing World*. Gainesville, FL: University Press of Florida.

717   Colp, H. (1997). *The Strangest Story Ever Told*. Petersburg, AK: Pilot Publishing. (Original work published 1953)

718   Noël, C. (2014). *Our Life with Bigfoot: Knowing Our Next of Kin at Habituation Sites* [Kindle edition]. US: CreateSpace Independent Publishing Platform.

719   Rife 2000.

720   Guttilla 2003.

721   Nunnelly 2011.

722   Rife 2000.

723   Lowery, R. (2011, May 26). Report #29294 (Class A): Sundown sighting by teen on bicycle in Eau Galle River bottoms. Retrieved December 1, 2015 from http://www.bfro.net/

724   Heuvelmans, B. (2016). *Neanderthal: The Strange Saga of the Minnesota Iceman*. (P. LeBlond, Trans.). San Antonio, TX: Anomalist Books.

725   Coleman, L. (2006). The Minnesota Iceman Cometh (and Goeth). In E. Dregni, M. Moran, & M. Scuerman (Eds.), *Weird Minnesota* (pp. 87-88). New York, NY: Sterling Publishing Co., Inc.

726   Bord & Bord 2006.

727   Harpur 2003.

728   Rogo, D.S., & Clark, J. (1982). *Earth's Secret Inhabitants*. New York, NY: Ace Books.

729   Taylor, S. (2008, May 10). Report #23771 (Class A): Young hunter sees and hears a Sasquatch near Applegate. Retrieved December 9, 2015 from http://www.bfro.net/

730   Hawkins, J. (2012). *Bigfoot and Other Monsters*. New York, NY: Rosen Publishing Group, Inc.

731   McMillan, B. (2006, April 27). Report #14511 (Class A): Sighting by snowmobilers outside Castlegar. Retrieved December 9, 2015 from http://www.bfro.net/

732   Gordon 2015.

733   Bayanov, D. (1993, February). Report from Moscow. In C. Cameron (Ed.), *Bigfoot Co-op Vol. 13*.

734   Emmer, R. (2010). *Creature Scene Investigator: Bigfoot – Fact or Fiction?* New York, NY: Chelsea House Publishers.

735   Bader, C.D., Mencken, F.C., & Baker, J.D. (2010). *Paranormal America: Ghost Encounters, UFO Sightings, Bigfoot Hunts, and Other Curiosities in Religion and Culture*. New York, NY: New York University Press.

736   Bord & Bord 2006.

737   Bigfoot Field Researchers Organization. (1996, December 21). Report #746 (Class A): Sighting by two newspaper deliverymen around 3:30 a.m. Retrieved December 1, 2015 from http://www.bfro.net/

738   Palmisano, A.C., & Barlaz, M.A. (1996). Introduction to Solid Waste Decompo-

sition. In A.C. Palmisano & M.A. Barlaz (Eds.), *Microbiology of Solid Waste* (pp. 1-30). Boca Raton, FL: CRC Press, Inc.

739   Alley 2007.

740   Rife 2000.

741   Bord 1989.

742   Meldrum 2006.

743   Steiger 2011.

744   Noël 2014.

745   Buschardt, C. (2012, October 28). Report #36838 (Class A): Man returns home at night to find a tall figure standing by his deer lick outside Farmington. Retrieved December 1, 2015 from http://www.bfro.net/

746   Nicholas, F. (2005). Appalachian Bigfoot Lacks Underarm Charm. In M. Lake, M. Sceurman & M. Moran (Eds.), *Weird Pennsylvania* (p. 92). New York, NY: Sterling Publishing Co., Inc.

747   Guiley 2012.

748   Greer, J.M. (2004). *Monsters: An Investigator's Guide to Magical Beings*. St. Paul, MN: Llewellyn Publications.

749   Clore 2015.

750   Craddock, G. (2014, June 29). Report #45665 (Class A): Memory told of a late night close encounter from a parked vehicle outside Gatlinburg. Retrieved December 3, 2015 from http://www.bfro.net/

751   Courtney, S. (2004, November 21). Report #9818 (Class A): Hiker has nighttime sighting at Minnehaha Falls. Retrieved December 3, 2015 from http://www.bfro.net/

752   Germer, W. (2016, April 17). *Sasquatch Chronicles Episode 211: Running right into a creature… literally*. [Audio podcast]. Retrieved April 20, 2016 from https://www.sasquatchchronicles.com

753   Kelleher, C.A. & Knapp, G. (2005). *Hunt for the Skinwalker: Science Confronts the Unexplained at a Remote Ranch*. New York, NY: Pocket Books.

754   Blackman, W.H. (1998). *The Field Guide to North American Monsters*. New York, NY: Three Rivers Press.

755   Estes, R.D. (1999). *The Safari Companion: A Guide to Watching African Mammals Including Hoofed Mammals, Carnivores, and Primates*. White River Junction, VT: Chelsea Green Publishing Company. (Original work published 1993)

756 Braun, C.A. & Anderson, C.M. (2007). *Pathophysiology: Functional Alterations in Human Health*. Philadelphia, PA: Lippencott Williams & Wilkins.

757 Gilbert, A. (2009, April 30). The Biochemistry of BO. Retrieved December 3, 2015 from http://www.firstnerve.com

758 Sams, C.E., & Conway, W.S. (2003). Preharvest Nutritional Factors Affecting Postharvest Physiology. In J.A. Bartz & J.K. Brecht (Eds.), *Postharvest Physiology and Pathology of Vegetables* (pp. 161-176). New York, NY: Marcel Dekker, Inc.

759 Anderson, B.C. (2010). *Cryptic Creatures*. Durham, CT: Strategic Book Publishing.

760 Noël, C. (2009). *Impossible Visits: The Inside Story of Interactions with Sasquatch at Habituation Sites*. US: Xlibris Corporation.

761 Bigfoot Field Researchers Organization. (2015). The 'Siege' at Honobia. Retrieved December 4, 2015 from http://www.bfro.net/

762 Gordon, S. (2010). *Silent Invasion: The Pennsylvania UFO-Bigfoot Casebook*. R. Marsh (Ed.). Greensburg, PA: Stan Gordon Productions.

763 Courtney, S. (2004, November 12). Report #9750 (Class A): Motorist observes bipedal animal shaking a pecan tree near Camp LeJeune. Retrieved November 27, 2015 from http://www.bfro.net/

764 Kimball, T.L. (2008, June 19). Report #24033 (Class B): Woman describes foul odor and possible vocalizations near home outside Charlevoix. Retrieved November 27, 2015 from http://www.bfro.net/

765 Curtis, C. (2004, April 2). Report #8435 (Class B): Incidents around a cabin near Greenburg. Retrieved November 27, 2015 from http://www.bfro.net/

766 Gordon 2015.

767 Keel 1976.

768 Gordon 2010.

769 Gordon 2010.

770 Gordon 2010.

771 Gordon 2010.

772 Johnson, P. G., & Jeffers, J.L. (1986) *The Pennsylvania Bigfoot*. Pittsburgh, PA: Johnson & Jeffers.

773 Steiger 2011.

774   Coleman, L. (2011, May 23). Joplin Bigfoot Report. Retrieved December 15, 2015 from http://cryptomundo.com/

775   Bord & Bord 2006.

776   Ramírez, M. (2012, May 16). Ovnis en Andalucía – Spain: A Humanoid at Fuengirola (CE-3, 1976) (S. Corrales, Trans.). Retrieved December 14, 2015 from http://inexplicata.blogspot.com/

777   Blackburn 2012.

778   Hudson, C. (2011). *Strange State: Mysteries and Legends of Oklahoma* (3rd ed.). US: CreateSpace Indepen- dent Publishing Platform.

779   McElyea, T. (2000, October 13). Report #451 (Class A). Young man has sighting near home. Retrieved December 14, 2015 from http://www.bfro.net/

780   Moneymaker, M. (1996, January 28). Report #928 (Class B): Hikers find tracks and a possible nest. Retrieved December 14, 2015 from http://www.bfro.net/

781   Monteith, R. (2013, July 21). Report #41782 (Class B): Man-like figure seen running along a tree-line off Hwy. 12 near Checkerboard. Retrieved December 14, 2015 from http://www.bfro.net/

782   Moneymaker, M. (2002, December 11). Report #5463 (Class A): Dusk sighting by hunter on Fort Hunter Liggett. Retrieved December 14, 2015 from http://www.bfro.net/

783   Clark, J. (2005). *Unnatural Phenomena: A Guide to the Bizarre Wonders of North America*. Santa Barbara, CA: ABC-CLIO, Inc.

784   Bord & Bord 2006.

785   Rife 2000.

786   Hucklebridge, R. (2008, September 1). Report #24648 (Class A): Man retells his close, visual encounter at dawn on Pine Mountain as a young deer hunter. Retrieved December 10, 2015 from http://www.bfro.net/

787   Dosen, C. (2002, October 27). Report #5172 (Class A): Multi-witness road-crossing sighting outside Fort St. John. Retrieved December 10, 2015 from http://www.bfro.net/

788   Sanders, K. (2009, February 22). Report #25531 (Class A): Witness recalls face to face encounter with creature near Myrtle Point. Retrieved December 10, 2015 from http://www.bfro.net/

789   Bindernagel 1998.

790   Guttilla 2003.

791 Citro, J.A. (1996). *Passing Strange: True Tales of New England Hauntings and Horrors*. Boston, MA: Houghton Mifflin Company.

792 Bigfoot Field Researchers Organization. (2002, February 6). Report #3731 (Class A): Child watches fawn being chased near Canadian River. Retrieved December 10, 2015 from http://www.bfro.net/

793 Fahrenbach, W.H. (2008, September 29). Report #24826 (Class A): Couple meets Sasquatch and finds nest in cave. Retrieved December 10, 2015 from http://www.bfro.net/

794 Bruns, T. (2010, April 11). Report #27568 (Class A): Daylight sighting of a Bigfoot outside Muscle Shoals. Retrieved December 10, 2015 from http://www.bfro.net/

795 Maisel, M. (2013, November 15). Report #42745 (Class A): Strange occurrences outside a home lead to a daylight sighting by a father and son near East Canton. Retrieved December 10, 2015 from http://www.bfro.net/

796 Bakara, D. (2013, June 17). Report #41448 (Class A): Motorist has daytime sighting along I-75 near Ruskin. Retrieved December 4, 2015 from http://www.bfro.net/

797 Brumfield, M. (2014, June 2). Report #45216 (Class A): Reoccurring activity on a farm outside Fort Stewart. Retrieved December 4, 2015 from http://www.bfro.net/

798 Bader, Mencken, & Baker 2010.

799 Fisher 2013.

800 Cornet 2005.

801 Cornet 2005.

802 Murphy, C.L. (2008). *Bigfoot Film Journal*. Blaine, WA: Hancock House Publishers.

803 Tourism Harrison. (n.d.). Harrison is Sasquatch Territory – about our Sasquatch. Retrieved March 28, 2016 from http://www.tourismharrison.com/

804 Keel 2002/1970.

805 Aubeck, C. (2004, March 21). Re: UFOs and Fairies/Legends/Supernatural – Pt. I. Retrieved December 14, 2015 from http://www.ufoupdateslist.com/

806 Hanks, M. (2014, February 19). Space Blobs: A Look at Jelly from the Stars. Retrieved May 2, 2016 from http://mysteriousuniverse.org/

807 Clark 2013.

808 Le Guérer 1994.

809   Rickard & Michell 2000.

810   Clark 2005.

811   Kelley, M. (2004). *Minor Histories: Statements, Conversations, Proposals*. J.C. Welchman (Ed.). Cambridge, MA: The Massachusetts Institute of Technology Press.

812   Bord & Bord 1989.

813   Guiley, R. (2008). *The Encyclopedia of Witches, Witchcraft & Wicca* (3rd ed.). New York, NY: Facts on File, Inc. (Original work published 1989).

814   Christiansen, R. (Ed.). (1964). *Folktales of Norway*. (R.M. Dorson, Trans.). Chicago, IL: University of Chicago Press.

815   Coleman, L. (2001). *Mysterious America: The Ultimate Guide to the Nation's Weirdest Wonders, Strangest Spots, and Creepiest Creatures*. New York, NY: Paraview Pocket Books.

816   Blackman 1998.

817   Smith 1996.

818   Steiger 2011.

819   Steiger 2011.

820   Redfern 2013.

821   Clark 2013.

822   No author. (1902, June 22). Sea Monster in Lake Superior. *Duluth News Tribune*.

823   Altman, E., & Samuels, M. (2015, July 19). *Beyond the Edge Radio: 7/19/2015 BTE Radio Creature Features presents – Katy Elizabeth and Dennis Hall of Champ Search* [Audio podcast]. Retrieved December 15, 2015 from http://beyondtheedge.planetparanormal.com/

824   Biobaum, C. (2012). *Awesome Snake Science: 40 Activities for Learning About Snakes*. Chicago, IL: Chicago Review Press.

825   San Francisco Call. (1895, April 21). An Embryonic Dragon Frightens a Party of Poppy Hunters at Sausalito. *The San Francisco Call*, p. 17.

826   Clark 2010.

827   Epoch Times. (2005, August 7). Dragons in the Sky. Retrieved December 15, 2015 from http://www.theepochtimes.com/

828   Clark 2013.

829   Gerhard, K. (2013). *Encounters with Flying Humanoids*. Woodbury, MN: Llewellyn Publications.

830   Strickler, L. (2015, July 20). Arcane Radio Live Show Archive 7.20.15 Guest Shannon LeGro [Audio podcast]. Retrieved December 15, 2015 from http://www.arcaneradio.com/

831   Keel 2002/1975

832   Bane 2012.

833   Nunnelly 2011.

834   Godfrey 2014.

835   Radford, B. (2011). *Tracking the Chupacabra: The Vampire Beast in Fact, Fiction, and Folklore*. Albuquerque, NM: University of New Mexico Press.

836   Radford 2011.

837   Corrales, S. (1997). *Chupacabras and Other Mysteries*. Murfreesboro, TN: Greenleaf Publications.

838   Stieven, M.A. (1999, Winter). "Chupacabras" Rampant in Brazil (1997). *Flying Saucer Review 44(4)*, pp. 13-16.

839   Corrales 1997.

840   Cowley, S., & Cox, G. (2012). *Searching for Bigfoot*. New York, NY: The Rosen Company.

841   Godfrey 2014.

842   Strickler, L. (2015, November 10). Arcane Radio Live Show Archive 11.10.15: Nick Redfern [Audio podcast]. Retrieved December 16, 2015 from http://www.arcaneradio.com/

843   Sieveking, P. (2003, February). Alien Big Cats: The Definitive Guide to a 40-Year Mystery. *Fortean Times 167*, p. 28.

844   Coleman, L. (1971, March). Mystery Animals in Illinois. *Fate Magazine*, pp. 48-54.

845   Breedlove, S. (2016, February 27). *Episode 81: With Loren Coleman* [Audio podcast]. Retrieved March 7, 2016 from http://saswhat.podbean.com/

846   Schaffner, R. (n.d.). Case 289. In A. Rosales (Ed.), *1978 Humanoid Sighting Reports*. Retrieved December 16, 2015 from http://www.ufoinfo.com/humanoid/humanoid-1978.pdf

847 McCarthy, E. (2014, July 11). 11 Ways Big Cats Are Just Like Domestic Cats. Retrieved December 15, 2015 from http://mentalfloss.com/

848 Le Guérer 1994.

849 Curley, M.J. (Trans.). (2009). *Physiologus: A Medieval Book of Nature Lore*. Chicago, IL: University of Chicago Press. (Original work published 1979)

850 Rickard & Michell 2000.

851 Hartland, E.S. (2000). *English Fairy and Folk Tales.* Mineola, NY: Dover Publications, Inc. (Original work published 1890)

852 Williams, D.S. (1997). *When Darkness Falls: Tales of San Antonio Ghosts and Hauntings*. Dallas, TX: Republic of Texas Press.

853 Redfern, N. (2014, October 12). Things That Go Bump in the Night Department – Black Dogs and UFOs. Retrieved December 17, 2015 from http://uforeview.tripod.com/

854 Clark, J. (2000). *Extraordinary Encounters: An Encyclopedia of Extraterrestrials and Otherworldly Beings*. Santa Barbara, CA: ABC-CLIO, Inc.

855 Coleman 2002.

856 Steiger 2011.

857 Redfern, N. (2004). *Three Men Seeking Monsters*. New York, NY: Paraview Pocket Books.

858 Godfrey, L.S. (2012). *Real Wolfmen: True Encounters in Modern America*. London, UK: Penguin Books Ltd.

859 Nunnelly 2011.

860 Steiger 2011.

861 Godfrey, L.S. (2003). *The Beast of Bray Road*. Madison, WI: Prairie Oak Press.

862 Nunnelly 2011.

863 Clore 2015.

864 Couch, J.N. (2014). *Goatman: Flesh or Folklore?* West Bend, WI: J. Nathan Couch.

865 Couch 2014.

866 Pugh, D.G., & Baird, A.N. (2012). *Sheep & Goat Medicine* (2nd ed.). Maryland Heights, MO: Elsevier Saunders.

867 Ellison, Q. (2011, August 31). That awful smell, yeah, that's me. Seriously. Retrieved December 21, 2015 from http://www.smokymountainnews.com/

868 Clark 2013.

869 Coleman 2003.

870 Rife, P.L. (2001). *America's Nightmare Monsters*. Lincoln, NE: Writers Club Press.

871 Steiger 2011.

872 Stringfield, L. (1977). *Situation Red—The UFO Siege!* Garden City, NY: Doubleday & Company, Inc.

873 Maruna, S. (2003). *The Mad Gasser of Mattoon: Dispelling the Hysteria* (2nd ed.). Jacksonville, IL: Swamp Gas Book Co.

874 Rife 2001.

875 Maruna 2003.

876 Maruna 2003.

877 Nunnelly 2011.

878 Maruna 2003.

879 Redfern, N. (2011). *The Real Men in Black*. Pompton Plains, NJ: New Page Books.

880 Bender, A.K. (2014). *Flying Saucers and the Three Men*. Point Pleasant, WV: New Saucerian Books. (Original work published 1962).

881 Bender 2014.

882 Redfern 2011.

883 Redfern 2011.

884 Keel 2002/1975.

885 Keel 2002/1975.

886 Keel 2002/1975.

887 Redfern, N. (2016). *Women in Black: The Creepy Companions of the Mysterious M.I.B.* US: Lisa Hagan Books [Kindle edition].

888 Redfern 2016 (*Women in Black*).

889 Noory, G. (2013, April 12). Coast to Coast AM - Black Eyed Children & Open

Endnotes 371

Lines. Retrieved December 17, 2015 from http://www.coasttocoastam.com/

890   Philson, K., & Hale, C. (2015, August 3). Expanded Perspectives - The Black Eyed Kids. Retrieved December 20, 2015 from http://www.expandedperspectives.com/

891   Bane, T. (2013). *Encyclopedia of Fairies in World Folklore and Mythology*. Jefferson, NC: McFarland & Company, Inc.

892   Bane 2013.

893   Morris, M.C.F. (1911). *Yorkshire Folk-Talk* (2nd ed.). London, UK: A. Brown & Sons, Ltd.

894   Morris 1911.

895   Converse, H.M. (1908). *Myths and Legends of the New York State Iroquois*. A.C. Parker (Ed.). Albany, NY: University of the State of New York.

896   Sanchez-Ocejo, V. (2003, July 28). Eyewitnesses to Incredible Winged Creatures, Imps. Retrieved December 20, 2015 from http://www.rense.com/

897   Johnson, M.T. (2014). *Seeing Fairies: From the Lost Archives of the Fairy Investigation Society, Authentic Reports of Fairies in Modern Times*. San Antonio, TX: Anomalist Books.

898   Native Languages of the Americas. (n.d.). Legendary Native American Figures: Pukwudgie (Puckwudgie). Retrieved December 20, 2015 from http://www.native-languages.org

899   Johnson 2014.

900   Thornber, W. (1985). *The History of Blackpool and Its Neighbourhood*. Blackpool, UK: The Blackpool and Fylde Historical Society. (Original work published 1837)

901   Cunliffe, H. (1886). *A Glossary of Rochdale-with-Rossendale Words and Phrases*. London, UK: John Heywood.

902   Arrowsmith, N. (2009). *Field Guide to the Little People*. Woodbury, MN: Llewellyn Publications. (Original work published 1977)

903   Johnson 2014.

904   Dr. Beachcombing 2013.

905   Johnson 2014.

906   Nunnelly 2011.

907   Deveraux 2003.

908   CICOANI Brazil. (n.d.). Case 109. In A. Rosales (Ed.), *1972 Humanoid Sighting Reports*. Retrieved December 20, 2015 from http://www.ufoinfo.com/humanoid/humanoid-1972.pdf

909   Vallee 1990.

910   Kelleher & Knapp 2005.

911   Clore 2015.

912   Vroon 1997.

913   Le Guérer 1994.

914   Larsson, M., Öberg-Blåvarg, C., & Jönsson, F.U. (2009). Bad Odors Stick Better Than Good Ones: Olfactory Qualities and Odor Recognition. *Experimental Psychology 56 (6)*, 375-380.

915   Germer, W. (2015, November 15). *Sasquatch Chronicles Episode 165: Calling 911* [Audio podcast]. Retrieved December 22, 2015 from https://www.sasquatchchronicles.com/

916   McKenna, T. (1990, July). The World Could Be Anything. [Lecture transcript]. Retrieved December 22, 2015 from https://terencemckenna.wikispaces.com

917   Schab 1995.

918   Kass, M.D., Rosenthal, M.C., Pottackal, J., & McGann, J.P. (2013) Fear learning enhances neural responses to threat-predictive stimuli. *Science* 342: 1389-1392.
919   Red Pill Junkie. Personal communication, February 8, 2016.

920   Granchi, I. (1995). *UFOs and Abductions in Brazil*. Madison, WI: Horus House Press, Inc. (Original work published 1992)

921   Dement, W.C. (2015). The Smell of Death During Sleep Paralysis. Retrieved December 29, 2015 from http://www.end-your-sleep-deprivation.com/

922   Raymond, C. (2011, December 6). Reports for Adair County, KY. Retrieved December 29, 2015 from http://www.kentuckybigfoot.com/

923   Rincon, P. (2005, April 21). Mice put in 'suspended animation.' Retrieved December 29, 2015 from http://news.bbc.co.uk/

924   Roth, M. (2010, February). Mark Roth: Suspended animation is within our grasp. Retrieved December 29, 2015 from http://www.ted.com/

925   Rincon 2005.

926   Roth 2010.

927 Kroonenberg 2013.

928 Dugbartey, G.J. (2015, July). The role of endogenous H2S production during hibernation and forced hypothermia: towards safe cooling and rewarming in clinical practice (Doctoral dissertation). Groningen, Netherlands: The University of Groningen.

929 Cornet 2005.

930 Guiley 2007.

931 Rolle, R. (1989). *The World of the Scythians* (F.G. Walls, Trans.). Berkeley & Los Angeles, CA: University of California Press (Original work published 1980 as *Die Welt der Skythen*)

932 Harvey, G., & Wallis, R.J. (2007). *Historical Dictionary of Shamanism*. Lanham, MD: The Scarecrow Press, Inc.

933 Stafford, P. (1993). Psychedelics Encyclopedia (3rd ed). Berkeley, CA: Ronin Publishing.

934 Browner, R. Personal communication, March 27, 2015.

935 Gholipour, B. (2015, April 22). Up to 90% of Your Perception Could Be Made Up Purely By the Brain. Retrieved December 30, 2015 from https://www.braindecoder.com/

936 Bishop, G. (2016, May 21). *Ufology – New Directions: Co-Creation*. Speech presented at New Mexico UFO/Paranormal Forum in Albuquerque, NM.

937 Hopkins, B., & Rainey, C. (2003). *Sight Unseen: Science UFO Invisibility and Transgenic Beings*. New York, NY: Atria Books.

938 Krebs 2006.

939 Zenz, C., Dickerson, O.B., & Horvath, E.P. (1994). *Occupational Medicine* (3rd ed.). St. Louis, MO: Mosby.

940 Stokes, D., Matthen, M., & Biggs, S. (2015). *Perception and Its Modalities*. Oxford, UK: Oxford University Press.

941 Hirsch, A.R. (2004). *What Your Doctor May Not Tell You About Sinusitis*. New York, NY: Warner Books.

942 Stokes, Matthen, & Biggs 2015.

943 Stokes, Matthen, & Biggs 2015.

944 Parker, G.H. (1922). *Smell, Taste, and Allied Senses in the Vertebrates*. Philadelphia, PA: J.B. Lippincott Company.

945   Hornung, D.E., Kurtz, D., & Youngentob, S.L. (1994) Anosmic Patients Can Separate Trigeminal and Nontrigeminal Stimulants. In K. Kurihara, N. Suzuki, & H. Ogawa (Eds.), *Olfaction and Taste XI: Proceedings of the 11th International Symposium on Olfaction and Taste and of the 27th Japanese Symposium on Taste and Smell* (p. 635). Tokyo, Japan: Springer.

946   Herz, R.S. (2001, October 1). Ah, Sweet Skunk! Why We Like or Dislike What We Smell. Retrieved January 4, 2016 from http://www.dana.org/

947   Feng, X., Zhou, Y.L., Meng, X., Qi, F.H., Chen, W., Jiang, X., & Xu, G.Y. (2013, February). Hydrogen sulfide increase excitability through suppression of sustained potassium channel currents of rat trigeminal ganglion neurons. *Molecular Pain 9(4)*.

948   Herz 2001.

949   Clore 2015.

950   Ramsbotham, J. (1999) Perfumes in Detergents. In G. Broze (Ed.), *Surfactant Science Series Volume 82: Handbook of Detergents – Part A: Properties.* (pp. 691-720). New York, NY: Marcel Dekker, Inc.

951   Ramsbotham 1999.

952   Ramsbotham 1999.

953   Conner, W.E., Alley, K.M., Barry, J.R., & Harper, A.E. (2007, December). Has vertebrate chemesthesis been a selective agent in the evolution of anthropod chemical defenses? *The Biology Bulletin 213(3)*, pp. 267-273.

954   Conner, Alley, Barry, & Harper 2007.

955   Conner, Alley, Barry, & Harper 2007.

956   Hornung, Kurtz, & Youngentob 1994.

957   Conner, Alley, Barry, & Harper 2007.

958   Conner, Alley, Barry, & Harper 2007.

959   Conner, Alley, Barry, & Harper 2007.

960   Conner, Alley, Barry, & Harper 2007.

961   Conner, Alley, Barry, & Harper 2007.

962   Conner, Alley, Barry, & Harper 2007.

963   Goldstein, E.B. (2010). *Encyclopedia of Perception* (Vol. 1). Thousand Oaks, CA: SAGE Publications.

Endnotes

964   Goldstein 2010.

965   Hirsch 2004.

966   Klenø, J., & Wolkoff, P. (2004). Changes in eye blink frequency as a measure of trigeminal stimulation by exposure to limonene oxidation products, isoprene oxidation products and nitrate radicals. *International Archives of Occupational and Environmental Health 77*, pp. 235-243.

967   Millen, J.K. (2001). *Your Nose Knows: A Study of the Sense of Smell*. Lincoln, NE: Authors Choice Press. (Original work published in 1960).

968   Conner, Alley, Barry, & Harper 2007.

969   Herz 2001.

970   Conner, Alley, Barry, & Harper 2007.

971   Turback, G. (1984, December). New Technologies Fight Wood-Stove Pollution. *Popular Science*, pp. 90-92.

972   Giriraj Pain Management Clinic. (n.d.). Trigeminal neuralgia. Retrieved January 4, 2016 from http://www.paingujarat.com/

973   Calunga, J.L., Paz, Y., Menéndez S., Martínez A., & Hernández A. (n.d.). Miscellaneous Studies for Ozone. Retrieved January 4, 2016 from http://drsozone.com/

974   Purves, D., Augustine, G.J., Fitzpatrick, D., Katz, L.C., LaMantia, A.S., McNamara, J.O., & Williams, S.M. (Eds.) (2001). *Neuroscience* (2nd ed.). Sunderland, MA: Sinauer Associates.

975   Hirsch 2004.

976   Hirsch 2004.

977   Wheless, J.W., Willmore, L.J., & Brumback, R.A. (2009). *Advanced Therapy in Epilepsy*. Shelton, CT: People's Medical Publishing House.

978   Briggs, K. (1976). *An Encyclopedia of Fairies: Hobgoblins, Brownies, Bogies, and Other Supernatural Creatures*. New York, NY: Pantheon Books.

979   Keel 2002/1975.

980   Deus Ex McKenna [Screen name] (2011, July 10). *Hermeticism & Alchemy (Terence McKenna)* [Video file]. Retrieved January 5, 2016 from https://www.youtube.com/watch?v=-YNdBpYh1eA

981   Hauck, D.W. (2008). *The Complete Idiot's Guide to Alchemy*. New York, NY: Alpha (Penguin Group).

982   Hauck 2008.

983   Hauck 2008.

984   Hauck 2008.

985   Hauck 2008.

986   Hauck 2008.

987   Dennis William Hauck quoted in Aromatico, A. (2000). *Alchemy: The Great Secret.* (J. Hawkes, Trans.). New York, NY: Harry M. Abrams, Inc.

988   Zeise, W.C. (1834). Ueber das Mercaptan. In *Annalen der Pharmacie* (Vol. 11-12). Heidelberg, Germany: Universitätsbuchhandlung von C.F. Winter.

989   Hauck 2008.

990   Hillman, J. (1991). The Yellowing of the Work. In M.A. Mattoon (Ed.), *Personal and Archetypal Dynamics in the Analytical Relationship: Proceedings of the Eleventh International Congress for Analytical Psychology, Paris, 1989* (pp. 77-96). Einsiedeln, Switzerland: Daimon Verlag.

991   Hauck 2008.

992   Harpur 2008.

993   Hauck 2008.

994   theduderinok2 [Screen name] (2011, February 6). *[Highly Recommended] Terence McKenna – Unfolding the Stone*. Retrieved January 8, 2016 from https://www.youtube.com/watch?v=zMPamVaTjJE

995   Hauck 2008.

996   Debus, A.G. (2002). *The Chemical Philosophy: Paracelsian Science and Medicine in the Sixteenth and Seventeenth Centuries* (Vol. 1). Mineola, NY: Dover Publications (Original work published 1977).

997   Debus 2002 Vol. 1.

998   Aromatico 2000.

999   Greenberg, A. (2007). *From Alchemy to Chemistry in Picture and Story.* Hoboken, NJ: John Wiley & Sons, Inc.

1000   Greenberg 2007.

1001   Rux, B. (1996). *Architects of the Underworld: Unriddling Atlantis, Anomalies of Mars, and the Mystery of the Sphinx.* Berkeley, CA: Frog, Ltd.

Endnotes

1002 Jung, C.G. (1977). *The Collected Works of Carl Jung: Mysterium Coniunctionis* (Vol. 14). (R.F.C. Hull, Trans.). H. Read, M. Fordham, G. Adler, W. McGuire (Eds.). Princeton, N.J.: Princeton University Press. (Original work published 1963)

1003 Jung, C.G. (1991). *Flying Saucers: A Modern Myth of Things Seen in the Skies.* (R.F.C. Hull, Trans.). Princeton, NJ: Princeton University Press. (Original work published 1978)

1004 Jung 1977.

1005 Greenberg 2008.

1006 Jung 1991.

1007 Harpur 2008.

1008 Jung 1991.

1009 Harpur 2008.

1010 Debus 2002 Vol. 1.

1011 Debus, A.G. (2002). *The Chemical Philosophy: Paracelsian Science and Medicine in the Sixteenth and Seventeenth Centuries* (Vol. 2). Mineola, NY: Dover Publications (Original work published 1977).

1012 Snuffin, M.O. (2007). *The Thoth Companion.* Woodbury, MN: Llewellyn Publications.

1013 Pope, N., Burroughs, J., & Penniston, J. (2014). *Encounter in Rendlesham Forest: The Inside Story of the World's Best-Documented UFO Incident.* New York, NY; Thomas Dunne Books.

1014 Dennett, P.E. (2008). *Mysteries, Legends, and Unexplained Phenomena: UFOs and Aliens.* R.E. Guiley (Ed.). New York, NY: Chelsea House Publishers.

1015 Hillman 1991.

1016 Hauck 2008

1017 Greenberg 2008.

1018 Von Franz, M.L. (1980). *Alchemy: An Introduction to the Symbolism and the Psychology.* Toronto, Canada: Inner City Books.

1019 Detienne, M. (1977). *The Gardens of Adonis: Spices in Greek Mythology.* (J. Lloyd, Trans.). Atlantic Highlands, NJ: The Humanities Press. (Original work published 1977 as *Les Jardins d'Adonis*)

1020 Von Franz 1980.

1021   Tonnies, M. (2012). *Posthuman Blues 2003-2004* (Vol. 1). Halifax, Nova Scotia: Redstar Books.

1022   theduderinok2 2011.

BIBLIOGRAPHY

Abe, S. (2011, December 17). The First Sulfur Eaters. Retrieved November 13, 2015 from https://astrobiology.nasa.gov

Academy of the Immaculate. (2008). *Mary at the Foot of the Cross, VII: Coredemptrix, Therefore Mediatrix of All Graces. Act of the Seventh International Symposium on Marian Coredemption.* New Bedford, MA: Franciscans of the Immaculate.

Aftel, M. (2001). *Essence and Alchemy: A Natural History of Perfume.* New York, NY: North Point Press.

Afrikaanse Sonntagzeitung Rapport - South Africa. (1995, April 2). Alien object lands to repair hole in its hull, says farmer. Retrieved November 3, 2015 from http://www.ufoevidence.org

Agency for Toxic Substances & Disease Registry. (2014, October 21). Toxic Substances Portal – Sulfur Dioxide. Retrieved October 19, 2015 from http://www.atsdr.cdc.gov

Allan, W.K. (n.d.). Case 100. In A. Rosales (Ed.), *1969 Humanoid Sighting Reports.* Retrieved September 15, 2015 from http://www.ufoinfo.com

Altman, E., & Samuels, M. (2015, July 19). *Beyond the Edge Radio: 7/19/2015 BTE Radio Creature Features presents – Katy Elizabeth and Dennis Hall of Champ Search* [Audio podcast]. Retrieved December 15, 2015 from http://beyondtheedge.planetparanormal.com

Altschule, H.G., & Vonnegut, B. (1997, April/May). The Smell of Tornadoes. *Weatherwise 50 (2),* pp. 24-25.

Allen, S. (2012, November 12). Report #37336 (Class B): Unexplained activity around a farm near Bondurant. Retrieved November 20, 2015 from http://www.bfro.net

Alley, J. R. (2007). *Raincoast Sasquatch*: *The Bigfoot/Sasquatch records of southeast Alaska, coastal British Columbia, & Northwest Washington from Puget Sound to Yakutat.* Blaine, WA: Hancock House. (Original work published 2003)

Ambraseys, N.N., & Melville, C.P. (1982). *A History of Persian Earthquakes.* Cambridge, UK: Cambridge University Press.

Amos, J. (2008, August 24). Solar plane makes record flight. Retrieved November 13, 2015 from http://news.bbc.co.uk

Anderson, B.C. (2010). *Cryptic Creatures.* Durham, CT: Strategic Book Publishing.

Anderson, C., & Chavez, E. (2009). *Our Lady of Guadalupe: Mother of the Civilization of Love.* New York, NY: Doubleday Religion.

Andrus, W. (1988, April). The Mundrabilla Incident – Part II. *MUFON UFO Journal 240*, pp. 14-17.

Angelucci, O. (1955). *The Secrets of the Saucers.* Amherst, MA: Amherst Press.

Anfalov, A. & Crimean Anomalous Phenomena Research Group. (n.d.). Case 199. In A. Rosales (Ed.), *2002 Humanoid Sighting Reports.* Retrieved October 19, 2015 from http://www.ufoinfo.com

Aromatico, A. (2000). *Alchemy: The Great Secret.* (J. Hawkes, Trans.). New York, NY: Harry M. Abrams, Inc.

Arrowsmith, N. (2009). *Field Guide to the Little People.* Woodbury, MN: Llewellyn Publications. (Original work published 1977)

Aubeck, C. (2004, March 21). Re: UFOs and Fairies/Legends/Supernatural – Pt. I. Retrieved December 14, 2015 from http://www.ufoupdateslist.com

Australian Government Department of the Environment. (2005). Sulfur Dioxide (SO_2). Retrieved October 22, 2015 from https://www.environment.gov.au

Bader, C.D., Mencken, F.C., & Baker, J.D. (2010). *Paranormal America: Ghost Encounters, UFO Sightings, Bigfoot Hunts, and Other Curiosities in Religion and Culture.* New York, NY: New York University Press.

Bailey, H. (2005). The Bush House. In J. Belanger (Ed.), *Encyclopedia of Haunted Places* (pp. 207-208). Franklin Lakes, NJ: New Page Books.

Baker, L. (2005). Former Jasper County Care Facility. In J. Belanger (Ed.), *Encyclopedia of Haunted Places* (pp. 138-139). Franklin Lakes, NJ: New Page Books.

Bakara, D. (2013, June 17). Report #41448 (Class A): Motorist has daytime sighting along I-75 near Ruskin. Retrieved December 4, 2015 from http://www.bfro.net

Baker, L. (2005). Port Arthur Historic Site. In J. Belanger (Ed.), *Encyclopedia of Haunted Places* (pp. 277-278). Franklin Lakes, NJ: New Page Books.

Baker, R.A., & Nickell, J. (1992). *Missing Pieces: How to Investigate Ghosts, UFOs, Psychics, and Other Mysteries.* Amherst, NY: Prometheus Books.

Bane, T. (2012). *Encyclopedia of Demons in World Religions and Cultures.* Jefferson, NC: McFarland & Company, Inc.

Bane, T. (2013). *Encyclopedia of Fairies in World Folklore and Mythology.* Jefferson, NC: McFarland & Company, Inc.

Barker, G. (1983). *The Year of the Saucer: Gray Barker's UFO Annual 1983.* Jane Lew, WV: New Age Press.

Bibliography

Barnes, C. (1996, December 2). A Perth mother and son's bizarre encounter's with another world. Retrieved November 5, 2015 from http://www.auforn.com

Barry, J.D. (1980). *Ball Lightning and Bead Lightning*. New York, NY: Plenum Press.

Bastien, J.L. (2008). *Ghosts of Mount Holly: A History of Haunted Happenings*. Charleston, SC: The History Press (Haunted America).

Bayanov, D. (1993, February). Report from Moscow. In C. Cameron (Ed.), *Bigfoot Co-op Vol. 13*.

Beckley, T.G. (1990). *The UFO Silencers*. New Brunswick, NJ: Inner Light Publications.

Belanger, J. (2005). RMS Queen Mary. In J. Belanger (Ed.), *Encyclopedia of Haunted Places* (p. 201). Franklin Lakes, NJ: New Page Books.

Belanger, J. (2005). South Bridge Underground Vaults. In J. Belanger (Ed.), *Encyclopedia of Haunted Places* (pp. 303-304). Franklin Lakes, NJ: New Page Books.

Belanger, J. (2007). *The Ghost Files*. Franklin Lakes, NJ: The Career Press, Inc.

Benavides, G.A, Squadrito, G.L., Mills, R.W., Patel, H.D., Isbell, T.S, Patel, R.P., Darley-Usmar, V.M., Doeller, J.E., Kraus, D.W. (2007, November 13). Hydrogen sulfide mediates the vasoactivity of garlic. *Proceedings of the National Academy of Sciences of the United States of America 104 (46)*, 17977–17982.

Bender, A.K. (2014). *Flying Saucers and the Three Men*. Point Pleasant, WV: New Saucerian Books. (Original work published 1962).

Berliner, D., & Friedman, S.T. (2010). *Crash at Corona: The U.S. Military Retrieval and Cover-Up of a UFO—The Definitive Study of the Roswell Incident*. New York, NY: Cosimo Books. (Original work published 1992)

Betz, C. (2009, October 31). Report #26823 (Class A): Daylight sighting by hunter and son in Richloam Wildlife Management Area. Retrieved November 20, 2015 from http://www.bfro.net/

Betz, C. (2011, June 10). Report #29414 (Class A): Woman walking her dogs has frighting early morning encounter near Charlotte Harbor. Retrieved December 9, 2015 from http://www.bfro.net/

BigfootEvidence [Screen name] (2011, July 10). *Melba Ketchum: Bigfoot is part lemur and part human* [Video file]. Retrieved March 7, 2016 from https://www.youtube.com

Bigfoot Field Researchers Organization. (1996, December 21). Report #746 (Class A): Sighting by two newspaper deliverymen around 3:30 a.m. Retrieved December 1, 2015 from http://www.bfro.net

Bigfoot Field Researchers Organization. (2001, July 8). Report #2770 (Class B): Couple has frightening encounter near Lake Shasta. Retrieved December 9, 2015 from http://www.bfro.net

Bigfoot Field Researchers Organization. (2002, January 11). Report #3529 (Class A): Daylight sighting by a wood cutter on a logging road in the Mts. above Oakley. Retrieved November 17, 2015 from http://www.bfro.net

Bigfoot Field Researchers Organization. (2002, February 6). Report #3731 (Class A): Child watches fawn being chased near Canadian River. Retrieved December 10, 2015 from http://www.bfro.net

Bigfoot Field Researchers Organization. (2015). The 'Siege' at Honobia. Retrieved December 4, 2015 from http://www.bfro.net

Bildhauer, B. (2003). Blood, Jews and Monsters in Medieval Culture. In B. Bildhauer & R. Mills (Eds.), *The Monstrous Middle Ages* (pp. 75-96). Bodmin, UK: MPG Books Ltd.

Bindernagel, J.A. (1998). *North America's Great Ape: the Sasquatch.* Courtenay, BC: Beachcomber Books.

Binnall, T. (2015, July 7). *Binnall of America Season IX: 7.7.15 – Carl DeMarco* [Audio podcast]. Retrieved October 19, 2015 from http://binnallofamerica.com

Biobaum, C. (2012). *Awesome Snake Science: 40 Activities for Learning About Snakes.* Chicago, IL: Chicago Review Press.

Bishop, G. (2016, May 21). *Ufology – New Directions: Co-Creation.* Speech presented at New Mexico UFO/Paranormal Forum in Albuquerque, NM.

Blackburn, L. (2012). *The Beast of Boggy Creek: The True Story of the Fouke Monster.* San Antonio, TX: Anomalist Books.

Blackman, W.H. (1998). *The Field Guide to North American Monsters.* New York, NY: Three Rivers Press.

Bloecher, T. (1978, February). CE-III Report from Montvale, N.J.: Preliminary Report. *MUFON UFO Journal 123*, pp. 4-7.

Bord, J., & Bord, C. (1984). *The Evidence for Bigfoot and Other Man-Beasts.* Wellingborough, UK: Aquarian Press.

Bord, J., & Bord, C. (1989). *Unexplained Mysteries of the 20th Century.* Lincolnwood, IL: Contemporary Books.

Bord, J., & Bord, C. (2006). *Bigfoot Casebook Updated: Sightings and Encounters from 1818 to 2004.* Enumclaw, WA: Pine Winds Press. (Original work published 1982)

Bouché, G. (2013, March 15). Report #40378 (Class B): Fishermen recount having large rocks thrown at them while fishing Steelhead on the Duckabush River. Retrieved November 24, 2015 from http://www.bfro.net

Braun, C.A. & Anderson, C.M. (2007). *Pathophysiology: Functional Alterations in Human Health*. Philadelphia, PA: Lippencott Williams & Wilkins.

Braenne, O.J. (n.d.). Case 27. In A. Rosales (Ed.), *1936 Humanoid Sighting Reports*. Retrieved October 21, 2015 from http://www.ufoinfo.com

Brake, D.A. (2005, June 24). Report #11956 (Class B): Unusual events at a remote family cabin near Keene Valley, NY. Retrieved November 20, 2015 from http://www.bfro.net

Brake, D.A. (2005, March 11). Report #44837 (Class A): Hunter has early morning encounter 8 miles north of Riverdale. Retrieved November 19, 2015 from http://www.bfro.net

Brandon, T. (2002). *The Ghost Hunter's Bible*. Mansfield OH: Zerotime Publishing.

Breedlove, S. (2016, February 27). *Episode 81: With Loren Coleman* [Audio podcast]. Retrieved March 7, 2016 from http://saswhat.podbean.com

Briazack, N.J., & Mennick, S. (1978). *The UFO Guidebook*. Secaucus N.J.: Citadel Press.

Briggs, K. (1976). *An Encyclopedia of Fairies: Hobgoblins, Brownies, Bogies, and Other Supernatural Creatures*. New York, NY: Pantheon Books.

Brown, A. (2006). *Ghost Hunters of the South*. Jackson, MS: University Press of Mississippi.

Brown, A. (2012). *The Big Book of Texas Ghost Stories*. Mechanicsburg, PA: Stackpole Books.

Brown, G. (2009). *The Bear Almanac: A Comprehensive Guide to the Bears of the World*. Guilford, CT: The Lyons Press.

Browner, R. Personal communication, March 27, 2015.

Bruce, R. (2012). *Astral Dynamics: The Complete Book of Out-of-Body Experience* (2nd ed.). Charlottesville, VA: Hampton Roads Publishing Company.

Brumfield, M. (2014, June 2). Report #45216 (Class A): Reoccurring activity on a farm outside Fort Stewart. Retrieved December 4, 2015 from http://www.bfro.net

Brunning, A. (2014, November 8). Why corpses stink – the science of smell. Retrieved October 1, 2015 from http://dyingwords.net

Bruns, T. (2010, April 11). Report #27568 (Class A): Daylight sighting of a Bigfoot outside Muscle Shoals. Retrieved December 10, 2015 from http://www.bfro.net

Brunvand, J.H. (2001). *Too Good to Be True: The Colossal Book of Urban Legends*. New York, NY: W.W. Norton & Company.

Bryan, C.B.D. (1995). *Close Encounters of the Fourth Kind*. New York, NY: Penguin Group (Arkana).

Bryant, Jr., V., & Trevor-Deutsch, B. (1980). Analysis of feces and hair suspected to be of Sasquatch origin. In M. Halpin & M.M. Ames (Eds.). *Manlike Monsters on Trial: Early Records and Modern Evidence* (pp. 291-300). Vancouver, CAN: University of British Columbia Press.

Budden, A. (1999). *The UFO Files: Psychic Close Encounters*. London, UK: Cassell & Co.

Bullard, T.E. (1987). *UFO Abductions: The Measure of a Mystery* (Vol. 1). Mount Rainier, MD: Fund for UFO Research.

Bullard, T.E. (1987). *UFO Abductions: The Measure of a Mystery* (Vol. 2). Mount Rainier, MD: Fund for UFO Research.

Burchum, J.R., & Rosenthal, L.D. (2016). *Lehne's Pharmacology for Nursing Care* (9th ed.). St. Louis, MO: Elsevier Saunders.

Buschardt, C. (2012, October 28). Report #36838 (Class A): Man returns home at night to find a tall figure standing by his deer lick outside Farmington. Retrieved December 1, 2015 from http://www.bfro.net

Bystrov, V. (1989, August 5). Case 234. In A. Rosales (Ed.), *1989 Humanoid Sighting Reports*. Retrieved November 5, 2015 from http://www.ufoinfo.com

Cadey, M. (2009). *Paranormal Bath*. Gloucestershire, UK: Amberley Publishing.

Calunga, J.L., Paz, Y., Menéndez S., Martínez A., & Hernández A. (n.d.). Miscellaneous Studies for Ozone. Retrieved January 4, 2016 from http://drsozone.com

Cannon, D. (1999). *The Custodians: Beyond Abduction*. Huntsville, AR: Ozark Mountain Publishers.

Cantrall, T. (2014, April 15). Candid Interview with Bob Gimlin by Thom Cantrall. Retrieved November 17, 2015 from http://bigfootevidence.blogspot.com

Carey, T.J., & Schmitt, D.R. (2007). *Witness to Roswell: Unmasking the 60-Year Cover-Up*. Franklin Lakes, NJ: New Page Books.

Carlson, R. W., Anderson, M. S., Mehlman, R., & Johnson, R. E. (2005). Distribution of hydrate on Europa: Further evidence for sulfuric acid hydrate. *Icarus 177 (2)*: 461.

Carter, C. (2010). *Science and the Near-Death Experience: How Consciousness Survives Death*. Rochester, VT: Inner Traditions.

Carter, L.A. (2014, August 25). Did you see flashes? Yep, an earthquake can create 'em (w/video). Retrieved November 13, 2015 from http://www.pressdemocrat.com

Casteel, S. (2012, January 20). A Conversation with Whitley Strieber. Retrieved November 5, 2015 from http://www.openminds.tv

Castillo, L.N. (n.d.). Case 83. In A. Rosales (Ed.), *1987 Humanoid Sighting Reports*. Retrieved September 15, 2015 from http://www.ufoinfo.com

Catholic Insight. (2008). Our Lady of Laus. Retrieved September 29, 2015 from http://www.thefreelibrary.com

CatholicTradition.org. (n.d.). Our Lady of Laus: Adapted from *Magnificat* Vol. XL, No. 5 and Vol. XXXVI. Retrieved September 29, 2015 from http://www.catholictradition.org

Centers for Disease Control. (n.d.). Occupational Health Guideline for Ammonia. Retrieved November 3, 2015 from http://www.cdc.gov

Centers for Disease Control. (n.d.). Occupational Health Guideline for Ozone. Retrieved October 30, 2015 from http://www.cdc.gov

Chalker, B. (1980, August). Australian "Interrupted Journeys." *MUFON UFO Journal 150*, pp. 3-8.

Chaloupek, H. (n.d.). Case 159. In A. Rosales (Ed.), *1987 Humanoid Sighting Reports*. Retrieved September 15, 2015 from http://www.ufoinfo.com

Chamish, B. (2000). *Return of the Giants*. Israel: Modiin House.

Chapman, C. (2014, November 8). Tek tek, the yeti of Cambodia. Retrieved November 17, 2015 from http://www.phnompenhpost.com

Charles, R.H. (Trans.). (2013). *The Book of Enoch*. London, UK: Society for Promoting Christian Knowledge Classics. (Original work published 1917).

Cheremisinoff, P.N., Morresi, A. C., & Young, R.A. (1975). Human Response and Effects of Odors. In Cheremisinoff, P.N. & Young, R.A. (Eds.), *Industrial Odor Technology Assessment* (pp. 1-25). Ann Arbor, MI: Ann Arbor Science Publishers Inc.

Chiras, D.D. (2015). *Human Biology*. Burlington, MA: Jones & Bartlett Learning.

Chorvinsky, M. (1997, Summer). Encounters with the Grim Reaper. *Strange Magazine 18*, pp. 6-12.

Christiansen, R. (Ed.). (1964). *Folktales of Norway*. (R.M. Dorson, Trans.). Chicago, IL: University of Chicago Press.

Cho, A. (2015, August 17). Stinky hydrogen sulfide smashes superconductivity record. Retrieved January 7, 2015 from http://news.sciencemag.org

CICOANI Brazil. (n.d.). Case 109. In A. Rosales (Ed.), *1972 Humanoid Sighting Reports*. Retrieved December 20, 2015 from http://www.ufoinfo.com

Citizens Against UFO Secrecy. (1986, January). Reported Killing of a UFO Entity. *Flying Saucer Review 31(2),* pp. 25-26.

Citro, J.A. (1996). *Passing Strange: True Tales of New England Hauntings and Horrors*. Boston, MA: Houghton Mifflin Company.

Clark, J. (1967, November). Why UFOs Are Hostile. *Flying Saucer Review 13(6)*, pp. 18-20.

Clark, J. (1997). *The UFO Book: Encyclopedia of the Extraterrestrial*. Canton, MI: Visible Ink Press.

Clark, J. (1998). *The UFO Encyclopedia: The Phenomenon from the Beginning* (Vol. 1: A-K, 2nd ed.). Detroit, MI: Omnigraphics, Inc.

Clark, J. (2000). *Extraordinary Encounters: An Encyclopedia of Extraterrestrials and Otherworldly Beings*. Santa Barbara, CA: ABC-CLIO, Inc.

Clark, J. (2005). *Unnatural Phenomena: A Guide to the Bizarre Wonders of North America*. Santa Barbara, CA: ABC-CLIO, Inc.

Clark, J. (2010). *Hidden Realms, Lost Civilizations, and Beings from Other Worlds*. Canton, MI: Visible Ink Press.

Clark, J. (2013). *Unexplained! Strange Sightings, Incredible Occurrences, and Puzzling Physical Phenomena* (3rd ed.). Canton, MI: Visible Ink Press.

Clean Diesel Fuel Alliance (n.d.). Guidance for Underground Storage Tank Management at ULSD Dispensing Facilities. Retrieved October 20, 2015 from http://www.clean-diesel.org

Clear, C. (1999). *Reaching for Reality: Seven Incredible True Stories of Alien Abduction*. San Antonio, TX: Consciousness Now.

Clore, D. (2015). Flying Saucers Stink: Alien Odors and Supernatural Smells. In D. Clore, *The Unspeakable and Others*. Odense, Denmark: H. Harksen Productions, pp. 293-309.

Cohen, I.B. (1996). *Ben Franklin's Science*. Cambridge, MA: Harvard University Press. (Original work published 1990)

Coleman, C.K. (1999). *Ghosts and Haunts of the Civil War*. Nashville, TN: Thomas Nelson.

Bibliography

Coleman, L. (1971, March). Mystery Animals in Illinois. *Fate Magazine*, pp. 48-54.

Coleman, L., & Clark, J. (1999). *Cryptozoology A to Z: The Encyclopedia of Loch Monsters, Sasquatch, Chupacabras, and Other Authentic Mysteries of Nature.* New York, NY: Fireside.

Coleman, L. (2001). *Mysterious America: The Ultimate Guide to the Nation's Weirdest Wonders, Strangest Spots, and Creepiest Creatures.* New York, NY: Paraview Pocket Books.

Coleman, L. (2002). *Mothman and Other Curious Encounters.* New York, NY: Paraview Press.

Coleman, L. (2003). *Bigfoot! The True Story of Apes in America.* New York, NY: Paraview Pocket Books.

Coleman, L. (2006). The Minnesota Iceman Cometh (and Goeth). In E. Dregni, M. Moran, & M. Scuerman (Eds.), *Weird Minnesota* (pp. 87-88). New York, NY: Sterling Publishing Co., Inc.

Coleman, L. (2006, December 13). Who Coined "Skunk Ape"? Retrieved November 19, 2015 from http://cryptomundo.com

Coleman, L. (2011, May 23). Joplin Bigfoot Report. Retrieved December 15, 2015 from http://cryptomundo.com

Collins, A. (2009). *The New Circlemakers: Insights Into the Crop Circle Mystery.* Virginia Beach, VA: 4th Dimension Press. (Original work published 1992)

Collins, A. (2012). *LightQuest: Your Guide to Seeing and Interacting with UFOs, Mystery Lights and Plasma Intelligences.* Memphis, TN: Eagle Wing Books.

Colombo, J.R. (1992). *UFOs Over Canada: Personal Accounts of Sightings and Close Encounters.* Willowdale, ON: Hounslow Press (Anthony Hawke). (Original work published 1991)

Colp, H. (1997). *The Strangest Story Ever Told.* Petersburg, AK: Pilot Publishing. (Original work published 1953)

Connally, K. (2005). The Baker Hotel. In J. Belanger (Ed.), *Encyclopedia of Haunted Places* (p. 183). Franklin Lakes, NJ: New Page Books.

Conner, W.E., Alley, K.M., Barry, J.R., & Harper, A.E. (2007, December). Has vertebrate chemesthesis been a selective agent in the evolution of anthropod chemical defenses? *The Biology Bulletin 213(3)*, pp. 267-273.

Converse, H.M. (1908). *Myths and Legends of the New York State Iroquois.* A.C. Parker (Ed.). Albany, NY: University of the State of New York.

Conway, G. (2002, January 12). The Guardians. Retrieved October 15, 2015 from http://www.ufobc.com

Cook, K.A. (2010). *Marian Apparitions Are Real: Visits of Jesus and Mary.* US: CreateSpace Independent Publishing Platform.

Cooper, L.A. (2010). *Gothic Realities: The Impact of Horror Fiction on Modern Culture.* Jefferson, NC: McFarland & Company, Inc.

Cornet, S. (2005, May 22). Vanishing Bigfoot and Anecdotal Accounts: Implications and Challenges for Researchers. Retrieved November 30, 2015 from http://www.nabigfootsearch.com

Corrales, S. (1997). *Chupacabras and Other Mysteries.* Murfreesboro, TN: Greenleaf Publications.

Couch, J.N. (2014). *Goatman: Flesh or Folklore?* West Bend, WI: J. Nathan Couch.

Coulombe, C.A. (2004). *Haunted Castles of the World: Ghostly Legends and Phenomena from Keeps and Fortresses Around the Globe.* Guilford, CT: The Lyons Press.

Courtney, S. (2004, November 12). Report #9750 (Class A): Motorist observes bipedal animal shaking a pecan tree near Camp LeJeune. Retrieved November 27, 2015 from http://www.bfro.net

Courtney, S. (2004, November 21). Report #9818 (Class A): Hiker has nighttime sighting at Minnehaha Falls. Retrieved December 3, 2015 from http://www.bfro.net

Courtney, S. (2005, June 17). Report #11911 (Class A): Campers have lengthy nightime encounter near Seneca. Retrieved November 20, 2015 from http://www.bfro.net

Courtney, S. (2012, December 17). Report #38337 (Class B): Possible nighttime sighting from a home by a young woman near Lake Lou Yaeger. Retrieved November 17, 2015 from http://www.bfro.net

Cowley, S., & Cox, G. (2012). *Searching for Bigfoot.* New York, NY: The Rosen Company.

Craddock, G. (2014, June 29). Report #45665 (Class A): Memory told of a late night close encounter from a parked vehicle outside Gatlinburg. Retrieved December 3, 2015 from http://www.bfro.net

Cranmer, B., & Manfred, E. (2014). *The Demon of Brownsville Road: A Pittsburgh Family's Battle with Evil in Their Home.* New York, NY: The Berkley Publishing Group.

Cryptozoology News. (2014, April 17). The Science Behind Bigfoot Odor. Retrieved November 30, 2015 from http://cryptozoologynews.com

Cunliffe, H. (1886). *A Glossary of Rochdale-with-Rossendale Words and Phrases.* London, UK: John Heywood.

Cunningham, S. (1989). *The Complete Book of Incense, Oils & Brews*. St. Paul. MN: Llewellyn Publications.

Curley, M.J. (Trans.). (2009). *Physiologus: A Medieval Book of Nature Lore*. Chicago, IL: University of Chicago Press. (Original work published 1979)

Curtis, C. (2004, April 2). Report #8435 (Class B): Incidents around a cabin near Greenburg. Retrieved November 27, 2015 from http://www.bfro.net

Cusik, D. (1828). *David Cusik's Sketches of Ancient History of the Six Nations (1828)*. P. Royster (Ed.). Lincoln, NE: Faculty Publications, UNL Libraries.

Cutchin, J. (2015). *A Trojan Feast*. San Antonio, TX: Anomalist Books.

Daily Galaxy. (2011, May 18). Stephen Hawking on Non-Carbon-Based Alien Life. Retrieved November 13, 2015.

Dains, D.K. (1974, December). Object in water checked in Pennsylvania. *MUFON UFO Journal 85*, p. 12.

Davis, J. (2005). Old New Castle. In J. Belanger (Ed.), *Encyclopedia of Haunted Places* (p. 52). Franklin Lakes, NJ: New Page Books.

Davis, T. (1998). *Why Dogs Do That*. Minocqua, WI: Willow Creek Press.

Davis, J.R., Johnson, R., Stepanek, J, & Fogarty, J.A. (Eds.) (2008). *Fundamentals of Aerospace Medicine* (4th ed.). Philadelphia, PA: Lippincott Williams & Wilkins. (Original work published 2002)

Debus, A.G. (2002). *The Chemical Philosophy: Paracelsian Science and Medicine in the Sixteenth and Seventeenth Centuries* (Vol. 1). Mineola, NY: Dover Publications (Original work published 1977).

Debus, A.G. (2002). *The Chemical Philosophy: Paracelsian Science and Medicine in the Sixteenth and Seventeenth Centuries* (Vol. 2). Mineola, NY: Dover Publications (Original work published 1977).

Degaudenzi, J.L. (1981). *Les OVNI en Union Soviétique*. Nice, FR: Alain Lefeuvre.

Dement, W.C. (2015). The Smell of Death During Sleep Paralysis. Retrieved December 29, 2015 from http://www.end-your-sleep-deprivation.com

Dennett, P.E. (2008). *Mysteries, Legends, and Unexplained Phenomena: UFOs and Aliens*. R.E. Guiley (Ed.). New York, NY: Chelsea House Publishers.

Detienne, M. (1977). *The Gardens of Adonis: Spices in Greek Mythology*. (J. Lloyd, Trans.). Atlantic Highlands, NJ: The Humanities Press. (Original work published 1977 as *Les Jardins d'Adonis*)

Deus Ex McKenna [Screen name] (2011, July 10). *Hermeticism & Alchemy (Terence McKenna)* [Video file]. Retrieved January 5, 2016 from https://www.youtube.com

Deveraux, P. (2003). *Haunted Land: Investigations into Ancient Mysteries and Modern Day Phenomena*. London, UK: Piatkus Books.

Devos, M., Patte, F., Rouault, J., Lafort, P., & Van Gemert, L.J. (Eds.). (1990). *Standardized Human Olfactory Thresholds*. Oxford, UK: IRL Press.

Dilks, D.D., Dalton, P., & Beauchamp, G.K. (1999) Cross-cultural variation in responses to malodors. *Chemical Senses 24*, 599.

Dosen, C. (2002, October 27). Report #5172 (Class A): Multi-witness road-crossing sighting outside Fort St. John. Retrieved December 10, 2015 from http://www.bfro.net

Dr. Beachcombing. (2013, October 10). Paranormal smells. Retrieved September 30, 2015 from http://www.strangehistory.net

Drake, R. (1977, July). Air Force Besieged by Saucers. *UFO Report*, p. 37.

Driscoll, R. (2011, September 5). Report #30573 (Class A): Bowhunter recalls dusk encounter on creek dike near Oak Grove. Retrieved November 20, 2015 from http://www.bfro.net

Druffel, A., & Sider, J. (2000, July). Onomastic research. *MUFON UFO Journal 387*, pp. 3-10.

Dugbartey, G.J. (2015, July). The role of endogenous H2S production during hibernation and forced hypothermia: towards safe cooling and rewarming in clinical practice (Doctoral dissertation). Groningen, Netherlands: The University of Groningen.

Duke Medicine News and Communications. (2012, February 6). Copper + Love Chemical = Big Sulfur Stink. Retrieved September 25, 2015 from http://corporate.dukemedicine.org

Durant, R.J. (1998, February). The Roswell debris testimony of Dr. Jesse Marcel, Jr. – Part 2: The I beam. *MUFON UFO Journal 358*, pp. 15-18.

Durant, R.J. (1998, July). Buzzes and smells in Strieber's *Majestic*. *MUFON Journal 363*, pp. 7-9.

Eberhart, G.M. (2002). *Mysterious Creatures: A Guide to Cryptozoology*. Santa Barbara, CA: ABC-CLIO, Inc.

Edwards, A. (1988). *On the (UFO) Road Again: Case Histories of Close Encounters of the Third Kind*. Seattle, WA: UFO Contact Center International.

Eldredge, D.M., Carlson, L.D., Carlson, D.G., & Giffin, J.M. (2007). *Dog Owner's Home Veterinary Handbook* (4th ed.). B. Adelman (Ed.). Hoboken, NJ: Howell Book House (Wiley Publishing, Inc.).

Ellis, M.M. (2014). *The Everything Ghost Hunting Book: Tips, Tools, and Techniques for Exploring the Supernatural World* (2nd ed.). Avon, MA: Adams Media.

Ellison, Q. (2011, August 31). That awful smell, yeah, that's me. Seriously. Retrieved December 21, 2015 from http://www.smokymountainnews.com

Ellwood, R.S. (1993). *Islands of the Dawn: The Story of Alternative Spirituality in New Zealand*. Honolulu, HI: University of Hawaii Press.

Emmer, R. (2010). *Creature Scene Investigator: Bigfoot – Fact or Fiction?* New York, NY: Chelsea House Publishers.

Encarnacao, J. (2013, May 9). *The Patriot Ledger*: 'Unbearable' smell in Quincy a mystery. Retrieved October 21, 2015 from http://www.patriotledger.com

Engen, T. (1982). *The Perception of Odors*. London, UK: Academic Press.

Engen, T. (1991). *Odor Sensation and Memory*. New York, NY: Praeger Publishers.

Epoch Times. (2005, August 7). Dragons in the Sky. Retrieved December 15, 2015 from http://www.theepochtimes.com

Epperson, I., & Kahlert, C. (1973, December). California Man Has Good View of UFO—And Occupant! *Skylook Magazine 73*, pp. 4-5.

Estes, R.D. (1999). *The Safari Companion: A Guide to Watching African Mammals Including Hoofed Mammals, Carnivores, and Primates*. White River Junction, VT: Chelsea Green Publishing Company. (Original work published 1993)

Fahrenbach, W.H. (1997). Sasquatch Smell / Aroma / Odor / Scent. Retrieved November 30, 2015 from http://www.bigfootencounters.com

Fahrenbach, W.H. (2008, September 29). Report #24826 (Class A): Couple meets Sasquatch and finds nest in cave. Retrieved December 10, 2015 from http://www.bfro.net

Faust, J.G. (1993). *The Black Raven*. (K.H. Welz, Trans.). Decatur, GA: Knights of Runes. (Original date unknown, alleged 1500s, published as *D.I.Fausti Schwartzer Rabe*)

Feindt, C. W. (2010). *UFOs and Water: Physical Effects of UFOs on Water Through Accounts by Eyewitnesses*. Bloomington, IN: Xlibris Corporation.

Feng, X., Zhou, Y.L., Meng, X., Qi, F.H., Chen, W., Jiang, X., & Xu, G.Y. (2013, February). Hydrogen sulfide increase excitability through suppression of sustained potassium channel currents of rat trigeminal ganglion neurons. *Molecular Pain 9(4)*.

Ferguson, J. (1977). *Les humanoides*. Montreal, CAN: Lémeac.

Feschino, Jr., F. (2013). *The Braxton County Monster – Updated & Revised Edition: The Cover-Up of the "Flatwoods Monster" Revealed*. USA: Lulu Enterprises.

Fields, H. (2012, April 12). Fragrant Flashbacks: Smells rouse early memories. Retrieved September 15, 2015 from http://www.psychologicalscience.org

Filer, G. (1999, November 4). Filer's Files #44-1999. Retrieved October 30, 2015 from http://www.ufoinfo.com

Filer, G.A. (2004, January). Filer's Files. *MUFON UFO Journal 429*, pp. 14-16.

Finch, L.I. (Ed.). (1908, December). Haunted House near London. *The Annals of Psychical Science VII (41)*, pp. 258-260.

Fisher, D. (2013, July 11). The Scent Of A Sasquatch: What's That Smell All About? Retrived November 30, 2015 from http://www.thecryptocrew.com

Flanders, F.B. (2012). *Exploring Animal Science*. Clifton Park, NJ: Delmar.

Fluet, M.R. (2009). *Our Brothers in the Skies: The Hidden Truth Revealed*. Bloomington, IN: AuthorHouse.

Fowler, R. & NICAP (n.d.). Case 81. In A. Rosales (Ed.), *1967 Humanoid Sighting Reports*. Retrieved October 21, 2015 from http://www.ufoinfo.com

Fowler, R.E. (1993, April). The Allagash Abductions. *MUFON UFO Journal 300*, pp. 3-6.

Fox, R.L. (2008). *Travelling Heroes: Greeks and their Myths in the Epic Age of Homer*. London, UK: Penguin Books Ltd.

Franklin, B. (1882). *The Works of Benjamin Franklin* (Vol. V). J. Sparks (Ed.). London, UK: Benjamin Franklin Stevens.

Frederickson, S.V. (1972, March). The Ängelholm Landing Report. *Flying Saucer Review 18(2)*, pp. 15-17.

Freeman, B. (2005). The Gravesite of James Dean. In J. Belanger (Ed.), *Encyclopedia of Haunted Places* (pp. 116-117). Franklin Lakes, NJ: New Page Books.

Freixedo, S. (1984). *¡Defendámonos de los Dioses!* Madrid, Spain: Editorial Posada, S.A.

Freud, S. *Civilization and Its Discontents*. (2005). New York, NY: W.W. Norton & Company, Inc. (Original work published 1930 as *Das Unbehagen in der Kultur*)

Friedman, S.T., & Marden, K. (2007). *Captured! The Betty and Barney Hill UFO Experience*. Franklin Lakes, NJ: New Page Books.

Fusch, E. (1992). S'cwene'y'ti and the Stick Indians of the Colvilles: The Interaction of Large Bipedal Hominids with American Indians. Retrieved November 17, 2015 from http://www.bigfootencounters.com

Gamlin, L., & Price, B. (1988, November 5). Bonfires and Brimstone. *New Scientist 1637*, pp. 48-51.

Gardenour Walter, B.S. (2015). *Our Old Monsters Witches, Werewolves, and Vampires from Medieval Theology to Horror Cinema.* Jefferson, NC: McFarland & Company, Inc.

Gater, P. (2003). *Living with Ghosts: An Investigation.* Staffordshire, UK: Anecdotes.

Gerard, T. (2001, August 17). Report #3008 (Class A): Gold dredgers have afternoon encounter in Cherokee National Forest. Retrieved November 19, 2015 from http://www.bfro.net

Gerhard, K. (2013). *Encounters with Flying Humanoids.* Woodbury, MN: Llewellyn Publications.

Gerhold, H.D. (2007). *A Century of Forest Resources Education at Penn State: Serving Our Forests, Waters, Wildlife, and Wood Industries.* University Park, PA: Pennsylvania State University Press.

Germer, W. (2015, March 29). *Sasquatch Chronicles Episode 90: Interview with Bob Gimlin* [Audio podcast]. Retrieved November 17, 2015 from https://www.sasquatch-chronicles.com

Germer, W. (2015, July 7). *Sasquatch Chronicles Episode 122: Sasquatch at my window Part two.* [Audio podcast]. Retrieved November 17, 2015 from https://www.sasquatchchronicles.com

Germer, W. (2015, August 2). *Sasquatch Chronicles Episode 132: A gold miners encounter* [Audio podcast]. Retrieved November 17, 2015 from https://www.sasquatch-chronicles.com

Germer, W. (2015, November 15). *Sasquatch Chronicles Episode 165: Calling 911* [Audio podcast]. Retrieved December 22, 2015 from https://www.sasquatchchronicles.com

Germer, W. (2015, November 22). *Sasquatch Chronicles Episode 167: That is when the rock throwing started.* [Audio podcast]. Retrieved November 24, 2015 from https://www.sasquatchchronicles.com

Germer, W. (2016, April 17). *Sasquatch Chronicles Episode 211: Running right into a creature... literally.* [Audio podcast]. Retrieved April 20, 2016 from https://www.sasquatchchronicles.com

Gholipour, B. (2015, April 22). Up to 90% of Your Perception Could Be Made Up Purely By the Brain. Retrieved December 30, 2015 from https://www.braindecoder.com

Gilbert, A. (2009, March 15). Proust with an Anal Probe: The Smells of An Alien Abduction. Retrieved November 5, 2015 from http://www.firstnerve.com

Gilbert, A. (2009, April 30). The Biochemistry of BO. Retrieved December 3, 2015 from http://www.firstnerve.com

Gilette, M.L., & Gloffke, W. (2006). *General, Organic, and Biochemistry: Connecting Chemistry to Your Life.* New York, NY: W.H. Freeman and Company.

Gill, G.W. (1980). Population Clines of the North American Sasquatch as Evidenced by Track Lengths and Estimated Statures. In M. Halpin & M.M. Ames (Eds.). *Manlike Monsters on Trial: Early Records and Modern Evidence* (pp. 265-273). Vancouver, CAN: University of British Columbia Press.

Giriraj Pain Management Clinic. (n.d.). Trigeminal neuralgia. Retrieved January 4, 2016 from http://www.paingujarat.com

Girvin, C.C. (1958). *The Night Has a Thousand Saucers.* El Monte, CA: Understanding Publishing.

Glanvil, J. (1689). *Sadiucismus Triumphatus: Full and Plain Evidence Concerning Witches and Apparitions.* London, UK: James Collins. (Original work published 1661)

Glassé, C. (2008). *The New Encyclopedia of Islam* (3rd ed.). Lanham, MD: Rowman & Littlefield Publishers, Inc.

Godfrey, L.S. (2003). *The Beast of Bray Road.* Madison, WI: Prairie Oak Press.

Godfrey, L.S. (2012). *Real Wolfmen: True Encounters in Modern America.* London, UK: Penguin Books Ltd.

Godfrey, L.S. (2014). *American Monsters: A History of Monster Lore, Legends, and Sightings in America.* New York, NY: The Penguin Group.

Goldstein, E.B. (2010). *Encyclopedia of Perception* (Vol. 1). Thousand Oaks, CA: SAGE Publications.

Good, T. (2007). *Need to Know: UFOs, the Military, and Intelligence.* New York, NY: Pegasus Books LLC.

Gordon, S. (1989, May). Pennsylvania Law Officer Reports CE2 Incident. *MUFON UFO Journal 253*, pp. 10-12, 23.

Gordon, S. (1999, January). Gordon reports on case that caused him to reconsider Bigfoot. *MUFON UFO Journal 369*, pp. 13-14.

Gordon, S. (2010). *Silent Invasion: The Pennsylvania UFO-Bigfoot Casebook.* R. Marsh (Ed.). Greensburg, PA: Stan Gordon Productions.

Gordon, S. (2015). *Astonishing Encounters: Pennsylvania's Unknown Creatures – Casebook Three.* Greensburg, PA: Stan Gordon Productions

Graber, G. (1976, February). Two occupants in craft. *MUFON Skylook: The UFO*

Monthly 99, pp. 3-4.

Granchi, I. (1995). *UFOs and Abductions in Brazil*. Madison, WI: Horus House Press, Inc. (Original work published 1992)

Greer, J.M. (2004). *Monsters: An Investigator's Guide to Magical Beings*. St. Paul, MN: Llewellyn Publications.

Greyling, S. (1968, Fall). The Modoc Man and Sasquatch, The Tulelake Story. *Many Smokes National American Indian Magazine*.

Gribble, B. (1987, November). Looking Back. *MUFON UFO Journal 235*, pp. 20-21.

Gribble, B. (1988, December). Looking Back. *MUFON UFO Journal 248*, pp. 14-16.

Gribble, B. (1989, June). Looking Back. *MUFON UFO Journal 254*, pp. 20-21, 23.

Gribble, B. (1989, July). Looking Back. *MUFON UFO Journal 255*, pp. 19-21.

Gribble, B. (1989, September). Looking Back. *MUFON UFO Journal 257*, pp. 13-15.

Gribble, B. (1989, November). Looking Back. *MUFON UFO Journal 259*, pp. 22-24.

Gribble, B. (1992, April). Looking Back. *MUFON UFO Journal 288*, pp. 17-19.

Green, J. (1995). On the Scent of the Sasquatch. Retrieved November 16, 2015 from http://www.sasquatchdatabase.com

Greenberg, A. (2007). *From Alchemy to Chemistry in Picture and Story*. Hoboken, NJ: John Wiley & Sons, Inc.

Greenburg, M.I., Hamilton, R.J., Phillips, S.D., and McCluskey, G.J. (Eds.). (2003). *Occupational, Industrial, and Environmental Toxicology* (2nd ed.). Philadelphia, PA: Mosby. (Original work published 1997)

Gross, P. (2014, October 2). The 1954 French Flap: October 2, 1954, Clermont-Ferrand, Puy-de-Dome. Retrieved November 5, 2015 from http://ufologie.patrickgross.org

Guiley, R.E. (2007). *The Encyclopedia of Ghosts and Spirits* (3rd ed.). New York, NY: Facts On File, Inc. (Original work published 1992)

Guiley, R. (2008). *The Encyclopedia of Witches, Witchcraft & Wicca* (3rd ed.). New York, NY: Facts on File, Inc. (Original work published 1989).

Guiley, R.E. (2009). *The Encyclopedia of Demons and Demonology*. New York, NY: Facts On File, Inc.

Guiley, R.E. (2012). *Monsters of West Virginia: Mysterious Creatures in the Mountain State*. Mechanicsburg, PA: Stackpole Books.

Guiley, R.E. (2014). *The Big Book of West Virginia Ghost Stories*. Mechanicsburg, PA: Stackpole Books.

Guttilla, P. (2003). *The Bigfoot Files*. Santa Barbara, CA: Timeless Voyager Press.

Habib, Y. (1975). Odor emission sources in the chemical and petroleum industries. In Cheremisinoff, P.N. & Young, R.A. (Eds.), *Industrial Odor Technology Assessment* (pp. 189-201). Ann Arbor, MI: Ann Arbor Science Publishers Inc.

Hagerty, B.B. (2009). *Fingerprints of God: The Search for the Science of Spirituality.* New York, NY: Riverhead Books.

Hairr, J. (2013). *Monsters of North Carolina: Mysterious Creatures in the Tar Heel State*. Mechanicsburg, PA: Stackpole Books.

Hall, M.A., & Coleman, L. (2010). *True Giants: Is* Gigantopithecus *Still Alive?* San Antonio, TX: Anomalist Books.

Hall, A.H., & Rumack, B.H. (1997, June). Hydrogen sulfide poisoning: an antidotal role for sodium nitrite? *Veterinary and Human Toxicology 39(3),* pp. 152-154.

Hall, R. (1975, October). Southern Africa reports several UFO sightings. *MUFON UFO Journal 95*, pp. 14-15.

Hall, R. (1976, April). Recapping and commenting. *MUFON UFO Journal 101*, p. 20.

Hall, R. (1980, November). Italian UFO wave of 1978. *MUFON UFO Journal 153*, pp. 12-15.

Hall, R. (1988). *Uninvited Guests: A Documented History of UFO Sighting, Alien Encounters, & Coverups.* Santa Fe, NM: Aurora Press.

Hall, R.H. (2001). *The UFO Evidence: A Thirty-Year Report* (Vol. 2). Lanham, MD: Scarecrow Press.

Hall, W.J. (2014). *The World's Most Haunted House: The True Story of the Bridgeport Poltergeist on Lindley Street*. Pompton Plains, NJ: New Page Books.

Hallenbeck, B.G. (2013). *Monsters of New York: Mysterious Creatures in the Empire State*. Mechanicsburg, PA: Stackpole Books.

Hamilton, S. (2008). *Monsters of Mystery*. Edina, MN: ABDO Publishing Company.

Hamilton, W.F. (1993, August). Area 51 Encounter. *MUFON UFO Journal 304*, pp. 14-17.

Hammonds, M. (2013, May 16). Does Alien Life Thrive in Venus' Mysterious Clouds? Retrieved November 13, 2015 from http://news.discovery.com

Han, B. (2014). *The Ghost Files*. Bloomington, IN: Booktango.

Hanks, M. (2014, February 19). Space Blobs: A Look at Jelly from the Stars. Retrieved May 2, 2016 from http://mysteriousuniverse.org

Hanson, J., & Holloway, D. (2011). *Haunted Skies: The Encyclopaedia of British UFOs: 1960-1965* (Vol. 2). Woolsery, UK: Fortean Words.

Hardtke, T. (2015). Deaths resulting from exorcism. In J.P. Laycock (Ed.), *Spirit Possession Around the World: Possession, Communion, and Demon Expulsion Across Cultures* (pp. 99-104). Santa Barbara, CA: ABC-CLIO, LLC.

Hargittai, I. (2011). *Drive and Curiosity: What Fuels the Passion for Science*. Amherst, NY: Prometheus Books.

Harpur, P. (2003). *Daimonic Reality: A Field Guide to the Otherworld*. Enumclaw, WA: Pine Winds Press. (Original work published 1994).

Hartland, E.S. (2000). *English Fairy and Folk Tales.* Mineola, NY: Dover Publications, Inc. (Original work published 1890)

Harvey, G., & Wallis, R.J. (2007). *Historical Dictionary of Shamanism*. Lanham, MD: The Scarecrow Press, Inc.

Hathaway, B.A. (2006). *Organic Chemistry the Easy Way.* Hauppauge, NY: Barron's Educational Series, Inc.

Haughton, B. (2012). *Famous Ghost Stories: Legends and Lore.* New York, NY: The Rosen Publishing Group, Inc.

Hauck, D.W. (2000). *The International Directory of Haunted Places*. New York, NY: Penguin Books.

Hauck, D.W. (2008). *The Complete Idiot's Guide to Alchemy*. New York, NY: Alpha (Penguin Group).

Hawkins, J. (2012). *Bigfoot and Other Monsters*. New York, NY: Rosen Publishing Group, Inc.

Hazelgrove, J. (2000). *Spiritualism and British Society Between the Wars*. Manchester, UK: Manchester University Press.

Healy, T. (2001, October 20). "High Strangeness" in Yowie Reports. In P. Cropper (Ed.). *Myths & Monsters 2001 Conference Papers*. Paper presented at Myths & Monsters 2001, Sydney, Australia (pp. 64-72).

Heasmer, C. (2015, February 3). I'm stalked by a ghost which smells of FISH when something bad is about to happen. Retrieved October 13, 2015 from http://www.mirror.co.uk

Helmholtz Centre for Environmental Research. (2006, October 20). Money does not smell—until it is touched. Retrieved January 13, 2016 from https://www.ufz.de

Hemminki, K., & Niemi, M.L. (1982). Community study of spontaneous abortions: relation to occupation and air pollution by sulfur dioxide, hydrogen sulfide, and carbon disulfide. *International Archives of Occupational and Environmental Health 51(1)*, pp. 55-63.

Herriot, J. (1976). *All Things Wise and Wonderful*. New York, NY: St. Martin's Paperbacks.

Herz, R.S. (2001, October 1). Ah, Sweet Skunk! Why We Like or Dislike What We Smell. Retrieved January 4, 2016 from http://www.dana.org/

Herz, R. (2011, January 6). Smell Manipulation: The subliminal power of scent. Retrieved September 15, 2015 from https://www.psychologytoday.com

Hesemann, M. (2000). *The Fatima Secret*. W. Strieber (Ed.). New York, NY: Dell Publishing.

Heuvelmans, B. (2016). *Neanderthal: The Strange Saga of the Minnesota Iceman*. (P. LeBlond, Trans.). San Antonio, TX: Anomalist Books.

Hiatt, L. (1975). *Australian Aboriginal Mythology: Essays in Honour of W.E.H. Stanner*. Canberra, AU: Australian Institute of Aboriginal Studies.

Hillix, W.A., & Rumbaugh, D. (2004). *Animal Bodies, Human Minds: Ape, Dolphin, and Parrot Language Skills*. New York, NY: Springer Science+Business Media.

Hillman, J. (1991). The Yellowing of the Work. In M.A. Mattoon (Ed.), *Personal and Archetypal Dynamics in the Analytical Relationship: Proceedings of the Eleventh International Congress for Analytical Psychology, Paris, 1989* (pp. 77-96). Einsiedeln, Switzerland: Daimon Verlag.

Hind, C.R. (1977, April). Orange UFO Over Rhodesia. *MUFON UFO Journal 113*, p. 18.

Hirsch, A.R. (2004). *What Your Doctor May Not Tell You About Sinusitis*. New York, NY: Warner Books.

Ho, O. (2008). *Mutants and Monsters*. New York, NY: Sterling Publishing Co., Inc.

Holleman, A.F., & Wiberg, E. (2001). *Inorganic Chemistry*. (M. Eagleson & W. Brewer, Trans.). B.J. Aylett (Ed.). San Diego, CA: Academic Press.

Holzer, H. (2004). *Ghosts: True Encounters from the World Beyond*. New York, NY: Black Dog & Leventhal.

Hood, R.E. (1994). *Begrimed and Black: Christian Traditions on Blacks and Blackness*. Minneapolis, MN: Augsburg Fortress.

Hopkins, B. (1981). *Missing Time*. New York, NY: Richard Marek Publishers.

Hopkins, B., & Rainey, C. (2003). *Sight Unseen: Science UFO Invisibility and Transgenic Beings*. New York, NY: Atria Books.

Hornung, D.E., Kurtz, D., & Youngentob, S.L. (1994) Anosmic Patients Can Separate Trigeminal and Nontrigeminal Stimulants. In K. Kurihara, N. Suzuki, & H. Ogawa (Eds.), *Olfaction and Taste XI: Proceedings of the 11th International Symposium on Olfaction and Taste and of the 27th Japanese Symposium on Taste and Smell* (p. 635). Tokyo, Japan: Springer.

Horváth, M. Bilitzky, L., & Hüttner, J. (1985). *Ozone*. New York, NY: Elsevier Science Publishing Co., Inc.

Howard, R.A. (2006). Realities and Perceptions in the Evolution of Black Powder Making. In B.J. Buchanan (Ed.), *Gunpowder, Explosives, and the State: A Technological History* (pp. 21-41). Bodmin, UK: MPG Books Ltd.

Hubbell, W. (1916). *The Great Amherst Mystery: A True Narrative of the Supernatural* (10th ed.). New York: Brentano's. (Original work published 1888)

Hucklebridge, R. (2002, November 10). Report #5284 (Class A): Hunter/Logger has a sighting in a closed logging area near Hilt. Retrieved November 19, 2015 from http://www.bfro.net

Hucklebridge, R. (2004, March 23). Report #8345 (Class A): Truck driver has a short but memorable encounter. Retrieved September 16, 2015 from http://www.bfro.net

Hucklebridge, R. (2008, September 1). Report #24648 (Class A): Man retells his close, visual encounter at dawn on Pine Mountain as a young deer hunter. Retrieved December 10, 2015 from http://www.bfro.net

Huggins, T. (October 13, 2009). Report #26746 (Class B): Hunter recalls strange incidents while camping near Valleyview. Retrieved November 17, 2015 from http://www.bfro.net

Hudnall, K. (2006). *Spirits of the Border: The History and Mystery of Tombstone*. Nashville, TN: Grave Distractions Publications.

Hudson, C. (2011). *Strange State: Mysteries and Legends of Oklahoma* (3rd ed.). US: CreateSpace Independent Publishing Platform.

Hullinger, J. (2014, September). What Does Space Smell Like? *Mental Floss 13(6)*, p. 40.

Huneeus, J.A. (1987, June 26-28). Historical Survey of UFO Cases in Chile. In W.H. Andrus & R. Hall (Eds.), *MUFON 1987 International UFO Symposium Proceedings*. Seguin, TX: MUTUAL UFO Network, pp. 181-219.

Hunt, A. (2013). *Dictionary of Chemistry*. New York, NY: Routledge. (Original work published 1998)

Husak, R. (2005). The Emmitt House. In J. Belanger (Ed.), *Encyclopedia of Haunted Places* (pp. 124-125). Franklin Lakes, NJ: New Page Books.

Hynek, J.A. (1966, December 17). Are Flying Saucers Real? *The Saturday Evening Post*, pp. 17-21.

Ikeya, M. (2004). *Earthquakes and Animals: From Folk Legends to Science*. Singapore: World Scientific Publishing Co. Pte. Ltd.

Illig, D. (2008, February 1). Report #23062 (Class B): Angler finds tracks, hears knocks and senses ominous presence east of North Bend. Retrieved November 17, 2015 from http://www.bfro.net

Inglis-Arkell, E. (2015, July 15). Why is a Compound That Smells Like Feces Put in Perfume And Chocolate? Retrieved October 19, 2015, from http://io9.com

Inman, M. (2010, October 10). Plane Exhaust Kills More People Than Plane Crashes. Retrieved November 13, 2015 from http://news.nationalgeographic.com

International Volcanic Health Hazard Network. (2015). Hydrogen Sulfide (H_2S). Retrieved October 23, 2015 from http://www.ivhhn.org

Iowa State University Extension. (2004, May). The Science of Smell Part 1: Odor perception and physiological response. Retrieved October 23, 2015 from https://store.extension.iastate.edu

Iskander, A. (365). *Nicene and Post-Nicene Fathers of the Christian Church, Volume IV: St. Athanasius Select Works and Letters – Life of St. Antony* (P. Schaff & H. Wace, Eds.). OrthodoxEBooks.org.

Ivanits, L.J. (1989). *Russian Folk Belief.* Armonk, NY: M.E. Sharpe.

Jastrow, Jr., M., McCurdy, J.F., Kohler, K., & Ginzberg, L. (1906). Burnt offering. In *Jewish Encyclopedia*. Retrieved September 21, 2015 from http://www.jewishencyclopedia.com

Johnson, J.C. (2010, August 31). The Harvest [Video file]. Retrieved November 30, 2015 from https://www.youtube.com

Johnson, M.T. (2014). *Seeing Fairies: From the Lost Archives of the Fairy Investigation Society, Authentic Reports of Fairies in Modern Times*. San Antonio, TX: Anomalist Books.

Johnson, P. G., & Jeffers, J.L. (1986) *The Pennsylvania Bigfoot*. Pittsburgh, PA: Johnson & Jeffers.

Jones, J. (1976, January). Possible E-M Case in Florida. *The APRO Bulletin 24(7)*, p. 2, 5.

Jung, C.G. (1977). *The Collected Works of Carl Jung: Mysterium* Coniunctionis (Vol.

14). (R.F.C. Hull, Trans.). H. Read, M. Fordham, G. Adler, W. McGuire (Eds.). Princeton, N.J.: Princeton University Press. (Original work published 1963)

Jung, C.G. (1989). *Memories, Dreams, Reflections*. (R. Winston & C. Winston, Trans.). A. Jaffé (Ed.). New York, NY: Random House. (Original work published 1961 as *Erinnerungen Träume Gedanken*)

Jung, C.G. (1991). *Flying Saucers: A Modern Myth of Things Seen in the Skies*. (R.F.C. Hull, Trans.). Princeton, NJ: Princeton University Press. (Original work published 1978)

Jung, C.G. (1997). *Jung on Synchronicity and the Paranormal*. R. Main (Ed.). London, UK: Rutledge.

Kass, M.D., Rosenthal, M.C., Pottackal, J., & McGann, J.P. (2013) Fear learning enhances neural responses to threat-predictive stimuli. *Science* 342: 1389-1392.

Keel, J.A. (1970). *UFOs: Operation Trojan Horse*. New York, NY: G.P. Putnam's Sons.

Keel, J. A. (1976). *The Eighth Tower: On Ultraterrestrials and the Superspectrum*. New York, NY: E.P. Dutton & Co. Inc.

Keel, J.A. (2002). *The Complete Guide to Mysterious Beings*. New York, NY: Tom Doherty Associates, LLC. (Original work published 1970 as *Strange Creatures from Time and Space*)

Keel, J. (2002). *The Mothman Prophecies*. New York, NY: Tom Doherty Associates, LLC. (Original work published 1975)

Keel, J.A. (2015). Savage Little Men From Outer Space – *Saga* Magazine – March 1969. In A. B. Colvin (Ed.), *The Book of Mothman: Everything You Wanted to Know About Reality Distortion But Were Afraid to Ask* (Kindle Location 1745-1971). Point Pleasant, WV: New Saucerian Books [Kindle Edition].

Kelleher, C.A. & Knapp, G. (2005). *Hunt for the Skinwalker: Science Confronts the Unexplained at a Remote Ranch*. New York, NY: Pocket Books.

Kelley, M. (2004). *Minor Histories: Statements, Conversations, Proposals*. J.C. Welchman (Ed.). Cambridge, MA: The Massachusetts Institute of Technology Press.

Kennedy, R.C. (2005). *Coffin Nails: The Tobacco Controversy in the 19th Century – Cigarettes: Women*. Retrieved October 13, 2015 from http://tobacco.harpweek.com

Keritsis, G.D., Bokelman, G.H., & Gooden, III, D.T. (1982, December 7). Tobacco curing method - US 4362170 A. Retrieved October 19, 2015 from www.google.com/patents

Keyhoe, D.E., & Lore, Jr., G.I.R. (Eds.). (1969). *UFOs: A New Look*. Washinton, D.C.: The National Investigations Committee on Aerial Phenomena.

Kimball, T.L. (2008, June 19). Report #24033 (Class B): Woman describes foul odor and possible vocalizations near home outside Charlevoix. Retrieved November 27, 2015 from http://www.bfro.net

Kimura, H. (2002, August 26). Hydrogen sulfide as a neuromodulator. *Molecular Neurobiology 26*, 13-19.

Klailova, M, & Lee, P.C. (2014). Wild Western Lowland Gorillas Signal Selectively Using Odor. *PLOS ONE 9*(7): e99554. DOI: 10.1371/journal.pone.0099554.

Kleen, M. (2010). *Haunting the Prairie: A Tourist's Guide to the Weird and Wild Places of Illinois*. Rockford, IL: Black Oak Press.

Klenø, J., & Wolkoff, P. (2004). Changes in eye blink frequency as a measure of trigeminal stimulation by exposure to limonene oxidation products, isoprene oxidation products and nitrate radicals. *International Archives of Occupational and Environmental Health 77*, pp. 235-243.

Knappert, J. (1995). *African Mythology: An Encyclopedia of Myth and Legend*. London, UK: Diamond Books.

Knol, A. S. (1985, December 7). Reliving the tale of the Big Muddy Monster. *Southern Illinoisan*, retrieved from http://www.bfro.net

Koch, K.E. (1986). *Occult ABC: Exposing Occult Practices and Ideologies*. Grand Rapids, MI: Kregel Publications (Original work published 1978 as *Satan's Devices*)

Krebs, R.E. (2006). *The History and Use of Our Earth's Chemical Elements: A Reference Guide*. Westport, CT: Greenwood Press.

Kroeber, A.L. (1976). *Handbook of the Indians of California*. New York, NY: Dover Publications, Inc.

Kroonenberg, S. (2013). *Why Hell Stinks of Sulfur: Mythology and Geology of the Underworld*. (A. Brown, Trans.). London, UK: Reaktion Books Ltd. (Original work published 2011 as *Waarom de hel naar zwavel stinkt*)

Kruszelnicki, K.S. (2007, June 27). Ozone Smell at the Seaside. Retrieved October 26, 2015 from http://www.abc.net.au

Kvideland, R., & Sehmsdorf, H.K. (Eds.). *Scandinavian Folk Belief and Legend*. (1988). Minneapolis, MN: University of Minnesota Press.

Lane, S. (2005). Ohio State Reformatory A.K.A. Mansfield Reformatory. In J. Belanger (Ed.), *Encyclopedia of Haunted Places* (pp. 126-127). Franklin Lakes, NJ: New Page Books.

Lara, O.R.P. (n.d.). Case 14. In A. Rosales (Ed.), *1945 Humanoid Sighting Reports*. Retrieved November 9, 2015 from http://www.ufoinfo.com

Largey, G.P., & Watson, D.R. (1972, May). The Sociology of Odors. *American Journal of Sociology 77(6)*, pp. 1021-1034.

Larsen, O.J. (n.d.). Case 288. In A. Rosales (Ed.), *1954 Humanoid Sighting Reports*. Retrieved November 9, 2015 from http://www.ufoinfo.com

Larsson, M., Öberg-Blåvarg, C., & Jönsson, F.U. (2009). Bad Odors Stick Better Than Good Ones: Olfactory Qualities and Odor Recognition. *Experimental Psychology 56 (6)*, 375-380.

Lawson, H. (2013, August 4). The river UNDER the sea: Haunting images of scuba diver exploring mysterious channel flowing in water-filled cavern. Retrieved October 24, 2015 from http://www.dailymail.co.uk

Lefer, D.J. (2007, November). A new gaseous signaling molecule emerges: Cardioprotective role of hydrogen sulfide. *Proceedings of the National Academy of Sciences of the United States of America 104 (46)*, 17907-17908.

Legro, S. (2015, November 19). *Into the Fray: Small Town Monsters* [Audio podcast]. Retrieved November 30, 2015 from https://intothefrayradio.com

Legro, S. (2015, December 31). *Into the Fray: Haunted Las Vegas* [Audio podcast]. Retrieved January 12, 2016 from https://intothefrayradio.com

Le Guérer, A. (1994). *Scent: The Essential and Mysterious Powers of Smell*. (R. Miller, Trans.). New York, NY: Kodansha International. (Original Work published 1988 as *Les Pouvoirs de L'Odeur*)

Lewis, C.S. (1964). *The Discarded Image: An Introduction to Medieval and Renaissance Literature*. Cambridge, UK: Cambridge University Press.

Lin, V.S., Lippert, A.R., & Chang, C.J. (2013, March 20). Cell-trappable fluorescent probes for endogenous hydrogen sulfide signaling and imaging H_2O_2-dependent H_2S production. *Proceedings of the National Academy of Sciences of the United States of America 110 (18)*, 7131-7135.

Lis-Balchin, M. (2006). *Aromatherapy Science: A Guide for Healthcare Professionals*. London, UK: Pharmaceutical Press.

Live Science. (2012, July 20). What Does Space Smell Like? Retrieved November 13, 2015 from http://www.livescience.com

Long, G. (2004). *The Making of Bigfoot: The Inside Story*. Amherst, NY: Prometheus Books.

Lorenzen, C.E. (1966). *Flying Saucers: The Startling Evidence of the Invasion from Outer Space*. New York, NY: The New American Library – Signet Books. (Original work published 1962 as *The Great Flying Saucer Hoax: The UFO Facts and Their Interpretation*)

Lorgen, E. (1998, May 2). Common Symptoms of Abduction – Chart. Retrieved November 5, 2015 from http://evelorgen.com

Lowery, R. (2011, May 26). Report #29294 (Class A): Sundown sighting by teen on bicycle in Eau Galle River bottoms. Retrieved December 1, 2015 from http://www.bfro.net

Lynch, G.J., Canwell, D., and Sutherland, J. (2012). *Famous Ghosts and Haunted Places*. New York, NY: The Rosen Publishing Group, Inc.

Machlin, M. & Beckley, T.G. (1981). *UFO*. Cape Town, South Africa: Quick Fox.

MacLaine, S. (2007). *Sage-Ing While Age-Ing*. New York, NY: Simon & Schuster, Inc. (Atria Books).

Mack, J. (1995). *Abduction: Human Encounters with Aliens*. New York, NY: Ballantine Books.

Mack, J. (1999). *Passport to the Cosmos*. New York, NY: Three Rivers Press.

MacPherson, M. (1999). *She Came to Live Out Loud: An Inspiring Family Journey Through Illness, Loss, and Grief*. New York, NY: Simon & Schuster (Scribner).

Maisel, M. (2013, November 15). Report #42745 (Class A): Strange occurrences outside a home lead to a daylight sighting by a father and son near East Canton. Retrieved December 10, 2015 from http://www.bfro.net

Malanowski, G. (2011). *The Race for Wireless*. Bloomington, IN: AuthorHouse.

Mallet, R. (1862). *Great Neapolitan Earthquake of 1857: The First Principles of Seismology* (Vol. 2). London, UK: Chapman and Hall.

Mann, S.A. (2014, March 28). Our Sunday Visitor: Who is Our Lady of Laus? Retrieved September 29, 2015 from https://www.osv.com

Marcuccio, P.R. (Ed.). (1992, August). *Federal Emergency Management Agency - Earthquakes: A Teacher's Package for K-6*. Washington, DC: The National Science Teachers Association.

Martin, G.N. (2013). *The Neuropsychology of Smell and Taste*. East Sussex, UK: Psychology Press.

Martin, J. (n.d.). Case 161. In A. Rosales (Ed.), *1982 Humanoid Sighting Reports*. Retrieved October 19, 2015 from http://www.ufoinfo.com

Martin, R. (1999, October 5). Great Zulu Shaman And Elder Credo Mutwa: A Rare, Astonishing Conversation. *The Spectrum, 1*(5), 1, 17- 32.

Maruna, S. (2003). *The Mad Gasser of Mattoon: Dispelling the Hysteria* (2nd ed.). Jacksonville, IL: Swamp Gas Book Co.

Mateja, P.J. (2005, November 1). Report #12951 (Class A): Possible encounter between a juvenile and a human child, near Gettysburg. Retrieved December 9, 2015 from http://www.bfro.net

Matthews, D. (2015, December 13). How a Weekend on Haunted Mackinac Island Resulted in Strange Insight Into the Nature of Ghosts. Retrieved January 15, 2016 from http://weekinweird.com

Maunder, M. (2007). *Lights in the Sky: Identifying and Understanding Astronomical and Meteorological Phenomena*. London, UK: Springer-Verlag.

Maxwell-Stuart, P.G. (2011). *Poltergeists: A History of Violent Ghost Phenomena*. Gloucestershire, UK: Amberly Publishing.

Maynard, D.G. (1998). *Sulfur in the Environment*. New York, NY Marcel Dekker, Inc.

McCampbell, J.M. (1973). *UFOlogy: New Insights from Science and Common Sense*. Belmont, CA: Jaymac-Hollman.

McCampbell, J. (1976). *UFOlogy: A Major Breakthrough in the Scientific Understanding of Unidentified Flying Objects*. Millbrae, CA: Celestial Arts.

McCarthy, E. (2014, July 11). 11 Ways Big Cats Are Just Like Domestic Cats. Retrieved December 15, 2015 from http://mentalfloss.com

McCall, G.J.H., Laming, D.J.C., & Scott, S.C. (Eds.). (1992). *Geohazards: Natural and Man-Made*. London, UK: Chapman & Hall.

McElyea, T. (2000, October 13). Report #451 (Class A). Young man has sighting near home. Retrieved December 14, 2015 from http://www.bfro.net

McKenna, T. (1990, July). The World Could Be Anything. [Lecture transcript]. Retrieved December 22, 2015 from https://terencemckenna.wikispaces.com

McMillan, B. (2006, April 27). Report #14511 (Class A): Sighting by snowmobilers outside Castlegar. Retrieved December 9, 2015 from http://www.bfro.net

McMillan, B. (2008, February 24). Report #23245 (Class A): Resting elk hunter smells and sees a Sasquatch near Whiteswan Lake. Retrieved November 19, 2015 from http://www.bfro.net

McTaggart, L. (2007). *The Intention Experiment: Using Your Thoughts to Change Your Life and the World*. New York, NY: Simon & Schuster, Inc. (Free Press).

Meikle, J.L. (1997). *American Plastic: A Cultural History*. New Brunswick, NJ: Rutgers University Press. (Original work published 1995)

Melamed, A. (n.d.). Case 49. In A. Rosales (Ed.), *1990 Humanoid Sighting Reports*. Retrieved October 19, 2015 from http://www.ufoinfo.com

Melanson, T. (2001). UFOs, Do They Smell? The Sulphur Enigma of Paranormal Visitation. Retrieved November 13, 2015 from http://www.conspiracyarchive.com

Meldrum, J. (2006). *Sasquatch: Legend Meets Science*. New York, NY: Forge Books.

Merry, A. (1908). Kilman Castle: The House of Horror. In R. Shirley (Ed.), *The Occult Review July-December 1908* (Vol. VIII, pp. 308-347). London, UK: William Rider & Son, Limited.

Mesnard, J., & Pavy, C. (1968, September). Encounter with "Devils": A strange account from the Cussac Plateau in France. *Flying Saucer Review 14(5)*, pp. 7-9.

Meyer, B. (1977). *Sulfur, Energy, and Environment*. Amsterdam, Netherlands: Elsevier Scientific Publishing Company.

Meyer, M. (2013). Yokai.com: An online database of Japanese ghosts and monsters. Retrieved October 13, 2015 from http://yokai.com

Meyer, O. (1994). Functional Groups of Microorganisms. In E.-D. Schulze & H.A. Mooney (Eds.), *Biodiversity and Ecosystem Function* (pp. 67-96). Berlin, Germany: Springer-Verlag.

Millen, J.K. (2001). *Your Nose Knows: A Study of the Sense of Smell*. Lincoln, NE: Authors Choice Press. (Original work published in 1960).

Mitzman, D. (2014, May 28). Do people experience smell in their dreams? Retrieved September 15, 2015 from http://www.bbc.com

Miles, J. (2000). *Weird Georgia: Close Encounters, Strange Creatures, and Unexplained Phenomena*. Nashville, TN: Cumberland House Publishing.

Monahan, B. (Ed.). (1997). *An American Haunting: The Bell Witch*. New York, NY: St. Martin's Griffin.

Moneymaker, M. (1996, January 28). Report #928 (Class B): Hikers find tracks and a possible nest. Retrieved December 14, 2015 from http://www.bfro.net

Moneymaker, M. (2002, December 11). Report #5463 (Class A): Dusk sighting by hunter on Fort Hunter Liggett. Retrieved December 14, 2015 from http://www.bfro.net

Monteith, R. (2012, December 16). Report #38287 (Class A). Dogs alert homeowner to a late night visitor outside Kamiah. Retrieved November 20, 2015 from http://www.bfro.net

Monteith, R. (2013, July 21). Report #41782 (Class B): Man-like figure seen running along a tree-line off Hwy. 12 near Checkerboard. Retrieved December 14, 2015 from http://www.bfro.net

Monteith, R. (2013, August 17). Report #41892 (Class A): Woman is startled to see a large hairy biped climbing her fence outside Clearwater. Retrieved November 17, 2015 from http://www.bfro.net

Monteith, R. (2014, April 16). Report #44837 (Class A): Years of South Florida Skunk Ape stories supported by witness accounts and newspaper articles. Retrieved November 19, 2015 from http://www.bfro.net

Moravec, M. (1980). *The UFO Anthropoid Catalogue*. Australia: Australian Center for UFO Studies.

Moravec, M.L. (1980, August). Psiufological Phenomena: UFOs and the Paranormal. *MUFON UFO Journal 150*, pp. 13-15.

Morris, M.C.F. (1911). *Yorkshire Folk-Talk* (2nd ed.). London, UK: A. Brown & Sons, Ltd.

Moseley, J.W., & Pflock, K.T. (2002). *Shockingly Close to the Truth: Confessions of a Grave-Robbing Ufologist*. Amherst, NY: Prometheus Books.

Mott, W.M. (2011). *Caverns, Cauldrons, and Concealed Creatures* (3rd ed.). Nashville, TN: Grave Distractions Publications.

Murphy, C.L. (2008). *Bigfoot Film Journal*. Blaine, WA: Hancock House Publishers.

Musgrave, J.B. (1979). *UFO Occupants & Critters*. Amherst, WI: Amherst Press.

National Research Council of the National Academies. (2009). *Emergency and Continuous Exposure Guidance Levels for Selected Submarine Contaminants* (Vol. 3). Washington, DC: The National Academies Press.

National UFO Reporting Center. (2003, March 4). Strange beam and apparition terrifies child. Retrieved October 13, 2015 from http://www.nuforc.org

National UFO Reporting Center. (2006, February 14). At about 2am, A freind [sic] and I were awoken in his country home south of Bragg Creek. Retrieved November 9, 2015 from http://www.nuforc.org

Native Languages of the Americas. (n.d.). Legendary Native American Figures: Oniare (Oniont). Retrieved September 15, 2015 from http://www.native-languages.org

Native Languages of the Americas. (n.d.). Legendary Native American Figures: Pukwudgie (Puckwudgie). Retrieved December 20, 2015 from http://www.native-languages.org

Nebraska Medical Center. (2010). Joann – Lung Cancer Patient: Fighting for Every Breath. Retrieved November 10, 2015 from http://www.nebraskamed.com

Newkirk, G. (2013, May 15). Week in Weird: Unidentified Foul Objects: Quincy, Massachusetts Plagued by Odd Aircraft and Awful Smells. Retrieved October 21, 2015 from http://weekinweird.com

Newton-Perry, L. (2015, September 22). The Original Post from Sophia about Dr. H.A. Miller. Retrieved December 1, 2015 from http://bigfootballyhoo.blogspot.com

Nicholas, F. (2005). Appalachian Bigfoot Lacks Underarm Charm. In M. Lake, M. Sceurman & M. Moran (Eds.), *Weird Pennsylvania* (p. 92). New York, NY: Sterling Publishing Co., Inc.

No author. (1902, June 22). Sea Monster in Lake Superior. *Duluth News Tribune*.

No author. (1973, June 26). Big, muddy 'critter' sighted at Big Muddy. *Southern Illinoisan*, p. 3.

Noël, C. (2009). *Impossible Visits: The Inside Story of Interactions with Sasquatch at Habituation Sites*. US: Xlibris Corporation.

Noël, C. (2014). *Our Life with Bigfoot: Knowing Our Next of Kin at Habituation Sites* [Kindle edition]. US: CreateSpace Independent Publishing Platform.

Noory, G. (2013, April 12). Coast to Coast AM - Black Eyed Children & Open Lines. Retrieved December 17, 2015 from http://www.coasttocoastam.com

Nunnelly, B.M. (2011). *The Inhumanoids: Real Encounters with Beings That Can't Exist*. Woolsery, UK: CFZ Press.

Okonowicz, E. (2010). *The Big Book of Maryland Ghost Stories*. Mechanicsburg, PA: Stackpole Books.

Olenik, T.J. (1975). Domestic Sewage and Refuse Odor Control. In Cheremisinoff, P.N. & Young, R.A. (Eds.), *Industrial Odor Technology Assessment* (pp. 117-146). Ann Arbor, MI: Ann Arbor Science Publishers Inc.

Olsen, T.M. (1980, November). UFO Odours and Origins. *Flying Saucer Review 26(4)*, pp. 12-13.

Omer, B. (2013, December 22). Report #43399 (Class A): Scientist skeptic has early morning encounter behind gas station near Las Vegas, NM. Retrieved November 19, 2015 from http://www.bfro.net

Orcutt, L. (2001). Catchpenny Mysteries: The Tulli Papyrus. Retrieved October 14, 2015 from http://www.catchpenny.org

Overmeire, G.V. (n.d.). Case 242. In A. Rosales (Ed.), *1995 Humanoid Sighting Reports*. Retrieved November 9, 2015 from http://www.ufoinfo.com

Owen, J. (2004, Spring). What Happened to That Hour? *Flying Saucer Review 49(1)*, pp. 6-7.

Paijmans, T. (2013, October 5). Spring-Heeled Jack in America. Retrieved April 20, 2016 from http://mysteriousuniverse.org

Palmisano, A.C., & Barlaz, M.A. (1996). Introduction to Solid Waste Decomposition. In A.C. Palmisano & M.A. Barlaz (Eds.), *Microbiology of Solid Waste* (pp. 1-30). Boca Raton, FL: CRC Press, Inc.

Parker, B.R. (1973, December). Strange Creature Stalls Auto in Georgia – Car Intensely Hot. *Skylook Magazine 73*, pp. 7-8.

Parker, G.H. (1922). *Smell, Taste, and Allied Senses in the Vertebrates*. Philadelphia, PA: J.B. Lippincott Company.

Pattskyn, H. (2012). *Ghosthunting Michigan*. Covington, KY: Clerisy Press.

Peterson, J.H. (Ed.). (2001). *The Lesser Key of Solomon: Detailing the Ceremonial Art of Commanding Spirits Both Good and Evil*. York Beach, ME: Weiser Books.

Pettit, D. (2003, May 13). Expedition Six: Space Chronicles #4 – The Smell of Space. Retrieved November 13, 2015 from http://spaceflight.nasa.gov

Phillips, T. (2005, June). Physical Traces. *MUFON UFO Journal 446*, pp. 15-17.

Phillips, T. (2005, September). Physical Traces. *MUFON UFO Journal 449*, pp. 18-19.

Phillips, T. (2005, December). Physical Traces. *MUFON UFO Journal 452*, pp. 18-19.

Phillips, T. (2006, January 30). The Mysterious Smell of Moondust. Retrieved November 13, 2015 from http://science.nasa.gov

Philson, K., & Hale, C. (2015, August 3). Expanded Perspectives - The Black Eyed Kids. Retrieved December 20, 2015 from http://www.expandedperspectives.com

Picknett, L. (2001). *The Mammoth Book of UFOs*. New York, NY: Carroll & Graf Publishers, Inc.

Playfair, G.L. (2011). *The Flying Cow: Exploring the Psychic World of Brazil*. Guildford, UK: White Crow Books.

Pope, N., Burroughs, J., & Penniston, J. (2014). *Encounter in Rendlesham Forest: The Inside Story of the World's Best-Documented UFO Incident*. New York, NY; Thomas Dunne Books.

Porter, H. (2006, Summer). Another Missing Week long Abduction, this time from Portsmouth England. *Flying Saucer Review 51(2)*, pp. 17-18.

Poulsen, K. (2009, March 13). Dangerous Japanese 'Detergent Suicide' Technique Creeps Into U.S. Retrieved October 23, 2015 from http://www.wired.com

Puckett, W. (2006, August). Sighting, odors, physical traces, and illness in Midwest encounter. *MUFON UFO Journal 460*, pp. 3-5.

Pugh, D.G., & Baird, A.N. (2012). *Sheep & Goat Medicine* (2nd ed.). Maryland Heights, MO: Elsevier Saunders.

Purves, D., Augustine, G.J., Fitzpatrick, D., Katz, L.C., LaMantia, A.S., McNamara, J.O., & Williams, S.M. (Eds.) (2001). *Neuroscience* (2nd ed.). Sunderland, MA: Sinauer Associates.

Pratt, B., & Luce, C. (1998, August). Varginha, Brazil ET crash, capture? *MUFON UFO Journal 364*, pp. 3-6.

Pratt, B., & Luce, C. (1998, September). Part Two: The Varginha ET Case. *MUFON UFO Journal 365*, pp. 8-13.

Pratt, B. (2004, February). UFOs still haunting Brazil's Valley of the Old Women. *MUFON UFO Journal 430*, pp. 3-8.

Price, H. (2012). *Poltergeist Over England: Three Centuries of Mischievous Ghosts.* Devon, UK: F&W Media.

Prieto, C.E.M.Y. (2006, December). *Distribution and Diversity of Sulfur-Reducing Prokaryotes in Sulfur-Rich Peat Soils* (Doctoral dissertation). The Pennsylvania State University: Department of Crop and Soil Sciences.

Project Blue Book. (1952, August 25). Desvergers case file. College Park, MD: National Archives.

Radford, B. (2011). *Tracking the Chupacabra: The Vampire Beast in Fact, Fiction, and Folklore.* Albuquerque, NM: University of New Mexico Press.

Rainbolt, D. (2007). *Ghost Cats: Human Encounters with Feline Spirits.* Guilford, CT: The Lyons Press.

Ramírez, M. (2012, May 16). Ovnis en Andalucía – Spain: A Humanoid at Fuengirola (CE-3, 1976) (S. Corrales, Trans.). Retrieved December 14, 2015 from http://inexplicata.blogspot.com

Ramsbotham, J. (1999) Perfumes in Detergents. In G. Broze (Ed.), *Surfactant Science Series Volume 82: Handbook of Detergents – Part A: Properties.* (pp. 691-720). New York, NY: Marcel Dekker, Inc.

Randles, J., & Whetnall, P. (1979, May). The Sunderland Family Encounters – Part 1. *Flying Saucer Review 25(3)*, pp. 11-18.

Randles, J. (1997). *UFOs & How to See Them.* New York, NY: Sterling Publishing Company, Inc.

Rawlings-Cody, A. (n.d.). Tolowa Indian stories... Del Norte County, California 1800's. Retrieved November 16, 2015 from http://www.bigfootencounters.com

Raymond, C. (2011, December 6). Reports for Adair County, KY. Retrieved December

29, 2015 from http://www.kentuckybigfoot.com

Redfern, N. (2004). *Three Men Seeking Monsters*. New York, NY: Paraview Pocket Books.

Redfern, N. (2011). *The Real Men in Black*. Pompton Plains, NJ: New Page Books.

Redfern, N. (2013). *Nick Redfern's Monster Files: A Look Inside Government Secrets and Classified Documents on Bizarre Creature and Extraordinary Animals*. Pompton Plains, NJ: New Page Books.

Redfern, N. (2014, October 12). Things That Go Bump in the Night Department – Black Dogs and UFOs. Retrieved December 17, 2015 from http://uforeview.tripod.com

Redfern, N. (2016). *The Bigfoot Book: The Encyclopedia of Sasquatch, Yeti and Cryptid Primates*. Canton, MI: Visible Ink Press.

Redfern, N. (2016). *Women in Black: The Creepy Companions of the Mysterious M.I.B.* US: Lisa Hagan Books [Kindle edition].

Red Pill Junkie. Personal communication, February 8, 2016.

Rémy, N. (2008). *Demonolatry: An Account of the Historical Practice of Witchcraft*. M. Summers (Ed.). Mineola, NY: Dover Publications, Inc. (Original work published 1930).

Revai, C. (2005). *Haunted New York: Ghosts and Strange Phenomena of the Empire State*. Mechanicsburg, PA: Stackpole Books.

Revai, C. (2009). *The Big Book of New York Ghost Stories*. Mechanicsburg, PA: Stackpole Books.

Ribera, A. (1986, May). The Jinn and the Dolmen: The Most Amazing Case of Abduction Yet. *Flying Saucer Review 31(4)*, pp. 2-10.

Rice, R.G., & Browning, M.E. (Eds.). (1976). *Ozone: Analytical Aspects & Odor Control*. New York, NY: Pan American Group/International Ozone Institute, Inc.

Rickard, B., & Michell, J. (2000). *Unexplained Phenomena: A Rough Guide Special*. London, UK: Rough Guides, Ltd.

Ridge, F. (2008, October 15). The 2003 UFO Chronology. Retrieved October 30, 2015 from http://www.nicap.org

Rife, P.L. (2000). *Bigfoot Across America*. Lincoln, NE: Writers Club Press.

Rife, P.L. (2001). *America's Nightmare Monsters*. Lincoln, NE: Writers Club Press.

Righi, B. (2008). *Ghosts, Apparitions, and Poltergeists*. Woodbury, MN: Llewellyn Publications.

Rimmel, E. (2005). *The Book of Perfumes*. Boston, MA: Adamant Media Corporation-Elibron Classics Series. (Original work published 1865)

Rincon, P. (2005, April 21). Mice put in 'suspended animation.' Retrieved December 29, 2015 from http://news.bbc.co.uk

Rizzi, W. (1980, September). Close encounter in the Dolomites. *Flying Saucer Review 26(3)*, pp. 22-27.

Rodgman, A., & Perfetti, T.A. (2013). *The Chemical Components of Tobacco and Tobacco Smoke* (2nd ed.). Boca Raton, FL: CRC Press.

Rodriguez, L.F., & Pereira, M.J. (n.d.). Case 134. In A. Rosales (Ed.), *1979 Humanoid Sighting Reports*. Retrieved October 19, 2015 from http://www.ufoinfo.com

Rogo, D.S., & Clark, J. (1982). *Earth's Secret Inhabitants*. New York, NY: Ace Books.

Rolle, R. (1989). *The World of the Scythians* (F.G. Walls, Trans.). Berkeley & Los Angeles, CA: University of California Press (Original work published 1980 as *Die Welt der Skythen*)

Romaniuk, P. (n.d.). Case 236. In A. Rosales (Ed.), *1972 Humanoid Sighting Reports*. Retrieved November 3, 2015 from http://www.ufoinfo.com

Rosales, A. (2014). Case 84. In A. Rosales (Ed.), *2014 Humanoid Sighting Reports*. Retrieved October 21, 2015 from http://www.ufoinfo.com

Roth, J. (2014). *Ghost Soldiers of Gettysburg: Searching for Spirits on America's Most Famous Battlefield*. Woodbury, MN: Llewellyn Publications.

Roth, M. (2010, February). Mark Roth: Suspended animation is within our grasp. Retrieved December 29, 2015 from http://www.ted.com

Rubin, J. (Writer), & Ohm, J. (Editor). (2009, January 24). Is That Skunk? [Television series episode]. In J. Donald (Producer), *Nature*. New York, NY: John Rubin Productions, Inc./Thirteen/WNET (Kravis Multimedia Education Center).

Rubin, M.B. (2001). The History of Ozone - The Schönbein Period, 1839–1868. *Bulletin for the History of Chemistry 26*, pp. 40-56.

Ruickbie, L. (2013). *Ghost Hunting: How to Identify and Investigate Spirits, Poltergeists and Hauntings*. London, UK: Constable & Robinson, Ltd.

Rullán, A.F. (2000, July 2). Odors from UFOs: Deducing Odorant Chemistry and Causation from Available Data. Retrieved October 14, 2015 from http://www.ufoevidence.org

Ruppelt, E.J. (2011). *The Report on Unidentified Flying Obects: The Original 1956 Edition*. C. Bennet (Ed.). New York, NY: Cosmo Classics. (Original work published 1956)

Russell, R. (2008). *Ghost Cats of the South*. Winston-Salem, NC: John F. Blair.

Rutkowski, C.R. (1999). *Abductions and Aliens: What's Really Going On?* Toronto, ON: Dundurn Press.

Rutkowski, C., & Dittman, G. (2006). *The Canadian UFO Report: The Best Cases Revealed*. Toronto, ON: Dundurn Press.

Rux, B. (1996). *Architects of the Underworld: Unriddling Atlantis, Anomalies of Mars, and the Mystery of the Sphinx*. Berkeley, CA: Frog, Ltd.

Saladin, K.S. (2013). *Human Anatomy* (4th ed.). New York, NY: McGraw-Hill Education.

Sanchez-Ocejo, V. (2003, July 28). Eyewitnesses to Incredible Winged Creatures, Imps. Retrieved December 20, 2015 from http://www.rense.com

Sanctuaire Notre-Dame du Laus. (2015). Retrieved September 29, 2015 from http://www.sanctuaire-notredamedulaus.com

Sanders, K. (2009, February 22). Report #25531 (Class A): Witness recalls face to face encounter with creature near Myrtle Point. Retrieved December 10, 2015 from http://www.bfro.net

Sanderson, I.T. (1974). *Uninvited Visitors: A Biologist Looks at UFO's*. London, UK: Universal-Tandem Publishing Company Ltd.

Sanderson, I.T. (2008). *Abominable Snowmen: Legend Come to Life*. New York, NY: Cosimo Classics. (Original work published 1961).

Sands, K.R. (2004). *Demonic Possession in Elizabethan England*. Westport, CT: Praeger Publishers.

Satti, J. (n.d.). *Miasma Analysis*. Retrieved September 15, 2015 from http://www.nanopathy.com

Satterfield, Z. (2004, Fall). What does ppm or ppb mean? *On Tap*, pp. 38-40.

Sams, C.E., & Conway, W.S. (2003). Preharvest Nutritional Factors Affecting Postharvest Physiology. In J.A. Bartz & J.K. Brecht (Eds.), *Postharvest Physiology and Pathology of Vegetables* (pp. 161-176). New York, NY: Marcel Dekker, Inc.

Sanchez-Ocejo, V. (n.d.). Case 42. In A. Rosales (Ed.), *1979 Humanoid Sighting Reports*. Retrieved October 21, 2015 from http://www.ufoinfo.com

Schab, F.R. (1995). *Memory for Odors*. Mahwah, NJ: Lawrence Erlbaum Associates.

Schacter, D., Gilbert, D., & Wegner, D. (2011). *Psychology* (2nd ed.). New York, NY: Worth Publishers.

Schaffner, R. (n.d.). Case 289. In A. Rosales (Ed.), *1978 Humanoid Sighting Reports*. Retrieved December 16, 2015 from http://www.ufoinfo.com/humanoid/humanoid-1978.pdf

Schmidt, R.A., Hillman, D., & UFORI. (n.d.). Case 79. In A. Rosales (Ed.), *1971 Humanoid Sighting Reports*. Retrieved October 30, 2015 from http://www.ufoinfo.com

Schmit, S. (2005). Franek Kluski's Casts. In *The Perfect Medium: Photography and the Occult*. New Haven, CT: Yale University Press. (Original work published 2004)

Schuessler, J. (1983, September). Cash-Landrum Case: Investigation of Helicopter Activity. *MUFON UFO Journal 187*, pp. 3-6.

Schuessler, J. (1998, February). Physiological effects from abductions. *MUFON UFO Journal 358*, pp. 13-15.

Schwarz, B.E. (1971, May). The Port Monmouth Landing. *Flying Saucer Review 17(3)*, pp. 21-27.

Schnabel, J. (1994). *Dark White: Aliens, Abductions, and the UFO Obsession*. London, UK: Penguin Books.

Scott, B. (2005, September 18). Report #12601 (Class B): Bow hunter hears vocalizations, smells foul odor. Retrieved November 17, 2015 from http://www.bfro.net

Seager, S., Bains, W., & Hu, R. (2013, October 1). A Biomass-Based Model to Estimate the Plausibility of Exoplanet Biosignature Gases. *The Astrophysical Journal 775*: 104 (28pp).

Severus, S. (1894). Martin is tempted by the Wiles of the Devil. In P. Schaff (Ed.), *A Select Library of Nicene and Post-Nicene Fathers of the Christian Church, Second Series* (Vol. 11). (A. Roberts, Trans.). New York, NY.

Shandera, J.H., & Moore, W.L. (1990, September). 3 Hours That Shook the Press. *MUFON UFO Journal 269*, pp. 3-10.

Sharpless, B., & Doghramji, K. (2015). *Sleep Paralysis: Historical, Psychological, and Medical Perspectives*. Oxford, UK: Oxford University Press.

Sherman, J. (2012, February 3). Report #32976 (Class B): Possible daylight sighting by a mountain biker in the Pere Marquette State Forest. Retrieved November 19, 2015 from http://www.bfro.net

Shields, B. (2013, May 9). WBZ-TV Boston: Mystery Aircraft Frightens Quincy Residents. Retrieved October 21, 2015 from http://boston.cbslocal.com

Shmueli, U. (2007). *Irritable Bowel Syndrome: Answers at Your Fingertips*. London, UK: Class Publishing.

Siegel, R.K. (1992). *Fire in the Brain: Clinical Tales of Hallucination*. Westminster,

UK: Penguin Books (Dutton Adult).

Sieveking, P. (2003, February). Alien Big Cats: The Definitive Guide to a 40-Year Mystery. *Fortean Times 167*, p. 28.

Sit, J. (2010, October 14). Edmond Woman Says She Can Predict Earthquake Activity. Retrieved November 13, 2015 from http://m.newson6.com

Sloan, D.L. (1998). *Ghosts of Key West*. Key West, FL: Phantom Press.

Smith, N.J.H. (1996). *The Enchanted Amazon Rain Forest: Stories from a Vanishing World.* Gainesville, FL: University Press of Florida.

Smith, Y.R. (2014). *Coronado: The President, The Secret Service, and Alien Abductions* [Kindle Edition].

Snuffin, M.O. (2007). *The Thoth Companion*. Woodbury, MN: Llewellyn Publications.

Sochka, Y.V., Anfalov, A., & UFODOS. (n.d.). Case 62. In A. Rosales (Ed.), *1995 Humanoid Sighting Reports.* Retrieved October 23, 2015 from http://www.ufoinfo.com/humanoid/humanoid-1995.pdf

Spengler, J. D., McCarthy, J. F., Samet, J.M. (2000). *Indoor Air Quality Handbook*. New York, NY, USA: McGraw-Hill Professional Publishing.

Stafford, P. (1993). Psychedelics Encyclopedia (3rd ed). Berkeley, CA: Ronin Publishing.

Steiger, B. (1988). *The UFO Abductors*. New York, NY: Berkley Books.

Steiger, B. (2011). *Real Monsters, Gruesome Critters, and Beasts from the Darkside*. Canton, MI: Visible Ink Press.

Steinberg, G., & O'Brien, C. (2015, October 4). *The Paracast: October 4, 2015 – Stan Gordon* [Audio podcast]. Retrieved November 3, 2015 from http://www.theparacast.com

Steinman, W.S., & Stevens, W.C. (1987). *UFO Crash at Aztec: A Well Kept Secret*. Tucson, AZ: UFO Photo Archives.

Stiles, D. (2007, April). Opinion: Bench Monkey. Retrieved January 5, 2016 from http://www.rsc.org

Stoddart, D.M. (1990). *The Scented Ape: The Biology and Culture of Human Odour*. Cambridge, UK: Cambridge University Press.

Stokes, D., Matthen, M., & Biggs, S. (2015). *Perception and Its Modalities*. Oxford, UK: Oxford University Press.

Strassman, R. (2000). *DMT: The Spirit Molecule*. Rochester, VT: Park Street Press.

Strickler, L. (n.d.). 'Sykesville Monster' Encounter. Retrieved November 20, 2015 from http://www.phantomsandmonsters.com

Strickler, L. (2015, July 20). Arcane Radio Live Show Archive 7.20.15 Guest Shannon LeGro [Audio podcast]. Retrieved December 15, 2015 from http://www.arcaneradio.com

Strickler, L., and Forker, S. (2015, October 12). *Arcane Radio Live Show Archive 10.12.2015: Mike Ricksecker* [Audio podcast]. Retrieved October 19, 2015 from http://www.arcaneradio.com

Strickler, L. (2015, November 10). Arcane Radio Live Show Archive 11.10.15: Nick Redfern [Audio podcast]. Retrieved December 16, 2015 from http://www.arcaneradio.com

Strieber, A. (2013, July 10). Russian Documents Reveal Many Underwater UFO Events. Retrieved October 26, 2015 from http://www.unknowncountry.com

Strieber, W. (1987). *Communion*. New York, NY: Avon Books.

Strieber, W. (1988, June). A Response to Critics. *MUFON UFO Journal 242*, pp. 7-8.

Strieber, W. (1997). *Transformation*. New York, NY: Avon Books. (Original work published 1988).

Stieven, M.A. (1999, Winter). "Chupacabras" Rampant in Brazil (1997). *Flying Saucer Review 44(4)*, pp. 13-16.

Stringfield, L., & Faria, J.E. (n.d.). Case 55. In A. Rosales (Ed.), *1950 Humanoid Sighting Reports*. Retrieved October 30, 2015 from http://www.ufoinfo.com

Stringfield, L. (1976, January). Cincinnati area has variety of sightings. *MUFON UFO Journal 98*, pp. 5-6.

Stringfield, L. (1977). *Situation Red—The UFO Siege!* Garden City, NY: Doubleday & Company, Inc.

Stromberg, J. (2014, January 2). Why Do Lights Sometimes Appear in the Sky During An Earthquake? Retrieved November 13, 2015 from http://www.smithsonianmag.com

Sulfur (n.d.). *University of Minnesota's Mineral Pages*. Retrieved September 24, 2015 from https://www.esci.umn.edu

Suttle, N.F. (2010). *Mineral Nutrition of Livestock*. Oxfordshire, UK: CABI.

Swancer, B. (2008, November 20). Japan's Yeti: Hibagon. Retrieved November 17, 2015 from http://cryptomundo.com

Swanton, J.R. (1926). Social and Religious Beliefs of the Chicasaw Indians. *44th Annual Deport*. Washington, DC: Bureau of American Ethnology.

Bibliography

Swindell, B. (2005). Yorktown. In J. Belanger (Ed.), *Encyclopedia of Haunted Places* (pp. 102-103). Franklin Lakes, NJ: New Page Books.

Swindler, D.R. (1998). *Introduction to Primates*. Seattle, WA: University of Washington Press.

Swords, M.D. (2013, November 21). Professor Michael D. Swords Reports of the Cash-Landrum UFO Investigation. Retrieved November 3, 2015 from http://www.blueblurrylines.com

Tangerman, A. (2009). Measurement and biological significance of the volatile sulfur compounds hydrogen sulfide, methanethiol and dimethyl sulfide in various biological matrices. *Journal of Chromatography B, Analytical technologies in the biomedical and life science 877*, 28.

Tasmanian UFO Investigation Centre. (1997). Tasmanian UFO Report – 1997. Retrieved November 5, 2015 from http://tufoic.eu.pn

Taylor, S. (2008, May 10). Report #23771 (Class A): Young hunter sees and hears a Sasquatch near Applegate. Retrieved December 9, 2015 from http://www.bfro.net

Taylor, T. (2007). Mineral Springs Hotel: The True Story of One of Alton's Most Haunted Locations. Retrieved September 29, 2015 from http://www.altonhauntings.com

theduderinok2 [Screen name] (2011, February 6). *[Highly Recommended] Terence McKenna – Unfolding the Stone*. Retrieved January 8, 2016 from https://www.youtube.com

Thomas, J. (n.d.). Case 379. In A. Rosales (Ed.), *1977 Humanoid Sighting Reports*. Retrieved October 30, 2015 from http://www.ufoinfo.com

Thomas, J.K. (1987, September). The Vehicle Interference Effect. *MUFON UFO Journal 233*, pp. 3-11.

Thompson, J.C. (n.d.). Case 153. In A. Rosales (Ed.), *1973 Humanoid Sighting Reports*. Retrieved November 5, 2015 from http://www.ufoinfo.com

Thompson, J.C. (1998). The Enigmatic Troup-Heard Corridor. Retrieved November 5, 2015 from http://www.mufonga.org

Thornber, W. (1985). *The History of Blackpool and Its Neighbourhood*. Blackpool, UK: The Blackpool and Fylde Historical Society. (Original work published 1837)

Tonnies, M. (2012). *Posthuman Blues 2003-2004* (Vol. 1). Halifax, Nova Scotia: Redstar Books.

Tourism Harrison. (n.d.). Harrison is Sasquatch Territory – about our Sasquatch. Retrieved March 28, 2016 from http://www.tourismharrison.com

Townsend, J. (2004). *Out There? Mysterious Monsters*. Chicago, IL: Raintree.

Trainor, J. (Ed.). (2000, July 13). UFO Roundup Volume 5, Number 28. Retrieved September 15, 2015 from http://ufoupdateslist.com

Trench, B.L.P. (1966). *The Flying Saucer Story*. London, UK: Neville Spearman.

Tucker, E. (2007). *Haunted Halls: Ghostlore of American College Campuses*. Jackson, MS: University Press of Mississippi.

Turback, G. (1984, December). New Technologies Fight Wood-Stove Pollution. *Popular Science*, pp. 90-92.

Turner, K. (1992). *Into the Fringe*. New York, NY: Berkley Books.

Turner, K. (1994). *Taken: Inside the Alien-Human Abduction Agenda*. Tallahassee, FL: Rose Printing Company, Inc.

Tyrrell, J. (2005). Market Square. In J. Belanger (Ed.), *Encyclopedia of Haunted Places* (p. 239). Franklin Lakes, NJ: New Page Books.

Tyson, P. (2012, October 4). Dogs' Dazzling Sense of Smell. Retrieved January 13, 2016 from http://www.pbs.org

UFOs Northwest. (2006, February 21). After 40 Years Woman Vividly Recalls Terrifying Encounter With Large UFO in Her Front Yard. Retrieved October 30, 2015 from http://www.ufosnw.com

UFOs Northwest. (2010, June). Security Guard Has Strange Encounter & Loses 3 Hours Time. Retrieved October 19, 2015 from http://www.ufosnw.com

Uhde, T.W., Cortese, B.M., & Vendeniapin, A. (2012). Sleep Disorders. In M. Hersen & D.C. Beidel (Eds.), *Adult Psychopathy and Diagnosis* (6th ed.) (pp. 717 - 747). Hoboken, NJ: John Wiley & Sons, Inc.

United States Department of Labor. (n.d.). Occupational Safety & Health Administration: Hydrogen Sulfide. Retrieved October 23, 2015 from https://www.osha.gov

United States Environmental Protection Agency – Office of Mobile Sources. (n.d.). Automobiles and Ozone. Retrieved October 30, 2015 from http://www3.epa.gov

Vallee, J., & Vallee, J. (1966). *Challenge to Science: The UFO Enigma*. Chicago, IL: Henry Regnery Company.

Vallee, J. (1990). *Confrontations: A Scientist's Search for Alien Contact*. New York, NY: Ballantine Books.

Vallee, J. (1991). *Revelations: Alien Contact and Human Deception*. New York, NY: Ballantine Books.

Vallee, J. (1992). *Forbidden Science* (2nd ed.). Berkeley, CA: North Atlantic Books.

Vallee, J. (1993). *Passport to Magonia.* Chicago, IL: Contemporary Books.

Vallee, J. (2008). *Dimensions: A Casebook of Alien Contact.* San Antonio, TX: Anomalist Books. (Original work published 1988)

Vallee, J., & Aubeck, C. (2010). *Wonders in the Sky: Unexplained Aerial Objects from Antiquity to Modern Times and Their Impact on Human Culture, History, and Beliefs.* New York, NY: Penguin Group (Jeremy P. Tarcher).

Van Utrecht, W. (2013, December 11). Cash-Landrum: The Light Pillar Theory Revisited by Wim VAN UTRECHT. Retrieved November 3, 2015 from http://www.blueblurrylines.com

Varner, G.R. (2007). *Creatures in the Mist: Little People, Wild Men and Spirit Beings around the World – A Study in Comparative Mythology.* New York, NY: Algora Publishing.

Verga, M. (2008). *When Flying Saucers Came to Earth: The Story of the Italian UFO Landings in the Golden Era of the Flying Saucers.* US: CreateSpace Independent Publishing Platform.

Verish, R. (2010, September 1). Planetary Body Odors. Retrieved November 13, 2015 from http://www.meteorite-times.com

Von Franz, M.L. (1980). *Alchemy: An Introduction to the Symbolism and the Psychology.* Toronto, Canada: Inner City Books.

Vosnaki, E. (2011, February 7). Mapping the vocabulary of scent: what smells like nail polish/metal/sweat/horses/hairspray/burnt toast/baby powder/dirty socks etc? Retrieved September 30, 2015 from http://perfumeshrine.blogspot.com

Vroon, P. A., van Amerongen, A., & de Vries, H. (1997). *Smell: The Secret Seducer.* (P. Vincent, Trans.). New York, NY: Farrar, Straus and Giroux. (Original work published 1994 as *Verborgen verleider*)

Walton, T. (1997). *Fire in the Sky: The Walton Experience* (3rd ed.). New York, NY: Marlowe & Company. (Original work published 1979)

Walters, E. (n.d.). Case 355. In A. Rosales (Ed.), *1990 Humanoid Sighting Reports.* Retrieved October 19, 2015 from http://www.ufoinfo.com

Ward, P.D. (2006, October). Impact from the Deep. Retrieved October 24, 2015 from http://www.scientificamerican.com

Warwick, T. (Ed.). *The Grand Grimoire: The Red Dragon.* (2015). US: CreateSpace Independent Publishing Platform. (Original date unknown, alleged 1750)

Waters, S. (2011). *Haunted Manitou Springs.* Charleston, SC: The History Press (Haunted America).

Webb, D. (1980, January). The Middleton Humanoids Affair. *MUFON UFO Journal 143*, pp. 7-10.

Webb, D.F., and Bloecher, T. (n.d.). Case 254. In A. Rosales (Ed.), *1975 Humanoid Sighting Reports*. Retrieved October 19, 2015 from http://www.ufoinfo.com

Weinhold, B. (2008). Ozone nation: EPA standard panned by the people. *Environmental Health Perspectives 116 (7)*, pp. 302–305.

Wheeldon, K. (2005, February). Family sights unusual object over home. *MUFON UFO Journal 442*, pp. 10-11.

Wherry, J.H. (1969). *Indian Masks & Myths of the West*. New York, NY: Bonanza Books.

Wheless, J.W., Willmore, L.J., & Brumback, R.A. (2009). *Advanced Therapy in Epilepsy*. Shelton, CT: People's Medical Publishing House.

Wicks, Jr., ZW., Jones, F.N., Pappas, S.P., & Wicks, D.A. (2007). *Organic Coatings: Science and Technology*. Hoboken, NJ: Wiley Interscience.

Williams, D.S. (1997). *When Darkness Falls: Tales of San Antonio Ghosts and Hauntings*. Dallas, TX: Republic of Texas Press.

Williams, W.F. (Ed.). (2013). *Encyclopedia of Pseudoscience: From Alien Abductions to Zone Therapy*. New York, NY: Routledge. (Original work published 2000)

Willison, J. (1820). *A Treatise Concerning the Sanctification of the Lord's Day*. Albany, NY: J. Boardman.

Wilson, P.A. (2010). *Monsters of Pennsylvania: Mysterious Creatures in the Keystone State*. Mechanicsburg, PA: Stackpole Books.

Windeatt, M.F. (1945). *The Children of Fatima and Our Lady's Message to the World*. St. Meinrad, IN: St. Meinrad's Abbey, Inc.

Winder, R.H.B. (1967, November). Vehicle Stoppage at Hook. *Flying Saucer Review 13(6)*, pp. 6-7.

Winter, R. (1976). *The Smell Book: Scents, Sex, and Society*. New York, NY: J.B. Lippincott Company.

Wolchover, N. (2011, February 2). What are the ingredients of life? Retrieved September 24, 2015 from http://www.livescience.com

Woodward, J. (2005, November). Animal reactions to UFO encounters. *MUFON UFO Journal 451*, pp. 8-12.

Woollaston, V. (2015, June 2). Why do wet dogs stink? Video reveals the chemistry behind your canine and how they're attracted to the smell of DEATH. Retrieved November 20, 2015 from http://www.dailymail.co.uk

World Health Organization. (1979). *Environmental Health Criteria 8: Sulfur Oxides and Suspended Particulate Matter*. UK: WHO.

Worley, D. (2004, September). While Blue Book slept. *MUFON UFO Journal 436*, pp. 5-6.

Wright, D. (1991, February). Current Case Log. *MUFON UFO Journal 274*, pp. 11-12.

Wright, D. (1994, February). The Entities: Initial Findings of the Abduction Transcription Project. *MUFON UFO Journal 310*, pp. 3-7.

Young, K. (2003, February). The Last Deed. *MUFON UFO Journal 418*, pp. 3-4.

Zaleski, C. (1987). *Otherworld Journeys: Accounts of Near-Death Experience in Medieval and Modern Times*. Oxford, UK: Oxford University Press.

Zeise, W.C. (1834). Ueber das Mercaptan. In *Annalen der Pharmacie* (Vol. 11-12). Heidelberg, Germany: Universitätsbuchhandlung von C.F. Winter.

Zenz, C., Dickerson, O.B., & Horvath, E.P. (1994). *Occupational Medicine* (3rd ed.). St. Louis, MO: Mosby.

Zwicker, R.J. (2007). *Haunted Portsmouth: Spirits and Shadows of the Past*. Charleston, SC: The History Press (Haunted America).

Index

3-hydroxy-3-methylhexanoic acid, 228
3-methyl-2-hexenoic acid, 228
3-methyl-3-sulfanylhexan-1-ol, 228

ABCs (see *Alien Big Cats*)
Abominable Snowman (see *yeti*)
Aborigine (Australia), 42
acetone, 157-158
acromegaly, 227-228
Adair County (Kentucky), 286
Adams County (Pennsylvania), 219
Adamski, George, 15, 114
Adirondack Mountains (New York), 211
Adkins, Brenda Ann, 186
Africa, 19, 28, 42, 47, 65, 75, 84, 97, 119, 137, 138, 146, 161, 215, 250, 251, 269, 270, 271, 306, 307, 311, 315
Age of Enlightenment, 11
Agni, 307
Aguilar, Alicia Rivas, 151
Aillen Mac Midhna, 302
Akin, James P., 280
akkorokamui, 248
Al-Khemia, 306
Alabama (see *United States*)
Alaska (see *United States*)
Alaska Highway, 237
Alberta (see *Canada*)
alchemy, 31, 304, 305-318
alcohol, 14, 49, 157, 265
aldehyde, 85, 157-158, 265, 298, 299, 300
Alexander the Great, 306
alfalfa, 260
Alien Big Cats, 253-254, 316
Alkali Lake (Nebraska), 248
Allegheny County (Pennsylvania), 202
Allegheny River (Pennsylvania), 215
Alley, J. Robert, 185, 198
alligators, 225
Alma (Colorado), 93
almonds, 112, 145, 154, 260, 307
Alton (Illinois), 54

Altschule, Howard G., 171
Alverton (Pennsylvania), 234
Alzheimer's disease, 18, 84
Amazon rainforest, 184, 217, 248, 291, 292
Amherst (Nova Scotia), 62-63
American Association for the Advancement of Science, 177
American Journal of Science (periodical), 171, 246
American Revolution, 72, 75
Amityville Haunting, 74, 84
ammonia, 36, 110, 146-148, 153, 170, 176, 199-201, 228, 242, 253, 254, 283, 297, 298, 301
Anderson, Gerald, 157
Andoversford (England), 64
Andreasson, Betty, 310-311
androstenol, 228
androstenone, 228
Angelucci, Orfeo, 114
Annals of Psychical Science, The (periodical), 70
Annals of Thutmose II, 97
anosmia, 16, 83, 297
Antietam National Battlefield, 79
Antony (Saint), 69-70
Apol, Mr. (MIB), 264
Apollo, 309, 313
Apollo 16, 179
Appalachian Trail (Pennsylvania), 225
apple pie, 81
Applegate (Oregon), 222
Arabian Peninsula, 307
Arabian sea, 99
Araçá cemetery, 68
Arawenté, 291
Area 51, 154-158
Arévalo, Wilfredo, 153
Argentina, 119, 142, 150, 153, 159
Arikha, Avigdor, 17
Aristotle, 9-11, 307

Arizona (see *United States*)
Arkansas (see *United States*)
arnica, 148
Arnold, Kenneth, 98
Ars Almadel, 48
Ars Notoria, 48
Arychuk, David, 12, 112
asbestos, 158
Asheville (North Carolina), 92
Ashtaroth, 31, 36
Asia, 11, 13, 21, 41, 49, 54, 68, 85, 89-90, 99, 112, 121, 124, 130, 140, 151, 171, 175, 184, 192, 193, 197, 213, 223, 240, 248, 250, 251, 285, 307
astral jelly (see *star jelly*)
astromyxin (see *star jelly*)
aswang, 251
Atlanta (Georgia), 292
atmospheric sulfur, 171-172
Aubeck, Chris, 99, 245
Australia, 26, 42, 107, 114, 120, 132, 156, 177, 184, 190, 212, 216
  Tasmania, 72
  Queensland, 165
Azhazha, Vladimir, 137
Aztec (New Mexico), 141
Aztecs, 47

baby powder (see *talcum powder*)
Babylon, 19
Bachelard, Gaston, 280
bacon, 15, 82
Bacon, Roger, 308
Baghdad (Iraq), 307
Bakelite, 156-157, 158, 159, 162, 212
Baker Hotel, 53
Baker, Robert Allen, 78, 91
Bakersfield (California), 250
ball lightning (see *lightning*)
Ball Lightning and Bead Lightning (book), 173
Ballechin House, 83
Bally's Casino, 63
Baltimore Street (Gettysburg), 82
Bantu tribe, 75
Barghest (see *black dogs*)
Bargtjest (see *black dogs*)

barmanu (see *Sasquatch*)
Barry, James Dale, 173
Basilicata (Italy), 175
Bath (England), 55
Battle of Bentonville, 3-4
Bauman, 209
Beast of Boggy Creek (see *Sasquatch*)
Beast of Boggy Creek, The (book), 235
Beast of Bray Road, The (book), 256
Beast of Bray Road, 256, 258
Beast of Gevaudan, 256
Beast of Land Between Lakes, 257
Beast of Whitehall (see *Sasquatch*)
Beckley, Timothy Green, 105
BEKs (see *Black Eyed Kids*)
Belanger, Jeff, 56
Belgium, 166, 316
Bell, Eugene, 152
Belo Horizonte (Brazil), 2
Bender, Albert K., 262-263
Benthal, Frederick, 157
Bentonville (North Carolina; see *Battle of Bentonville*)
benzaldehyde, 299
benzene (see *hydrocarbons*)
benzyl acetate, 299
benzyl mercaptan (see *sulfur*)
Bermuda Triangle, 315
Bernard (Saint), 46
Bethel Church Road (West Virginia), 258
BFRO (see *Bigfoot Field Researchers Organization*)
Bhowmick, Sunin, 124-125
Big Muddy Monster (see *Sasquatch*)
Bigelow, Robert, 274
Bigfoot (see *Sasquatch*)
Bigfoot Casebook (book), 194
Bigfoot Field Researchers Organization, 187, 194, 196, 199, 211, 216, 222, 229, 232, 235
Bigfoot Film Journal (book), 240
Biltmore House, 92
Bindernagel, John, 191
Biography of Satan, The (book), 29
Bird Cage Theatre, 60
Birth Memories Hypothesis, 176

Index

Bishop, Greg, 294
black dogs, 254-255, 277, 313
Black Eyed Kids, 266-267
Black Plague, 11
Black Shuck (see *black dogs*)
Blackman, W. Haden, 227, 248
Blennerhassett Hotel, 61, 91
Blessed Virgin Mary, 6, 15, 43, 44, 45-52, 90, 113-114, 159
    Our Lady of Fátima, 51-52
    Our Lady of Guadalupe, 46
    Our Lady of Laus, 45-46
Bloecher, Ted, 260
Bloody Lane, 79
Bloom, John Howard, 161
Bluff Creek (California), 189
Blythburgh (England), 254
boggard stones, 270
Boggart (see *faeries*)
bogwish (see *Sasquatch*)
Bolos, 306
Book of Enoch, 26-27
Book of Revelation (Bible), 23, 26-27
Bord, Janet and Colin, 192, 194
Borley Rectroy, 62
Botetourt County (Virginia), 261
Bottle Hollow, 227
Bourne, Geoffrey, 215
Bowling Green (Missouri), 13
Bracken County (Kentucky), 236
Bradley family, 81
Brake, D.A., 211
Brandon, Trent, 76
brass, 151, 250
Braxton County (West Virginia), 162-163
Bray Road (Wisconsin), 256, 258
Brazil, 2, 36, 68, 115, 118, 123, 124, 148, 192, 257, 272, 273, 285
bread, 45, 81
Breedlove, Seth, 208
Brenner, Iris, 152
Briazack, Norman J., 100
Bridgeport (Connecticut), 78
Bridgewater Triangle, 315
brimstone (see *sulfur*)
British Army intelligence, 163

British Columbia (see *Canada*)
Brogan, Des, 73
Brooke, Graham, 272
Brooksville (Florida), 240
Brown Mountain Lights, 174
Brown, Virginia, 53
brownies (see *faeries*)
Bruce, Robert, 89
Bryant, Jr., Vaughn, 214
BTMM (see *Bukit Timah Monkey Man*)
Buchanan, Charles, 259
Buckinghamshire (England), 87
Buenos Aires (Brazil), 148
Bukit Timah (Singapore), 197
Bukit Timah Monkey Man, 197
Bukit Timah Nature Reserve, 197
Bullard, Thomas, 19, 100
Bungay (England), 254
Burr, John, 60
Burrville Cider Mill, 60
Busby, Mike, 253
Bush House, 53
Bushylease Farm, 253
butyric acid, 298
BVM (see *Blessed Virgin Mary*)
Byers, Thomas, 206
Byng (Oklahoma), 238

C. nerteros pacificus (see *Sasquatch*)
cabbage, 100, 103, 187, 224, 279
cacosmia, 16
Cairo (Egypt), 52
Cairo (Illinois), 201, 253
Calama (Chile), 269
calcium, 121, 179
calcium carbonate, 150
Calcutta Statesman (periodical), 193
Calgary (Alberta), 12
California (see *United States*)
Call, The (periodical), 250
Cambodia, 184
Cambridge (England), 61
Cambridgeshire (England), 255
Cameron, John, 72
Camp Lejune Marine Corps Base, 231
camphor, 31, 148, 175, 298

Canada, 5, 12, 33, 105, 114, 141-142, 145, 150, 161, 185, 197
   Alberta, 12, 187, 194, 195
   British Columbia, 107, 191, 194, 196, 216, 222, 240
   Manitoba, 141, 148, 298
   Newfoundland, 89
   Nova Scotia, 62, 122
   Ontario, 63, 150
   Quebec, 165, 249
Cannock Chase, 255, 263
Cannon, Dolores, 160
Cape Cod (Massachusetts), 112, 154
Caracas (Venezuela), 151
carbide, 151
carbon, 33, 179
carbon dioxide, 73, 78
carbon disulfide (see *sulfur*)
carbon monoxide, 9
carbon tetrachloride, 261
carbonyl sulfide (see *sulfur*)
carborundum (see *silicon carbide*)
cardboard, 108-109, 111, 160, 211
Cardenas, Filiberto, 121
Carlsson, Gösta, 140
Carmichael, Rosa, 76
Carnegie Mellon University, 292
Carpenters Knob, 206
Cash Landrum Incident, 149-150, 164, 165
Cash, Betty, 149-150
Castillo de San Marcos, 55
Castle Stuart, 72
cats (see also *alien big cats*), 31, 55, 84, 199, 214, 215, 236, 253-254, 282, 316
Cave of Dogs, 288
Cedar Grove, 61
cenotes, 131-132
Central African Republic, 215
Cerberus, 254
Ceres, 129
CH₃SH (see *methyl mercaptan*)
Chadwick-Ciccone, Cathy, 75
Champ, 249
Chancellor, William N., 61
charcoal, 77
Charlevoix (Michigan), 232
Chastel, Jean, 256
cheese, 25, 111, 228, 299
Chelsea House, 59
Cheremisinoff, Paul N., 9
Cherokee National Forest (Tennessee), 200
cherry, 25
Cherry Creek (New York), 148, 163
chewing gum, 42, 82
Chiasson family, 165
Chicago (Illinois), 53, 56
Chickasaw tribe, 185
chicken, 100, 105, 200, 201, 229, 259
Childress, Adele, 257
Chile, 14, 165, 245, 269, 273
chimpanzee, 223, 227, 240
China, 89-90, 250
chlorine, 127, 136
chloroform, 146
Cho, Adrian, 177
Choctaw tribe, 185
Chopic, Gary J., 115
Chorvinsky, Mark, 71
Christ, Jesus (see *Jesus of Nazareth*)
Christianity, 11, 20, 25-26, 32, 42, 47-49, 51, 69, 70, 124, 131, 254, 267, 308, 309, 315,
Chrysostom, John (Saint), 69-70
Chupacabras and Other Mysteries (book), 252
chupacabras, el, 251-252, 269, 277, 299
chupas, 118
CICOANI, 2, 272
cigar (see *tobacco*)
cigarette (see *tobacco*)
Cincinnati (Ohio), 17, 163
Cincinnati Enquirer (periodical), 234
cinnabar, 33
cinnamaldehyde, 299
cinnamon, 42, 49, 109-111, 299
Cintron, Migdalia, 113
Civil War (United States), 3, 43, 54, 72, 77
Civilization and Its Discontents (book), 10
Clackamas County (Oregon), 238
Clanda, 247
Clark, Jerome, 131, 194

Clarke, Hugh, 29
Clayton, Evelyn, 253
Clelland, Mike, 241-242
Clermont (France), 153
Cleveland County (North Carolina), 206
Clinton County (Pennsylvania), 220
Clore, Dan, 176, 278
clove, 49
coal, 31, 78, 79, 252
Cohen, Maury, 215
Cole, C.E., 261
Coleman, Christopher K., 3-4
Coleman, Loren, 193, 194, 203, 253
Colley, B.J., 156
Colorado (see *United States*)
Colp, Harry, 217
Communion (book), 108-112
Comoros islands, 28
Complete Guide to Mysterious Beings (book), 5
Confrontations (book), 118, 138, 273
Connecticut (see *United States*)
Connersville (Indiana), 119
Conway, Graham, 107
Conyers (Georgia), 52
Cooper, L. Andrew, 92
Copake (New York), 74
Copiapó (Chile), 245-246
copper, 35, 85, 125, 128, 151, 152, 245
Cordes, Carl and Beulah, 261
Corinthians (Bible), 48
Cornet, Sharon, 194-195, 239, 289
Cornu, Gilbert, 51
Cornwallis, Charles, 72
Corrales, Scott, 235, 252
Cortina tribe, 273
COS (see *carbonyl sulfide*)
Coulthard, Fred & Wayne, 114
Council of Toledo, 30
Courtenay-Latimer, Marjorie, 250
Courtney, Stan, 187
Cox, Esther, 62
Crash at Corona (book), 157
Creath, Randy, 3
Cromartie, Shirley, 264-265
crop circles, 121-122
Crowe, Richard, 189

Crowley, Aleister, 247
Crypto 4 Corners, 207
Cryptozoology News (website), 215
CS_2 (see *carbon disulfide*)
culantro (see *Eryngium foetidum*)
Cupid, 48
Curse of Chains, 31
Cussac (France), 119
Custodians, The (book), 160
cyanide, 112
Czechoslovakia, 89

da Silva, Liliane, 36
da Silva, Valquíria, 36
da Souza, Carlos, 146
Dai-el-Aouagri (Morocco), 119
Daimonic Reality, 52, 312
Dallas (Oregon), 119
Dames Vertes (see *faeries*)
Dan, Frank, 185-186
Dante, 16, 67
Darby family, 67
Darby, Mildred, 67-68
Dartmoor (England), 254
Darya-ya Namak (Iran), 175
Dauphin County (Pennsylvania), 119
Davenport, Peter, 89, 140
Davidson, Benjamin, 17
Davis, Sherry, 237
Dayton (Texas), 149
de Rachewiltz, Boris, 97
Dean, James, 60
Death Car, 71
Debus, Allen G., 309, 314
Decatur (Illinois), 186
Delaware (see *United States*)
Delgado family, 59
Delphi (Greece), 291
Demler, John H., 119
Demon of Brownsville Road, The (book), 74
Derry Township (Pennsylvania), 229
DesVergers, "Sonny", 106-107, 135, 167
Detienne, Marcel, 316
devil stones, 270
Devil's Island (Wisconsin), 249
diarrhea, 148, 149, 215, 239
Dickson, Laura, 91

Diego, Juan, 46
diesel, 123, 127, 170, 261
diethylamine, 299
Dietrich, Andrea, 85
Dimensions (book), 118
dimethyl sulfide (see *sulfur*)
dimethyl trisulfide (see *sulfur*)
Divinópolis (Brazil), 285
djinn, 20
DMT (see *N,N-Dimethyltryptamine*)
dogs (see also *Texas Blue Dogs* and *black dogs*), 12, 56, 83-84, 87, 90, 105, 129, 152, 162-163, 187, 188, 189, 190, 195, 198, 200, 201-205, 206, 207, 208, 210, 211, 212, 213, 214, 215, 216, 220, 221, 222, 223, 232, 242, 249, 282, 286, 288, 297
   German Shepherd, 255
   Labrador, 190, 253
   Pit Bull, 255
dogman, 256-257
Dolomite Mountains (Italy), 115, 164
Downes, Jon, 252
Dr. Beachcombing, 56
dragons, 25, 28, 36, 249-250, 254, 256, 259, 268, 310, 311, 315
   lindorms, 36
Drake, Rufus, 128
drakes (see *faeries*)
Drew, Leon, 195
Drinnon, Dale, 195, 214, 239
drones, 170
   Zephyr-6 drone, 176-177
Druffel, Ann, 36
Drummer of Tedworth, 23-24
Duckabush River (Washington), 211
duendes (see *faeries*)
Duke University Medical Center, 35
Duke, Charlie, 179
Duluth News Tribune (periodical), 249
Durant, R.J., 102
Durbin, Jim, 59
d'wende (see *faeries*)
dybbuk box, 55
dysosmia, 16

Ealing (England), 76
earthlights (see *earthquake lights*)
earthquake lights, 174-175
earthquakes, 174-175
East Canton (Ohio), 238
East Lancashire (England), 270
East Peoria (Illinois), 201
East Squantum Street (Quincy, Massachusetts), 117
Eaton (Ohio), 235
Eau Galle (Wisconsin), 220
ectoplasm, 65, 86
Edinburgh (Scotland), 73
Eggman, 76
eggs, 6, 14, 25, 28, 34, 37, 68, 76, 77, 100, 103, 117, 118, 126-131, 133, 142, 165, 167, 175, 187, 193, 212, 215, 231, 235-238, 240, 247, 257, 263, 264, 268, 277, 279, 282, 283, 285, 290
Egypt, 19, 28, 47, 97, 306, 307, 311, 315
Eighth Tower, The (book), 24, 26, 100, 105, 124, 127
El Constituyente (periodical), 245
Elfers (Florida), 198, 240
Eliot (Maine), 256
Elizabeth, Katy, 249
Elkhorn (Wisconsin), 256, 258
Elliott, Meagan, 138-139
Emmitt House, 82
Encyclopedia of Ghosts and Spirits, The (book), 90
Engen, Trygg, 17, 18, 104
England (see also Ireland, Scotland, and Wales), 23-24, 29, 55, 61, 62, 64, 75, 76, 87, 91, 112, 120, 132, 136, 156, 160, 166, 172, 253, 254, 255, 256, 268, 270, 272, 277
English Fairy and Other Folk Tales (book), 254
entheogens, 290-296
epilepsy, 175, 263, 301
Erie Canal (Ohio), 82
Eryngium foetidum, 21
ether, 146, 163
ethyl mercaptan (see *sulfur*)
Europa, 179

Index 429

Europe (see also Belgium, Czechoslovakia, England, Finland, France, Germany, Greece, Italy, Norway, Poland, Portugal, Spain, Sweden, Switzerland, Ukraine) 5, 12, 26, 31, 33, 56, 267, 293, 308, 309
Evan City (Pennsylvania), 139
exorcism, 31, 86, 133

faeries, 4, 5, 6, 19, 28, 32 41, 43, 99, 113, 130, 160, 267-273, 278, 290, 293, 302, 318
   Boggart, 270
   brownies, 267
   Dames Vertes, 271
   drakes, 268
   duendes, 21, 269
   dwendes, 267
   kataw, 267
   mermaids, 267
   orculli, 267-268
   pooka, 268
   pukwudgies, 269
   troll, 271-272, 312-313
   Tuatha Dé Danann, 302
   woodwose, 267
Fahrenbach, W.H., 188, 195, 215
fairies (see *faeries*)
Fairy Investigation Society, 269
fairy stones, 270
Fairyland, 32, 318
Famous Ghost Stories: Legends and Lore (book), 42
Fátima (Portugal), 51
Faust, Johann Georg, 31
Feindt, Carl W., 122
Felipe, Ivete Clemência, 2
Felix, Felito, 113
Fernandez, Julio, 139
Field Guide to North American Monsters, The (book), 227
fig, 112
Final Events (book), 36
Finland, 130,
Finn of the Fianna, 302
First Matter (see *Prima Materia*)
Flamel, Nicolas, 309

Flatwoods Monster, 12, 162-164
Flixton (England), 256
Florida (see *United States*)
Florida State University, 84
flowers, 15, 42, 45-47, 49, 53-55, 59, 68, 89, 91, 113-115, 260, 269, 270
   gardenias, 102, 261
   gilly-flower, 46
   honeysuckle, 54, 55, 57, 155, 208
   hyacinth, 115
   jasmine, 50, 54-55, 57, 265, 299
   lavender, 53
   lilac, 42, 46, 54
   lily, 46, 49, 50, 115
   roses, 4, 11, 14, 46, 48, 49, 50-53, 55, 90, 93, 113-115, 300
   violets, 46, 49, 50, 93, 115
Flying Saucer Review (periodical), 101, 115, 131
Flying Saucers Stink: Alien Odors and Supernatural Smells (article), 176
Flying Saucers: A Modern Myth of Things Seen in the Skies (book), 311
Fontana (California), 221
Forbes family, 68
Forli (Italy), 99
formaldehyde, 157-158, 265, 298, 299, 300
formalin (see also *formaldehyde*), 265
formic acid, 299
Fort Constitution, 79
Fort Duchesne (Utah), 227
Fort Salisbury, 248
Fort St. John (British Columbia), 237
Fort Worth (Texas), 53, 156, 258-259
Fort, Charles, 4
Fossey, Dian, 215
Foster Cabin (see *Log Cabin Village*)
Fouke (Arkansas), 206, 210, 235
Fouke Monster (see *Beast of Boggy Creek*)
Fowler, Mary, 52
Fowler, Raymond, 124
fox fire (see *swamp gas*)
foyson, 19
France, 45, 46, 64, 81, 86, 119, 124, 130, 153, 256, 271, 280
Francisco (Fátima witness), 51

frankincense, 110
Franklin, Benjamin, 136
Fred Hutchinson Cancer Research Center, 287
Freeman, Bob, 60
Freeport (Illinois), 75
Freud, Sigmund, 10, 241
Friedman, Stanton T., 154, 157
Fuengirola (Spain), 235
Fusch, Ed, 192

gadarrah, 257
Galdikas, Birutė, 191
Galen of Pergamon, 11
galena, 33
Gandarewa, 36
gardenias (see *flowers*)
Gardner, Gerald B., 247
Garfield, James A., 75
garlic, 20, 31, 129, 142, 148, 192, 249, 258, 279
Garrett, Bob, 188
gasoline, 150
Gaspar, Luis and Marianna, 55
Gater, Paul, 41
Gaufridi, Louis, 30
Gavleborg County (Sweden), 186
Gehenna, 28, 132, 257
Genesis (Bible), 26
George Fox University, 113
Georgia (see *United States*)
geraniol, 300
Gerhard, Ken, 252
Germany, 75, 177, 309, 311
German Shepherd (see *dogs*)
Gettysburg (film), 77
Gettysburg (Pennsylvania), 43, 76, 82, 212
Gettysburg orphanage, 76-77
Gevaudan (France), 256
ghosts (see *spirits*)
Ghost Files, The (book), 56
Ghost Hunter's Bible, The (book), 76
Gibbs, George, 184
Gigantopithecus blacki, 183
Gilbert, Avery, 111
gilly-flower (see *flowers*)

Gimlin, Robert, 189-190
ginger, 49
Girvin, Calvin C., 114
Glanvill, Joseph, 24
Glindemann, Dietmar, 85
globsters, 247-248
Goatman, 257-258
goats, 31, 218, 249, 251
God helmet (see *Persinger, Michael*)
Godfrey, Alan, 112, 255
Godfrey, Linda, 198-199, 203, 256
Goethe, 31
Gold Hill Hotel, 53
Goloveshko, Tatyana, 151
Gomorrah, 26
Gonzales, Cariaga, 14
Gordon, Stan, 103, 125-126, 202, 228, 231, 233
gorilla, 190, 215, 228, 239
Gothic Realities, 92
Gould, Douglas, 123
Gowan, Bill, 106
Graham (Washington), 114
Grand Grimoire, 31
Grantsburg (Wisconsin), 232
Graves, Kersey, 29
Graves, Rufus, 246
Greece, 10, 19, 27, 28, 48, 85, 115, 136, 254, 258, 306, 314, 316
Green, Andrew Malcolm, 76, 90
Green, John, 194-195, 204, 223, 224
Green, Norah, 90-91
Greenburg, Arthur, 310
Greensburg (Pennsylvania), 234
Gregory of Tours, 47
Grey Lady of Bath (see *Theatre Royal*)
Grey, Margot, 16, 108
Grim Reaper, 71
Grimaud, François, 45-46
Groom Lake Air Force Base (see *Area 51*)
Grotta de Cani (see *Cave of the Dogs*)
Guadalupe (Mexico), 46
Guatemala, 161
Guiley, Rosemary Ellen, 5, 42, 90
Guiteau, Charles, 75
Gul-Biavan (see *Sasquatch*)
Gulf Breeze (Florida), 110

Gulf Coast Bigfoot Research
  Organization, 201
Gulf of Mexico, 33
gunpowder, 3, 34, 43, 65, 77-79, 125, 171,
  179, 273, 279
Gwydir Castle, 72, 73

H$_2$S (see *hydrogen sulfide*)
H$_2$SO$_3$ (see *sulfurous acid*)
H$_2$Te (see *hydrogen telluride*)
Hagerty, Barbara Bradley, 50
Haining, Peter and Philippa, 64
hair loss, 112, 115, 149, 166
Halkomelem tribe, 184
Hall, Dennis, 249
Hall, Mark, 203
Hall, Richard, 138
Hall, William, 191-192
Halloween, 63, 302
Hamilton, Alexander, 171
Hamilton, Bobby, 201, 216
Hamilton, William F., 89
Hansen, Frank, 220-221
Hara, 307
Harada, Reiko, 192
Harare (Rhodesia/Tanzania), 137
Harper's Ferry (West Virginia), 79
Harpur, Patrick, 52, 312, 313
Harrison Hot Springs, 240
Harrison, Edgar, 189
Hartland, Edwin Sidney, 254-255
Harvard University, 297
Harvey-Wilson, Simon, 177
Hauck, Dennis William, 307-309, 315
Haughton, Brian, 42-43
Haverhill (Massachusetts), 124
Healy, Tony, 212
Hebrew (see *Judaism*)
hedonics (olfaction), 14-26, 20, 34, 42, 46,
  47, 49, 65, 69, 94, 106, 123, 130, 187,
  192, 280
Heilongjiang province (China), 250
Helgøy Island, 248
Helgöy Island (see *Helgøy Island*)
Henry County (Georgia), 107
heptanol, 300
Hermes, 306, 309, 313, 317

hermeticism (see *alchemy*)
Hernandez, Candelaria, 160-161
Herodotus, 28
Herriot, James, 18
Herz, Rachel, 297
Heuvelmans, Bernard, 221
hexanol, 300
hibagon (see *Sasquatch*)
Hill, Betty, 127, 255
Hillman, James, 308
Himalayan Mountains, 193
Hinduism, 47, 307
Hines, Sarah, 105
Hirsch, Alan R., 300-301
*History of Blackpool and its Neighborhood,
  The* (book), 270
HMS *Rob Roy*, 248
Holocaust, 17
Holt, Jane, 54
Holtville (California), 9
Holy Ghost, 48, 308
Homer, 27, 48
honey, 188
honeysuckle (see *flowers*)
Honobia (Oklahoma), 229, 234
Hoover, Herbert, 43
Hopkins, Budd, 133, 138, 167, 294, 299
Horton, Virginia, 133
Houston (Texas), 71
Howard-Bury, C.K., 193
Hubbell, Walter, 62
Huchnom tribe, 2
Huggins, Tyler, 187
hulk'ilal, 1-2
Hunnicutt, Robert, 259-260
Hunt for the Skinwalker, The (book), 274
Huon Valley (Tasmania), 151-152
Huron-Manistee National Forest
  (Michigan), 203
hyacinth (see *flowers*)
hydrazine, 170
hydrocarbons, 100, 101, 135, 150, 151,
  153, 178
  benzene, 100, 152-154, 170, 176, 312
  nitrobenzene, 298
hydrofluoride (see *hydrogen fluoride*)
hydrogen, 33, 153, 205, 295

hydrogen fluoride, 127
hydrogen sulfide (see *sulfur*)
hydrogen telluride, 192
Hyer, Tommy, 162
Hynek, J. Allen, 172
hypnagogia (see *sleep paralysis*)
hypnosis, 104, 105, 111, 112, 123, 128, 138, 149, 160, 184, 241, 293, 295, 303
hypnotic regression (see *hypnosis*)

Idaho (see *United States*)
IFSB (see *International Flying Saucer Bureau*)
Iliad (poem), 27, 48
Illinois (see *United States*)
Illinois River (Illinois), 201
In the Beginning (book), 137
incense, 19-20, 110, 115, 268
Incorruptibles, 50-51, 84
incubus, 70
Index (Washington), 53
India, 11, 124, 307
Indiana (see *United States*)
Indianapolis (Indiana), 120
indole, 33, 55, 57, 73, 129, 212
Indonesia, 54
Inferno (poem), 16, 67
infrasound, 191
International Flying Saucer Bureau, 262-263
International Space Station, 178
International Union of Pure and Applied Chemistry, 24
Inverness (Scotland), 72
Iowa (see *United States*)
Iran, 175
Iraq, 307
Ireland, 67
iron, 85, 151, 178, 179
Iroquois confederation, 268
Irtysh River (Russia), 13
Isaiah (Bible), 26
Isidore the Laborer (Saint), 50
Isis, 307
Islam, 28, 47, 308
Islamapur (India), 124
Israel, 28, 121

Israelsson, Fat-Mats, 32, 50
Italy, 19, 25, 33, 52, 56, 97, 99, 115, 119, 199, 175, 267, 288, 306
iunx (see *jynx*)
Ivanov, V.A., 13
Ivory Coast (Africa), 84

Jabir, 307, 309
Jacinta (Fátima witness), 51
jack-o'-lantern (see *swamp gas*)
Jahannam (see *Gehenna*)
Janzen, Lavern, 165
Japan, 21, 41, 68, 85, 130, 184, 192, 197, 213, 248
jasmine (see *flowers*)
Jasmine Woman (spirit), 54-55
Jasper County (Iowa), 84, 205
Jasper County Care Facility, 84
Jeannette (Pennsylvania), 234
Jell-O, 262
Jequitiba (Brazil), 272
Jerusalem (Israel), 28
Jesus of Nazareth, 11, 48, 69, 175, 254, 308, 309, 314, 315
Jews (see *Judaism*)
jinx (see *jynx*)
John (Bible), 48
Johnson & Johnson, 56
Johnson, Basil, 69
Johnson, J. Bond, 156
Johnson, J.A., 248
Johnson, J.C., 207
Johnson, Marjorie, 269
Johnson, Ronald E., 134
Johnston, Joseph E., 3
Jonestown (Pennsylvania), 119, 148, 298
Joplin (Missouri), 234
Joseph (alien), 255
Joyce, Carolyn, 166
Judaism, 11, 55, 257, 306
Judas (Bible), 11
Jung, Carl, 48, 87-88, 283, 308, 311-313, 315, 317
Jupiter, 169, 179
jynx, 316-317

Kamiah (Idaho), 206

Kampung, 197
Kargopol (Russia), 223
Katahdin Mountain (Maine), 238
kataw (see *faeries*)
Kazakhstan, 140
Kearney, Mrs., 260-261
Keel, John, 1, 40-5, 24-25, 27, 65, 100, 105, 118, 124, 127, 129-130, 183, 193, 197, 242, 250, 264, 265, 302-303
Kekulé, Auguste, 312
Kelleher, Chris, 176
Kelleher, Colm, 273-274
Kent (England), 91, 132
Kentucky (see *United States*)
Kentucky Bigfoot Research Organization, 286
keratin, 126, 229, 269
kerosene, 170
Ketchikan (Alaska), 202
ketone, 85, 158
ketosis, 49
Kettle Moraine (Wisconsin), 198
Kewaksum (Wisconsin), 258
Key Biscayne (Florida), 264
Key West (Florida), 59
kikiyaon, 250
Kimball, T.L., 232
Kingesfielde, Mistress, 74
Kingston (Pennsylvania), 234
Kircher, Athanasius, 288
Kitimaat tribe, 191
Klailova, Michelle, 215-216
Klamath (California), 201
Klein, John, 61
Kline, Lavena and Theresa, 213
Kluski, Franek, 86
Knapp, George, 273-274
Knife Island, 249
Knobby (see *Sasquatch*)
Knowles family, 132
Koch, Kurt E., 75
Koch, Tom, 117
Kopov, Nazar, 128
Koren, Stanley, 49
Kourianof (Russia), 171
Krishna, 47
kubikajiri (see *yokai*)

Kubo, Albert, 213
kuchi-sake-onna (see *yokai*)
Kucinich, Dennis, 114
kuntilanak, 54
kushtakaa (see *Sasquatch*)

Lady of the Rosary (see *Our Lady of Fátima*)
Lake Bardawil (Egypt), 28
Lake Champlain (United States/Canada), 249
Lake Huron (North America), 83
lake monsters, 11, 83, 131, 247-249, 299
Lake Ontario (North America), 11, 131
Lake Sirbonis (see *Lake Bardawil*)
Lake Superior (North America), 249
Lake Worth (Texas), 258-259
Lake Worth Monster, 258-259
Lampasas (Texas), 81
Landrum, Vickie, 149-150, 164, 165
Lanier, Ray, 152
Las Cruces (New Mexico), 138
Las Vegas (Nevada), 63, 108
Las Vegas (New Mexico), 199
laurel, 148, 291
Laus (France), 45-46
lavender (see *flowers*)
Lawson, Alvin, 176
Lazarus (Bible), 48
Le Guérer, Annick, 10, 11, 20, 47, 254, 280
Leap Castle, 67, 70
Leavy, Alice, 123, 128
LeBlond, Paul, 221
Lechuguilla (Mexico), 287
Ledger, Don, 122
Lee, Phyllis C., 215-216
Lee, Robert E., 3
Lefevre, Nicholas, 314
Lemon, Eugene, 162-163
lemurs, 200
Leo, 315
Lesser Key of Solomon (book), 48
Lethe River, 47
Levelland (Texas), 134
Lewis, C.S., 4
Library of Alexandria, 306-307

Lidwina (Saint), 49
Liège (Belgium), 166
lighter fluid, 149-150
lightning, 27, 86, 136, 171
  ball lightning, 141, 154, 173-174
lilac (see *flowers*)
lily (see *flowers*)
liminality, 312-313
limonene, 299
lindorms (see *dragons*)
Linnaeus, Carolus, 32
lipid peroxides, 85
lithium-sulfur batteries, 176-177
Livingston County (Kentucky), 257
lofa (see *Sasquatch*)
Log Cabin Village, 53-54
Long Beach (California), 61
Long Island (New York), 129, 264, 303
Long, Jesse, 121
Longmont (Colorado), 135
Lorgen, Eve, 108
Los Angeles (California), 88
Loudun Possessions, 11, 31
Louisiana (Missouri), 189
Louisiana (see *United States*)
Louisville (Kentucky), 81
Love, Bob, 55
Loveland (Ohio), 259-260
Loveland frogs, 259-260, 299
Lowell (Massachusetts), 247
LSD (see *lysergic acid diethylamide*)
Luca, Bob, 134
Lúcia (Fátima witness), 51
Lucretius, 11
Ludowici (Georgia), 238
Luke (Bible), 48
Lutz family, 84
lymphocyte, 100, 144, 289
Lyra (alien), 114
lysergic acid diethylamide, 16, 291

Maceiras, Venture, 148
Mack, John, 107, 127, 128, 166, 317
Mackie, Andrew, 62
Mackinac Island (Michigan), 83, 297
MacKinnon, John, 215
MacLaine, Shirley, 114

Mad Gasser of Mattoon, 12, 260-261, 289
Madeira-Loveland Pike, 259
Madrid (Spain), 50
magnesium, 179
Magnus, Albertus, 308
Maine (see *United States*)
Majestic (book), 102
Makumba (gorilla), 215
Malaysia, 197
mandala, 311
Manitoba (see *Canada*)
Manitou Springs (Colorado), 76, 77
Manner family, 78
mapinguari (see *Sasquatch*)
Marcel, Jesse, 156
Marcel, Jr., Jesse, 156-157
Marian apparition (see *Blessed Virgin Mary*)
Mariemont (Ohio), 258
marijuana, 62
Marine Naval Air Station (San Diego), 131
Market Square, 63
Marshall (Michigan), 237
Martin of Tours (Saint), 69, 70
Mary (Bible; see also *BVM*), 11, 51
Mary of Bethany (Bible), 48
Maryland (see *United States*)
Massachusetts (see *United* States)
Massachusetts Institute of Technology, 180
matah kagmi (see *Sasquatch*)
Mather, Cotton, 75
Matthews, Dana, 83
Mattoon (Illinois), 12, 260-261, 289
Mattoon Journal Gazette (periodical), 261
Maubeuge (France), 153
Maximus (Saint), 47
May, Fred and Edward, 162
Mayans, 131
McCampbell, James, 100, 125, 145, 152-154, 173, 298
McCleary, Edward Brian, 248
McGuire Air Force Base, 147
McKenna, Terence, 280-281, 285, 304, 305, 309, 318

Index 435

McMillan, Blaine, 216, 222
McMullen family, 147
McPike Mansion, 61
Melanson, Terry, 177
Memphis (Tennessee), 74, 81
Men-in-Black, 262-265, 303
Mendenhall, Jerri, 221
Mendoza (Argentina), 159
Menghi, Girolamo, 31
Mennick, Simon, 100
menthol, 145
mercaptan (see *thiol*)
Mercury (alchemy; see *Sophic Sulfur*)
mermaids (see *faeries*)
Merrittstown (Pennsylvania), 234
Merry, Andrew (see *Darby, Mildred*)
mesquite, 160
Messengers, The (book), 241
met-teh kang-mi (see *yeti*)
metch-kangmi (see *yeti*)
meteors, 171, 178-179, 246
methane, 33, 173, 174, 175
methanethiol (see *sulfur*)
methyl mercaptan (see *methanethiol*)
metoh-kangmi (see *yeti*)
Mexico, 46, 121, 287,
Meyersdale (Pennsylvania), 222
MGM Grand Hotel and Casino, 63
Miami (Florida), 121
Miasma Theory, 11-12, 28, 130-131, 174, 246
MIB (see *Men-in-Black*)
Michael (angel), 30
Michalak, Stefan, 141-142, 167
Michigan (see *United States*)
Miller Document, 216-217
Miller, H.A., 216
Miller, Jason, 258
Mills, Joan, 205
Milwaukee (Wisconsin), 220
Mineral Springs Hotel, 54
Mineral Wells (Texas), 53
Minerva (Ohio), 200, 253
Minerva Monster (film), 200
Minnehaha Falls, 226
Minnesota iceman, 220-221
Mirabelli, Carmine Carlos, 68

Miracle of the Sun (see *Our Lady of Fátima*)
Missing Pieces (book), 78
Mississippi (see *United States*)
Missouri (see *United States*)
Missouri Monster (see *Momo*)
Modoc tribe, 209
Molalla (Oregon), 203
Momo (see *Sasquatch*)
Mompesson, John, 23-24
Monetho, 306
Monongahela (Pennsylvania), 234
Monster Files (book), 163
Montana (see *United States*)
Monteagle Mountain (Tennessee), 186
Monteith, R., 199
Moreno family, 150
Morocco, 119
Morris, M.C.F., 268
Morse, Jeff, 147
Moscow (Russia), 285
Moses, 306
Mothman, 65, 103
Mothman Prophecies, The (book), 118, 129, 250, 264
Mount Hiba (Japan), 184
Mount Holly (New Jersey), 75
Mount Karthala (Comoros islands), 28
Mount Misery (Long Island), 303
Mr. Boots (spirit), 73
MSH (see *3-methyl-3-sulfanylhexan-1-ol*)
Mudan River (China), 250
MUFON (see *Mutual UFO Network*)
mummy, 250
Mundus Subterraneus (book), 288
Murchison (Australia), 114
Murphy, Christopher L., 240
Murphy, Jane, 106
Murphysboro (Illinois), 2
Muscle Shoals (Alabama), 238
Museum of Natural History (New York), 178
mushrooms, 271, 285, 291, 292
mustelids, 214
Mutual UFO Network, 36, 100, 101, 102, 110, 166, 194, 239
Mutwa, Credo, 127, 152

Myrtle Point (Oregon), 237
Myths & Legends of our Own Land (book), 74
Myths & Monsters (conference), 212

N,N-Dimethyltryptamine, 16, 129, 162, 293, 295
Namibia, 250
National Observer, The (periodical), 194
NC-172, 231
Neanderthal: The Strange Saga of the Minnesota Iceman (book), 221
Nebraska (see *United States*)
Nelson House, 72
Nelson, Bob, 219
Nepal, 193
nepenthe, 47
neurotheology (see *Persinger, Michael*)
Nevada (see *United States*)
Neville, Joe, 82
New Boston (Michigan), 134
New Hampshire (see *United States*)
New Jersey (see *United States*)
New Mexico (see *United States*)
New York (see *United States*)
New Zealand, 69, 138, 299
Newfoundland (see *Canada*)
Newkirk, Greg, 117
Newman, Henry, 193
NH$_3$ (see *ammonia*)
NO (see *nitric oxide*)
Nicholas, Fred, 225
Nickell, Joe, 78
Niemtzow, Richard, 149
Nile River (Egypt), 29, 306
nitric oxide, 152, 153, 173
nitrobenzene (see *hydrocarbons*)
nitrogen, 33, 78, 153
nitrogen dioxide, 154
nitrogen oxides, 135, 170, 174, 175
Nixon, Richard, 264
NO$_2$ (see *nitrogen dioxide*)
Noël, Christopher, 218
NORAD, 36
Norfolk (England), 255
North America's Great Ape (book), 191
North Berwick (Scotland), 108

North Carolina (see *United States*)
North Dakota (see *United States*)
North Tongass Highway, 198
Northampton (England), 29
Northwest River Park (Virginia), 237
Norway, 160, 248
Nova Scotia (see *Canada*)
Noxie (Oklahoma), 37
Nunley, Neil, 162
nuppeppō (see *yokai*)
nuribotoke (see *yokai*)

O.K. Corral, 60
O'Bannon family, 67
O'Donnell, Richard, 271-272
Oak Hill (Florida), 224
Oakley (Idaho), 188
Oakville (Ontario), 63
Occult Review (periodical), 67
Ochopee (Florida), 193, 206
octopus, 281
Odyssey (poem), 27, 33
Ohio (see *United States*)
Ohio State Reformatory, 53
Oishi, Jeff, 178
Ojai (California), 237
Ojibwe tribe, 69
Oklahoma (see *United States*)
Old Hag (see *sleep paralysis*)
Old New Castle (Delaware), 61
Old Sausalito (California), 250
Old Shuck (see *black dogs*)
olivine, 179
Olsdotter, Margareta, 32
Olsen, Thomas M., 101, 102, 135
Omaha (Nebraska), 166
Omer, Boyd, 199
Onion Lake, 150
onions, 81, 228, 279, 300
Ontario (see *Canada*)
opium, 61, 250
orangutan, 191
orculli (see *faeries*)
Oregon (see *United States*)
Oregon Regional Primate Research Center, 188
Orogrande (New Mexico), 165

Index

orris, 50
Osiris, 307
Oswald, Luli, 199
Ouija board, 74
Our Lady of Fátima (see *Blessed Virgin Mary*)
Our Lady of Guadalupe (see *Blessed Virgin Mary*)
Our Lady of Laus (see *Blessed Virgin Mary*)
Our Life with Bigfoot (book), 218
ourobouros, 311-312
Overstrand (England), 255
owls, 241-242
oxygen, 33, 34, 86, 126, 139, 153-154, 167, 174, 236, 287-288
ozone, 6, 27, 85-86, 89, 100, 101-102, 113, 133-143, 148, 152, 159, 167, 170-171, 173, 176, 179, 180, 250, 282, 284, 300

Padre Pio (see *Pio of Pietrelcina*)
paint, 34, 60, 145
paint thinner, 252, 299
Pakistan, 184
Paladino, Carl, 14
Pamir Mountains (Central Asia), 184
Pan, 258
Paniago, Heítor, 252
panther (mythology), 254, 315-316
Parham, Beauford E., 146
Paris (France), 81, 86, 130
Parker (Arizona), 258
Parker, G.H., 297
Parkersburg (West Virginia), 61
Paro, Jaye P., 129, 302-303
Passaic County (New Jersey), 198
Passport to the Cosmos (book), 127
Patapsco River (Maryland), 208
patchouli, 258
Patterson-Gimlin film, 189-190
Patterson, Roger, 189-190
Pauling, Linus, 192
Pekin (Illinois), 201
Pela, Honore, 46
Pennsylvania (see *United States*)
Pensacola Bay (Florida), 248

Pentagon, The, 5
peppermint, 82
Peppertown (Indiana), 135
Permian-Triassic boundary, 130
Perry, Datus, 223, 239
Persia (see *Iran*)
Persinger, Michael, 49-50, 175
Perthshire (Scotland), 83
Pettit, Don, 178
phantosmia, 16, 90-91, 263
phenyl ethyl alcohol (see *roses*)
Philippines, 251, 267
Phillips, Dottie, 120
Philosopher's Stone, 307, 309, 310
Phoenix (Arizona), 108
Phoenix (mythology), 310, 311
phosphine, 148
phosphorus, 33
photochemistry, 135, 139-141
Pienaar, Jan, 146
Pike County (Georgia), 280
Pikes Peak Journal (periodical), 76
Pio of Pietrelcina, 49
pipe (see *tobacco*)
piperidine, 299
Pit Bull (see *dogs*)
Pittsburgh (Pennsylvania), 74
Plato, 10-11, 14
plesiosaur, 249
Pliny the Elder, 33
Plutarch, 47
Point Pleasant (West Virginia), 258
Poland, 49
pomegranate, 48, 112
pooka (see *faeries*)
Pope Gregory, 15
Pope John Paul II, 51
popo bawa, 251
Port Arthur (Tasmania), 72
Portsmouth (England), 166
Portsmouth (Ohio), 17
Portugal, 51
pot (see *marijuana*)
potassium carbonate, 78
potassium nitrate, 77
potassium sulfate (see *sulfur*)
Poulton Church, 270

Pratt, Bob, 2
Prima Materia, 307, 309, 312
Prince of Wales Island (Alaska), 183
Princess Moon Owl, 129, 302
Project Blue Book, 5, 106, 172
Puerto Rico, 113, 251-252
pukwudgies (see *faeries*)
pwdr sêr (see *star jelly*)
Pyrenees mountains (Europe), 31
pyrite, 33
pyroxene, 179

Qu'ran, 28, 47
Quail, Salina, 107
Quazgaa, 310
Quebec (see *Canada*)
Queens (New York), 163
Queensland (Australia), 121, 165
Querétaro (Mexico), 121
Quincy (Massachusetts), 117
Quincy Shore Drive (Quincy, Massachusetts), 117

raccoon, 201, 210
Racine (Wisconsin), 257
Radford, Benjamin, 251
Raef, Urban, 260
Ragusa (Italy), 119
Raincoast Sasquatch (book), 185
Ramey, Roger, 156
Ramírez, Manuel, 235
Ramón y Cajal, Santiago, 136-137
Randles, Jenny, 109-110
Rath, Cheryl, 3
Ray, Cheryl (see *Rath, Cheryl*)
Raymer, A.H., 28
Reagan, Fred, 134, 142
Real Men in Black, The (book), 263
Red Headband, 28
Red Lion pub, 53
Red Pill Junkie, 283
Red Rooster Inn, 59
Redfern, Nick, 36, 163, 263, 265
Reichart, John, 258
Rémy, Nicholas, 27
Rencurel, Benôite, 45-46
Rendlesham Forest incident, 314

Revilla Road (Alaska), 202
Rhodes (Greece), 115
Rhodesia, 137, 161, 270
Richards, Andrea, 120
Richloam Wildlife Management Area, 210
Rios, Zenon Carlos, 285
River Styx, 132
Rivera, Aida, 113
Rizzi, Walter, 115
RMS *Queen Mary*, 61
Roachdale (Indiana), 222
Roccagloriosa (Italy), 52
rocket fuel, 150, 170
Rodrigues, Ubirajara Franco, 36
Rogers, Randy and Lou, 222
Rollins, Ed, 258
Rome (Italy), 11, 19, 306
Roosevelt, Theodore, 209
rosemary, 148
roses (see *flowers*)
Rosie (spirit; see *Gold Hill Hotel*)
Ross (Ohio), 119
Roswell (New Mexico), 102, 154-158, 299
Roth Lab, 287
Roth, Mark, 287-288, 302
Routh, Guy, 64
Royal Air Force, 18
Royal Canadian Mounted Police, 141
Rule, Margaret, 75
Rullán, Antonio F., 102, 104, 125, 126, 139, 174, 195, 298
Ruppelt, Edward J., 135
Ruskin (Florida), 238
Russell, Randy, 55
Russia, 13, 49, 130, 151, 171, 223, 285
Rutgers University, 282
Rutherford (New Jersey), 205
Rutland (Vermont), 186
Ryan, Mary, 205

S-alk(en)yl-L-cyestine, 228
S'cwene'y'ti (see *Sasquatch*)
Sabirov, Alisher, 112
saffron, 20, 47
Salisbury (Tanzania; see *Harare*

(Rhodesia))
Salt Springs (Florida), 152
saltpeter (see *potassium nitrate*)
Samhain Eve (see *Halloween*)
San Antonio (Texas), 138, 152, 255
San Diego (California), 81, 131
San Francisco (California), 250
San Jose Mission, 255
sandalwood, 81, 130
Sander, Irene, 107
Sanderson, Ivan, 100, 151, 153, 163, 185, 221
São Paulo (Brazil), 68
São Vicente (Brazil), 10,
Saquarema (Argentina), 119
Sasquatch, 5, 6, 9-10, 14, 25, 28, 36-37, 125-126, 183-242, 259, 280, 284, 286, 289, 290, 298, 301, 303, 312
   barmanu, 184
   Beast of Boggy Creek, 206, 235, 210
   Beast of Whitehall, 234
   Big Muddy Monster, 2-3
   bogwish, 191
   C. nerteros pacificus, 217
   Gul-Biavan, 184
   hibagon, 184, 192, 213
   Knobby, 206
   kushtakaa, 202
   lofa, 185
   mapinguari, 184, 192, 217
   matah kagmi, 210
   Momo, 189, 205
   S'cwene'y'ti, 192
   ses'quac, 184
   shampe, 185
   Skunk Ape, 193, 194, 198, 199, 203, 206, 210, 213, 217, 222, 224, 225, 227, 238, 240, 298
   tek tek, 184
   tsiatko, 184
   yeti, 193
   Yowie, 184, 190, 212, 216
SasWhat (podcast), 253
Satan, 11, 26, 27, 28, 29-32, 33, 35, 36, 47, 69, 74, 78, 246, 254, 265, 308, 314
Saturday Evening Post, The (periodical), 172

Saturn, 114, 169
Satus Pass (Virginia), 226
Scandinavia (see also *Finland, Norway, Sweden*), 36, 49, 160, 167
Scarberry, Linda, 65
Scent (book), 10
Scented Ape, The (book), 204
Schab, Frank, 282
Schackelman, Mark, 257
Schaffner, Ron, 253
Schaller, George, 215
Schönbein, Christian Friedrich, 136
Science (periodical), 177
scopolamine, 265
Scotland, 62, 72, 73, 83, 108, 124, 270
Scott, Brian, 108
screen memories, 111, 240-242, 294
Scythians, 291
Seige of Honobia, 229, 234
Sekhmet, 315
Selkirk (Manitoba), 148
Seminole tribe, 193
Senate, Richard, 53
Seneca (Illinois), 210
Sense and Sensibilia (treatise), 9-10
Serbonian Bog (see *Lake Bardawil*)
ses'quac (see *Sasquatch*)
Severus, Sulpicius, 69
Sevier County (Tennessee), 226
Shag Harbour (Nova Scotia), 122, 255
shampe (see *Sasquatch*)
Sharpsville (Indiana), 220
Shaver, Ronnie, 162
Shealy, David, 193-194
Sherman Ranch, 273, 278
Sherman, William Tecumseh, 3
Sherpas, 193
Sherry, Sam, 211
Shoback, Doug, 61-62
Shuck's Lane, 255
Shulgin, Alexander, 304
Sicily (Italy), 33
Sider, Jean, 36
Siegel, Ronald K., 88
Sierra Nevada Mountains, 219
Sierra, Miguel, 139
Sight Unseen (book), 294

Silbury Hill, 120
Silent Invasion (book), 233
silicon, 127
silicon carbide, 150
silicon dioxide, 179
Silver Dolphin Mobile Home Court, 234
Silver Springs (Maryland), 194
Simi Valley (California), 115
Singapore, 197
Singleton family, 270
Skåne County (Sweden), 118
skatole, 33, 55, 57, 73, 212
Skinner, Charles M., 74
Skinwalker Ranch (see *Sherman Ranch*)
skunk, 9, 121, 187, 190, 193, 197, 199, 202, 203, 205-208, 210, 214, 216, 218, 224, 232, 249, 279
Skunk Ape (see *Sasquatch*)
Skunk-Ape Research Headquarters, 193
skunk cabbage, 224
sleep paralysis, 41, 88-90, 107, 271, 285, 290, 295, 302
Smell & Taste Treatment and Research Foundation, 300
Smell, Taste, and the Allied Senses in Vertebrates (book), 297
Smith, Marion, 134
Smith, Martha C., 269-270
Smith, Yvonne, 123
Sni-A-Bar Creek (Missouri), 205
Snitowsky, George and Edith, 163
Snyder, Bob, 203
SO_2 (see *sulfur dioxide*)
Sobrinho, Joao Alves, 272-273
Sochi (Russia), 151
Socorro (New Mexico), 103, 315
Socorro incident, 103, 315
Sodom, 26
Solganda, 36
Song of Solomon, 11
Sonoma County (California), 174
Sophic Mercury, 309-310, 313, 317
Sophic Salt, 309, 310
Sophic Sulfur (see *sulfur*)
South Africa, 75, 138, 146
South Ashburnham (Massachusetts), 310
South Dade (Florida), 298

South Middleton (Massachusetts), 123
Spain, 50, 120, 128, 136, 139, 235, 245, 267, 308
Spanish Peaks (Colorado), 188
Spare, Austin Osman, 247
Sparks, Brad, 149
Species (film), 251
Spinbrook (Queensland), 212
spirits, 3-4, 5, 6, 15, 16, 20, 23, 25, 41-94, 99, 101, 106, 113, 123, 126, 130, 131, 147, 161, 166, 175, 180, 188, 192, 194, 228, 241, 242, 247, 265, 268, 269, 270, 278, 280, 289, 290, 291, 293, 294, 301, 303, 317
Spokane tribe, 184, 192
Springbrook (Australia), 190
Springfield (Illinois), 82
Springfield Theatre Center, 82
Squire, Nathaniel G., 236
St. Augustine (Florida), 55
St. Coletta convent, 257
St. Louis College of Pharmacy, 30
St. Mary's Coptic Church, 52
Staining (England), 270
Stampa, Piero Antonio, 31
star jelly, 246-247, 277
star rot (see *star jelly*)
star shot (see *star jelly*)
Star-Telegram (periodical), 156
steel, 150
Steiger, Brad, 225
Stewart, Jimmy, 221
Stinky (spirit), 60
Stockdale, Captain, 248
Stockton, Steve, 63
Stoddart, David Michael, 204
Stoeckman, Charlie, 203
Stokes, James, 165
Stone Mountain (Georgia), 108
Stoney Ghosty, 61
Stoystown (Pennsylvania), 78
Strange Magazine (periodical), 71
Strickler, Lon, 54, 155, 192, 208-209
Strieber, Whitley, 102, 107-112, 160, 273, 299
Stringfield, Leonard, 142, 146, 245
Stuart, John, 69

Sturdevant, Harry, 123
Sturgis (Michigan), 247
Suffolk (England), 64
sulfur (see also *atmospheric sulfur*), 2, 23-37, 41, 42, 65, 74-80, 75, 81, 85, 86, 93, 99, 100, 101, 102, 103, 106, 108, 111, 117-132, 134, 135, 136, 137, 141-142, 147-148, 150, 151, 159, 163, 165-166, 167, 170, 171-173, 174-175, 176, 177, 179-180, 187, 202, 205, 212, 213, 221, 223, 224, 228, 229, 231-242, 246, 247, 250, 252, 254, 255, 257, 258, 263, 264, 266, 267-268, 269, 270, 274, 277-279, 283, 284, 286, 295, 296, 298, 300, 302, 306-311, 313-317
    benzyl mercaptan, 165
    brimstone, 23, 24, 25, 26-32, 34, 48, 74, 78, 93, 124, 136, 229, 251-252, 254-256, 270, 277
    carbon disulfide, 103, 127
    carbonyl sulfide, 103
    dimethyl sulfide, 137, 224, 247, 248
    dimethyl trisulfide, 73
    ethyl mercaptan, 35
    hydrogen sulfide (see also *eggs*), 14, 28, 33, 34, 35, 73, 77, 78, 103, 118, 123, 125-132, 142, 165, 173, 174, 177, 180, 212, 213, 236-239, 252, 261, 277, 284, 287-290, 291, 295-296, 297, 300-303, 315, 316
    methanethiol, 35, 73, 120, 213
    potassium sulfate, 77
    Sophic Sulfur, 308-317
    sulfur dioxide (see also *gunpowder*), 33, 34, 77-80, 91, 100, 103, 124-125, 135, 142, 148, 152, 170, 180, 236, 252, 268, 300, 315
    sulfuric acid, 33, 34, 120, 179, 298
    sulfurous acid, 78
    thiocresol, 35
    thiol, 27, 121, 205, 308
sulfur dioxide (see *sulfur*)
sulfur lamps, 177
sulfuric acid (see *sulfur*)
sulfurous acid (see *sulfur*)
sulphur (see *sulfur*)
Sulphur Creek (Alabama), 235
Sulphur Creek Camp (Washington), 235
Sulphur River (Arkansas), 235
Sulphur Spring Road (California), 235
Sunderland family, 161
Sunderland, Gaynor, 161
Surrey (England), 253
suspended animation, 287-290, 291, 295-296, 301-302, 303
swamp gas, 172-173
Sweden, 32, 118, 140, 160, 186, 280
Switzerland, 309, 315
Swords, Michael D., 150
Symons's Monthly Meteorological Magazine (periodical), 172
synchronicity, 241, 312

Taikomol, 1-2
talcum powder, 56, 116
Tallulah Falls (Georgia), 146
Tampa (Florida), 265
tanystropheus, 249
Taoist, 307
tapir nymph, 248
tar-grass, 163
Tara, 302
Tasmania (see *Australia*)
Taua (Brazil), 257
Taylor, Bob, 145
Taylor, Troy, 82
Tedworth (England), 23-24
Teed family, 62
Teed, Olive, 62
tek tek (see *Sasquatch*)
Tennessee (see *United States*)
Teresa of Ávila (Saint), 50
terpineol, 300
Texas (see *United States*)
Texas Blue Dogs, 252
Texas Canyon (California), 257
Thames Ditton (England), 172
The Patriot Ledger (periodical), 117
Theatre Royal, 255
Theophrastus, 11
thiocresol (see *sulfur*)
thiol (see *sulfur*)
Thomas Bay (Alaska), 217
Thomas saloon, 93

Thomas, Joe Kirk, 164
Thompson, John C., 110
Thornber, William, 270
Thornton Heath, 68
Thoth, 306
Three Secrets (see *Our Lady of Fátima*)
threshold (olfaction), 14-15, 35, 73, 130, 136, 148, 296
thyme, 270
Tibet, 193, 210
Tidworth (England; see *Tedworth*)
tigers, 191
tilma, 46
timpan, 302
tip-of-the-nose (olfaction), 18, 106, 111, 137-138, 153, 163, 185, 190, 282
tobacco, 6, 17 , 42, 59-61, 65, 78, 79-80, 89, 246, 291
Toledo (Spain), 30, 120
Tolowa tribe, 185
toluene, 299
Tombstone (Arizona), 60
Tonnies, Mac, 277, 317
Tosh, Kenneth, 37
Townshend (Vermont), 140
Transformation (book), 111-112
Trenton (New Jersey), 124
Trevor-Deutsch, Burleigh, 214
Tria Prima, 309-310, 313
trigeminal nerve, 296-304
Trismegistus, Hermes, 306, 309, 313, 317
Trojan Feast, A (book), 7, 19
troll (see *faeries*)
tryptophan, 55
tsiatko (see *Sasquatch*)
Tuatha Dé Danann (see *faeries*)
Tucker, Elizabeth, 71
Tule Lake, 209
Tulli Papyrus, 97-99
Tulli, Alberto, 97
Tully (Queensland), 121
Turkey, 99
Turner, Karla, 19, 107, 145
turpentine, 145
Twisp (Washington), 200
Two Contraries, 307-308, 309, 311, 312, 313-314, 317

Typhon, 28
Tyrrell, Jennifer, 63

UFO Abductions: The Measure of a Mystery (book), 19, 100
UFO British Columbia, 107
UFO Crash at Aztec (book), 141
UFO Silencers (book), 105
UFOlogy: A Major Breakthrough in the Scientific Understanding of Unidentified Flying Objects (book), 145, 152
UFOs, 2, 5-6, 12-13, 19, 36, 52, 97-180, 233-235, 241, 245, 246, 247, 249, 250, 253, 255, 257, 259, 260, 262, 263, 265, 270, 272, 273, 274, 277, 278, 280, 284, 289, 290, 292, 293, 294, 298-300, 301, 303, 311-312, 313, 314-315, 316, 317
chupas, 118
UFOs and Water (book), 122
UFOs Northwest, 113
Ukraine, 128
Unidentified Submersible Objects, 122, 137, 248
Uninvited Visitors (book), 100
United Kingdom (see *England*)
United States, 5, 15, 36, 75, 77, 79, 114, 154, 157, 177, 195, 216, 253, 257
Alabama, 235, 238
Alaska, 183, 185, 198, 202, 217
Arizona, 60, 108, 258
Arkansas, 206, 210, 235
California, 2, 9, 61, 81, 88, 115, 131, 174, 185, 189, 201, 202, 209, 221, 235, 237, 250, 257, 273
Colorado, 62, 76, 77, 93, 135, 138, 139, 188, 195
Connecticut, 78
Delaware, 61
Florida, 55, 59, 84, 106, 110, 121, 147, 152, 167, 188, 193-194, 198, 199, 203, 206, 210, 213, 222, 224, 227, 238, 240, 248, 152, 264, 265, 298
Georgia, 52, 107, 108, 146, 164, 226, 238, 257, 280, 292
Idaho, 188, 206
Illinois, 2, 12, 53, 54, 56, 61, 75, 82, 186, 187, 201, 210, 253, 260-261,

Index 443

289
Indiana, 60, 119, 120, 135, 220, 222, 224
Iowa, 84, 134, 139, 205, 251
Kentucky, 78, 81, 236, 257, 286
Louisiana, 33, 201
Maine, 238, 256
Maryland, 54, 188, 194, 208-209
Massachusetts, 112, 117, 121, 123, 124, 154, 180, 247, 310
Michigan, 60, 83, 134, 172, 203, 232, 237, 247, 259, 297
Mississippi, 61
Missouri, 13, 189, 205, 225, 234
Montana, 209, 235
Nebraska, 166, 248
Nevada, 53, 63, 108, 154-158
New Hampshire, 79, 89
New Jersey, 75, 123, 124, 132, 147, 198, 205
New Mexico, 102, 103, 112, 138, 141, 154-158, 165, 199, 207, 299, 315
New York, 11, 14, 60, 74, 88, 108, 129, 134, 148, 163, 178, 211, 234, 249, 264, 268, 303
North Carolina, 3, 92, 106, 174, 206, 231
North Dakota, 165
Ohio, 17, 53, 82, 119, 140, 154, 163, 200, 213, 235, 238, 250, 253, 258, 259-260, 294
Oklahoma, 37, 229, 234, 235, 238
Oregon, 113, 119, 184, 188, 203, 222, 237
Pennsylvania, 43, 74, 76, 78, 82, 103, 119, 120, 125, 139, 147, 148, 161, 171, 187, 190, 202, 203, 211, 212, 215, 219, 220, 222, 225, 229, 233, 234, 237, 298
Texas, 33, 53, 54, 71, 81, 106, 134, 138, 149, 152, 156, 218, 225, 235, 252, 255, 258-259
Utah, 227, 273
Vermont, 140, 186, 249
Virginia, 72, 85, 237, 261, 114
Washington, 53, 184, 185, 187, 200, 211, 224, 226, 235, 287

Washington DC, 157
West Virginia, 61, 75, 79, 103, 162, 225, 258
Wisconsin, 198, 220, 223, 232, 249, 256, 257, 258
United States Air Force, 5, 106, 112, 128, 147, 154, 156, 158, 165
United States Department of Defense, 177
United States Department of Energy, 177
University of Albany, 35
University of Bogotá, 121
University of California, Los Angeles, 88
University of Leipzig, 85
University of Massachusetts-Boston, 117
University of Northern Colorado at Greeley, 62
University of Stirling, 215
University of Washington, 287
Upland (Pennsylvania), 161
Urgench (Uzbekistan), 112
urine, 35, 49, 55, 73, 89, 187, 197, 198-201, 207, 209, 224, 226, 229, 257, 258, 283, 298, 299
Ursuline, 11
US-17, 231
USOs (see *Unidentified Submersible Objects*)
USS *Constellation*, 79
Utah (see *United States*)
Ute tribe, 227, 273
UV rays, 135, 136, 139, 180
Uzbekistan, 112

Valentine, Basil, 315
valeric acid, 299
Vallee, Jacques, 52, 99, 118, 121, 123, 124, 138, 155, 272, 273
Valley of the Son of Hinnom (see *Gehenna*)
Vallon des Fours (France), 45
Valparaiso (Chile), 165
vampires, 20, 73, 129, 251
Van Meter (Iowa), 251
Van Meter Visitor, 251
van Tassel, George, 36
Vanderbilt II, George Washington, 92

vanilla, 82, 297
Vanity Fair, 65
Varginha (Brazil), 36, 146
Vehicle Interference Effect, The (article), 164
Velikovsky, Immanuel, 137
Venezuela, 151
Venus, 6, 48, 102, 180, 315, 318
Verish, Robert, 178
Vermont (see *United States*)
Versailles, 256
Verstynen, Timothy, 292
Vicksburg (Mississippi), 61
vinegar, 167, 297, 299
violets (see *flowers*)
Virginia (see *United States*)
Virginia City (Nevada), 253
Virginia Polytechnic Institute and State University, 85
Visayan Islands (Philippines), 267
volatile organic compounds, 139
von Franz, Marie-Louise, 315, 317
Vonnegut, Bernard, 171
Vonnegut, Kurt, 171
Vroon, Piet, 14, 34, 279
Vulcanization process, 34, 126, 165, 229

Wales, 72, 161
Walker, James, 84
Wallace, LeRoy, 155, 192
Walter, Brenda S. Gardenour, 30
Walters, Ed, 110
Walton, Travis, 107
Ware, Brandon, 227
Washington (see *United States*)
Washington D.C. (see *United States*)
water jaguar, 248
Waters, Stephanie, 76
Waverly (Ohio), 82
Waverly Hills Sanatorium, 81
WBZ-TV Boston, 117
Weatherly, David, 266
Weatherwise (periodical), 171
Webel, Patrick, 166
Week In Weird (website), 83
wendigo, 69
Werewolf of Flixton, 256

West Virginia (see *United States*)
West Virginia State Penitentiary, 75-76
Westhope (North Dakota), 165
Whaley House, 81
whiskey, 60
White Sulphur Springs (Montana), 235
White, Robert, 5
Whitefish Point Lighthouse, 60
Whitehall (New York), 234
Widecombe-in-the Moore (England), 136
wil-o'-the-wisp (see *swamp gas*)
Wilderness Hunter (book), 209
Wilkinson, Doreen, 69
William (spirit; see *Gold Hill Hotel*)
William of Ockham, 277
Williams Air Force Base, 128
Williams Lake (Michigan), 259
Willison, John, 29
Wilton (Arkansas), 206
Winnipeg (Manitoba), 141
Wisconsin (see *United States*)
witches, 20, 23, 30-31, 224
witch balls, 31
Witness to Roswell (book), 155
Wonders in the Sky (book), 99
Woodward, Joan, 100
woodwose (see *faeries*)
Woolcott, Francis, 74
Wooten, Raymond, 194
World War I, 51, 124, 287
World War II, 51, 103, 163, 197
Wortley (England), 272
Wright Patterson Air Force Base, 147, 154-158
Wright, Carolina, 206

Xavier, Kátia, 36

yeti (see *Sasquatch*)
yin-yang, 307
yogis, 49
yokai, 41, 42, 43, 69
 kubikajiri, 85
 kuchi-sake-onna, 21
 nuppeppō, 69
 nuribotoke, 68

York County (Maine), 237
Yorkshire (England), 112, 268
Yorktown (Virginia), 72
Youngstown (Pennsylvania), 237
Yowie (see *Sasquatch*)
Yuki (see *Huchnom*)

Zanzibar Islands, 251
Zeise, William Christopher, 308
Zephyr-6 drone (see *drones*)
Zeus, 27, 28
Zimbabwe (see *Rhodesia*)
zinc, 160
zombies, 68, 73
Zoroastrianism, 36
Zosimus, 306

www.ingramcontent.com/pod-product-compliance
Lightning Source LLC
Chambersburg PA
CBHW020047170426
43199CB00009B/196